Financial Elites and European Banking

Financial Elites and European Banking

Historical Perspectives

Edited by
Youssef Cassis and Giuseppe Telesca

OXFORD
UNIVERSITY PRESS

OXFORD
UNIVERSITY PRESS

Great Clarendon Street, Oxford, OX2 6DP,
United Kingdom

Oxford University Press is a department of the University of Oxford.
It furthers the University's objective of excellence in research, scholarship,
and education by publishing worldwide. Oxford is a registered trade mark of
Oxford University Press in the UK and in certain other countries

© Oxford University Press 2018

The moral rights of the authors have been asserted

First Edition published in 2018

Impression: 1

All rights reserved. No part of this publication may be reproduced, stored in
a retrieval system, or transmitted, in any form or by any means, without the
prior permission in writing of Oxford University Press, or as expressly permitted
by law, by licence or under terms agreed with the appropriate reprographics
rights organization. Enquiries concerning reproduction outside the scope of the
above should be sent to the Rights Department, Oxford University Press, at the
address above

You must not circulate this work in any other form
and you must impose this same condition on any acquirer

Published in the United States of America by Oxford University Press
198 Madison Avenue, New York, NY 10016, United States of America

British Library Cataloguing in Publication Data

Data available

Library of Congress Control Number: 2018931820

ISBN 978-0-19-878279-7

Printed and bound by
CPI Group (UK) Ltd, Croydon, CR0 4YY

Links to third party websites are provided by Oxford in good faith and
for information only. Oxford disclaims any responsibility for the materials
contained in any third party website referenced in this work.

Contents

List of Figures   vii
List of Tables   ix
List of Contributors   xi

Introduction   1
Giuseppe Telesca

1. Financial Crises and the Public Discourse on Financial Elites: A Comparison between the Great Depression and the Great Recession   17
Youssef Cassis and Giuseppe Telesca

2. Reshaping Strategies: Merchants and Bankers at the Time of the French Revolution   40
Niccolò Valmori

3. Adjusting to Financial Instability in the Interwar Period: Italian Financial Elites, International Cooperation, and Domestic Regulation, 1919–1939   61
Giandomenico Piluso

4. Financial Elites and the Italian Corporate Network, 1913–2001   92
Alberto Rinaldi and Michelangelo Vasta

5. French Bankers and the Transformation of the Financial System in the Second Half of the Twentieth Century   117
Laure Quennouëlle-Corre

6. Trust and Regulation in Corporate Capital Markets before 1914   134
Leslie Hannah

7. Financial Elites, Law, and Regulation: A Historical Perspective   158
T. T. Arvind, Joanna Gray, and Sarah Wilson

Contents

8. Central Bankers in Twelve Countries between 1950 and 2000:
   The Making of a Global Elite　　182
   Mikael Wendschlag

9. Basel Banking Supervisors and the Construction of an International
   Standard-Setter Institution　　209
   Alexis Frédéric Drach

Index　　237

List of Figures

3.1	Aggregate total assets and loans on net-worth of the banking system as a whole, 1896–1940	67
4.1	Density (per cent) and isolated and marginal firms (per cent)	101
4.2	Density (per cent) of the top 250 firms in selected countries	101
8.1	Central bankers' background in public sector and government	190
8.2	Central bankers' background in private sector and academia	198
8.3	Academic background of central bank governors in office, 1950–2000	201

List of Tables

3.1	The four largest Italian banks (C4) and banks of issue: volatility (standard deviation) of indicators of capital adequacy and profitability, 1919–1939	68
3.2	Italian delegates at the International Financial Conference at Brussels, 1920	85
3.3	Italian delegates at the Monetary and Economic Conference, London 1933	86
4.1	Descriptive statistics of the network	99
4.2	Firms by sector	99
4.3	Top twenty firms by number of interlocks and sector of activity	102
4.4	IDs generated by the top twenty BLs	105
4.5	BLs by age	105
4.6	BLs by region of birth	107
4.7	BLs by level of education	108
4.8	BLs with seats in at least one bank and one industrial firm	109
4.9	Financial elite by type of BLs	110
5.1	Lead management and co-lead management of capital raising by the first hundred ranked French firms in 1963—credit and issuing	120
5.2	Funds raised by the SICAV of the three big deposit banks (millions of francs)	121
8.1	Central bank governors in twelve countries, in office 1950–2000	186

List of Contributors

T. T. Arvind is Professor of Law at Newcastle Law School, having entered academia after several years as a commercial practitioner. He has published extensively in the areas of legal history and private law. His recent work has explored the connections and boundaries between the worlds of common law and regulatory action. He is the author of *Contract Law* (Oxford University Press, 2017), and the joint editor, with Jenny Steele, of *Tort Law and the Legislature: Common Law, Statute and the Dynamics of Legal Change* (Hart, 2013). He was awarded the ICLQ Young Scholar Prize in 2010, and the Society of Legal Scholars Best Paper Prize in 2009.

Youssef Cassis has been Professor of Economic History at the European University Institute, Florence since January 2011. His work mainly focuses on banking and financial history, as well as business history more generally. His most recent publications on the subject include *Capitals of Capital. A History of International Financial Centres, 1780–2005* (Cambridge University Press, 2006, expanded paperback edition, 2010); *Crises and Opportunities. The Shaping of Modern Finance* (Oxford University Press, 2011); and, with Philip Cottrell, *Private Banking in Europe: Rise, Retreat and Resurgence* (Oxford University Press, 2015). He has also recently co-edited *Infrastructure Finance in Europe. Insights into the History of Water, Transport and Telecommunications*, with Giuseppe De Luca and Massimo Florio (Oxford University Press, 2016); *The Performance of European Business in the Twentieth Century*, with Andrea Colli and Harm Schröter (Oxford University Press, 2016); and *The Oxford Handbook of Banking and Financial History*, with Richard Grossman and Catherine Schenk (Oxford University Press, 2016). He was the co-founder and co-editor (1994–2004) of *Financial History Review* (Cambridge University Press), a long serving member of the Academic Advisory Council of the European Association for Banking and Financial History, and President (2005–7) of the European Business History Association.

Alexis Frédéric Drach is Research Associate at Glasgow University. He holds a PhD in history from the European University Institute in Florence. His interests lie in the history of banking regulation and supervision, banks' internationalization, European integration, globalization, and expertise. He is part of the project EURECON, 'The Making of a Lopsided Union: European Economic Integration, 1957–1992', funded by a grant from the European Research Council.

Joanna Gray is Professor of Financial Law and Regulation at Birmingham Law School, University of Birmingham. She qualified as a solicitor in the City of London in the 1980s and has many years' experience lecturing, publishing, and consulting in

List of Contributors

the broad areas of banking and financial markets law and corporate finance law. She has conducted executive education and CPD activity for City of London law firms, for clients in the banking and finance sectors, and for the IMF and Reserve Bank of India. She has participated in policy seminars as an academic expert with the Bank of England, European Central Bank, the UK Financial Services Authority, the Bank of England's Prudential Regulatory Authority, the Central Bank of Russia, and the Australian Prudential Regulatory Authority. Her publications include (with Jenny Hamilton), *Implementing Financial Regulation: Theory and Practice* (John Wiley, 2006) and, more recently, 'Lawyers and Systemic Risk in Finance: Could (and Should) the Legal Profession Contribute to Macroprudential Regulation?', *Legal Ethics* 19.1, 2016, 'Behavioural Finance and the Macroprudential Dimension', *Journal of Banking Regulation* 17.3, 2016, and 'Toward a More Resilient Financial System?', *Seattle University Law Review* 36, 2013.

Leslie Hannah is Professor Emeritus of Business History at the London School of Economics and formerly Dean of Cass Business School, London. Now living in Tokyo, he works on comparisons of American, European, and Japanese business. His latest article (with Makoto Kasuya) is 'Twentieth-Century Enterprise Forms: Japan in Comparative Perspective', *Enterprise & Society* 17, 2016.

Giandomenico Piluso is Associate Professor in Economic History at the University of Siena, Department of Economics and Statistics. He has been a visiting fellow at King's College, University of Cambridge, in 2011 and at Nuffield College, University of Oxford, in 2015, and Jean Monnet Fellow at the European University Institute, Florence, in 2016–17. He has published extensively on financial and business history. His publications include (with Leandro Conte) 'Finance and Structure of the State-Owned Enterprise in Italy: IRI from the Golden Age to the Fall', in F. Amatori, R. Millward, and P. A. Toninelli (eds.), *Re-appraising State-Owned Enterprise: A Comparison of the UK and Italy* (Routledge, 2011), and 'Italy: Building on a Long Insurance Heritage', in P. Borscheid and N. V. Haueter (eds.), *World Insurance: The Evolution of a Global Risk Network* (Oxford University Press, 2012).

Laure Quennouëlle-Corre is director of research at the CNRS in Paris (Centre de Recherches Historiques) and teaches economic history at the Paris1-Pantheon-Sorbonne University. She received her PhD from the Ecole des Hautes études en sciences sociales (EHESS) in 2000 and published her first book, *La direction du Trésor. L'Etat-banquier et la croissance 1947–1967*, the same year. Her work focuses on monetary and financial history, especially international capital flows, financial policies and regulation. Her recent book, *La place financière de Paris au XXe siècle. Des ambitions contraries* (2015), deals with the role of Paris as an international financial centre and explores the role of different financial institutions throughout the century.

Alberto Rinaldi is Associate Professor of Economic History at the University of Modena and Reggio Emilia. He has published extensively on Italian contemporary economic history, focusing in particular on industrial districts, trade, growth, institutions, and the structure of the corporate system. His works are published in leading international journals, such as *Explorations in Economic History*, *Cliometrica*, *Business History*, *Enterprise & Society*, and *Journal of Policy Modelling*.

List of Contributors

Giuseppe Telesca focuses in his research and teaching on economic and financial history. He obtained his PhD in economic and social history at the University of Florence (Italy) and undertook post-doctoral research as Jean Monnet Fellow at the Robert Schuman Centre for Advanced Studies of the European University Institute (EUI) in Fiesole (Italy). After his stay as Visiting Fellow at the University of Reading (UK) he held the position of Research Associate at the EUI where he collaborated with Professor Youssef Cassis on a project on the 'Memories of Financial Crises'. He has published on the history of the Italian banking system, the evolution of Italian financial elites, and the economic and urban impact of big sport events on host cities/countries.

Niccolò Valmori obtained his PhD at the European University Institute in 2016 and is currently post-doctoral fellow at the EHESS in Paris. In 2017 he was awarded the Gustave Gimon Fellowship (Stanford University) and the Earhart Fellowship in Early American History (University of Michigan). Since 2016 he has been teaching at the Institut d'études politiques. Beyond French history his research interests include economic history, Atlantic history, global history, and cultural history.

Michelangelo Vasta received his DPhil at the University of Oxford. He is Professor of Economic History at the Department of Economics and Statistics of the University of Siena. Most of his research work has dealt with Italian economic development from the Unification to the present. His fields of research range over macro and micro perspectives and focus on technical change, institutions, international trade, corporate networks, and entrepreneurship. He has been published extensively in major economic and business history journals such as *Economic History Review*, *European Review of Economic History*, *Explorations in Economic History*, *Journal of Economic History*, *Business History*, and *Enterprise & Society*.

Mikael Wendschlag is a researcher at the Department of Economic History at Uppsala University. Since defending his thesis in 2012 he has received several major research grants to conduct research projects related to the history of central banks, financial supervision, and white-collar crime in financial history. For two years, 2015–17, he was employed by the Swedish FSA as an independent researcher. He has been a visiting researcher at the European University Institute, the Swedish House of Finance, and the Swedish Riksbank.

Sarah Wilson is a Senior Lecturer in Law at York Law School, University of York in the UK. She holds degrees in both law and history, and her key research interests lie in financial law (financial regulation including banking, and financial crime), trusts law, and a 'law and history' combination of legal history (both traditional and critical) and modern British history. Sarah has published widely in the sphere of financial law. Her recent monograph, *The Origins of Modern Financial Crime: Historical Foundations and Current Problems in Britain* (Routledge, 2014) provides a multidisciplinary analysis of financial crime from 1830 to the present. She is currently writing (with Gary Wilson) a monograph on Banking and Society in 21st Century Britain. She is also a long-standing contributor to Lloyds Law Reports Financial Crime, and has helped to shape its new International Section. Sarah's research agenda in financial law is also strongly internationally focused, drawing in the USA and Canada and especially the APAC region.

Introduction

Giuseppe Telesca

I.1 Introduction

The 2008 financial meltdown, which degenerated into the Great Recession, provided the starting point for the research project presented in this book. We observed that while the post-Lehman Brothers financial debacle had spawned a large wave of anger and mistrust towards the financial sector, and had brought about a wealth of accounts of financial elites' responsibilities, in most cases this flurry of literature was lacking historical depth.[1] Less transient reasons, independent from the Lehman collapse, were behind the idea of gathering contributions of colleagues—mostly business historians—interested in financial elites. Looking at the last thirty to forty years we noticed that inequality, whether measured in terms of income or in terms of wealth distribution, was approaching levels last seen before the First World War.[2] At the same time we observed that financial elites occupied little space in historians' research agenda for the last two decades or so. The fading state of the study of elites was in sharp contrast with the popular hostility against a new business plutocracy at the top end of the income distribution that, with different degrees of intensity, depending on the country, was seizing growing

---

[1] See, for instance, Georgina Murray and John Scott (eds.), *Financial Elites and Transnational Business: Who Rules the World?* (Cheltenham, 2012); Heinrich Best and John Higley (eds.), *Political Elites in the Transatlantic Crisis* (Basingstoke, 2014); Andrés Solimano, *Economic Elites, Crises, and Democracy: Alternatives beyond Neoliberal Capitalism* (Oxford, 2014); Stephen Bell and Andrew Hindmoor, *Masters of the Universe and Slaves of the Markets* (Cambridge, MA and London, 2015).

[2] For a bird's-eye view on inequality see Anthony Barnes Atkinson and François Bourguignon (eds.), *Handbook of Income Distribution*, vol. 1 (Amsterdam, 2000). Inequality has become a topical theme in recent years, as demonstrated by the success of the book by Thomas Piketty, *Capital in the Twenty-First Century* (Cambridge, MA, 2014).

shares of national income.[3] In the wake of the Great Recession, which had intensified the fury against financial elites, we felt that the time was ripe to put them at the centre of scholarly attention again, trying to offer a new historical perspective on the topic.

It is the ambition of this book to combine different bodies of scholarship that in the past have been interested in (1) providing social/structural analysis of financial elites, (2) measuring their influence, or (3) exploring their degree of persistence/circulation. The final goal of this effort is to investigate the adjustment of financial elites to institutional change, and to assess financial elites' contribution to institutional change, in the short and in the long term. For this purpose, the volume looks at financial elites' role in different European societies and markets over time, and provides historical comparisons and country and cross-country analysis of their adaptation and contribution to the transformation of the national and international regulatory/cultural context in the wake of a crisis and in a long-term perspective.

On the one hand, a wide definition of financial elites is adopted in this book, in order to mirror the complexity of today's financial world. On the other hand, most of the chapters concentrate on banking elites because they represent the most relevant component of the financial systems examined in this volume. The focus on European bankers complements the post-crisis literature mainly focused on American (or Anglo-Saxon) bankers while allowing for a fruitful comparison between the two sides of the Atlantic Ocean. The vast array of methodological approaches, without affecting the overall coherence of the book, turns this volume into a useful tool for different segments of the academic community: from business and financial historians to lawyers, from economists to sociologists and political scientists. Research results are presented in an accessible way with the aim to render this volume beneficial for regulators, policy-makers, and the general public as well.

I.2 Literature Review

The scholarship on financial elites has traditionally been interested in either measuring financial elites' influence on, and proximity to, other elites (namely the political elite), or providing a description of financial elites' background, education, network of relationships, political tendencies, and cultural values. Even though it is admittedly difficult to completely separate these two approaches, the former strand of literature can be traced back to the works of

---

[3] For the American case see Steven N. Kaplan and Joshua Rauh, 'Wall Street and Main Street: What Contributes to the Rise in the Highest Incomes?', *Review of Financial Studies* 2010 (23.3): 1004–50.

Introduction

John Atkinson Hobson, Rudolf Hilferding, and Louis Brandeis, which will be analysed elsewhere in this volume.[4] The first systemic attempt to measure the influence of bankers, however, was pursued by the British journalist Percy Arnold during the interwar years. Arnold put together a list of directors of prestigious British financial institutions—the Bank of England, the London merchant banks, the so-called 'Big Five' high street banks, the major discount houses, and Glyn, Mills & Co (the then biggest British private bank)—to see who was simultaneously holding directorships in other financial firms.[5] Albeit rudimentary in its methodology and naïve in its conclusions, Arnold's work provided a template for the following academic efforts aimed at measuring the influence of financial/business elites.[6]

If the measurement of influence has traditionally been the favourite research goal of social scientists, historians have added to this body of scholarship, at a later stage, a wealth of social/structural analyses of financial elites. The study of the bourgeoisie in the years of its ascent and consolidation—from the beginnings of the nineteenth century to the First World War—acquired a prominent position in historians' agenda during the 1980s.[7] In the light of the economic crisis of the previous decade, the diminishing faith in state interventionism and Keynesian prescriptions triggered a strong interest towards 'wealth creators' such as entrepreneurs and bankers, which coincided with a reduced attention towards the working class in the field of social history, and a shift from macro to microanalysis in the field of economic history.[8] It is not by chance that Britain—where the politically polarizing and socially costly process of deindustrialization was accompanied by the spectacular growth of the financial sector in the 1980s—was at the forefront of this wave of historical studies dedicated to financial elites. William Rubinstein elicited a controversial debate over the relationship between the City of London and the industrial sector by pointing out that City bankers and merchants were

---

[4] See Chapter 1 by Cassis and Telesca and Chapter 4 by Rinaldi and Vasta.

[5] Percy Arnold, *The Bankers of London* (London, 1938).

[6] On Arnold's work and its shortcomings see Youssef Cassis, 'Financial Elites Revisited', in Ranald Michie and Philip Williamson (eds.), *The British Government and the City of London in the Twentieth Century* (Cambridge, 2004), 76–95. As the literature on this subject is considerable, and a full exploration of it would go beyond the scope of this introduction, we limit ourselves to mentioning Philip Stanworth and Antony Giddens (eds.), *Elites and Power in British Society* (Cambridge, 1974), Michael Useem, *The Inner Circle: Large Corporations and the Rise of Business Political Activity in the US and the UK* (Oxford, 1984), and John Scott, *Corporations, Classes, and Capitalism* (Oxford, 1997).

[7] The discovery of 'the discreet charm of the bourgeoisie' offered the opportunity to revise old established stereotypes. Among other things, the idea that the alleged weakness of the German bourgeoisie, in comparison to the British and the French ones, stemmed from the peculiar historical pattern of its affirmation was nuanced, if not discarded; see the work edited by Jürgen Kocka, *Bürgentum in 19. Jahrhundert. Deutschland im europäischen Vergleich*, 3 vols. (Munich, 1988).

[8] Herman Van Der Wee, 'Economic History: Its Past, Present and Future', *European Review* 2007 (15.1): 33–45.

far wealthier than the British northern industrialists.[9] Were Rubinstein's surprising conclusions supported by credible empirical evidence? Was the economic power of City bankers and financiers, asserted in Rubinstein work, automatically convertible into social prominence and political influence? And, if this was the case, had the socio-political supremacy of the City of London turned into a systematic priority of financial interests over industrial ones since the second half of the nineteenth century? What was the link between this alleged supremacy and the British industrial decline? These questions inspired many socio-historical analyses dedicated to the British financial elite. Youssef Cassis's analysis of English bankers from 1890 to 1914 demonstrated that during the Edwardian period the City aristocracy had merged on equal terms with the landed aristocracy to form a renewed, powerful elite.[10] José Harris and Pat Thane confirmed Cassis's findings applying to the most successful London merchant bankers the concept of 'aristocratic bourgeoisie'. Building on Arno Mayer's idea that neither the aristocracy, nor the bourgeoisie constituted coherent classes, they concluded that 'in Britain by the end of the nineteenth century the most successful merchant bankers were totally integrated with the indigenous landholding aristocracy, and not simply on the aristocracy's terms'.[11] Michael Lisle-Williams, interested in the continuity of family capitalism in English merchant banking until the 1960s, reached similar conclusions over a longer time frame.[12] Eventually Peter Cain and Anthony Hopkins, concerned with the underlying motives and dynamics of British imperialism from the Glorious Revolution to mid-twentieth century, coined the concept of 'gentlemanly capitalism', which summarizes what, at the time, was polemically described as the 'new orthodoxy' of British economic history.[13] Cain and Hopkins saw in the emerging middle-class of the financial sector and services, centred upon London and the south-east of the country, the bulk of a renewed 'gentlemanly capitalism' that started arising from 1850 onwards. As in the case of the first

---

[9] William Rubinstein, *Men of Property: The Very Wealthy in Britain since the Industrial Revolution* (London, 1981).
[10] Youssef Cassis, *Les banquiers de la city à l'époque eduardienne* (Geneva, 1984).
[11] José Harris and Pat Thane, 'British and European Bankers, 1880–1914: An "Aristocratic Bourgeoisie"?', in Pat Thane, Geoffrey Crossick, and Roderick Floud (eds.), *The Power of the Past: Essays for Eric Hobsbawm* (London and New York, 1984), 215–34, quote at p. 228. This indicates a significant divergence between Harris's and Thane's, or Cassis's thesis on the one hand, and Mayer's thesis on the other. Mayer, in fact, argued that the convergence between aristocracy and bourgeoisie had left the former in a position of dominance and control; Arno Mayer, *The Persistence of the Old Regime: Europe to the Great War* (New York and London, 1981).
[12] Michael Lisle-Williams, 'Beyond the Market: The Survival of Family Capitalism in the English Merchant Banks', *British Journal of Sociology* 1984 (35.2): 241–71 and Michael Lisle-Williams, 'Merchant Banking Dynasties in the English Class Structure: Ownership, Solidarity and Kinship in the City of London, 1850–1960', *British Journal of Sociology* 1984 (35.3): 333–62.
[13] Martin J. Daunton, '"Gentlemanly Capitalism" and British Industry, 1820–1914', *Past and Present* 1989 (122): 119–58.

version of 'gentlemanly capitalism', based on capitalist agriculture, this new form of gentlemanly capitalism, based on finance and services, was able to merge with the powerful British landholding aristocracy, hence forming a new, relatively coherent elite, whose interests and values diverged from the ones of the northern industrial capitalists.[14] Despite the qualms of its adversaries, the 'new orthodoxy'—which had the merit of overcoming the until then prevailing neoclassical interpretation of British economic history that excluded social and political considerations—did not go unchallenged and stimulated a passionate debate during the 1980s and early 1990s.[15]

During the same period the interest about financial elites spread over the British borders, and collective biographies of French, German, and Swiss bankers were published in combination with European comparative studies.[16] If these works focused on different themes, depending on the country in which they were produced, the social status enjoyed by bankers and financiers, their higher or lower degree of autonomy/separation compared with other business elites, and their political and economic weight within the society represented the core concerns of this body of scholarship.

---

[14] Peter J. Cain and Anthony G. Hopkins, 'Gentlemanly Capitalism and British Expansion Overseas, I: The Old Colonial System 1688–1850', *Economic History Review* 1986 (39.4): 501–25 and Peter J. Cain and Anthony G. Hopkins, 'Gentlemanly Capitalism and British Expansion Overseas, II: New Imperialism 1850–1945', *Economic History Review* 1987 (40.1): 1–26.

[15] On economic power, social status, and political influence of City bankers see Stanley D. Chapman, 'Aristocracy and Meritocracy in Merchant Banking', *British Journal of Sociology* 1986 (37.2): 180–93; Youssef Cassis, 'Merchant Bankers and City Aristocracy', *British Journal of Sociology* 1988 (39.1): 114–20; Stanley D. Chapman, 'Reply to Youssef Cassis', *British Journal of Sociology* 1988 (39.1): 121–6. On 'gentlemanly capitalism' see Daunton, ' "Gentlemanly Capitalism" '; William Rubinstein, ' "Gentlemanly Capitalism" and British Industry, 1820–1914', *Past and Present* 1991 (132): 150–70; Martin J. Daunton, ' "Gentlemanly Capitalism" and British Industry, 1820–1914: Reply', *Past and Present* 1991 (132): 170–87.

[16] For the national case studies see Alain Plessis's books on the stockholders, regents, and governors of the Bank of France during the Second Empire: *La Banque de France et les deux cent actionnaires sous le Seconde Empire* (Geneva, 1982) and *Régents et gouverneurs de la Banque de France sous le Second Empire* (Geneva, 1985); Youssef Cassis and Fabienne Debrunner, 'Les élites bancaires suisses', *Schweizerische Zeitschrift für Geschichte-Revue Suisse d'Histoire-Rivista Storica Svizzera* 1990 (40.3): 259–73; Morton Reitmayer, *Bankiers im Kaiserreich. Sozialprofil und Habitus der deutschen Hochfinanz* (Göttingen, 1999); Hubert Bonin, *Le monde des banquiers français au XXe siècle* (Brussels, 2000). A comparative perspective on European bankers is in Youssef Cassis, 'Financial Elites in Three European Centres: London, Paris, Berlin, 1880s–1930s', *Business History* 1991 (33.3): 53–71 and in the book edited by the same author, *Finance and Financiers in European History, 1880–1960* (London and Paris, 1992). A few late works on national or comparative collective biographies of bankers deserve to be mentioned here: Youssef Cassis, 'Before the Storm: European Banks in the 1950s', in Stefano Battilossi and Youssef Cassis (eds.), *European Banks and the American Challenge: Competition and Cooperation in International Banking under Bretton Woods* (Oxford, 2002), 36–52; Youssef Cassis, 'European Bankers in the Interwar Years', in M. Kasuya (ed.), *Coping with Crisis: International Financial Institutions in the Interwar Period* (New York, 2003), 21–42; Samuel Tilman, *Les grands banquier belges (1830–1935). Portrait collectif d'une élite* (Brussels, 2005); Iurgen Köhler, 'Redesigning a Class of its Own: Social and Human Capital Formation in the German Banking Elite, 1870–1990', *Financial History Review* 2007 (14.1): 63–87.

The already recalled decline of studies on financial elites in the field of history has various explanations. If one looks at the British case, the dismal performance of the country financial institutions after the 'Big Bang' of the 1980s—namely in the field of investment banking, where the once mighty leading merchant houses have been subjugated by foreign banks—has changed the terms of the old debate, raising questions about the death of 'gentlemanly capitalism'[17] or the desirability of the City of London's so-called 'Wimbledonization'.[18] More generally, two main reasons account for the fading state of the historical studies on elites. On the one hand, the accumulation of knowledge over the subject and the reiterated use of the collective biographies methodology have provoked a physiological process of rejection. On the other hand, other academic approaches within the field of history—cultural history in particular—have gained momentum.[19]

I.3 Not Mere 'Dependent Variables': Financial Elites and Financial Regime Change

Our volume partly goes back to the classical research questions recalled in section 1.2, and partly moves away from them to explore the adaptation of financial elites and their contribution to institutional change. Elites in general, and financial elites in the specific case of this book, have always been seen either as active key agents who effect social change, playing a significant role in shaping the course of history, or as mere supports of particular structural determinants.[20] We decided to adopt an intermediate position between these two strands, as we consider the two dimensions to be interrelated. We claim that not only do the legal/regulatory architecture of the financial markets and the governance of the financial organizations affect financial elites' actions, but also financial elites' actions in turn affect the legal framework of financial markets and the governance of financial organizations.

---

[17] Paul Thompson, 'The Pyrrhic Victory of Gentlemanly Capitalism: The Financial Elite of the City of London, 1945–1990' (two parts), *Journal of Contemporary History* 1997 (33.3): 283–304 and (33.4): 427–40; Philip Augar, *The Death of Gentlemanly Capitalism: The Rise and Fall of London's Investment Banks* (London, 2000).

[18] The concept of 'Wimbledonization' refers to the oldest tennis tournament in the world. It is not the nationality of the winner that matters for the organizers of Wimbledon, but the capacity of the tournament to attract the best players of the world. On the 'Wimbledonization' of the City of London see Richard Roberts, 'London as an International Financial Centre, 1980–2000: Global Powerhouse or Wimbledon EC2?', in Youssef Cassis and Eric Bussière (eds.), *London and Paris as International Financial Centres in the Twentieth Century* (Oxford, 2005), 287–312.

[19] Cassis, 'Financial Elites'.

[20] The antagonism between 'humanism' and 'instrumentalism' within the social sciences is discussed by Mike Savage and Karel Williams, 'Elites: Remembered in Capitalism and Forgotten by Social Sciences', in Mike Savage and Karel Williams (eds.), *Remembering Elites* (Oxford, 2008), 1–24.

Introduction

The shaping of the financial system has been described as a continuous dialectic between the state, which imposes regulation of financial activities in order to stabilize the financial system (a necessity that becomes particularly compelling after a crisis), and the regulatees, who try to circumvent the regulator's intentions. According to Edward Kane, once the legal framework has been set up, the regulatees try to shortcircuit regulator intentions, both by finding loopholes and by simply disobeying the law. In the continuous tension between regulation and regulatory avoidance, a third component plays a crucial role. Financial innovation represents, in Kane's view, the tool par excellence that regulatees use to circumvent regulation. Being fuelled by regulation, financial innovation becomes in turn a determining factor for a new wave of re-regulation.[21]

The authors consider the 'regulatory dialectic' approach an interesting starting point; at the same time they are aware of the necessity to recognize that reality is more complex than a scheme in which there are legislators and bureaucrats who seek to impose regulation, and elite bankers and financiers who try to escape the costs of regulation. At least two other hypotheses should be encompassed for a correct understanding of the financial system's evolution and the financial elites' adaptation/contribution to it. First, there are the beliefs shared by individuals who are in a position to make policies (dominant beliefs).[22] Regulators do not always have confidence in the benefits of a strictly regulated financial system: on the contrary, as the experience of the last decades demonstrates and is discussed elsewhere in the book, at times they believe that deregulated financial markets can be more efficient, and even fairer, than regulated ones. Second, as several chapters of the book implicitly or explicitly assume, regulatees contribute to designing and implementing legal and political reforms that affect the financial system through a process of interaction with governments and policy-makers. The way in which this interaction is carried out may range from lobbying to corruption, passing by the regulatory capture of financial services' supervisors in a process in which the role of financial elites is far from being marginal.

For this reason, the book devotes particular attention to financial elites' reaction to financial regime change. A financial regime change can be defined as a deep transformation in the hierarchy of goals to be pursued, and in the institutional design and the set of tools employed by banks, financial institutions, and financial elites to reach these goals. A financial regime change generally occurs over a long period of time. However, the depth of the

---

[21] Edward J. Kane, 'Good Intentions and Unintended Evil: The Case against Selective Credit Allocation', *Journal of Money, Credit and Banking* 1977 (9.1): 55–69, Edward J. Kane, 'Accelerating Inflation, Technological Innovation, and the Decreasing Effectiveness of Banking Regulation', *Journal of Finance* 1981 (31.2): 355–67.

[22] Douglass C. North, *Understanding the Process of Economic Change* (Princeton, NJ, 2005).

post-Lehman slump and its effect on the real economy, the resolute crisis response deployed by politicians and policy-makers, the coordinated crisis management effort displayed on the occasion of the G20 leaders' summits held in Washington (November 2008) and London (April 2009), and the bold reform agenda put forward by the world's leading economies afterwards, brought about the feeling that a 'Bretton Woods moment' was in the making. Bretton Woods (New Hampshire) was the place where 730 delegates from 44 Allied nations met, in the summer 1944, to agree on the rules of the game of the post-war international monetary system. Bretton Woods became also the formula to design the post-war Keynesian equilibrium built around the idea of a market economy mitigated, and constrained when necessary, by a political process (embedded liberalism).[23] This regime postulated that the state played a crucial role, vis-à-vis the financial system and the corporate sector, when it came to allocating resources, promoting economic growth, fostering public good, and curbing private interests and speculation. The post-war regime responded to problems that the old laissez-faire system had been unable to address during the interwar years, and was the result of unique wartime circumstances, which permitted the building of a large consensus between powerful state actors and international experts.[24]

From the mid-1970s onwards—while the world economy was facing the daunting stagflation challenge—the post-war financial regime was supplanted, through a slow and incremental process, by a neoliberal one, which preached a limited and non-interventionist role for the state, expanded market allocation in economic life, favoured monetarist policies and supply-side reforms, and promoted a regime of free trade and free capital mobility. Neoliberalism, in a significant move away from classic forms of laissez-faire, promoted market solutions beyond the economic sphere and displayed a tendency to accept 'the idea that competition [was] not the "natural" state of affairs, and that the market [could] produce sub-optimal results wherever producers [had] monopoly power'. In the aftermath of the 2008 financial debacle, the time seemed ripe for a new shift from a financial regime of free market and commodification to a regime in which increasing regulation and de-commodification emerged as a response to a profound crisis. Against the expectation of a Polanyian social 'countermovement', some observers predicted that the likely outcome of the 2008 collapse would be a legitimacy crisis of the old financial regime rather than the establishment of a new regime.[25] This phase of navigation in uncharted waters would have probably rendered finance, to use Winston Churchill's

---

[23] John Ruggie, 'International Regimes, Transactions and Change: Embedded Liberalism in the Postwar Economic Order', *International Organization* 1982 (36.2): 379–405.

[24] Erich Helleiner, 'A Bretton Woods Moment? The 2007–2008 Crisis and the Future of Global Finance', *International Affairs* 2010 (86.3): 619–36.

[25] Robert Wade, 'Financial Regime Change', *New Left Review* 2008 (53): 5–21, quote at p. 5.

formula of the mid-1920s, 'less proud' (and more regulated) than it had been from the 1980s onwards. At the same time, it was difficult to say whether structural reforms such as the separation of commercial and investment banking, or the reduction in the size and complexity of institutions too big and interconnected to fail would be implemented.[26] Ten years after Lehman collapse we seem still to be facing a situation in which 'the old is dying and the new cannot be born'.[27] This consideration represents the departing point of our book.

I.4 Presentation of the Volume

The nine chapters of this volume complement each other, either thematically or by period. The collection of essays is organized along thematic blocks within which a chronological order is followed. Youssef Cassis's and Giuseppe Telesca's chapter opens the book because of its immediate link with the post-Lehman collapse debate. Why were elite bankers and financiers demoted from 'masters' to 'servants' of the society after the Great Depression, a crisis to which they contributed only marginally? Why, in contrast, do they seem to have got away with the recent crisis, in spite of their more palpable responsibility in triggering it and the generalized blame unleashed against them? And, finally, were the bankers of the 'first' and the 'second' globalization 'Masters of the Universe' in the same manner? Cassis and Telesca argue that the (relative) mildness of the Great Recession, also due to the already recalled response to the panic generated by the Lehman collapse, has certainly contributed to preserve elite bankers' and financiers' status, income, wealth, and influence, in spite of the considerable loss of their reputational capital. They then draw a distinction between the reality of bankers' and financiers' position and responsibility with regard to the Great Depression and the Great Recession, and the public discourse on bankers and financiers before and after the two crises. The disentanglement of these two levels demonstrates that the narration of a financial crisis can match social and economic reality with a major or minor degree of adherence to authenticity. In the meantime, discursive struggles (blame games) aimed at offering to the public opinion the scapegoat of a crisis have only a limited, and not always positive, impact on the post-crisis process of reform that, contrary to what one may think, represents the exception

---

[26] Martin Wolf, 'Seeds of Its Own Destruction', *Financial Times*, 8 March 2009.
[27] 'La crisi consiste appunto nel fatto che il vecchio muore e il nuovo non può nascere; in questo interregno si verificano I fenomeni morbosi più svariati' (Antonio Gramsci, *Quaderni del carcere*, vol. 1 (Turin, 1975), 311). This famous quote from the *Prison Notebooks* refers to the 1930s crisis, when the Italian Marxist theorist and political activist observed an elite aloof, deprived of any moral authority, and able to cling to power only by means of pure coercion.

rather than the rule after a financial crisis. The chapter provides an in-depth analysis of the differences existing between the bankers of the Great Depression and their colleagues of the late twentieth/early twenty-first century regarding their position within the firm, their attitude towards the firm, and, more generally, their work culture, mental models, and codes of conduct. This comparison allows Cassis and Telesca to discuss, *inter alia*, the topic of remuneration packages and incentives, which has occupied a significant space of the post-crisis debate because of its eye-catching nature—after all, the image of the 'greedy' banker is one of the typical stereotypes of the 'Masters of the Universe'—and, most of all, because the flawed structure of incentives offered to elite bankers has been considered a crucial determinant of the 2008 financial debacle.[28] Apart from the opening chapter, the rest of the book makes but scant reference to a topic that, with a few exceptions, appears to become less relevant when going back in time. This does not mean that elite bankers in the past were not wealthy (and/or greedy), but simply that in the last decades, for the first time in history, a very large number of bankers hired as salaried managers have been able to enjoy a level of remuneration which had previously been reserved only to owner-managers—a phenomenon that has had a strong impact on the governance of banks and financial institutions.

If Cassis and Telesca deal with a potential financial regime change that has not happened yet (and may never take place), the following two chapters deal with two moments of extraordinary transformation: the French Revolution and the Great Depression. What happens to elite bankers and financiers when dramatic political, institutional, and socio-economic transformations occur? Here the big divide is between scholars who believe that elites, even when confronting a systemic crisis, have the ability to reproduce themselves, and conflict theorists, who see history as the 'graveyard of aristocracy' and argue that a systemic upheaval hastens the number of 'deaths' and 'casualties' among elites. On the one hand we have Pierre Bourdieu, who looking at the French experience maintains that elites manage to reproduce themselves. According to Bourdieu, individuals can count on different capitals, which

---

[28] A thorough analysis of the topic goes beyond the scope of this introduction. We can only briefly remind, here, of the two contrasting interpretations regarding the rationale of high remunerations and, most of all, the design of pay structures. According to the agent theorists, pay structures are crucial in aligning executives' interests (agent) to that of the shareholders (principal); see the classic works of Michael C. Jensen and William H. Meckling, 'Theory of the Firm: Managerial Behavior, Agency Costs and Ownership Structure', *Journal of Financial Economics* 1976 (3.4): 305–60 and Eugene F. Fama and Michael C. Jensen, 'Separation of Ownership and Control', *Journal of Law and Economics* 1983 (26.2): 301–25. An opposite strand of thought maintains, instead, that the level and design of top executives' remunerations has nothing to do with an economic rationale and, in reality, mirrors power relationships within the firms; see, for instance, Lucian Bebchuk and Jesse Fried, *Pay Without Performance: The Unfulfilled Promise of Executive Compensation* (Cambridge, MA and London, 2004).

Introduction

can be seen as the 'aces in a game of cards' that define the chances of an individual to 'profit in a particular field'.[29] Bourdieu identifies four types of capital: (1) cultural capital, represented by knowledge and technical skills obtained throughout intergenerational transmission, education, and training; (2) social capital, made up by social networks and influences that one can mobilize when pursuing one's aims; (3) economic capital, made of material goods, money, and properties; (4) symbolic capital, consisting of prestige and good image. Elites' ability to convert one type of capital into another allows them to adjust to a changing environment through the modification of the volume and distribution of their assets.[30] On the other end of the spectrum we have Vilfredo Pareto, who argues that when major motivations of human actions (residues) change, a more or less comprehensive circulation of elites is inevitable and 'foxes', more inclined to innovations, take the place of 'lions', more inclined to consolidation, or vice versa.[31] The Italian Pareto identified a process of political elites circulation that culminated with the ascent of the fascist regime, from 1922 onwards. With this scenario in mind he writes: 'the history of man is the history of the continuous replacement of certain elites: as one ascends, another declines'.[32]

Niccolò Valmori's chapter looks at the biographical experiences of three foreign bankers confronted with the challenge of the French Revolution and the political and economic collapse of the *ancien régime*. The Scottish Walter Boyd, the Anglo-French James Bourdieu, and the Swiss Jean-Conrad Hottinguer saw in the events that brought about the revolution, and in the vicissitudes of the ensuing years, an opportunity to enter new fields of business. Like Machiavelli's Prince, they tried to offset their *fortuna* (the revolution's vicissitudes) with as much *virtù* as they were able to deploy.[33] Their efforts were rewarded with contrasting results. In an account that, at times, evokes (Pierre) Bourdieu's theory of human capital, Valmori insists particularly on the bankers' use of their embedded resources in social networks to ease the flow of information and maximize their connections. Boyd, for instance, in a volatile

---

[29] Pierre Bourdieu, 'The Social Space and the Genesis of Groups', *Theory and Society*, 1985 (14.6): 723–44, quote at p. 724.
[30] Pierre Bourdieu, *Distinction: A Social Critique of the Judgement of Taste* (London and New York, 2010 [1980]).
[31] The division between 'foxes' and 'lions' refers, in Pareto's work, to the political elites, while for the economic elites Pareto distinguishes between 'speculators', with a penchant for innovation, and 'rentiers', with a proclivity towards consolidation (Vilfredo Pareto, *Mind and Society* (New York, 1936), originally published in 1916, with the title *Trattato di sociologia generale*).
[32] Vilfredo Pareto, *The Rise and Fall of the Elites: An Application of Theoretical Sociology* (Totowa, NJ, 1968), 36, originally published in 1901 with the title 'Un'applicazione di teorie sociologiche', in the *Rivista Italiana di Sociologia*.
[33] Machiavelli distinguishes between *fortuna*, say all the circumstances that human beings cannot control, and *virtù*, say the ability to apply the right strategy to counterbalance *fortuna* and, under the circumstances, reach a certain goal (Niccolò Machiavelli, *Il Principe*).

context in which information was in great demand, used his insight into the French political scene to reinforce his business relationship with a leading European financial house such as the Dutch bank Hope and Co. If information is a possible benefit which emerges from the network of an individual, the ascent of Hottinguer illustrates that political influence is another potential gain stemming from relations which are not open to others.[34] But connections can also play ambivalently in times of chaos and turmoil, when political fortunes can rise and fall very quickly, as (James) Bourdieu found out when his business ambitions were fatally wounded by the fall of Jacques Necker, in charge as the Minister of Finance for a second spell, between 1788 and 1790.

Giandomenico Piluso's chapter looks at the interwar years in Italy and adopts a broad definition of financial elites, which encompasses central bankers, senior bankers and managers, and high-ranking civil servants and technocrats. The period under scrutiny—from the early 1920s to the mid-1930s, when a decade-long process of transformation of the Italian financial system's regulatory architecture came to a close—is characterized by growing financial instability. Piluso identifies a dramatic process of circulation within the Italian financial elite during these years, and a shift from the previous dominance of 'cosmopolitan' private bankers and financiers, to a generation of civil servants and high bureaucrats who played, from the mid-1920s onward, an increasing role in the top-down process of organization, regulation, and management of the Italian economy. The prestige of the former was undermined, *inter alia*, by the incapacity of the semi-private mechanisms of international financial/monetary cooperation in which they were involved to solve contentious issues such as the war reparations and the inter-allied debt. The standing of the latter was reinforced by their participation in new forms of international cooperation—for instance, the international conferences of the 1920s and 1930s. The very different profile of the delegates called to represent the Italian interests at the Brussels International Financial Conference, in 1920, and at the London Monetary and Economic Conference, in 1933, epitomizes the extent of the transformation. Piluso's findings are (indirectly) supported by the long-term network analysis of the Italian financial elite provided in the following chapter.

Moving from a short- to a long-term perspective, Chapters 4 and 5 of the volume are devoted to two countries whose 'variety of capitalism' falls in between the two ideal-type models of 'liberal market economy' and 'coordinated market economy' identified by Peter Hall and David Soskice.[35] Consistently

---

[34] Nan Lin, 'Building a Network Theory of Social Capital', in Nan Lin, Karen S. Cook, and Ronald S. Burt (eds.), *Social Capital: Theory and Research* (New York, 2001), 1–29.

[35] Peter A. Hall and David S. Soskice (eds.), *Varieties of Capitalism: The Institutional Foundations of Comparative Advantage* (Oxford, 2001).

Introduction

with the inspiration of the book recalled at the beginning of this introduction, both the chapter by Alberto Rinaldi and Michelangelo Vasta, which deals with the Italian financial elites, and the chapter of Laure Quennouëlle-Corre, which deals with the French financial elites, assume that financial actors are more than 'dependent variables'. The financial system evolves also as a consequence of the structure of the corporate system and the behaviour, within it, of financial elites: that is why Rinaldi and Vasta concentrate on the structure of the corporate system, and Quennouëlle-Corre focuses on the behaviour of financial agents.

Rinaldi's and Vasta's chapter adopts a long-term perspective and looks at the board members of the top 250 Italian companies by total assets; one-fifth of the companies for each benchmark year (1913, 1927, 1936, 1960, 1972, 1983, and 2001) are financial firms. By making use of interlocking directorates (IDs), the authors identify multiple directors and big linkers for each benchmark year. Their assumption is that big linkers—the individuals who hold the largest number of board positions within the companies included in the sample—represent a crucial factor of cohesion: they are the opinion leaders of the business community, operate as a vehicle through which information is collected and spread among banks and companies, and act as the main channel connecting business and political worlds. Rinaldi's and Vasta's reconstruction of the map of bankers' linkages obtained through the use of IDs is also an indirect way to look at the topic of the persistence/circulation of elites explored by Piluso in Chapter 3. In this case the authors' focus is on bankers' centrality within the Italian corporate network during the twentieth century. As clearly emerges from their analysis, bankers' influence picked up in 1927, when the universal banks still played a crucial role within the economic system. The banking legislation of the 1930s, by splitting commercial and investment banking activities and implicitly prohibiting the presence of bank fiduciaries on company boards, pushed the bankers to the periphery of the system. Elite bankers recovered a central position within the Italian corporate system only at the beginning of the twenty-first century, following the return of universal banking in the 1990s. The analysis has the merit of showing that a clear link exists between institutional change and the hierarchies within the corporate system: each institutional transformation favours a new equilibrium in which some components of the economic elites thrive at the expense of others.

Quennouëlle-Corre's chapter considers the French financial elites during the second half of the twentieth century. First, she looks at the years of strict financial regulation in France, between 1950 and 1980, and provides an account of this period that goes beyond the cliché of the cosy cohabitation between banking elites and the French political and regulatory elites, eased by their common background (the *grandes écoles*) and revolving doors practices—for instance the tradition of appointing high civil servants such as the *inspecteurs*

13

des finances to the helm of the big French banks. The picture that emerges from Quennouëlle-Corre's chapter is more nuanced than one would expect, and is one in which financial elites do not always accept strict regulation in exchange for protection from potential competition, but they also try to bypass domestic rules through innovation and the expansion of banking activity beyond borders (the two things being often synonymous), and modify regulation by means of pressures and lobbying in various guises. The second part of the chapter looks at the reaction of the French bankers to the double shock of the 1980s—the nationalization of a large part of the banking system at the beginning of the decade and the liberalization of the financial system between 1984 and 1986—and reflects on the consequences of these events vis-à-vis French financial elites.

Leslie Hannah's chapter takes us back to Victorian Britain in a tale that represents a powerful antidote to agent theorists' tendency to oversimplify the intricacy of human motivation. Hannah notices that shareholders in Victorian Britain were willing to invest their money in public companies in spite of the fact that, at the time, formal corporate governance standards were poorer than the ones set up in the last twenty years or so. Yet, Victorian financial intermediaries did better than their modern counterparts when it came to charging (lower) fees and insuring (better) performance to their investors, and also financial depredations were less significant in magnitude than the ones which have emerged during and after the 2008 financial debacle. According to Hannah, this 'alchemy' occurred as a consequence of a reiterated game of interaction between investors, financial intermediaries, and directors of public companies, in which cooperative and mutually beneficial solutions prevailed, in the longer term, over short-term considerations about directors' maximization of advantages to the detriment of shareholders. Hannah's chapter, by underlining how a series of complex causes and 'a large element of contingency' permitted the alignment of shareholders' and directors' interests in Britain before 1914, casts serious doubts on the ability of state supervision alone to eliminate financial frauds and unethical behaviour by financial elites.

The last three chapters of the book, written respectively by T. T. Arvind, Joanna Gray, and Sarah Wilson, Mikael Wendschlag, and Alexis Drach, focus on the definition of financial elite 'as repository of specialist knowledge';[36] they deal, in other words, with the (in)famous 'experts' whose authority and impartiality has recently been so emphatically questioned in the political battleground. Besides differences in scope (the first chapter has a national, the second an international/comparative, and the third a transnational

---

[36] Arvind, Gray, and Wilson, Chapter 7 in this volume.

Introduction

dimension) and approach (cultural/legal historical the first, more oriented towards the idea of collective biographies the other two), these chapters share a fundamental interest in issues related to the experts' desirable degree of social embeddedness, the difficult search for a balance between their autonomy and their accountability, and the features that render them credible in the eyes of other financial actors, policy-makers, and public opinion.

Like Hannah in Chapter 6, Arvind, Gray, and Wilson focus on Victorian England. Their chapter offers fascinating insights into 'the magic circle of legal advisers who work in the City' (lawyers, practitioners, academics) and the judges and arbitrators tasked with adjudicating financial sector disputes. They analyse their role, influence, and accountability, before comparing the current situation with that of the nineteenth century, when common law's rules and conventions permitted Victorian criminal courts to be structurally insulated from the risk of being captured by financial elite groups. Very little remains today of those rules and conventions. In particular, the authors identify in the process of commercial law reshaping in a more business-friendly direction, between the 1980s and the 1990s, the factor that has profoundly changed the culture and *modus operandi* of the modern civil courts towards banking cases. This difference has clearly emerged in the approach to the post-2008 crisis prosecutions; very different from the one adopted by the Victorian criminal courts in the second half of the nineteenth century.

Wendschlag's chapter analyses a sample of eighty-five bankers at the helm of the central banks of twelve developed economies between 1950 and 2000. The author looks at their political, academic, and professional profile and tries to identify the typical background that renders a central banker credible. The answer, obviously, differs over time and depending on the country. Nonetheless, Wendschlag detects four different shifts during the period under scrutiny, which correspond to the emergence of four different central banker profiles: (1) during the 1950s–60s the typical central banker is endowed with a 'civil servant' background; (2) during the 1970s the typical central banker has the marks of a 'politician'; (3) in the 1980s a 'marked-oriented' kind of governor rises from the ashes of Keynesianism; (4) during the 1990s the figure of the independent academic central banker becomes more and more fashionable, in correspondence with the emergence of an allegedly rule-based, technocratic, and depoliticized monetary policy. According to the author, the major drive of central bankers' profile change is to be detected in the performance of the economy: economic conditions that change for the worse are likely to bring about a new type of central banker.

Drach's chapter should be placed in the context of social scientists' work on policy networks, in particular transnational networks of knowledge-based

Financial Elites and European Banking

experts that share common values (so-called epistemic communities).[37] Historical research has investigated the role of these networks as crucial actors in the development of the European economic project, for instance, or in the setting up of the post-Bretton Woods regulatory/supervisory framework of the international financial system.[38] Drach builds on this body of scholarship to look at the Basel Committee on Banking Supervision, set up to respond to the post-Bretton Woods episodes of financial instability in Britain, Germany, and the United States between 1973 and 1974.[39] The author provides information about the educational profiles and background of fifty of the 127 individuals who took part in the Basel Committee's activities between 1974 and 1988, when the capital adequacy agreement, the first international standard in banking regulation, was achieved. This information is useful to establish the degree of homogeneity within the Basel Committee in the period 1974–88, and the relationship of the components of the Committee—prevalently coming from central banks' supervisory or foreign exchange departments—with the national central banks/regulatory authorities. The second part of the chapter is a Bourdieusian account of the transformation of the Basel Committee from a club of middle-ranked figures who try to learn from each other by means of exchanging ideas and information, to an influential and respected standard setting institution endowed with the task of harmonizing banking regulation and supervisory practices at international level.

As should already be clear after reading this brief introduction, different views are expressed in the book regarding the responsibilities of financial elites in provoking financial crises, their destiny in the aftermath of a systemic crisis, the desirability of having financial elites socially embedded, the appropriate balance that should be found between their autonomy and accountability, and the need for more or less financial regulation. We believe that the plurality of viewpoints expressed in this volume does not result in a mere cacophony of voices and we welcome this element of pluralism, for this is a book that, far from attempting to bring the discussion on financial elites to a close, aims at reviving it among historians.

---

[37] David Marsh and Rod Rhodes, *Policy Networks in British Government* (Oxford, 1992); Peter M. Haas, 'Introduction: Epistemic Communities and International Policy Coordination', *International Organization* 1992 (46.1), 1–35; Martin Marcussen, *Ideas and Elites: The Social Construction of Economic and Monetary Union* (Aalborg, 2000).

[38] See Drach's Chapter 9 in this volume for relevant literature.

[39] The establishment of the Basel Committee in 1974 was part of the reaction of the G10 central bank governors to the challenges of the post-Bretton Woods era.

1

Financial Crises and the Public Discourse on Financial Elites

A Comparison between the Great Depression and the Great Recession

Youssef Cassis and Giuseppe Telesca

1.1 Introduction

In his short novel *O Banqueiro Anarquista*, published in 1922, Fernando Pessoa imagines a dialogue, in the rarefied atmosphere of a gentlemen's club, between a wealthy banker and his deferential after-dinner companion—possibly a junior colleague. In this dialogue the former reveals the mechanics of anarchism to the latter. The banker, who comes from a poor background, claims that he is still the anarchist he used to be when, at the age of 21, he was fighting the 'social fictions' of the bourgeois society. He demonstrates through the use of sophisms and subterfuges that his whole life represents a form of theory and practice of anarchism more coherent than the one pursued by 'the men who throw bombs and form trade unions'.[1] Pessoa plays with an oxymoron, sketching the profile of a banker who does not worry about the means through which his fortune has been acquired and is increased, while fighting bourgeois society's 'social fictions'. Intriguingly, the Portuguese writer uses a banker to represent a type of capitalist who accumulates a huge fortune to set himself free from 'the power and tyranny of money'—that Pessoa identifies as the worst form of bourgeois social fiction of his epoch. Would Pessoa have chosen

---

[1] Fernando Pessoa, 'The Anarchist Banker', in Eugénio Lisboa (ed.), *The Anarchist Banker and Other Portuguese Stories* (Manchester, 1997), 88–114.

another kind of capitalist if he were to write his novel a decade later, in the midst of the Great Depression?

To use the formula of the American economist Paul Sweezy, the type of banker who had symbolized the concentrated economic power of the 'roaring 1920s', had been dismissed 'in the short space of a single decade' because of 'an atrophy of his functions'.[2] Sweezy's work referred to American bankers, the same people tackled by the Senate Committee on Banking and Currency in a probe that resulted in 'the bankruptcy of an elite—of its beliefs, traditions and sense of entitlement'.[3] The German Bank Enquête, at its height in September 1933, was the coeval European version of the Wall Street probe. Even though it did not provoke any relevant changes within the banking legislation of the country, the Bank Enquête brought about a dramatic purge of bankers, often racially and/or politically motivated.[4] If similar public trials did not occur in Britain, France, and Italy, other symptoms—from the suspicion that a 'banker ramp' was behind the fall of the Labour government in 1931,[5] to the French *légende noire* of the 'two-hundred families',[6] to the frequent anti-finance tirades of some of the fascist hardliners in Italy[7]—highlighted that also in these countries bankers were experiencing a shortage of reputational capital. One could be tempted to think that, also as a result of this loss of credibility, bankers were downgraded from 'masters' to 'servants' of the economy and society, and should conclude that something similar will happen, and indeed is already happening, as a consequence of the financial crisis triggered by the collapse of Lehman Brothers in September 2008.

This representation would be historically inaccurate and possibly misleading. The financial crises of the Great Depression were unevenly felt by the world's largest economies, the regulatory responses to them were less uniform than one would imagine,[8] and bankers' responsibilities with regard to the crises were differentiated depending on the countries concerned. Moreover, even though the attempt to hold elite bankers responsible for the crisis was nearly universal, the blame game did not find purchase in popular sentiment everywhere. Nonetheless, the interwar years triggered a financial regime change in banking that can be defined as a fundamental adjustment in the

---

[2] Paul M. Sweezy, 'The Decline of the Investment Banker', *Antioch Review* 1941 (1.1): 63–8.
[3] Steve Fraser, *Wall Street: A Cultural History* (London, 2005), 390.
[4] Harold James, *The German Slump: Politics and Economics, 1924–1936* (Oxford, 1986), 317–23.
[5] We will come back to this point in section 1.4.
[6] René Sédillot, *Les Deux Cents Familles* (Paris, 1988).
[7] Matteo Di Figlia, *Farinacci: il radicalismo fascista al potere* (Rome, 2007).
[8] They went from the timely and severe measures implemented in the United States, to the delayed and mild ones taken by France, to the almost inexistent changes in Britain's legislation; Youssef Cassis, 'Regulatory Responses to the Financial Crises of the Great Depression: Britain, France, and the United States', in Edward J. Balleisen, Lori S. Bennear, Kimberly D. Krawiec, and Jonathan B. Wiener (eds.), *Policy Shock: Recalibrating Risk and Regulation after Oil Spills, Nuclear Accidents, and Financial Crises* (Cambridge, 2017), 349–70.

hierarchy of goals to be pursued, and in the institutional design and the set of tools employed by banks, financial institutions, and financial elites to reach these goals. If compared with the financial crises of the Great Depression, the financial crisis triggered by the collapse of Lehman Brothers has been more global in its consequences, despite primarily affecting the United States and Western Europe, provoking the so-called Great Recession; it has stimulated a more homogeneous effort to promote financial reform in the world's leading economies, and has spawned a large and generalized wave of anger and mistrust towards the financial sector. The contradictory implementation of the reform agenda, and a series of scandals and malfeasances in the banking and financial sector that have emerged since 2008, however, seem to question the assumption that we are witnessing a transformation comparable to that experienced after the Great Depression. In Europe, both the single countries and the European Union have endeavoured to implement a complex set of legislative and regulatory reforms put forward by specialized panels of policy advisers (e.g. the Liikanen Commission for the EU or the Vickers Commission for the United Kingdom). The European Parliament has adopted a series of reforms designed to merge the control of Eurozone lenders under a banking union and end the era of taxpayer bailouts.[9] A perhaps more coherent financial reform effort has been displayed in the United States, through the approval of the 2010 Dodd-Frank Wall Street Reform and Consumer Protection Act.[10] However, the election of Donald Trump at the end of 2016, his promise to soften financial sector regulation, and a series of appointments to senior government and regulatory positions of people linked to Wall Street, seem to hint that a significant reversal of the policies pursued since 2008 could be under way.[11]

---

[9] Recent events, for instance the winding up of two failing regional banks in Italy (June 2017), have been interpreted as an infringement of the Bank Recovery and Resolution Directive, which was aimed at ruling out the use of public funds for bank rescues (Lucrezia Reichlin, 'The European Banking Union Falls Short in Italy', *Financial Times*, 27 June 2017).

[10] A scholarly evaluation of the financial reform process in Britain, France, Germany, the European Union, and the United States is in Renate Mayntz (ed.), *Crisis and Control: Institutional Change in Financial Market Regulation* (Cologne, 2012). For an in-depth analysis of the American legislation see Viral V. Acharya, Tom Cooley, Matthew Richardson, and Ingo Walter (eds.), *Regulating Wall Street: The Dodd-Frank Act and the New Architecture of Global Finance* (Hoboken, NJ, 2011).

[11] Trump called the Dodd-Frank Act 'a disaster' during the presidential campaign. In February 2017 he signed an executive order asking the Treasury to conduct a 120-day review of it and other American financial regulations ('The Right Way to Redo Dodd-Frank', *The Economist*, 11 February 2017). In June 2017 he nominated an avowed enemy of the Dodd-Frank Act at the helm of the Federal Deposit Insurance Corporation, one of the United States' most powerful bank regulators (Barney Jopson, 'Trump Nominates Dodd-Frank Opponent to Police Wall Street', *Financial Times*, 18 June 2017). Also the November 2017 disavowal of Janet Yellen—traditionally Fed chair are offered a second term—has been interpreted as a further sign of the President's willingness to loosen the post-crisis financial regulation ('The Unfortunate Exit of an Exemplary Fed Chair', *Financial Times*, 29 November 2017).

Political scientists have been puzzled by the duration and contradictory direction of the post-crisis transition and have been looking for reasons that help to make sense of this *strange non-death of (neo) liberalism*.[12] A structural motive has been proposed, which maintains that the forces that have benefited most from the neoliberal financial regime remain powerful actors, particularly in the political field. This would explain, for instance, why banks and financial institutions were permitted to become too big to fail before the crisis, and were bailed out at the expenses of taxpayers after.[13] Another explanation focuses on neoliberalism's institutional embeddedness, which would render difficult its replacement. To put it simply, the institutionalization of neoliberal ideas and the existence of organizations imbued with neoliberal ideas have played a crucial role in ensuring the persistence and supremacy of neoliberalism. The argument of institutional embeddedness would contribute to explain why the bold reform agenda envisaged in the aftermath of the financial debacle has been only partially implemented, or is currently under scrutiny where the process of reform has gone further (as is the case of the United States). Other justifications look more in a cultural/ideological direction, emphasizing neoliberalism's extraordinary flexibility and adaptability, but also its capacity to win over alternative competitors when it comes to developing and communicating its ideas in the policy arena and political sphere.[14]

Historians have emphasized that the Great Depression marked a turning point in the foundation of a 'well-tempered' capitalism because of the exceptional conjuncture of a period characterized by two world wars, a devastating economic crisis, a series of political turbulences, a massive process of re-nationalization of the world economic system, and the abrupt end of the process of globalization.[15] When compared to the Great Depression, the Great Recession has been so far milder in its political, economic, and social consequences. Moreover, better crisis management has been put in place, building on the lessons of past financial crises.[16] If this awareness has avoided a new

---

[12] We play with the title of Colin Crouch, *The Strange Non-Death of Liberalism* (Cambridge, 2011) who, in turn, evokes George Dangerfield's classic *The Strange Death of Liberal England* (New York, 1935).

[13] The second part of this critique ignores that the alternative would have been even worse—as the panic triggered by Lehman collapse clearly showed.

[14] An in-depth analysis of the reasons for the neoliberal paradigm's resilience, with a complete state-of-the-art review of the relevant literature is in Vivien A. Schmidt and Mark Thatcher, 'Theorizing Ideational Continuity: The Resilience of Neo-Liberal Ideas in Europe', in Vivien A. Schmidt and Mark Thatcher (eds.), *Resilient Liberalism in Europe's Political Economy* (Cambridge, 2013), 1–50.

[15] Youssef Cassis, *Crises and Opportunities: The Shaping of Modern Finance* (Oxford, 2011), 104–12.

[16] This is particularly true if one looks at the monetary policy. Following the 2008 financial turmoil, central bankers have maintained the solemn promise made by Ben Bernanke in 2002, for the 90th birthday of Milton Friedman, the first scholar who pointed out at the responsibilities of the monetary authorities in transforming 1929 in the Great Depression (Milton Friedman and Anna J. Schwartz, *The Great Contraction 1929–1933* (Princeton, NJ, 1965)). On that occasion,

Great Depression, it has also allowed for a quick return to mainstream ideas, policies, and attitudes as soon as the conclusion that the worst scenarios had been averted had been reached.[17] As a side effect of this return to 'business as usual', elite bankers and financiers have been spared the destiny of their colleagues during the interwar years.

We believe that such explanations might be helpfully integrated by looking at bankers' and financiers' position and responsibility with regard to the Great Depression and the Great Recession, on the one hand, and by analysing the shaping of the public discourse on bankers and financiers before and after the crises, on the other. Section 1.3 deals with financial elites' responsibility in the Great Depression and in the Great Recession, comparing and contrasting themes such as banks' and financial institutions' ownership and control, weight (in), links (with), and contribution to the 'real economy'. Section 1.4 looks at the prevailing narratives prior to the crises and at the discursive struggles triggered by the latter. Which responsibilities did journalists, politicians, policy-makers, scholars, and interest groups ascribe to bankers and financiers during the Great Depression? Did the discursive struggles triggered by the Great Depression affect bankers and financiers in the 1930s? Are they likely to affect them after the Great Recession?

As a preliminary step to this analysis, we need to justify the comparison between the Great Depression and the Great Recession and say more about the theoretical framework of this chapter.

1.2 Theoretical Framework

It can be admitted that financial crises share similar characteristics—from their deep causes to their unfolding and eventual denouement—whatever the specific context within which they take place. One thinks, for example, of the various stages of a typical crisis identified by Charles Kindleberger (displacement, bubble, financial distress, crisis, revulsion and discredit) or the level of excessive indebtedness emphasized by Reinhart and Rogoff.[18] More specifically, the Great Recession approaches the Great Depression in magnitude and

---

the future Chair of the Board of Governors of the Federal Reserve when the 2008 crisis unfolded, said to Friedman: 'You were right. We did it. We are very sorry. But thanks to you, we won't do it again' ('Remarks by Governor Bernanke at the Conference to Honor Milton Friedman', University of Chicago, 8 November 2002, <http://www.federalreserve.gov/boarddocs/Speeches/2002/20021108/default.htm>, last accessed 3 December 2016).

[17] Barry J. Eichengreen, *Hall of Mirrors: The Great Depression, the Great Recession, and the Uses and Misuses of History* (Oxford, 2015), 1–14.

[18] Charles P. Kindleberger, *Manias, Panics and Crashes: A History of Financial Crises* (London, 1978); Carmen M. Reinhart and Kenneth S. Rogoff, *This Time is Different: Eight Centuries of Financial Folly* (Princeton, NJ, 2009).

resonates with macroeconomic, microeconomic, and geopolitical issues that emerged during the 1920–30s with regard to the causes of the crises and the context in which they took place. One should not forget, however, the differences between the two events and, with regard to the Great Depression, we should distinguish between the Wall Street Crash of 1929 and the banking crises of the early 1930s. Often evoked in the wake of the Lehman collapse, the former presents less convincing analogies with the recent turmoil than the latter, which provide a demonstration of the fragility of financial systems and their connections with the real economy.[19] We decided to compare the Great Depression and the Great Recession because we believe that the recent financial debacle shares with the Great Depression—at least potentially—the features of

> a singular, accelerating process in which many conflicts, bursting the system apart, accumulate so as to bring about a new situation after the crisis has passed [...] the crossing of an epochal threshold, a process that can repeat itself *mutatis mutandis*. Even if history always remains unique in individual cases...[20]

Severe financial crises such as the ones we decided to explore entail not only tangible economic, social, and political consequences that have the potential to provoke large-scale transformations; they also encompass a cultural dimension in that they may 'strain the metaphors that construct the cognitive framing of economic life'. The socio-economic context is framed in cognitive maps that help us make sense of what happens. An acute financial crisis may 'invalidate the existing maps', and trigger discursive struggles in which different actors contribute to produce alternative frames of meaning in order to mobilize support for their position. Most of the time these alternative maps are already on offer before a crisis occurs, even though they are usually confined to the margins of the prevailing, undisputed orthodoxy.[21] A financial crisis has the potential to challenge a culturally constructed dominant narrative, and might allow for the emergence of other ways to make sense of the reality.[22] When a crisis occurs, journalists, politicians, policy-makers, scholars, and interest groups engage in the 'dynamic process of accusations and counter accusations', so-called blame games, to identify the actor/actors that can

---

[19] Harold James, *The Creation and Destruction of Value: The Globalisation Cycle* (Cambridge, MA and London, 2009), 36–97.
[20] Reinhart Koselleck, *The Practice of Conceptual History: Timing History, Spacing Concepts* (Stanford, CA, 2002), 240.
[21] Mark D. Jacobs, 'Financial Crises as Symbols and Rituals', in Karin Knorr Cetina and Alex Preda (eds.), *The Sociology of Finance* (Oxford, 2012), 376–92, quotation 377.
[22] Peer C. Fiss and Paul M. Hirsh, 'The Discourse of Globalization: Framing and Sensemaking of an Emerging Concept', *American Sociological Review* 2005 (70.1): 29–52. The authors explain that the meaning of events can be socially constructed by actors who produce frames of meaning to mobilize support for their position (framing perspective), or can result from social-psychological and epistemological processes through which actors develop an understanding of the situation which they are in (sense-making perspective).

be held responsible for the crisis. Blame games allow the members of a society to 'express indignation at acts that offend the collective conscience' and to 're-establish a disrupted social order'.[23] Moreover, as crises narratives are constructed simultaneously to the denouement of the events, the way in which crises are written and perceived contributes to shaping the responses to them, hence determining the way in which crises unfold.[24] Crises narratives are eventually reconstructed and reinterpreted ex-post, when the discursive struggles move to the historical battlefield and crises are remembered differently, depending on the sensitivity of the day. In section 1.4 we touch upon the latter point only briefly (we will come back to the topic in a future work),[25] while we concentrate on coeval representations of bankers' responsibilities with regard to the crises of the Great Depression, and draw some lessons for today's debate. Our goal is to test the idea according to which narratives 'co-construct and legitimize social reality', hence creating 'order out of chaos by assigning meaning and causality to seemingly incomprehensible and unconnected events'.[26] But before delving into the socio-cultural representation of the financial crises under scrutiny, we need to say more about financial elites' position and responsibility then (Great Depression) and now (Great Recession).

1.3 Financial Elites' Position and Responsibilities

Financial elites should hold a similar level of responsibility in major financial crises (as opposed to isolated events such as the failure of a single bank) such as those of the Great Depression or the financial debacle of 2008 and the ensuing Great Recession. This is often implicitly assumed in the comparisons between the two crises. Interestingly, it has been observed that the level of remuneration of American bankers had reached inordinately high levels, by comparison with other sectors, in the 1920s and since the 1990s.[27] Comparisons have also been made between the losses, mainly in terms of reputation, suffered by

---

[23] Olivia Nicol, 'The Blame Game for the Financial Crisis (2007–2010): A Sociological Theory of Fields of Accusation', EUI Working Paper MWP 2016/03.
[24] Colin Hay, 'Chronicles of a Death Foretold: The Winter of Discontent and Construction of the Crisis of British Keynesianism', *Parliamentary Affairs* 2010 (63): 446–70.
[25] We are currently working on a project dedicated to The Memory of Financial Crises supported by the Research Council of the European University Institute, Florence.
[26] Per Hansen, 'From Financial Capitalism to Financialization: A Cultural and Narrative Perspective on 150 Years of Financial History', *Enterprise and Society* 2014 (15.4): 605–42, quotation 608. On the performative role of economics in shaping economic reality, a topic that will be dealt with later, see also Donald Mackenzie, *An Engine, Not a Camera: How Financial Models Shape Markets* (Cambridge, MA and London, 2008), 6–25.
[27] See Thomas Philippon and Ariell Reshef, 'Wages and Human Capital in the U.S. Finance Industry: 1909–2006', *Quarterly Journal of Economics* 2012 (127.4): 1551–1609.

bankers as a consequence of the financial crises of the 1930s and those of 2008 (see section 1.4).

But how much did the banking elite in the 1920s and in the decade or so preceding the collapse of Lehman Brothers actually have in common—in terms of socio-professional status, income and wealth, as well as involvement in the financial turbulence of their time? The issue remains rather blurred, and yet it is an essential dimension of a comparison between the two periods. Given that both crises were 'global', though in a different way, it is important to consider the position of leading bankers and financiers in the world's major advanced economies, namely the United States, Britain, France, and Germany. Japan will be left aside as it did not really belong to this group in the 1920s and experienced a different financial crisis in the late twentieth century. Differences were more marked in the first half of the twentieth century than at the turn of the twenty-first, so closer attention will be paid to the earlier period.

The socio-professional status of bankers, like that of other business leaders, is primarily determined by their position in the firm: as owner-manager or salaried manager. Banks were the first companies, alongside railways, where ownership was separated from control. The 'banking revolution' of the nineteenth century saw the advent of the joint stock bank, in England in the 1830s and in continental Europe in the 1850s. By the late nineteenth century, a group of large commercial banks had emerged in most European countries and were extending their network of branches nationwide.[28] These 'new banks' had several thousand shareholders and were managed by a board of directors who usually delegated the running of the bank's daily business to full-time salaried managers. Big banks had thus become managerial enterprises.[29] In the United States, where banks were smaller (opening branches in another state was prohibited by law), the separation between ownership and control was less pronounced than in Europe. The presidents of the largest banks often had a controlling stake in the company—as late as the early twentieth century in a bank such as National City Bank, for example, the country's largest bank.[30] Nevertheless, by the 1920s, managerial capitalism had become more firmly established in the banking world in both Europe and America, in line with the general trend in big business development.[31]

---

[28] See Philip L. Cottrell, 'Aspects of Commercial Banking in Northern and Central Europe, 1880–1931', in Sara Kinsey and Lucy Newton (eds.), *International Banking in an Age of Transition* (Aldershot, 1998), 90–135; Youssef Cassis (ed.), *Finance and Financiers in European History, 1880–1960* (Cambridge, 1992).
[29] See Alfred D. Chandler, Jr, 'The Emergence of Managerial Capitalism', *Business History Review* 1984 (58.4): 473–503.
[30] Harold van B. Cleveland and Thomas F. Huertas, *Citibank 1812–1970* (Cambridge, MA, 1985).
[31] See Cassis, *Crises and Opportunities*, 79–82.

The rise of the big banks did not entirely eradicate the influence of family owned and controlled private banks. Powerful banks, organized as partnerships, were able to survive and prosper in the world's two leading financial centres: the merchant banks in London and the investment banks in New York. They included such famous names as Rothschilds, Barings, Morgan Grenfell, Schroders, Kleinwort, and Hambros in the former; J. P. Morgan, Kuhn Loeb, Speyer, Seligman, Kidder Peabody, Lee Higginson, and Dillon Read in the latter.[32] They were still at the apex of international finance in the 1920s, and managed to survive the Great Depression, state intervention and regulation, and the decline in international capital flows; although no longer regal, they still enjoyed a degree of prestige and influence. A change took place in the 1960s, with the conversion of most merchant banks and investment banks into public companies. Some had done so earlier, but they had remained in family hands. What changed in the 1960s, in Britain and the United States, was the opening of both ownership and control, on a large scale, to outside interests—not only outside the family, but also outside the traditional networks of relationships.

It would be wrong to assume that these banks retained a partnership form of organization because they were engaged in investment banking, a banking activity deemed more risky than commercial banking. The German universal banks, which combined commercial banking and investment banking and, unlike their American counterparts, were not barred from doing so in the 1930s, were typical managerial enterprises. In the same way, the French leading investment bank, the Banque de Paris et des Pays-Bas, established in 1872, had been run from an early stage by salaried managers. The merchants banks' and investment banks' survival as partnerships was primarily due, especially in Britain, to the specialization of the banking system, which continued until the 1980s. In the United States, investment banks were facing increasing competition from the securities affiliates of the commercial banks in the 1920s and were undoubtedly protected by the Glass-Steagall Act of 1933. Their conversion into public companies offered a number of advantages—tax advantages to partners; no risk of large capital withdrawals following a partner's death; better incentives to valued employees; and wider resources required by new activities, especially trading and principal investment, as well as new technology.[33]

---

[32] See Vincent Carosso, *Investment Banking in America: A History* (Cambridge, MA, 1970); Stanley D. Chapman, *The Rise of Merchant Banking* (London, 1984).

[33] See Alan D. Morrison and William J. Wilhelm, Jr, *Investment Banking: Institutions, Politics, and Law* (Oxford, 2007), 89–92 and 267–92. Morrison and Wilhelm link investment banks' forms of organization to the type of skills required to perform their activities: partnerships are best adapted to 'tacit knowledge' characteristic of traditional investment banking, joint stock companies to 'technical expertise', increasingly predominant in modern investment banking.

The difference between owner-managers and salaried managers was reflected in their respective levels of income and wealth. Figures are mainly available for the pre-1914 years, but things had not fundamentally changed a decade or so later. Not surprisingly, the highest incomes and largest fortunes in the financial sector were made by investing one's own money—in other words as a partner of a private bank rather than as a manager of a joint stock bank. The wealthiest were the partners in the most prominent firms. In the United States, John Pierpont Morgan was the richest banker, though the $80 million estate he left on his death in 1914 fell short of the greatest fortunes made in industry by the likes of Carnegie or Rockefeller.[34] In Europe, the Rothschilds, as a family, came first by a significant margin, while individually the French Rothschilds ($50 million each for Alphonse and Gustave) came ahead of their English cousins. In the City of London, most of the multimillionaires (more than $5 million) were partners in a leading merchant bank.[35] In Germany, private bankers in both Frankfurt and Berlin were far wealthier than the managing directors of the big Berlin credit banks. Interestingly, however, the latter were the richest amongst European banks' salaried managers, with several fortunes in excess of $2 million. This reflected the governance structure of German business. Profit-sharing plans and bonuses are difficult to compare for this period. However, unlike their counterparts in Britain and France, senior managers in German banks sat on, and often chaired, the supervisory boards of a myriad of companies (usually at least twenty for the managing directors of the big Berlin banks) for which they received a not insignificant fee. However, this was not enough to bridge the gap with owner-managers.[36]

The contrast is striking with the position of the senior executives of today's leading banks. Even though this new financial elite is almost entirely made up of salaried managers, it has been able to retain some of the prerogatives of the partners of the old family owned investment banks—in the first place the remuneration packages they have been able to secure and hence the wealth they have been able to accumulate. The scale of the highest rewards might not have exceeded that achieved by the financial magnates of the first globalization and such opportunities have remained the preserve of a fairly small elite. However, the proportion of bankers benefiting from an exceptionally high income might well be higher, because of the vast expansion of the financial sector and the far greater complexity of financial transactions. Moreover, not only top managers, but also star traders and others in sales

---

[34] William D. Rubinstein (ed.), *Wealth and the Wealthy in the Modern World* (London, 1980), 19.
[35] Youssef Cassis, *City Bankers, 1890–1914* (Cambridge, 1994), 197–200.
[36] Morton Reitmayer, *Bankiers im Kaiserreich. Sozialprofil und Habitus der deutschen Hochfinanz* (Göttingen, 1999), 112–20.

(of equity or structured products), or mergers and acquisitions have been able to make their fortune—thanks not only to salaries but, especially, to incentives such as bonuses and stock options.

More importantly, for the first time in history, salaried managers have been able, on a grand scale, to enjoy a level of remuneration which had previously been the preserve of owner-managers. In other words, bankers risking other people's money have benefited from the same privileges as those risking their own capital. There are some exceptions that confirm the rule. Hedge fund managers, for example, have been risking their own capital, and made huge fortunes,[37] while instances of stratospheric remuneration of top managers can be found in the 1920s.[38] Nevertheless, this is a new phenomenon, and a significant difference between now and then.

Interestingly, these differences have been reflected in the way financial elites have been held responsible for the two crises. Bankers have fallen from their pedestal for different reasons. Admittedly, the financial debacle of 2008 was different from the banking crises of the Great Depression. To put it in a nutshell, the various crises that broke out between 1931 and 1934 were primarily a *consequence* of the economic depression, even though they contributed to exacerbate the situation, whereas the financial disaster of 2008 was clearly the *cause* of the ensuing Great Recession. Moreover, we have already said that unlike the 2008 crisis, those of the 1930s retained a distinctly national character. They did not break out simultaneously in all countries, with some countries, like Britain, escaping them altogether, and others, such as France, experiencing a protracted but never acute crisis. Not surprisingly, the most serious banking crises occurred in the two countries where the economic crisis was most severe: the United States and Germany.[39]

As a consequence, the perception of the nature of the financial crises and the causes of the depression was different—between countries and between periods. In the 1930s, far more emphasis was put on the stock market crisis in the United States than in Europe. The Wall Street Crash of 1929 had no equivalent in Europe, neither the excesses of the 1920s, characterized by the euphoria of growth, speculative fever, inexperience and also, at

---

[37] See for example the popular account of Sebastian Mallaby, *More Money than God: Hedge Funds and the Making of a New Elite* (London, 2010).
[38] At National City Bank, for example, a bonus plan, known as the management fund, was adopted in 1923, linking the remuneration of senior executives to the bank's performance. In practice, after a deduction of 8 per cent, senior executives shared between themselves 20 per cent of the bank's profits. The president, Charles Mitchell, had a $25,000 fixed salary, but his total pay package was far higher, especially in the boom years of the late 1920s, reaching $3.5 million between 1927 and 1929, to which must be added his individual participations in the bank's flotations. See Cleveland and Huertas, *Citibank*, 111; John Kenneth Galbraith, *The Great Crash 1929* (London, 1975 [1954]), 171; Carosso, *Investment Banking*, 333–4.
[39] See Cassis, *Crises and Opportunities*, 22–30.

times, fraud;[40] nor the depth and length of the market collapse, down 89 per cent from its 1929 peak when it bottomed out in July 1932.[41] Moreover, with the democratization of share ownership in the United States, losses were borne by a much wider investing public than in France or even Britain. There might have been as many as 15 million holders of securities in America in 1925 (the highest estimate), though no more than 600,000, or barely 4 per cent, were believed to own 75 per cent in value. Nevertheless the figure of the small investor held a central place in the collective imagination of the day, and his or her participation in subscriptions was sought after, as shown by the low value of various shares.

In the United States bankers' responsibility in the crisis was judged from the perspective of stock market operations and the deception of small investors by unscrupulous bankers. The hearings of the Senate investigation on banking and stock exchange practices went on for two years, from April 1932 to May 1934, and took a particularly energetic turn with the appointment, in January 1933, of Ferdinand Pecora as counsel for the Senate Committee on Banking and Currency. The Senate investigation into banking and stock exchange practices greatly contributed to the pillorying of Wall Street's leading bankers and financiers, with its findings echoed in the popular press and resonating with the public.[42] These Wall Street grandees were not held responsible for bringing their banks to the brink of collapse: the major banks had indeed survived four banking crises and, however weakened, still stood firm in the depth of the Depression. They were mainly accused of malpractices judged harmful to investors and condemned by a public opinion increasingly hostile to the financial world, with abuses, breach of trust, and self-enrichment, in various guises, being recorded.[43]

---

[40] See Galbraith, *The Great Crash*, who more than anyone else popularized this view. For Galbraith, the raging bull market from early 1928 was conditioned by a popular belief in the market's perpetual rise, by the forming of investment trusts and holding companies, and by the tremendous leverage caused by the increasingly widespread practice of margin buying.

[41] In Paris, by contrast, stocks had fallen by 59 per cent during the same period, while in London, they never lost more than a third of their value; Alfred Sauvy, *Histoire économique de la France entre les deux guerres*, 3 vols. (Paris, 1984), vol. III, 398–405.

[42] Witnesses included Charles Mitchell, chairman and former president of National City Bank and its investment bank affiliate, National City Company; Albert Wiggin, his counterpart at Chase National Bank and Chase Securities Corporation; Jack Morgan, senior partner of J. P. Morgan & Co., and Thomas Lamont, the firm's foremost partner; Albert Kahn, a senior partner in Kuhn Loeb & Co., Wall Street's second largest investment bank; Clarence Dillon, senior partner of Dillon Read & Co., another top investment bank, which rose to prominence in the 1920s; Richard Whitney, chairman of the New York Stock Exchange; and others. See Carosso, *Investment Banking*, 330–48; Fraser, *Wall Street*, 381–4; Ron Chernow, *The House of Morgan: An American Banking Dynasty and the Rise of Modern Finance* (London, 1990), 360–74; Cleveland and Huertas, *Citibank*, 172–85.

[43] National City Company, for example, advised investors to buy South American stock (especially two loans for Minas Geraes, a state in the Brazilian Republic, and three Peruvian government loans) that it had issued, and knew to be low grade, with no information about risks or market conditions. Kuhn Loeb issued investors in a holding company (the Pennroad Corporation) not with actual shares but with certificates carrying no voting rights. Dillon Read

In Germany, opinions were divided between those who directly attributed the crisis to the banks and their leaders—excessive foreign liabilities, insufficient equity, and ultimately the pernicious effects of universal banking—and those who saw the problem in the international politico-economic context—German foreign policy on reparation.[44] In France, politico-financial scandals (failure of the Banque Oustric, Stavisky affair) tended to overshadow a series of fairly minor banking crises. Britain was more concerned with the fate of the pound than its fairly stable banking system.

1.4 Discursive Struggles

The context within which the Great Depression and the Great Recession took place looks similar, once the disruption brought about by the First World War is discounted. A growing degree of global financial markets' integration and the increasing salience of finance in the economy of the major industrialized countries are recorded in the periods preceding the two crises.[45] Both during the so-called 'first' and during the 'second' globalization, bankers and financiers played a remarkable role in spreading and accelerating those structural transformations, hence becoming the 'heroes' of the narratives that considered those processes beneficial, and the 'villains' of the narratives that maintained a critical view on those developments.

Joseph Alois Schumpeter's famous definitions of the banker as the 'capitalist par excellence' and the 'ephor of the exchange economy' were coined in his

---

structured the capital of two of its investment trusts (United States and Foreign Securities Corporation and United States and International Securities Corporation) in such a way as to exert complete control with less than 10 per cent of their capital. J. P. Morgan allocated the stock of one its holding companies (the Alleghany Corporation) to a 'preferred list' of influential friends; see Carosso, *Investment Banking*, 330–48.

[44] See Theo Balderston, 'The Banks and the Gold Standard in the German Banking Crisis of 1931', *Financial History Review* 1994 (1.1): 43–68.

[45] The first phenomenon was the consequence of a wave of innovations in communication technologies that, in the second part of the nineteenth century, stimulated an increasing movement of goods, capital, and people, promoted a significant convergence in living standards within the countries that experienced industrialization first, and created a climate favourable to further economic opening (Kevin H. O'Rourke and Jeffrey G. Williamson, *Globalization and History: The Evolution of a Nineteenth-Century Atlantic Economy* (Cambridge, MA and London, 1999), 1–7). As for the growing weight of finance relative to the real economy—a physiological phenomenon in a mature economy—various studies have documented this trend during the first wave of globalization (for the British case see Philip L. Cottrell, 'The Domestic Commercial Banks and the City of London, 1870–1939', in Cassis, *Finance and Financiers*, 39–62). Between 1987 and 2007 the degree of financial intensity of economies such as the British and the American ones—as measured by indices such as the Financial Interrelation Ratio—went through a dramatic acceleration and reached unprecedented levels (Alessandro Roselli, *Financial Structures and Regulation: A Comparison of Crises in the UK, USA and Italy* (London, 2012), 145–9).

1912 *Theorie der Wirtschaftlichen Entwicklung*.[46] In the same year, the publicist and future Nobel Prize winner Norman Angell was invited to talk about his book at the London Institute of Bankers.[47] According to Angell, the idea that militarism, wars and conquests were beneficial for national economies represented a *Great Illusion*, a reality cancelled by the growing economic interdependence between industrial countries.[48] In his address to the British banking community, Angell underlined how bankers and financiers, far from being the 'sinister' representatives of a mysterious and unaccountable 'money power' depicted in certain caricatures, were the agents called to show concretely the economic futility of war between nation states through the provision of international credit to an interconnected world.[49]

Bankers and financiers did not attract only benevolent scrutiny, and were often depicted as the 'villains' by narratives that maintained strong reservations against the process of globalization. In the wake of the First World War and during the conflict, for instance, far-right writers such as the French J. E. Favre and the Italian Giovanni Preziosi, considered that crucial national industries were under the control of financial institutions such as the French Banque de Paris et des Pays-Bas and the Banca Commerciale Italiana, which had been created in the heyday of the first globalization and were international in their capital, management, directors, scope, and nature of business.[50] If one moves towards the left of the political spectrum, the often more sophisticated arguments utilized by left-wing writers against bankers and financiers were certainly not less corrosive. The British economist John Atkinson Hobson, for instance, argued that the investments of his country had been biased by an influential financial elite intermingled with the political leadership and foreign interests.[51] Rudolf Hilferding, bearing in mind the continental European experience of the mixed banks, wrote about the power of the banks (*die Bankenmacht*), which through corporate ownership and interlocking directorates had become the masters of industrial capital. Hilferding predicted that a merger between industry and finance would have marked the final stage

---

[46] Joseph Alois Schumpeter, *The Theory of Economic Development: An Inquiry into Profits, Capital, Credit, Interest, and the Business Cycle* (Cambridge, MA, 1955), 74.

[47] Norman Angell, *The Great Illusion* (New York and London, 1910). The book had been first published in 1908, with the title *Europe's Optical Illusion*.

[48] J. D. B. Miller, 'Norman Angell and Rationality in International Relations', in David Long and Peter Wilson (eds.), *Thinkers of the Twenty Years' Crisis* (Oxford, 1995), 100–21.

[49] Norman Angell, 'The Influence of Banking upon International Relations', *Journal of the Institute of Bankers* 1912 (33.1): 50–75.

[50] Giovanni Preziosi, *La Germania alla conquista dell'Italia* (Florence, 1916); J. E. Favre, *Le capital français au service de l'étranger: un cas, la Banque de Paris et des Pays-Bas et sont oeuvre anti-nationale* (Paris, 1917). These authors targeted particularly leading figures of these banks—either foreign-born or with foreign origins—with arguments often imbued with racist and anti-Semitic motives that resonate with far-right populist narratives against the cosmopolitan financial elites that have emerged after 2008.

[51] John A. Hobson, *Imperialism: A Study* (London 1938 [1902]).

of capitalism.[52] On the other side of the Atlantic Ocean, Louis Brandeis decided to investigate New York bankers' use of other people's money, in line with the 1912 Pujo inquiry into the so-called 'Money Trust'.[53]

Both positive and negative narratives developed during the 'second globalization' often rhyme with arguments utilized a century before. If anything, a less pluralistic debate in the field of economics characterized the 1990s–2000s. To limit our analysis to bankers' and financiers' position within the economy and society, no Schumpeter versus Hilferding divide can be identified in a period during which critical strands of literature such as 'financialization' proved to be more popular among sociologists, political scientists, and anthropologists than economists and economic historians.[54] The lack of pluralism was possibly related to the emergence of financial economics and, more generally, the post-1970s growing role of statistics, mathematics, and modelling in the wider field of economics. This process coincided with the crisis of Keynesianism and the metamorphosis of economists from engineers called to dominate the economic cycle, to experts called to defend the tenets of 'the most scientific of the social sciences'.[55] To use the words of a scholar sympathetic with this process, while after 1929 'bankers walked away from the argument on greed', as a consequence of the already mentioned Senate investigation into banking and stock exchange practices, from the 1970s onwards 'economists performed a process of purification of bankers' discourse [...] They brought their stuff with them—models, data, editors and referees—and started making themselves at home.'[56] This intellectual revolution was accompanied by a dramatic wave of financial innovations, which had started already in the 1950s–60s with the Eurodollar and Eurobond markets, and accelerated impressively from the 1980s onwards with the spread of new financial products and so-called 'securitization'.[57]

---

[52] Rudolph Hilferding, *Finance Capital: A Study in the Latest Phase of Capitalist Development* (London, 1981 [1910]).
[53] Louis D. Brandeis, *Other People's Money and How Bankers Use It* (New York 1933 [1914]).
[54] The concept of 'financialization' has been used to describe different phenomena such as the ascent of a *rentier* class (William Greider, *One World, Ready or Not: The Manic Logic of Global Capitalism* (New York, 1997); Gérard Duménil and Dominique Lévy, 'Neoliberalism: The Crime and the Beneficiary', *Review* 2002 (25.4): 393–400), the dominance of the 'shareholder value' ideology and its implications (see *Economy and Society* 2000 (29.1), special issue on shareholder value), the growing relevance of capital markets over bank-based finance (Kevin Phillips, *Wealth and Democracy: A Political History of the American Rich* (New York, 2002)), and the increasing role of financial channels, instead of trade and commodity production, in the process of accumulation and profit-making (Giovanni Arrighi, *The Long Twentieth Century: Money, Power, and the Origins of Our Times* (London, 1994)).
[55] Mary S. Morgan, 'Economics', in Theodore M. Porter and Dorothy Ross (eds.), *The Cambridge History of Science*, vol. VII (Cambridge, 2003), 275–305, quotation 277.
[56] Marc Flandreau, 'The Vanishing Banker', *Financial History Review* 2012 (19.1): 1–19, quotation 11.
[57] See Stefano Battilossi, 'Financial Innovation and the Golden Ages of International Banking: 1890–1931 and 1958–1981', *Financial History Review* 2002 (7.2): 141–75. An overview on the

Did the financial revolution create, to use the formula of the late historian Gerald Feldman, a 'new breed of bankers'?[58] This question will be dealt with in the concluding remarks of this chapter, but it brings us back to the cultural dimension of the phenomenon we are analysing. Not only did financial economics, in fact, provide the intellectual foundations of the financial revolution of the last forty years, but it offered a crucial contribution to financial elites' understanding of the markets. In this sense one could say, with Donald Mackenzie, that financial economics: 'did more than analyse markets; it altered them'.[59] Initially confined to the United States, the financial revolution affected all major economies in the twenty years that preceded the Lehman collapse—even though with different degrees of speed and intensity.[60] This process gave rise to a global financial elite whose culture and approach to banking business—when it comes to investment banking[61]—was more uniform than it had been in the past.

When the financial crisis broke out in 2007–8, the repudiation of a generation of derivative specialists who had come to the fore in the decades of the financial revolution became part of a complex blame game directed at reversing the (until then) successful narrative of bankers and financiers as 'heroes' of society and vital contributors to its overall well-being.[62] The 'Pecora

'securitization' revolution is in Gillian Tett, *Fool's Gold: How Unrestrained Greed Corrupted a Dream, Shattered Markets and Unleashed a Catastrophe* (London 2009).

[58] 'The fact that most of my financial assets are being handled by an investment house also does some banking business [...] and belongs to a "group", that is a holding company whose name vaguely corresponds to a big bank whose name is more familiar to most people but is not the bank itself strikes me as an interesting and relatively novel situation [...] Most of the money in my pension fund is invested in mutual funds. Mutual funds or investment trusts are, to be sure, not new [...] but the dependence of millions of persons, at least in the US, on institutional investors dealing in mutual funds is quite new' (Gerald D. Feldman, 'Is the Sun Setting on Banking History as We Have Known and Practiced It?', in Edwin Green and Monika Pohle Fraser (eds.), *The Human Factor in Banking History: Entrepreneurship, Organization, Management and Personnel* (Athens, 2008), 281–95, quotation 281–2).

[59] Mackenzie, *An Engine, Not a Camera*, 12.

[60] In spite of the process of convergence brought about by financial innovation since the 1980s, significant variety endured on the eve of 2008 depending on the country, the segment of the market in which banks and financial institutions operated, and the management of the single financial institutions considered. For this reason, Australian and Canadian financial institutions were less involved than their British and American counterparts in the financial crisis while, within the same country, HSBC and Standard Chartered fared better than RBS or HBOS (Stephen Bell and Andrew Hindmor, *Masters of the Universe, Slaves of the Markets* (Cambridge, MA and London 2015)).

[61] While the formal line between different types of bank became blurred, investment and commercial banking remained profoundly divided.

[62] A comprehensive appraisal of this narrative would deserve a work on its own. We can only observe that examples of this rhetoric can be found among journalists and opinion-makers (see, for instance, Thomas Friedman, *The Lexus and the Olive Tree* (London, 1999), 47–53, on the link between financial innovation and the democratization of finance) as well as policy-makers and politicians, as highlighted by the 2006 British Minister for Financial Services' speech on the achievements of the financial sectors in Britain, on light-touch financial regulation, on the refusal 'to treat banks just like utilities', while preferring 'to rely on market forces and competition policy to promote efficiency through open and competitive markets' (Ed Balls, 'Speech at the British Bankers

moment' this time was not performed by the Financial Crisis Inquiry Commission (FCIC) of the United States that, in spite of the damning conclusions reached at the end of its hearings, did not attract the same attention commanded by the Senate Committee on Banking and Currency eight decades earlier.[63] In an era of social media dominance, political disenfranchisement, and ideological disillusion, the outrage against 'banksters' was expressed through new forms and mobilized by different political and social actors.[64] The outcome of this global wave of indignation and resentment, however, appears to be less univocal than one would expect. According to scholars who suggest that financial crises have little impact on institutions and regulation, once the outrage is exhausted, the financial industry manages to water down the complex and time-consuming reform process.[65] Another strand of thought believes, instead, that financial crises can display a far-reaching transformative effect. For this to happen, however, a political entrepreneur à la Schumpeter needs to emerge.[66]

The evocation of the political entrepreneur brings us back to Pecora and the Senate Committee on Banking and Currency. Pecora has been at times depicted as a demagogue 'more interested in generating headlines than in laying the factual groundwork for legislation in the public interest',[67] and at other times as a conscientious official who, with a 'non sensational, non

Association', 11 October 2006, <http://www.edballs.co.uk/blog/speeches-articles/my-speech-to-the-british-bankers-association-11th-october-2006>, last accessed 18 January 2017).

[63] The Financial Crisis Inquiry Commission was established, in May 2009, to 'examine the causes, domestic and global, of the current financial and economic crisis in the United States'. This independent, ten-member panel was composed of six members appointed by the Democratic leadership of Congress and four by the Republican leadership. The Commission produced its final report in 2011 (see US Financial Crisis Inquiry Commission, *Financial Crisis Inquiry Report*, <https://fcic.law.stanford.edu/report>, last accessed 23 January 2017).

[64] The fury against bankers and financiers has been epitomized by movements such as 'Occupy Wall Street', which emerged, in the aftermath of the Lehman collapse, with an agenda demanding radical (though generic) change and performed several episodes of occupation of public spaces, culminating in the 'Declaration of the Occupation of New York City' on 30 September 2011. Like many of the coeval movements that spread in Spain (*Indignados*), Greece (anti-austerity movement), Egypt and other Middle Eastern and North African countries (Arab Spring), 'Occupy' maintained a deliberate distance from the traditional political actors (to look at the transnational dimension of this phenomenon, and at its relationship with other experiences of mobilization of the recent past, see Donatella Della Porta and Alice Mattoni (eds.), *Spreading Movements in Times of Crisis* (Colchester, 2011)).

[65] Russell Hardin, *Collective Action* (Baltimore, MD, 1982), 20–2 and Todd Sandler, *Collective Action: Theory and Applications* (New York and London, 1992), 3–7. Those books have clearly been influenced by Mancur Olson's work on the smaller organized groups, which are likely to prevail over larger but more dispersed ones (Mancur Olson, *The Logic of Collective Action: Public Goods and the Theory of Groups* (Cambridge, MA, 1965)).

[66] Jonathan R. Macey, 'Wall Street in Turmoil: State-Federal Relations Post Eliot Spitzer', *Brooklyn Law Review* 2004 (70): 117–39.

[67] Bradford J. De Long, 'Morgan's Men Add Value? An Economist's Perspective on Financial Capitalism', in Peter Temin (ed.), *Inside the Business Enterprise: Historical Perspectives on the Use of Information* (Chicago and London, 1991), 205–36, quotation 213. Another work that reappraises the role of the American bankers, namely the ones in charge of the big national banks and their

confrontational style', managed to produce a 'grammar of motives' that made sense of the crisis of the American economy and society and promoted the ensuing regulatory legislation on finance and banking.[68] In these antithetical interpretations—an excellent example of the battle of ideas transferred to historical ground—both the supporters of Pecora's approach, and its detractors, tend to overemphasize the Senate Banking and Currency Committee's role and to forget the severity of the economic distress in the United States during the 1930s—not comparable to the one experienced after the Great Recession.

As we have seen in section 1.3, the British clearing banks escaped major crises in between the two world wars.[69] British merchant bankers were affected by events such as the collapse of the central European banks and the Bank of England's abandonment of the Gold Standard, but they did not experience the moral bankruptcy of American bankers.[70] This does not mean that British bankers were let off the hook. On the contrary, during the 1920s–1930s they were submitted to what one could describe as a constant, even though not intensive, wave of criticism. The first charge against British bankers held them responsible for the industrial and trading deflation policy of the 1920s, culminating in the 1925 decision to return to the Gold Standard with the pre-war parity. By restricting credit and enforcing the return of sterling to the Gold Standard, bankers had contributed to precipitating, and then protracting, the industrial depression.[71] This accusation went hand in hand with the rhetoric about the divide between London (and the interest of the City's merchant banks in particular) on the one hand, and industrial Britain on the other, an image popularized by works that reached out beyond the financially literate section of public opinion.[72] The other charge against the British banking

---

securities affiliated, is Thomas F. Huertas and Joan L. Silverman, 'Charles E. Mitchell: Scapegoat of the Crash?', *Business History Review* 1986 (60.1): 81–103.

[68] Jacobs, 'Financial Crises as Symbols and Rituals', 388.

[69] Mark Billings and Forrest Capie, 'Financial Crises, Contagion, and the British Banking System between the Two World Wars', *Business History* 2011 (53.2): 193–215.

[70] David Kynaston, *The City of London*, vol. III, *Illusion of Gold 1914–1945* (London, 1999), 222–4, 357–60, and 490–2; Oliver Accominotti, 'London Merchant Banks, the Central European Panic, and the Sterling Crisis of 1931', *Journal of Economic History* 2012 (72.1): 1–43. Merchant banking thrived during the first globalization in a context of free international trade, unhindered capital movements, and supremacy of sterling as international currency. The changing of perspectives in the interwar year raised concerns within the British banking community about the destiny of their established and successful merchant banks (see, for instance, Paul Einzig, 'Internal vs International Banking', *The Banker* 1933 (8.11): 97–100 and Paul Bareau, 'Eclipse of the Merchant Banker', *The Banker* 1941 (16.8): 82–7).

[71] 'Banking and Currency', *The Banker* 1927 (2.11): 431–45; A. Appleton, 'The TUC and Bankers', *The Banker* 1931 (6.10): 35–40. The reality was more complex if one considers that bankers such as the then chairman of Midland Bank, Reginald McKenna, dissented from the so-called 'Treasury view' (see for instance 'The Bankers' Speeches', *The Economist*, 29 January 1927).

[72] J. B. Priestley, *English Journey* (London, 1934) and Thomas Johnston, *The Financiers and the Nation* (London, 1934).

system—which principally targeted the clearing banks—was that it was too conservative when it came to providing support to the manufacturing sector, namely to small and medium-sized enterprises. Here the universal banking model of continental Europe was evoked as an example to be followed.[73] If this critique against the British bankers was abandoned after 1931—when the collapse of the Austrian Credit-Anstalt and the difficulties of the German *D-Banken* rendered the universal banking model less fashionable—a new allegation came to the fore in the same year: the idea that a 'bankers' ramp' was behind Ramsay MacDonald and Philip Snowden's 'betrayal' of the Labour Party and the creation of the National coalition government. The accusation was published by *The Daily Herald* on 25 August 1931 and opened one of the most turbulent phases in the controversial history of the relationship between the City and the Labour Party. The fight against the British bankers went on until the mid-1930s but—unlike what was happening in the United States—it was not rewarding in electoral terms: Labour, in fact, underwent two painful defeats in October 1931 and November 1935.[74] Historians' opinion diverges on the long-term impact of this battle of ideas. Philip Williamson argues that the notion of the 'bankers' ramp', not very successful vis-à-vis British public opinion, was crucial in bringing about the post-1945 British financial regulation (in particular the nationalization of the Bank of England and the control of the Treasury and the Bank of England of British clearing banks).[75] Martin Daunton maintains that the interwar years attempt by the Labour Party to blame bankers did not translate either in electoral success, or in policy and legislative actions (for instance, there was no trace of the National Investment Bank in the policies pursued by the Labour government after 1945).[76] We tend to share the scepticism of this second interpretation towards the effectiveness of the interwar campaign against British bankers.

The narration of a financial crisis can match social and economic reality with a major or minor degree of adherence to authenticity, depending on the capacity of political entrepreneurs to make sense of a crisis, identify scapegoats, and mobilize and organize public opinion towards certain policy and legislative goals—the United States of the 1930s being a case in point. The British experience of the same period, however, shows that there is a limit to the possibility of writing and representing financial crises—and offering to public opinion the relative culprits. Between the two world wars a financial regime change occurred in several countries. This shift was only marginally

---

[73] See 'Banking in England and Germany: Some Misunderstandings', *The Economist*, 30 November 1929 and 'Banks and Industry in England and Germany', *The Economist*, 1 March 1930.
[74] Kynaston, *Illusions of Gold*, 358–74.
[75] Philip Williamson, 'A Bankers' Ramp? Financiers and the British Political Crisis of August 1931', *English Historical Review* 1984 (99.393): 770–806.
[76] Martin Daunton, 'Finance and Politics: Comments', in Cassis, *Finance and Financiers*, 283–90.

linked to the blame games discussed in this section: it is not by chance that it occurred both in countries where the criticism of bankers was successful, and in countries where anti-banker rhetoric was not politically rewarding. As suggested earlier, the shift was linked to the world wars, the Great Depression, the radicalization of politics, and the collapse of globalization. All these circumstances marked the beginning of a profound redefinition of the relationship between the state, the financial system, and the corporate sector on the one hand, and triggered the crisis of the liberal narrative which had dominated the decades prior to the First World War on the other. In this context, the downgrading of bankers and financiers from 'masters' to 'servants' of the economy and society happened as a corollary of a more fundamental change, defined by the ascent of a financial regime that contemplated a different and more active role for the state as economic actor.

1.5 Conclusion

Evidence of a radical shift similar to the one experienced during the interwar years is still contradictory, but a swing of the pendulum from the camp of financial deregulation to that of financial regulation is, at the time of writing, a reality—even though it is difficult to determine where the pendulum will stop. How dramatic would the adjustment be for today's bankers and financiers in the (remote) hypothesis of a drastic financial regime change? This hypothetical question allows us to go back to Feldman's doubt as to whether the financial revolution of the last forty years has created a 'new breed of bankers'. In a recent video installation that revisits the *Anarchist Banker*, the novel mentioned at the beginning of the chapter, a TV moderator interviews Arthur Ashenking, the former CEO of BG Bank, a fictional financial institution that, because of its involvement in the derivative markets, has applied for a government bailout after years of sensational performances.[77] During the interview Ashenking, a former community organizer and anti-Vietnam War demonstrator, claims that he has found the embodiment of his radical anarchism in the ideal of the free market.[78] Even though Pessoa in the 1920s did not

---

[77] The name of the banker represents a loose translation of the dodgy financier who, allegedly, inspired Pessoa's novel. Artur Alves dos Reis, founder of the Angola Metropole Bank, mounted a huge fraud in 1925 on the Portuguese escudo. In December 1925, the Portuguese police found at the Oporto branch of the bank a large number of fake 500 escudo banknotes, displaying the marks of a well-known London firm specialized in printing banknotes ('Forged Bank Notes in Portugal', *Financial Times*, 14 December 1925). Alves Reis confessed to the police that the signatures to documents and to letters sent to the London firm Waterlow and Sons were forged, and that the whole plan of the fraud was his own work ('Bank Notes Affaire: Alleged Confession of a Lisbon Banker', *Financial Times*, 28 December 1925).

[78] Jan Peter Hammer, *The Anarchist Banker*, 2010. We would like to thank the author who gave us the opportunity to watch the video installation.

mean to criticize the world of finance per se—his targets being rather some of the crucial principles of modern political and economic theory: from Locke to Rousseau, and from Smith to Marx[79]—the reinterpretation of the *Anarchist Banker* as a neoliberal (libertarian?) banker in the aftermath of the Lehman collapse makes perfect sense. But were the bankers of the 1920s–30s captivated by 'the tyranny of money'—to use Pessoa's expression—in the same manner as their colleagues during the 1990s–2000s?

To answer this question, and measure all the distance existing between the bankers of the 'first' and the bankers of the 'second' globalization, it is worth listening to the banker who, arguably, was the most representative of the 1920s–30s. J. P. Morgan, the senior partner of the eponymous wealthiest and most powerful investment bank of Wall Street, testified in front of the Senate Committee on Banking and Currency on 23 May 1933. He built a strong defence of his firm's business on the idea that credit—his 'most valuable possession'—was at the centre of 'a code of professional ethics and customs' that 'could never be expressed in legislation, but [had] a force far greater than any law'. The acquisition of credit, in Morgan's words, came from the respect and esteem of the community and was the result of 'years of fair and honourable dealings': it could, however, be suddenly lost and, once lost, could not be restored for a long time. The fact that Morgan and his partners had 'skin in the game'—in that they were risking not only their customers', but also their own money—lent credibility to his claim that the private banker who 'makes a public sale and puts his own name at the foot of the prospectus [...] has the continuous obligation of the stronger kind to see, so far as he can, that nothing is done which will interfere with the full carrying out by the obligor of the contract with the holder of the security'.[80] Reputation as an honest and competent broker was an invaluable competitive advantage for the Morgan partnership. It would have been extremely unwise to endanger this asset for the sake of a short-term gain.[81]

Financial economists have elaborated on this idea, building models in which big financial institutions—even in a context of imperfect information and lacklustre regulation—are judged able to monitor themselves because of their size and the connected risk to compromise their reputational capital. In other words, according to this approach, the argument that a banker who fools 'one thousand persons once [...] would be unlikely to succeed again' was true in the 1920s and is still true in the twenty-first century, and the only difference between then and now is that, meanwhile, this argument has

---

[79] K. David Jackson, *Adverse Genres in Fernando Pessoa* (Oxford, 2010), 110–12.
[80] United States Senate, 'Opening statement submitted by J. P. Morgan on 23 May 1933', *Hearings Before the Committee on Banking and Currency* (Washington, 1934), 879–81.
[81] De Long, 'Morgan's Men Add Value?'

received a name (rational expectation) and a Nobel Prize (in 1995).[82] In the aftermath of 2008 some partial disavowal to this argument has emerged among financial economists who have recognized that if firms' monitoring is entrusted to individuals, the quality of the monitoring will eventually depend on the position within the firm, the attitude towards the firm, and the ideas of those individuals.[83]

As we have seen in section 1.3, the new elite bankers are mostly salaried managers able to enjoy the income and wealth of the old family owned investment banks' partners without bearing their risks. Moreover, they work in a volatile context of job insecurity.[84] This condition of uncertainty, partially offset by the high level of remuneration enjoyed by these senior executives, inevitably results in the weakening of bankers' corporate identity.[85] If one adds to the picture that the new bankers make sense of the financial markets through the eyes of financial economics,[86] as we have seen in section 1.4, the distance between J. P. Morgan and his contemporary colleagues is difficult to understate, and can be illustrated by the words of one of the most representative new bankers.

Lloyd Blankfein is currently the chairman and CEO of Goldman Sachs. He already was at the helm of the biggest and wealthiest investment bank of the United States at the time of the 2008 crisis. Since the end of 2006, Blankfein's bank had started reducing its exposure to the increasingly volatile subprime market by means of the creation of mortgage-related products then distributed to the bank's less sophisticated clientele. If this decision allowed Goldman Sachs to outperform its rivals and avoid the humiliation of Bear Stearns (bought by JPMorgan Chase with the backing of the Federal Reserve in March 2008), Merrill Lynch (rescued by Bank of America in

---

[82] Flandreau, 'The Vanishing Banker', 12.

[83] Daron Acemoglu, 'The Crisis of 2008: Lessons for and from Economics', *Critical Review* 2009 (21.2/3): 185–94.

[84] Karen Ho, 'Disciplining Investment Bankers, Disciplining the Economy: Wall Street's Institutional Culture of Crisis and the Downsizing of "Corporate America"', *American Anthropologist* 2009 (111.2): 177–89. This work—which describes bankers as perpetrators of the process of big companies' downsizing aimed at extracting 'shareholder value' from them, but also as victims of this practice—refers to Wall Street investment bankers at the end of the 1990s. However, job insecurity combined with high remuneration has been a characteristic of the last decades in the most dynamic sectors of the banking system.

[85] The new bankers' lack of corporate identity is underlined by Feldman, 'Is the Sun Setting?'

[86] The political philosopher Sergio Caruso argues that the financial revolution has produced a new Economic Theology centred on a Holy Trinity in which Rational Choice Theory represents the Father, Homo Economicus the Son, and the Efficient Market Hypothesis the Holy Spirit. According to Caruso, Homo Economicus, introduced to the Temple of economic thought by the authors of classical economics with clear explanatory limits, has grown far beyond its bounds in the last forty years. Back to the Temple as an adult, Homo Economicus has invited the merchants into the Temple, instead of throwing them out of it. The metaphor indicates a reality in which the boundaries between economics as a science and the empirical knowledge and experience of bankers and financiers have faded (Sergio Caruso, 'L'homo oeconomicus come figura teologica e Seconda Persona della Trinità contemporanea', *Lessico di etica pubblica* 2013 (4): 16–39).

September 2008), and Lehman Brothers (which filed for bankruptcy on 15 September 2008), it also constituted—in the words of a structured finance expert consulted by the FCIC—'the most cynical use of credit information' he had ever seen, a practice akin to buying 'fire insurance on someone's house and then committing arson'.[87] On the occasion of his testimony before the FCIC, on 13 January 2010, Blankfein's refusal to recognize any responsibility for the financial crisis, and his insistence on the 'tremendous liquidity' of his bank, which 'never anticipated government help' (in reality, Goldman had converted itself into a bank holding company to get the backing of the federal government), provoked the irritated reaction of the Commission's chairman Phil Angelides and the media.[88]

Ten years after the Lehman collapse, banks appear to be better regulated and capitalized than in 2007. Moreover, some of them have been severely humbled by the billions of dollars, pounds, or euros paid in fines related to past wrongdoings. Yet, more fundamental issues—first of all the question of banks' size and complexity—are still waiting for a clear regulatory definition. These contradictions, combined with the probably less relevant, but certainly eye-catching question of the excessive pay of elite bankers and financiers, explain the sense of distrust that continues to surround the financial sector and which has been evoked in this chapter and in the introduction to the volume. How this feeling will affect financial elites' long-term position within the financial system and society is not for historians to assess. If the past can provide some guidance, the answer to this question will probably depend on how fast the next financial crisis will break out, and how serious it will be. Meanwhile, the significant remunerations that elite bankers and financiers continue to enjoy, and the lack of discernment displayed by some of them,[89] will provide new opportunities for political entrepreneurs to stir up hostile public opinion against the 'Masters of the Universe'.

---

[87] Inquiry Commission, *Inquiry Report*, 235–8, quotation 236.
[88] See, for instance, Michael Skapinker, 'The Sorry Business of Corporate Apologies', *Financial Times*, 12 January 2010; John McKinnon and Michael R. Crittenden, 'Panel Rips Wall Street Titans', *The Wall Street Journal*, 14 January 2010; Dana Milbank, 'Sorry Still Seems to be the Hardest Word on Wall Street', *The Washington Post*, 14 January 2010; Paul Krugman, 'Bankers without a Clue', *The New York Times*, 15 January 2010.
[89] The last example in this sense arrived in November 2017, when the CEO of the Swiss bank UBS, Sergio Ermotti, declared that efforts to put bankers' pay under control were motivated by envy among less well paid officials (Martin Arnold, Caroline Binham, and Patrick Jenkins, 'UBS Chief Blasts Regulators' Drive to Curb Banker Pay', *Financial Times*, 1 December 2017).

2

Reshaping Strategies

Merchants and Bankers at the Time of the French Revolution

Niccolò Valmori

2.1 Introduction

The momentous political consequences that the French Revolution brought to France inevitably affected the entire economy of what was at the end of eighteenth century the most populous country in Europe. France, which was struggling with the burden of a heavy debt greatly increased by the support offered to the rebels in North America, seemed to be set on a new track by the abolition of feudalism and of all the venal offices which characterized the old French monarchy. However, the issue of *assignats* and their transformation into paper money caused a dire inflation which worsened the state of French finances, now additionally strained by the war efforts against the Austrian Empire and the other European monarchies.[1] Market actors such as merchants and bankers not only had to face a grim outlook for the French economy but also had to deal with the open distrust of the revolutionary authorities. During the Terror this distrust would cost many bankers their lives, especially if they were foreigners or were suspected of being agents of foreign powers.

---

[1] The issue of creating *assignats* has always fascinated many historians working in economic history or on the history of French Revolution. A milestone in the broad historiography on the *assignats* remains the work by Seymour Edwin Harris, *The Assignats* (Cambridge, 1930). A good overview of the historiography on this topic is offered by Manuela Albertone, 'Une histoire oublié: les assignats dans l'historiographie', *Annales historiques de la Révolution française* 1992 (287): 87–104. The most recent contribution on the subject is the recent book by Rebecca L. Spang, *Stuff and Money in the Time of the French Revolution* (Cambridge, MA and London, 2015).

In the months before and after the fall of the Bastille, bankers active on the Parisian market looked attentively at the political events that were taking place in the French capital. How did market operators conceive their business in a time of such wide-ranging changes? Did the general appreciation for the coming of the French Revolution change at a certain point? What were the strategies adopted to diversify risk in the aftermath of the fall of old-regime institutions? Once General Bonaparte came to power in 1799, and later established the French Empire, did bankers succeed or fail in promoting their interests in the new political framework? As shown in this study, the reactions of bankers towards the changing political scenario were more the outcome of their direct knowledge of the political choices taken by the political actors rather than the stability of political institutions in itself. The direct access to information was the only key to remaining prominent actors in a critical time like the French Revolution.

After a description of the Paris market and its main features at the end of the eighteenth century, the focus will be on foreign bankers and merchants who followed the activities of the Assembly of Notables (1787) and later of the National Assembly (1790–1). Foreign market actors will be examined in depth for their perspective as outsiders on what was taking place in France, and how they perceived risks and opportunities for their business. Section 2.4 will be devoted to the case of a Swiss banker who not only was successful in his business activities but also climbed the social ladder to become Baron of the Empire and *regent* of the Banque de France.

Before presenting the bankers at the centre of this study, it is worth recalling the importance of Paris as a financial market at the end of the eighteenth century. At that time Amsterdam was the most important financial market for the placement of loans opened by a growing number of monarchies in financial difficulty, such as the Swedish Crown and the Russian Empire ruled by Catherine the Great.[2] Nonetheless the primacy of the Dutch financial market was openly challenged by the rise of Paris and London as 'capitals of capital'.[3]

In fact, the Parisian Stock Exchange offered a wide variety of financial products which attracted an increasing number of foreign investors from all corners of the European continent. In particular, Dutch and Swiss bankers were attracted by the annuities circulating on the French market which

---

[2] For a description of the long-term relevance of the Amsterdam capital market through the eighteenth century, see James C. Riley, *International Government Finance and the Amsterdam Capital Market, 1740–1815* (Cambridge, 1980).

[3] The expression is taken from a book written by Youssef Cassis, *Capitals of Capital: A History of International Financial Centres, 1780–2005* (Cambridge, 2006). On the development of London's and Amsterdam's financial markets in the eighteenth century, see Ann M. Carlos and Larry Neal, 'Amsterdam and London as Financial Centers in the Eighteenth Century', *Financial History Review* 2011 (18.1): 21–46.

yielded incredibly high interest rates.[4] The most interesting product was the *rente viagère* (life annuity) that could yield up to 8–10 per cent interest per year, and that could be assigned to young people, thus assuring longer profits to the capitalist who bought them.[5] This market offered endless opportunities as life annuities had been launched to finance the ever-growing debt of the French Crown, which had increased after France's active participation in the American War of Independence. Even after Robespierre's fall, the conundrum of debt repayment haunted France: in 1797 the Directory chose to repudiate two-thirds of the entire debt, which in 1789 the National Assembly had pledged to refund entirely.[6]

As emerges from this description of the Paris market, opportunities and risks were equally balanced, and foreign investors needed to have a continuous flow of information directly from the French capital to avoid reckless decisions concerning their investments in annuities or in other securities. Therefore business correspondences are essential sources for appreciating the level of understanding of market actors of the political evolution that was taking place in France at the end of the eighteenth century.

2.2 Brokering Information between Bankers at the Eve of 1789: The Case of Walter Boyd and Henry Hope

In December 1786, when the first rumours of the king's order to call the Notables were circulating, Walter Boyd was 33 years old and had recently settled in the French capital.[7] This Scottish banker had been apprenticed

---

[4] For an appreciation of the 'global' character of the Parisian market at the eve of the revolution, see Lynn Hunt, 'The Global Financial Origins of 1789', in Suzanne Desan, Lynn Hunt, and William Max Nelson (eds.), *The French Revolution in Global Perspective* (Ithaca and London, 2013), 32–43. For a general overview of the role of private bankers in Europe during the early modern period, see Youssef Cassis and Philip L. Cottrell, *Private Banking in Europe: Rise, Retreat, and Resurgence* (Oxford, 2015).

[5] The best essay on the French financial difficulties in the second half of the eighteenth century is probably François R. Velde and David R. Weir, 'The Financial Market and Government Debt Policy in France, 1746–1793', *Journal of Economic History* 1992 (52.1): 1–39. Other articles which offer economic elements to help to understand the weight of public finance in the French Revolution are: François R. Velde, 'Macroeconomic Features of the French Revolution', *Journal of Political Economy* 1995 (103.3): 474–518; and Eugene Nelson White, 'The French Revolution and the Politics of Government Finance, 1770–1815', *Journal of Economic History* 1995 (55.2): 227–55.

[6] For a comparative view of French finances and British finances during this period, see Michael D. Bordo and Eugene N. White, 'A Tale of Two Currencies: British and French Finance During the Napoleonic Wars', *Journal of Economic History* 1991 (51.2): 303–16.

[7] On the life of Walter Boyd, see Sidney Raymond Cope, *Walter Boyd, a Merchant Banker in the Age of Napoleon* (London, 1983). Cope's work is rich in details of Boyd's career but it is mostly focused on the activity of the Scottish banker during Napoleonic times as the title suggests. Another publication which offers many elements on Boyd's activity in Paris during the revolutionary period is Jean Bouchary, *Les manieurs d'argent à Paris à la fin du XVIIIe siècle* (Paris, 1939–43). This research focuses on the banker's activity during the Terror, using the documents left by the police and the revolutionary tribunal.

in the British bank Herries & Co and later had worked as a clerk in the Compagnie d'assurance de la Flandre autrichienne (Assurance Company of the Austrian Flanders).

After this experience Boyd worked in the Banque particulière dans les Pays Bas autrichiens (Private Bank in the Austrian Low Countries) which was under the control of his chief William Herries and Édouard de Walckiers, whose mother was at the head of the bank Veuve Nettine & C. responsible for financial operations for the Imperial Court of Vienna.[8] The private bank had as its core business the investment of private savings in commercial activities. It was founded in Brussels and survived only two years, from 1782 to 1784. At the end of the Anglo-Dutch War in 1784 the assurance company and the bank created by Herries were put into liquidation and Walter Boyd moved to Paris.

The Scottish banker rapidly made his entrance into the Parisian banking system, acting as a private financier in the first period and later founding his personal bank with the name of Boyd & Ker & Co, which was included in the official list of operative banks published in the *Almanach Royal* in 1787.[9]

While Boyd was struggling to emerge as a banker in the Paris market, an already well-established Dutch bank, Hope & Co, was making large investments in French annuities. Traditionally, Dutch investors had always been prudent in their operations, preferring the British stock market to the French one. However, during the last two decades of the eighteenth century, Dutch bankers and investors decided to put their money in the more risky French market. There were three main reasons for this significant change: the political dissension with England, the higher interest rates available on French annuities (by far the most profitable in Europe), and, lastly, the fact that the French monarchy's finances were considered more stable than the British royal finances.[10]

Hope's bank had become a leading European financial actor in the speculative field of dealing in foreign loans launched by the different monarchies

---

[8] The most complete work on bankers of the eighteenth century from a biographical perspective is Thierry Claeys, *Dictionnaire biographique des financiers en France au XVIIIe siècle* (Paris, 2008). For the bankers operative on the Paris financial market during the last decades of the eighteenth century a remarkable piece of research has been written by Jean Bouchary, *Les compagnies financières à Paris à la fin du XVIII siècle* (Paris, 1940-2). A very detailed monograph written on a bank active during the Revolution is Guy Antonetti, *Une Maison de Banque à Paris au XVIIIe siècle: Greffulhe Montz et Cie, 1789-1793* (Paris, 1963).

[9] During this first period of activity Boyd was particularly active in lending money to those who aspired to be invested with offices in the administration of the public finances. Thus, Boyd furnished the significant sum of 150,000 livres to Bataille de Tancarville who needed this sum for being appointed tax farmer (*regisseur général*). For this operation, see Archives Nationales (henceforth, AN), Étude notarial (henceforth ET)/XLVIII/305, 3 July 1786.

[10] On Dutch investments in France see James C. Riley, 'Dutch Investment in France, 1781-1787', *Journal of Economic History* 1973 (33.4): 732-60 and Alice Carter, 'Dutch Foreign Investment, 1738-1800', *Economica* 1953 (20): 322-40.

who badly needed money for their continuous war efforts.[11] Thus the Dutch bank took the opportunity to invest in the French annuities through their agent, the Dutch bank Vandenyver Frères & C. in Paris.

Even if Boyd was not the correspondent agent of Hope & Co in Paris he well knew how much news coming directly from the French capital might be appreciated.[12] From the correspondence between Boyd and Henry Hope clear evidence emerges of how the merchants, who resided in two different cities, relied on confidential news about what was taking place in the foreign city where they had economic interests at stake. Moreover, within this flow of news Boyd never forgot to review the different political positions that were emerging from the Assembly of Notables.

Louis XVI called this assembly, gathering together the most influential people in his kingdom, in the hope of finding possible solutions to the threatening problem of the public debt.[13] The first aim of Boyd was to communicate to his Dutch peer how well he was connected with the Court where he could have direct access to first-hand information, even if he remained a foreign actor.[14] Boyd clearly expressed his intention to offer his colleague the best information available on the debates that were taking place at Versailles, and in that situation the possibility to have direct information was crucial:

> I consider this political epoch as extremely important to every person possessed [sic] French stocks or likely to become so, and therefore, I will continue to get the best and earliest information for my government and that of my friends in which number your house possessed a distinguished place.[15]

When the Assembly of Notables opened its work at Versailles Boyd shared the great hopes that this event had produced in France and could not resist

---

[11] On the Hope's activity in the placement of foreign loans, see Marten G. Buist, *At spes non fracta. Hope & Co. 1770–1815, Merchant Bankers and Diplomats at Work* (The Hague, 1974), 14–38.

[12] On the role of information within merchant networks see Dominique Margairaz and Philippe Minard, *L'information économique, XVIe–XIXe siècle: journées d'études du 21 juin 2004 et du 25 avril 2006* (Paris, 2008).

[13] On the Assembly of Notables there have been many publications. Here we report only the monographs and the works read and used to present the subject here. On the French side it is fundamental to know the work of Aimé Cherest, *La chute de l'ancien regime, 1787–1789* (Paris, 1884). In the twentieth century Albert Goodwin's 'Calonne, the Assembly of French Notables of 1787 and the Origins of the "Révolte Nobiliaire"', *English Historical Review* 1946 (61): 203–46 gives appropriate attention to the revolutionary features of the Notables' attitude. In more recent times another work which is valuable is John Hardman, *Overture to Revolution: The 1787 Assembly of Notables and the Crisis of France's Old Regime* (Oxford, 2010).

[14] 'We furnish to Government the sum of six millions on advantageous terms [...] we must also mention that the affair of the six millions furnished to the Government is the most profound secret to every person but the Minister and us. We confide it to you with the most perfect satisfaction, convinced of your attachment to us and your discretion in the affair committed to you', Gemeente Amsterdam Stadsarchief (henceforth, GAS), Archief van de Firma Hope en co, Ingekomen stukken, 123, document (henceforth, d.), 12, letter of 22 December 1786.

[15] GAS, 123, d. 45, letter of 13 March 1787.

comparing that assembly to the one which ended with Magna Carta in England.[16] Notwithstanding this shared enthusiasm, Boyd recognized the distance between the Minister of the Finances, Charles-Alexandre de Calonne, and the Notables who wanted to safeguard their fiscal privileges at any cost.

Calonne had blatantly challenged Necker's *Compte rendu* released in 1781 in which the former Minister of the Finances had asserted the stability of the French financial system. This challenge was short-sighted because Necker could count on many followers among the Notables, especially in the clergy where such figures as Loménie de Brienne and Champion de Cicé were staunch antagonists of Calonne's reforms. Boyd's letter emphasized that the Notables were strongly opposed to the proposed innovations in the fiscal sphere, such as the suggested land tax and the enlargement of provincial assemblies on the basis of wealth, while only the abolition of the different *corvées* and the freeing of the corn trade had met with positive responses. The disagreement between Calonne and the Notables became an open conflict after the meeting held in the Comte de Provence's room on 2 March 1787.[17]

During that consultation Calonne had revealed the huge size of the Crown's debt: 113 million livres. At the general meeting held on 12 March Calonne announced the other reforms asked for by the king, expressing his thanks for the collaboration offered by the Notables with the previous reforms. Boyd gave an accurate report of the session on 12 March, which is worth including here:

> The notables have behaved with great dignity and firmness; but they have, in my opinion, on more than one occasion forget [sic] that they were only <u>counsellors</u> and by no means <u>legislators</u>. I know they mean to oppose the land tax in money, until they have seen the accounts called for. I knew well that these accounts would not be produced [...] The Clergy and the nobility (two powerful bodies) are decidedly against him (Calonne) because his measures tend to render them liable to taxes which they have no mind to bear; but we are well assure that the King is aware of all this and has positively determined to support his minister in the great and glorious work which he has undertaken and which is complicated, must give a stability to the Credit of France which it has never yet possessed.[18]

---

[16] 'We continue to augure well of this meeting, and if our ideas are well founded, we are not without hope that Frenchmen will in future ages cite this epoch of their history with the same enthusiasm that Englishmen do the famous assembly of Runneymede in the reign of King John. This is a roundabout, respect being always had to the differences between the two countries', GAS, 123, d. 26, letter of 22 January 1787.

[17] The account of the meeting in the Monsieur's room to discuss Calonne's proposals is edited by Pierre Renouvin, *L'assemblée des notables de 1787. La conférence du 2 mars* (Paris, 1920). The Comte de Provence later became Louis XVIII.

[18] GAS, 123, d. 45, letter of 13 March 1787. The words underlined are such in the original letter to Hope.

In this letter Boyd expressed his personal opinion and he wanted to offer his correspondent not just a simple report but also his view on the political developments which had occurred in France. The political aspects were literally underlined by the Scottish banker who understood well the revolutionary attitude shown by the Notables: called simple 'counsellors', they considered themselves 'legislators'. On the one hand, Boyd grasped the king's position: Louis XVI did not want further discussion over the plans proposed by Calonne and he envisaged a swift approval of the proposals in order to rescue his kingdom from its financial difficulties. On the other hand, Boyd was surprised by Calonne's approach: he wanted to introduce new taxes without presenting the current situation of public finances with accurate balances and more detailed documents to show the necessity to create the land tax.

This way of dealing with the members of the first two estates procured total isolation for Calonne, with the sole exception of the king. Louis XVI shared with his *controlleur des finances* the worry about French credit, which held little credibility at that moment. Boyd's appraisal of French credit was not obvious to all: in Europe the image of French finances was based on the *Compte rendu* published by Necker in 1781, where it was declared that France had a surplus of 13 million livres for that year. Boyd's doubts over the assessment of the Crown's obligations hint that the Scottish banker was at least critical of Necker's policy of opening loans with high interest owed to the creditors.

The Scottish banker started to call into question the stability not only of the French debt but also of the political situation in the country where he lived. In fact, Boyd understood well that behind the Notables' resistance to the in-kind taxation there was what would later be called the 'aristocratic revolution', which challenged the royal power to levy taxes without the vote of a permanent assembly.[19] Boyd clearly perceived the revolutionary consequences of the resistance shown by the Notables to the enforcement of a new tax, which reminded him of the political dynamic of Westminster:

> They [the Notables] are firm and manly but much more adapted to the meridian of S. Stephen's Chapel than to that of the Hall of Versailles.[20]

---

[19] 'I am further assured that the whole body of notables is firmly and decidedly against the minister, and that it will be impossible for him to hold his place. That the general sentiment of the meeting is to give literally the necessary supplies and to resolve that it shall be understood that they as well as every subject of France as well every acre of property in the Kingdom are pledged for the pay of the public debt; but that they will not vote a single shelling until they know the real state of the finances and that a perfect and effectual check be established upon the public accounts. In this protest they say that they never can give an opinion upon a Land-tax until they are satisfied with regard to the causes which have rendered it necessary, the extent of its produces and the length of its duration', GAS, 123, d. 46, letter of 16 March 1787.

[20] Ibid.

In this passage Boyd drew the comparison between the English system, where discussions on any issues, not in the least on fiscal matters, took place in the House of Commons, and the French one which was not used to broad discussion on fiscal decisions made by the Crown. Furthermore, fiscal decisions, like the land tax, were not part of the tasks entrusted to the Assembly of Notables. In France only the Estates General could offer remarks and advice on fiscal subjects. Under the Bourbon monarchy the English principle of the sovereign rule of 'King in Parliament' did not exist and thus the King of France was not asked to share his fiscal decisions with anyone.

From what emerges from the correspondence between Boyd and Hope it is evident that the Scottish banker had clearly in mind that the fiscal knot was more than an economic debate: the Notables opposed Calonne's plans because they wanted to limit the royal power, primarily in the fiscal sphere. At least from Boyd's point of view, the political evolution set in motion by the resistance of the Notables to the reforms was as important as the financial interests which he and his Dutch friend had at stake in France. The correspondence between the Scottish banker and his Dutch colleague shows the central role of information at the eve of revolutionary changes: on the one hand the exchange of information was not limited to the economic situation of the country but provided political evaluations of the changing scene in the French capital; on the other hand sharing information was the way followed by Walter Boyd to gain ground with the stronger and more prominent banker Henry Hope.

2.3 Sliding Doors: New Opportunities and Disillusion for Bankers in the Early Period of the French Revolution

Once the Estates General gathered in Versailles and the Third Estate proclaimed itself as the National Assembly, the entire French system of political and economic institution was completely changed: new opportunities were at hand for those market actors willing to run the risk of investing in a country in the middle of such consequential change. Foreign investors needed reliable sources of information on the daily activities of the National Assembly and its decisions concerning economic issues such as the repayment of the debt, the destiny of the French East India Company, or the nationalization of the lands belonging to the Church or to the Crown.

The Anglo-French banker James Bourdieu found himself in the favoured position of being a confidential correspondent with Barthélémy Huber, a merchant of Genevan origins, who was one of the closest advisers of the French Finance Minister Jacques Necker. James Bourdieu's father was a Huguenot who fled to England after the revocation of the Edict of Nantes in 1685.[21] In 1789 Jacques Necker had asked Bourdieu to furnish the corn needed in the Paris region, and thus the English merchant was personally well-known to Necker. Bourdieu intended to capitalize on the services that he had rendered to Necker in resolving the crisis caused by the poor harvest of the summer of 1789.

As a matter of fact the English banker had personal interests at stake in three main areas: the activities of the French East India Company, the tobacco trade, and the acquisition of the *biens nationaux*, the old ecclesiastical and royal lands. Since all these issues were under revision by the National Assembly, Bourdieu hoped to gain some personal returns, counting on his good relationship with Jacques Necker. Regarding the activities of the National Assembly the English banker did not share the pessimistic vision so widely diffused in England; instead he hoped for the complete success of the revolution in France. In Bourdieu's view the success or failure of the revolution, like his personal economic affairs, was in Necker's hands. Only the Genevan minister could propose the right balance between new rights and old institutions which might work in a new political system.

Throughout the year 1790 Bourdieu showed many times his concern about the possibility that Necker might resign from the office of Minister of Finances. The English merchant was particularly worried by the growing influence that Mirabeau, a declared enemy of Necker, had gained over the Assembly. When it was clear that the Assembly mistrusted the minister and that the committees were completely disregarding Necker's suggestions, Bourdieu started to express some critical remarks on the French situation.

When Necker resigned from his post in September 1790, Bourdieu started to lose his faith in the possibility of the French people establishing a stable new political system. Necker's resignation confirmed his mistrust towards the French people:

> The French have really shown themselves to be a sanguinary people; fickle and changeable they always were, of which there never was a more fatal instance than their demanding the head the man whom they had recalled, and was in fact the author of the late revolution.[22]

---

[21] Bourdieu confirms Huber's hypothesis on his origins: 'You are right in conjecture about my origin. My father was one of the refugees at the Revocation of the Edict of Nantes', AN, T 38, II cahier, letter of 15 June 1790.

[22] AN, T 38, III cahier, letter of 10 September 1790. Bourdieu recalled many times in his letters the untrustworthy character of French people: 'He (Necker) is by this time as much forgot in France as if he never existed, such is the fickle inconsistent character of the people', in a letter of 24 September 1790.

Bourdieu's disappointment is also easily understood in the light of his attempt to acquire the agency in London from the new French East India Company.[23] The destiny of the commercial company was in the Assembly's hands: a prorogation or end of the privilege to trade between France and the East Indies or the complete abolition of the Company depended on the Assembly's deliberations. The Assembly after a brief debate chose to abolish the privilege without suggesting more definite measures for the future of the trading company.[24] The Board of the Company decided on 12 April to continue its commercial operations with the Indies.

As a consequence Bourdieu faced the challenging task of gaining the confidence of the majority of the Board in order to be nominated as the sole agent of the Company in London. In the new Board Bourdieu could count on Louis Monneron, who was nominated as commissar, but at the same time his opponent and rival Thomas Simon Bérard was confirmed as administrator.[25] Bourdieu offered his credit to Monneron who had greatly lost on his shares of the Caisse d'Escompte, which he had bought at 4,500 livres per share; now their value was tumbling down at 3,350 livres.[26]

Bourdieu wanted to be the only agent in London of the French East India Company, but being the sole agent of such a company was highly demanding. The agent of a trade company needed to have abundant capital to loan to the company and at the same time to guarantee credit over all the different trade centres in Europe. Furthermore in the Indian trade the agent had to cover all the ships and loads engaged in the transoceanic trade with assurances. Bourdieu was well aware of the difficulties ahead, especially if he had to equal Charles Herries and his incredible network of bankers in the main European trade centres:

> if we were to undertake to make any payments for domiciles, or other objects originally address'd to the H's (Herries), we might not find the same resource, as they had at Paris and Amsterdam. The house of Boyd, which is become considerable by the support of the Hope's of Amsterdam, the Nettine of Brussels and La Borde of

---

[23] On the French East India Company, see Philippe Haudrère, *La compagnie française des Indes au XVIIIe siècle* (Paris, 2005).

[24] For the assembly debate on the abolition of India Company privilege see *Archives Parlementaires de 1787 à 1860*, ed. Jérôme Mavidal and Émile Laurent, vol. XII (Paris, 1867), 221–36.

[25] Bourdieu showed his satisfaction for Monneron's nomination to the Board in the following letter: 'I am very happy to hear that Mr. Louis Monneron is of the Party, because he is the reverse of the Sabatier, Perier and Gourlade. He is as liberal, as they are mesquin, and will never support the idea of reducing the usual established commission upon India Business, such as he had always paid us himself', AN, T 38, letter of 20 April 1790.

[26] AN, T 38, letter of 30 July 1790: 'We have told him he was welcome to draw on us for the sum he wanted between 13 to 140.000 sterling without requiring a deposit, which he offers. We were glad of the opportunity of obliging him at this juncture, tout ceci entre nous, and for your government in case you should have occasion to solicit his interference in our favor for the India agency. At the same time we trust your discretion, not to give him the least suspicion of this communication.'

Paris, had always a portefeuille to assist upon occasion; besides which the E.I.C. had opened a very extensive credit at the Hope's in favor of the H's. [...] They have been able to provide for such immense sums as they must have had to pay for the East India Company.[27]

The situation of the French East India Company was far from being completely settled: Bérard had resigned, Herries remained the sole agent of the company, and the National Assembly did not take a final position on the future of the trade company. The East India Company needed to decide whether to continue its trade or to liquidate all its affairs.

The main problem to solve for the trading company was to pay the debt towards Herries & Co, which amounted to around 100,000 pounds. Huber, once he had become commissioner of the Company, insisted to Bourdieu that he must pay this debt if he was to hold the office of agent of the company. At first the English merchant refused to engage his scarce capital in this operation; moreover Bourdieu was not confident of being named as the sole agent, but rather felt that he should share this responsibility with someone else. When eventually Bourdieu agreed to risk this operation, the National Assembly decided to liquidate the Company and to secure the shares on the tobacco duty.

The tobacco trade was the other business in which Bourdieu had a solid interest. At that time the import of tobacco into France was regulated by the deal reached by the Ferme Générale, the company of tax farmers, and the Philadelphia merchant Robert Morris, who was the only dealer allowed to sell up to 60,000 tobacco hogsheads to the French market.[28]

Bourdieu hoped that the tobacco trade would remain in the Ferme's control because only in this situation could he get tobacco orders directly from France, otherwise he would have to compete against many other competitors in the field. The National Assembly could revoke the privilege given to the Ferme as it had done with the East India Company.[29] The National Assembly did not hurry to determine the future of the Ferme and this uncertainty considerably influenced Bourdieu's plans. The English merchant communicated to his French correspondents that the right moment to buy tobacco from America had come: the tobacco crop had been incredibly abundant and if France

---

[27] AN, T 38, cahier III, letter of 13 August 1790.
[28] On the Morris deal with France see Frederick L. Nussbaum, 'American Tobacco and French Politics 1783–1789', *Political Science Quarterly* 1925 (40.4): 497–516. An important monograph on the tobacco trade between the United States and France is Jacob Michael Price, *France and the Chesapeake: A History of the French Tobacco Monopoly, 1674–1791, and of its Relationship to the British and American Tobacco Trades* (Ann Arbor, MI, 1973).
[29] AN, T 38, cahier IV, letter of 20 April 1790: 'It remains to know whether the national Assembly after taking away the Privilege of the East India Company and making that trade free, mean to make any regulation in the department of the Farmers General, which brings in so great a revenue to Government. I should suppose it must be soon known what the intentions of the national assembly are, upon this Business.'

remained neutral in the war between Spain and Great Britain they could profit from all the advantages of being a neutral country.

Waiting for the final decision of the National Assembly, Bourdieu promoted with every means the possibility to furnish tobacco through London, which would bring him large profits from the activity of intermediary in this trade. The English merchant had to battle against two major competing factors in the tobacco trade: first, the American merchant Robert Morris, second, the possibility of an increase in tobacco growing in French regions such as Alsace, Artois, or Lorraine where the cultivation of tobacco was widely diffused.

Bourdieu made clear that he did not want a personal emolument for the tobacco loads which he would have sent to France, but preferred a simple 2 per cent commission on the future order coming from the Ferme on other goods. All hopes harboured by Bourdieu were destroyed by the decision of the Assembly in March 1791 to liberalize the tobacco trade.

Both in the case of the French East India Company and in the case of the tobacco trade held by the Ferme Générale, Bourdieu had striven to obtain commercial orders from two institutions of the Old Regime which were attacked by the general offensive against privileges launched by the National Assembly. Fortunately for him Bourdieu's interests were larger than just these two fields.

Bourdieu showed great interest in the possibility of buying the *biens nationaux*, lands confiscated from the Church which had become national patrimony. The decree of 19 December 1789 created a Caisse de l'Extraordinaire, where it was estimated that at least 400 million livres might be collected by the sale of these lands. Bourdieu advanced his candidacy to become the official merchant charged with the offers made by British investors to buy the national lands. Bourdieu knew that he needed some guarantees to proceed in this field:

> When a regular plan is finally settled by your National Assembly for the sale of Church Lands and foreigners can form a proper idea of the probable advantages by purchasing, there is no doubt but our monied people will become adventurers.[30]

When Bourdieu was informed that the sale of the lands would be done through the different municipalities he proposed himself as broker for the Paris municipality. The English merchant could present himself to the English market as a keen specialist in the French market because of his business with Necker, who was at that time still in charge. Moreover, if the sale of the lands was in the charge of the municipalities it was in their interest to have a prestigious banker like Bourdieu acting as a broker. Nevertheless, the English banker's plans were dashed by another decision made by the National Assembly: on 14 May 1790 the Assembly decreed that no intermediaries were needed

---

[30] AN, T 38, letter of 23 March 1790.

to sell national lands. While Bourdieu had suffered many drawbacks in his particular economic interests, what really made him distrust the French political course was a political consideration: the weakness of the executive. The reasoning of the English merchant was clear: without a solid executive power which could assure the enforcement of contracts and the clear will to maintain internal order, no one could think it wise to invest capital in a country like France where there was no effective power to protect economic deals.

The English merchant saw with great anguish that the distrust towards France and its stock market had rapidly increased. Bourdieu's concern over the lack of real executive power in revolutionary France was shown to be well founded: the weakness of executive power became apparent when disorder broke into open rebellion in towns like Lyons and Nancy; and the Assembly displayed itself as incredibly slow in taking economic decisions in strategic fields like the future of the East India Company or the regulation of tobacco trade. If a strong and respected executive power had existed these delays might have been avoided.

These political considerations had direct effects on the financial choices made by Bourdieu: he moved his capital away from France and returned to invest in the less risky English stock market. Bourdieu's case was not unique and many other market actors withdrew their capital from Paris and looked for other markets. However, what happened to the Anglo-French merchant underlines how in turbulent times the access to information and the existence of political connections were not sufficient to protect or allow investments: on the contrary these assets can easily became fateful liabilities and impede any further venture. Nonetheless, the Paris market did not lose all its potential for foreign bankers willing to settle in the French capital. Of course, such a move required some luck in avoiding the turbulent effects of events such as the Terror, but the Paris market under the Directory, and later during the Napoleonic Empire, could offer wide opportunities for profit and social advance. The trajectory of the Swiss banker Jean-Conrad Hottinguer is a good example of the new phase that the Paris market entered after the end of the Terror.[31]

2.4 Living through Revolution: Hottinguer's Rise to the Haute Banque

Jean-Conrad Hottinguer was born in 1764 in Zurich where he served his apprenticeship as a bookkeeper for his uncle. Later he moved to Paris where

---

[31] To my knowledge only one biography has been dedicated to Hottinguer, that by Max Gérard, *Messieurs Hottinguer, banquiers à Paris* (Paris, 1972). Gérard had the possibility to use the archives of the bank which is still active with branches in Zurich, New York, and Paris.

he started to work in the financial house of Lecouteulx & C., which was led by the future director of the Banque de France, Jean-Barthélémy Le Couteulx de Canteleu. After this experience in a well-known French house of commerce, Hottinguer moved to work with another Swiss banker, Denis Rougemont. This banker was one of the main agents for Swiss bankers and merchants who had interests in the Paris market. Rapidly, Hottinguer became Rougemont's partner, but he was close to failure when Rougemont went into bankruptcy for a badly conceived speculation on colonial goods in 1792. When Rougemont committed suicide this tragic event forced Hottinguer to leave Paris for London where he started to collect back the credit he had personally opened for his associate. In London he recovered part of his fortunes, and he also met his future wife: Martha Redwood, the young daughter of a rich American planter and shipowner.

After a short period in Zurich, where he had escaped to from Paris when the Terror imposed by the Jacobin authorities openly persecuted foreign bankers, he decided to seek refuge in the United States where he remained until the beginning of the Directory. However, the instability of this regime found little favour among financiers and Hottinguer is thought to have been one of the bankers who personally helped Napoleon with financial aid to succeed in his coup d'état on 18 Brumaire 1799, although no clear evidence of this support has been found. In the meantime, Hottinguer became involved in the activities of supplying food and garments for the army, which seemed a profitable field of investment, given France's endless state of war under the Directory and the Consulate. Moreover, Hottinguer became a close adviser on financial matters to Charles-Maurice de Talleyrand-Périgord, whom he had met for the first time in the United States.

Hottinguer was also always interested in the Atlantic trade with the United States where he sent his friend and associate Henry Escher, another Zurich merchant. For this reason, Hottinguer opened branches of his house of commerce, Hottinguer & C., at Le Havre and Nantes.[32] These two subsidiaries were the terminals of a very profitable Atlantic commerce which turned on the export of French wine to American ports. The Swiss banker rapidly became one of the financial elite who composed the ranks of the Bank of France and in 1803 he became a member of the *regents* of this young institution. Hottinguer's ascent to this office was not the last significant accomplishment in his life: in 1808 the emperor Napoleon appointed Hottinguer a Baron of the Empire for his fidelity and services towards France.

---

[32] On the French–American trade during the last years of the eighteenth century and the first decade of the nineteenth, see Silvia Marzagalli, *Bordeaux et les États-Unis, 1776–1815: politique et stratégies négociantes dans la genèse d'un réseau commercial* (Geneva, 2015).

During the last years of the Napoleonic Empire Hottinguer reduced his activities to the trade relations with the United States and limited his financial operations to small discounting activities on the Paris market. Even though his successful career was mostly due to Napoleon's favour, the Swiss banker, like his personal friend Talleyrand, was accepted both in Restoration France and also during the reign of Louis Philippe. At the end of his life (he died in 1844) Hottinguer could be proud of having established a well-respected and widely known bank which could enjoy a large measure of credit due to the remarkable success of its founder.

From this brief description of Hottinguer's life, it is clear that he was truly cosmopolitan banker who was capable of navigating the turbulent seas of different political regimes and financial situations thanks to his political and personal connections, which helped him climb to the top of the social ladder. However, what really makes the case of Hottinguer noteworthy is his ability to maintain a very wide and international group of clients whom he had met during his travels in England, the United States, Switzerland, and, last but not least, France.

Moreover, from a study of notarial documentation concerning Hottinguer's activity during the Napoleonic Empire it appears that Dutch clients continued to play an important role in the business run by the Swiss banker. The persistent relevance of Dutch capital on the Paris Stock Exchange is a clear sign of a twofold development: on the one hand Dutch capital remained significant even after the partial decline of Amsterdam as a financial centre; on the other hand, the weighty investments put up by Dutch firms in the French debt signalled the importance of Paris as a truly European stock exchange during the first years of the nineteenth century.

Hottinguer profited from his travels abroad to enlarge his clientele beyond the Swiss clients for whom he had moved to Paris before the outbreak of the revolution. The case of the Escher family is an example of the long-term trust shown by Swiss clients towards their fellow countryman in Paris: Jean Escher had appointed the bank Rougemont & C. as his attorney in Paris and later he entrusted all the business interests of his family members to Hottinguer.[33] The Escher family was not an isolated case of long-term fidelity towards Hottinguer expressed by his fellow citizens throughout the years of revolution. Even though the Swiss remained a constant presence among Hottinguer's clientele, a larger number of his clients were American or Dutch merchants.

Hottinguer acquired American clients probably partly as a consequence of his marriage to the daughter of a rich American merchant, but also as a result

---

[33] See the power of attorney passed to the notary Gibé in Paris where Jean Conrad Escher nominated Hottinguer attorney for his three daughters and his brothers. AN ET LV, 205, 25 Prairial year 10.

of his direct engagement in the American trade, especially in the profitable whale hunting business which required large sums of capital to buy assurance on the ship load, advance wages due to the sailors, and, more generally, to be ready to suffer large losses in case of pirate attacks or seizure of the ship by a foreign navy.[34] The largest group of American clients was from Boston, but other commercial cities such as New York, Charleston, and Baltimore were also well represented.

The American clientele charged the Swiss banker with one vital mission: the recovery of different credits that they had opened towards the French Republic. This assignment is easily understandable in the light of the troubled relationships between the two young republics: after a short period of alliance during the War of Independence, the United States had started to readdress their diplomatic relations with their former colonial power, and to move their allegiance away from the now revolutionary France. This situation risked ending with an open war between the United States and France under the Adams presidency, which advanced the Alien Sedition Act to protect the country from any foreign influence, especially any widespread diffusion of revolutionary ideals. During this period not only were diplomatic relations between the two countries mostly strained, but also commercial exchanges were jeopardized by open acts of piracy perpetuated by privateers on both sides of the Atlantic.

An improvement in the relationship between the two young republics came only when Thomas Jefferson became president of the United States, and when concurrently the coup d'état of 18 Brumaire brought Napoleon to power. Jefferson's well-known Francophile attitude and the pragmatic approach showed by Napoleon regarding the sale of Louisiana to the United States both favoured a general reappraisal of the commercial relationships between the two states. The general appeasement was sanctioned in a convention between the two nations which included a commission to which merchants could appeal to settle their reclaims or credits towards the other nation.

One of the main sources of contention for American merchants regarding their commercial relationships with France were all the commercial bills that remained unpaid by the French authorities, who had employed all sorts of bills of exchange to pay for the goods and provisions needed for the supply of the island of Haiti. The French Caribbean colony was the theatre of a cruel and violent war between French forces and the slaves, who were supplied and armed by the British navy. American merchants played an important role in the process of assuring the necessary supply of food to the French army and to that part of the population which had remained loyal to the colonial

---

[34] See AN, ET XV, 1174, 7 Nivose year XIV.

authorities. Numerous American merchants appointed Hottinguer as their personal attorney with the specific aim of recovering their credits with the French republican authorities.

Even if Hottinguer had had only to face a single problem, credit recovery, this presented multifaceted aspects related to the specific situation of each American merchant. Nonetheless, there were some common features which characterized the situation of Hottinguer's American clients: the majority of them complained about unpaid bills of exchange which dated back to 1794 or 1796. Many American merchants not only were confident that their capital would be entirely paid back by French authorities, but also expected to receive the interest due on the sum that they had advanced.[35] In some cases the French authorities on the island of Haiti had partially covered the sum they owed to the American merchants by paying with other goods, such as the typical staples of the Caribbean, sugar, molasses, and coffee, which were much appreciated by their counterparts. Sometimes the credit recovery was particularly complicated when the American client claimed that the entire cargo had been seized and sold by privateers.[36]

Hottinguer was also charged with the duty of recovering credit from the United States in favour of French citizens.[37] This responsibility was a clear sign of the significant position acquired by Hottinguer in the transatlantic trade between the two republics: the Zurich banker was recognized by merchants and private citizens as a reliable and efficient attorney in dealing with business concerning the two countries.

The most significant group of foreign clients of the Hottinguer bank was composed of Dutch merchants and bankers, both of which had relevant interests at stake on the Paris market. Almost all the Dutch merchants and bankers with whom Hottinguer had to deal came from the three main cities of the Batavian Republic, later the Kingdom of Holland: Amsterdam, The Hague, and Utrecht. This is easily understood in light of the relevance of Amsterdam as a financial centre, The Hague as the political centre of the country, and Utrecht one of the major cities of the area. Nevertheless private citizens from

---

[35] David Spear, a Bostonian merchant, and Asa Higgins, master of the ship *Washington*, were waiting for the payment of 21,135 livres which was due to them for the cargo delivered to Cap François, capital of French Haiti. See AN, ET XV, 1178, 7 Prairial year XIII (28 May 1805).

[36] A case of this nature is that regarding Eben Parson, a Boston merchant, who had lost his cargo taken by French privateers. These French pirates sold the cargo at Lorient to another buyer. As a consequence Parson did not receive anything from the selling of his cargo. See AN, ET XV, 1170, 25 Messidor year XIII (15 July 1805).

[37] This was the case of Salvi Victor Genton—citizen of Amarens, in the Gaillac department, South of France—who had been named as universal heir of Jean Louis Ambroise Genton. Jean Louis had fought for the United States as colonel and he had a credit towards them of $6,409. His brother Salvi, therefore, had appointed Hottinguer to recover this important sum from the American authorities. See AN, ET XV, 1177, 15 Germinal year XIII (6 April 1805).

small urban centres, such as Deventer and Workum in the agricultural region of Friesland, can also be found among Hottinguer's Dutch clients.[38]

An analysis of the notarial records regarding Hottinguer's Dutch clients shows that the main activity for all these businessmen was the French public debt. In 1793 the Grand Livre de la dette publique was created to offer a solid guarantee to the creditors of the state that all obligations made by the previous government would be lawfully met. However, in 1797, the situation of public finance remained critical and led the Directory to default partially in order to be able at least to pay one-third of the entire debt. Moreover, it was stated that all French bonds could yield a 5 per cent interest and not more, as had been the case before this reform, which was euphemistically called 'consolidation of one-third' but was universally known as the 'bankruptcy of the two-thirds'.[39]

Hottinguer's Dutch clientele included not only some small merchants but also important bankers such as Voombergh, Halmael and Borski, and Van Staphorst, Willink & Co. These two banks were specialized in dealing with foreign loans, especially the placement of American bonds for the European buyers. Hottinguer became the agent of Voombergh, Halmael and Borski from the winter of 1805.[40] Until that time Hottinguer was more inclined to work with Zurich bankers who asked him to act as their agent in Paris. Voombergh was not the first Dutch banker to employ Hottinguer as his agent in Paris but he rapidly became Hottinguer's most important client.[41]

Voombergh, Halmael and Borski, who constituted a bank syndicate, entrusted to Hottinguer a single task: to sell their French bonds which were registered in the Grand Livre de la dette publique. Only once during the decade considered in this chapter did Hottinguer buy French bonds directly from his Dutch colleague; otherwise the Swiss banker simply followed the orders to sell French bonds on the Paris Bourse.[42]

---

[38] Two clients coming from small centres were Petrus Hockema, citizen of Workum, and Willem Shimmelpenninck, citizen of Deventer. Even if these two clients were not part of the business community of Amsterdam, Shimmelpenninck was one of the shareholders of the Banque de France—in fact he gave full powers to represent his interest in the assembly of the bank to Hottinguer—and Hockema asked to sell his French bonds which amounted to 4,500 francs. See AN, ET XV, 1232, 22 May 1810 for Hockema and AN, ET XV, 1204, 22 December 1807.

[39] Far from being easily resolved, the payment of life annuities continued until the present day as revealed by François R. Velde, 'The Case of the Undying Debt', *Financial History Review* 2010 (17.2): 185–209.

[40] The first act concerning the business between Hottinguer and Voombergh took place on 1 November 1805, see AN, ET XV, 1181, 25 Frimaire year XIV (17 December 1805).

[41] Hottinguer was the agent of the Dutch banker Réné Berenbrock, working for the Dutch firm Vanderhoeven & Co, in the liquidation of the credits of the French bankers Geyler and Jordan. See AN, ET XV, 1160, 18 Fructidore year XI (5 September 1803).

[42] On 20 June 1806 Hottinguer bought from Voombergh French bonds up to a total value of 37,625 francs. See AN, ET XV, 1186, 30 June 1806.

During the time frame discussed here, there were some occasions when Hottinguer received a higher number of sell orders than in other periods when his Dutch peers seemed less interested in selling their French bonds. An example of this unstable trend in the sell orders is that of spring 1807: Hottinguer had received sell orders for a value of 178,000 francs during the entire month of April and the first half of May, whereas just in the week from 20 to 27 May Hottinguer was asked to sell French bonds for a value of 676,000 francs.[43]

What caused Voombergh and his associate to sell in one week an amount of bonds valued three and a half times their sell orders of the previous month and a half? One possible reason for these financial operations can be found in the news of the opening of a loan in favour of Spain on the Dutch market. This loan was a consequence of the emperor Napoleon requiring payment of the sum due by Spain to France: since the Spanish Crown could not find the capital for this, it turned to the Dutch market. After the direct pressure of the French Foreign Minister, on 21 May 1806 the king Louis Bonaparte gave the order to open a loan in favour of Spain.[44] The decision to sell so many French bonds can be correlated with the need to have enough capital for the new loan.[45]

2.5 Conclusion

The French Revolution unsettled the economic world just as it unsettled the entire political framework of Old Regime France. Some market actors, such as Bourdieu and Boyd, looked at this turmoil as an opportunity to enter into fields of business that were impossible for them before the outbreak of the revolution. For this reason Bourdieu was ready to take advantage of a situation of free trade, as in the case of the French East India Company, as well as of protected trade, as in the case of tobacco.

Bourdieu failed in his various attempts to gain a position in these two businesses, but what really turned him away from the French market was his

---

[43] See AN, ET XV, 1196–7 (May–June 1806).
[44] In a letter addressed by Talleyrand to the French ambassador at The Hague it is clear how relevant was this loan that would enable Spain to pay the money due to France: 'Ne neglegez rien, Monsieur, pour engager le Gouvernement hollandais à se preter au voeu de la Cour d'Espagne', letter sent by Talleyrand to Dupont-Chaumont, ambassador at The Hague, in Ministère Affaires Etrangères [MAE] Corneuve, Correspondance politique [CP], 611, d. 17. In a letter sent by Dupont on 21 May 1806 the opening of the loan was communicated: 'Le Roi [...] a rendu un decret pour permettre l'emprunt d'Espagne; il sera expedié aujourd'huj à Amsterdam', MAE, CP, 611, d. 89.
[45] I am not suggesting a unequivocal correlation between the incredibly high number of sell orders and the new loan for Spain, nonetheless it seems one of the best reasons to explain Voombergh's attitude in that period.

analysis of the political situation of the country in which he wanted to invest. Bourdieu started to lose his faith in the stabilization of the French economy during 1790, which is usually considered a calm and positive period, before the flight of the king in 1791 and the outbreak of war in spring 1792. Again Bourdieu's concern about the stability of French economy did not derive from the issuing of the *assignats*, the paper money circulating on the security of the national lands sold, but from the lack of effective power in the hands of the king.

Both Boyd and Bourdieu were directly engaged in the national French market in those sectors, such as the obligations market or the international trade, which required large investments and were thus particularly open to the activity of foreign actors. More particularly the French market was part of a great circulation of capital, which turned on the three 'capitals of capital', Amsterdam, Paris, and London. In the specific cases that we have considered here Amsterdam was the pivotal financial market where it was possible to raise large sums, which could be invested in the French stock market, *in primis* in life securities, while London offered a wide market for marine assurances which were essential in long distance trade such as the tobacco trade or the Indies trade.

Whereas Bourdieu failed to acquire new business within the French market, Hottinguer succeeded in becoming one of the most prominent bankers on the Paris market. Of course, Hottinguer was lucky in avoiding the Terror, and his travel to the United States allowed him to create new networks and so enlarge his clientele. Bourdieu, as later also Hottinguer, tried to diversify his investment in various fields, but the high volatility of the National Assembly hindered any further possible advancement. In contrast, Hottinguer was able to profit from the improvement in the relationship between France and the United States to settle different businesses that his American clients had entrusted to him. Moreover, the Swiss banker played an important role in representing Dutch interests on the Paris annuities market within the new empire framework.

Hottinguer's case shows how the three 'capitals of capital'—Amsterdam, Paris, and London—were always connected notwithstanding the almost endless state of war in Europe during the first years of the nineteenth century. The rise of London as the main European financial centre appears to have been gradual, and not a swift development as has sometimes been suggested, and this long process did not prevent Paris continuing to be an attractive market for bankers at least until the end of the Empire.

On the whole the trajectories of these bankers have highlighted the importance of gaining access to information and strengthening connections with other bankers or political actors able to offer insightful views on the ever-shifting French political life. In a time of unpredictable changes like the

French Revolution connections and information became highly valuable and strategic assets in shaping investment in the volatile Parisian market. Information and connections came at a price, however: the rapid political changes enacted by the National Assembly put an end to the investing plans of Bourdieu as well as Hottinguer's tie with Talleyrand which had developed while both were exiled in the United States.

3

Adjusting to Financial Instability in the Interwar Period

Italian Financial Elites, International Cooperation, and Domestic Regulation, 1919–1939

Giandomenico Piluso

3.1 Introduction

Financial instability phenomena are defining moments in the history of regulation and in the very way elites consider themselves and their role in politics, as responses to such phenomena are essentially a political issue and a government matter in a broad sense.[1] Major instability cases, such as those that occurred in the interwar period, may entail changes in the character of the elites and in the definition of their own contours. In times of high instability, when the existing set of rules is usually extremely under pressure for exogenous shocks, the complex interplay between elites and institutions is more apparent and the necessity to adjust the individual financial systems may involve an adaptive selection of the respective elites.[2] Such a process may

---

I would like to express my gratitude to the Warden, Sir Andrew Dinot, and Fellows of Nuffield College at the University of Oxford, where I spent a splendid period of research and study as a Jemolo Fellow in 2015. In particular, my thanks go to Professor Laurence Whitehead and the entire staff at the College's Library for their invaluable support and assistance.

[1] This point was implicitly considered by Gerald Feldman when comparing individual figures of bankers and civil servants within their own institutional settings in Germany and Italy in the 1920s and 1930s. See Gerald Feldman, 'Political Disputes about the Role of Banks', in Harold James, Hakan Lindgren, and Alice Teichova (eds.), *The Role of Banks in the Interwar Economy* (Cambridge, 1991), 16–17.

[2] In a sense this argument partly echoes that by Daron Acemoglu, Simon Johnson, and James A. Robinson, 'Institutions as a Fundamental Cause of Long-Run Growth', in Philippe Aghion and Steven N. Durlauf (eds.), *Handbook of Economic Growth* (Amsterdam and London, 2005), vol. 1, 389–96.

cause notable changes in the very nature of elites, as to their structure, qualities, networks, and boundaries.[3] From this viewpoint, the interwar period can be regarded as an interesting case on how financial elites cope with a highly uncertain environment and adjustment processes when external shocks severely affect economies, alter market stability, and disrupt international relations.[4] The end of the first globalization after the Great War redefined the international financial environment and financial elites as a whole, ranging from central bankers to banking sector managers, had to muddle through a disorderly context. Throughout the post-war decade ineffective attempts to stabilize international financial and currency markets were again and again made by design, according to an explicit plan centred on the restoration of the Gold Standard.[5] As correlated economic policies proved to be unsuitable in fixing instability, all over Europe financial elites were bound to deal with mounting uncertainty, whilst their peculiar cosmopolitanism was eroding. From the mid-nineteenth century financial elites tended to assume a well-defined international nature as capital markets increasingly acquired an international dimension, at least up to 1914.[6] As in the 1920s a string of shocks related to the First World War dramatically altered the progress of markets' integration processes, financial elites adapted themselves to tendencies to a more 'intense national consciousness',[7] shifts that impaired international monetary cooperation and implied alterations within the roles and composition of financial elites, although without losing their international penchant all at once.[8] In the end, financial instability called for more intensive regulation reallocating responsibilities and regulatory powers from the private sector to the public sphere. In this process, as private sector representatives tended to mingle with public bodies and agencies, financial elites somewhat changed

---

[3] This kind of approach would coincide with a sort of Namierization of the study of financial elites.

[4] See Harold James, 'Introduction', in James, Lindgren and Teichova (eds.), *The Role of Banks in the Interwar Economy*, 1–12.

[5] There is an enormous literature, as well as an ongoing debate, on the shortcomings of monetary policies in the interwar years in relation to the reconstruction of the pre-1914 Gold Standard. See Peter Temin, *Lessons from the Great Depression* (Cambridge, MA, 1989); Barry Eichengreen, *Golden Fetters: The Gold Standard and the Great Depression, 1919–1939* (Oxford, 1992); Harold James, *The End of Globalization: Lessons from the Great Depression* (Cambridge, MA, 2001).

[6] See Maurice Obstfeld and Alan M. Taylor, 'Globalization and Capital Markets', in Michael D. Bordo, Alan M. Taylor, and Jeffrey G. Williamson (eds.), *Globalization in Historical Perspective* (Chicago, 2003), 122–5.

[7] Thus, referring to the then 'present state', Michiel Hendrik De Kock, deputy governor of the South African Reserve Bank, expressed himself reflecting on the possibility of the Bank for International Settlements becoming a 'real central bank of central banks' that it would have involved 'the subordination of the monetary sovereignty of individual nations'. See Michiel H. De Kock, *Central Banking* (London, 1939), 165–6.

[8] This could be regarded as a consequence of an intergenerational adjustment where competences (and powers) still rely upon older and more experienced individuals whilst junior (and younger) members have still to gain access to top posts. Paradoxically, at least in the Italian case, a lesser internationalized financial elite would occupy the domestic scene in the post-war decades.

their contours and boundaries as a result of major changes in their own environment. In general terms, what emerges is a tendency of financial elites to adjust their behaviour and professional profiles to the shift towards a more regulated context, by cooperating or even merging with public agencies or technocracies.[9]

In fact, at least in the Italian case, the old elites and the new were gradually overlapping rather than the latter ones substituting the former ones mechanically, whilst a serious change occurred in the early 1930s when institutional innovation deeply modified the regulatory architecture of the whole financial system. In the 1920s the most important attempts to stabilize the international financial and monetary systems were made, in effect, by intermingled financial elites from private institutions and public bureaucracies, according to a common pattern of the pre-war financial world. Yet, financial elites addressed the main factors of instability, such as war reparations, inter-allied debts, and volatile exchange rates and capital flows, by adopting policies which proved to be an ineffective deflationary strategy. Thus, resulting macroeconomic imbalances within the international environment required recurring adjustment policies and stimulated central authorities to intervene by progressively regulating more markets and intermediaries. This process was related to the efforts to strengthen international financial cooperation mechanisms undertaken after the Treaty of Versailles. The very concept of international financial cooperation emerged through economic and monetary conferences (from the Brussels and Genoa conferences in 1920 and 1922 to London in 1933), bilateral agreements on inter-allied debts, and intergovernmental organizations, such as the League of Nations or the Bank for International Settlements (BIS). On these grounds, regulation appears as a complex response to domestic instability, as commonly maintained in literature, *and* to external shocks which stimulated forms of cooperation between senior civil servants and financial elites. In this regard, such a change could be considered not just as a mere top-down process achieved by central authorities and lawmakers, but, rather, as a reaction to domestic *and* international instability by a wider group of policy-makers, in which financial elites encompassed senior bankers and top bank managers, central bankers, and high-ranking civil servants and technocrats as well.[10]

---

[9] Such a process would have the same hybrid character observed by David Landes for innovation processes within nineteenth-century financial Europe. See David Landes, 'Vieille banque et banque nouvelle: la révolution financière du dix-neuvième siècle', *Revue d'Histoire Moderne et Contemporaine* 1956 (3.3): 207–22.

[10] Here financial elites are defined as a composite group at the very apex of power and responsibility. This definition is actually a rather narrow definition, related to policy-making and adjustment strategies or to the 'power of influence' of policy-makers as advisers, thus referring to a relatively small and open group of individuals, subject to changes in structure and boundaries. Such a definition partially coincides, especially in terms of amplitude, with that assumed by

The chapter considers how and according to which rationales and purposes the Italian financial elites played their part within the international arena in the interwar period. As was common at that time, Italian governments and central monetary authorities tended to co-opt prominent or competent representatives from the private sector onto special committees dealing with these issues at home, at international conferences, or in bilateral negotiations. The demand for technical competences and bargaining abilities rose strongly by favouring cooperation amongst senior officials, central bankers, private bankers, and top bank officials.[11] The Treasury and the Bank of Italy enlisted financiers and bank officials when they had to join international committees, or to take part in international stabilization programmes organized by central banks, as well as turning to an influential in-between figure, Alberto Beneduce, for the Special Advisory Committee of the BIS. Besides, bankers and managers played an important role in settling inter-allied debts. Indeed, the way central authorities and financial elites cooperated during the 1920s in order to adjust sectors and institutions to an unstable international environment was a major factor in the reshaping process of the Italian economy as it emerged from the crisis of the early 1930s, with its winners and losers. As a major result, a financial technocracy, with an established reputation in international organizations, largely replaced the previous cosmopolitan financial elite, weakened within its very international foundations, by affirming a different regulatory model which aimed at guaranteeing internal stability from external shocks as its main objective.[12]

This perspective may offer a different view on the underlying forces which led to redefining financial regulation, usually assumed as an institutional response to domestic instability. From this perspective the financial regulation of the 1930s will be analysed as a result of a more complex process, embracing adjustment responses to international instability and the changing contours of financial elites. The chapter considers three main points: (i) how Italian financial elites coped with the twin domestic crises of the early 1920s by

---

Youssef Cassis, 'Financial Elites in Three European Centres: London, Paris, Berlin 1880s–1930s', *Business History* 1991 (33.3): 53–71, but is quite different from that recently adopted by Andrés Solimano, *Economic Elites, Crises, and Democracy: Alternatives beyond Neoliberal Capitalism* (New York, 2014), 17. Andrés Solimano rigidly separates financial sector elites (bankers, big investors, hedge fund owners and managers) from their regulators (central bankers, finance ministries, and governments). Thus, Solimano opts for a dualistic definition centred on sector and wealth, more than influence and roles, which induces to ignore complex processes of overlapping in policy-making that were typical of the interwar years.

[11] In this regard see the letter sent by Alberto Pirelli, then at the Peace Conference in Versailles, to Bonaldo Stringher, from Paris, on 3 March 1919, in Marcello De Cecco (ed.), *L'Italia e il sistema finanziario internazionale, 1919–1936* (Rome and Bari, 1993), 499–500.

[12] In this sense Italian financial elites differed from other European cases: cf. Youssef Cassis, 'Financial Elites Revisited', in Ranald Michie and Philip Williamson (eds.), *The British Government and the City of London in the Twentieth Century* (Cambridge, 2004), 76–95.

promoting financial innovation and fostering central banking, from the international conferences of the early 1920s up to mounting capital controls of the 1930s; (ii) how they took part in reparations and inter-allied debt negotiations and with what purposes they acted within international institutions such as the BIS; (iii) how they re-regulated the national financial system vis-à-vis external constraints from the mid-1920s onwards. This approach aims to provide an unconventional perspective on financial regulation as it evolved from the mid-1920s onwards, by connecting international constraints with the rationale behind central monetary authorities' choices. Such a rationale, which reshaped the financial sector and had a long-term impact on markets and intermediaries, evidences deeper relationships than is commonly understood within the complex array of international constraints.

3.2 Banks and Instability in Italy between the World Wars

At the end of the First World War the Italian economy was severely hit by three twin crises. During the war the aggregate public debt literally sky-rocketed doubling from 80 per cent on GDP on the eve of the conflict up to 160 per cent in 1921 inducing an unprecedented fiscal crisis.[13] At the same time a banking crisis, largely fuelled by the end of the wartime high liquidity, occurred as all the major manufacturing firms were in the middle of a financial overstretching which in the end affected their lenders.[14] This double shock was accompanied by an exchange rate crisis, as the lira significantly depreciated against both the British pound and the US dollar after 1919. These intertwined crises emerged in a context of increased volatility of the GDP, which in the interwar years was higher compared with previous and ensuing periods.[15]

In the 1920s the main indicators of size and activity of the banking sector fluctuated robustly as a consequence of alternating phases of inflation and deflation. Besides an increase in the total number of banks (and other intermediaries such as special credit institutions) and an overall dramatic surge of their total assets at constant values and as a percentage of GDP up to the early 1930s,[16] some indicators that allow us to stress the impact of inflation on

---

[13] On these variables new estimates are provided by Maura Francese and Angelo Pace, 'Il debito pubblico italiano dall'Unità a oggi. Una ricostruzione della serie storica', Banca d'Italia, *Questioni di Economia e Finanza*, occasional paper, no. 31, 18–19, 21. See also Roberto Artoni and Sara Biancini, 'Il debito pubblico dall'Unità ad oggi', in Pierluigi Ciocca and Gianni Toniolo (eds.), *Storia economica d'Italia* (Rome and Bari, 2004), vol. 3, 269–380.

[14] See Gianni Toniolo, 'Italian Banking, 1919–1936', in Charles H. Feinstein (ed.), *Banking, Currency, and Finance in Europe between the Wars* (Oxford, 1995), 298–300.

[15] See Domenico Delli Gatti, Mauro Gallegati, and Marco Gallegati, 'On the Nature and Causes of Business Fluctuations in Italy, 1861–2000', *Explorations in Economic History* 2005 (42.1): 90–1.

[16] According to estimates by Gianni Toniolo total bank assets and bank assets as percentage of GDP escalated, the former ones, from 42,946 million lire in 1919 to 114,103 million lire in 1932

banking dynamics, such as the aggregate total assets and loans on net-worth, provide an even more interesting tale of longer-term phenomena from the late nineteenth century to the outbreak of the Second World War.[17] These two indicators seem to be particularly sensitive to inflationary and deflationary phenomena in accordance with the relative rigidity of equity capital to catch up with the total assets growth rate in times of high liquidity and/or inflation.[18] In terms of size, the ability of the Italian banking system to lend grew significantly in comparison with its net-worth, almost doubling throughout the entire war period before contracting during the severe deflationary juncture of 1921–2.[19] The ensuing junctures were influenced by monetary policies as well: a short reflation in 1923–4 was followed by a sharp reduction after 1925 when the return to the Gold Standard was announced and Italy was bound to adjust to it by adopting a harsh deflationary monetary policy with 'quota novanta' (that is, ninety lire against one British pound). The relative contraction of the total assets and overall loans to net-worth ratios was also partially the result of the introduction of the first measures of bank capital adequacy in 1926. In the 1930s both ratios appear to achieve a smoother trend, although at a higher level in comparison with the pre-war dynamics, confirming that inflation was due to produce again a surge in either ratios related to military expenditures (see Figure 3.1).

In the 1930s, after the inflationary outcomes related to the war finance affected either time series, both ratios shift to a higher mean, as shown in Figure 3.1, and a more pronounced shift could be observed for the loans to net-worth ratio, which stabilized at an average 50 per cent higher in comparison with that of the pre-war years. This effect may be considered as a good measure of the overall impact of the war-related inflationary and instability phenomena on the structural features of the Italian banking system as a whole.[20]

(at 1938 prices) and the latter ones, from 30.7 per cent of GDP to 68.9 per cent (cf. Toniolo, 'Italian Banking, 1919–1936', 301, Table 10.1).

[17] These indicators of capital adequacy of the banking systems can offer a gauge of the leverage practised by banks avoiding distortions which could originate from the level of simple capitalization related to the equity capital component.

[18] Although different in its causes, a rather similar phenomenon has been experienced in the last two decades by most banking systems.

[19] This deflationary pressure was ascribed to a 'policy [pursued by the large banks] which aimed at rendering their resources more liquid'. See 'Report on the Application in Italy of the Resolutions of the International Financial Conference held in Brussels in 1920', League of Nations—Brussels Financial Conference 1920, *The Recommendations and their Application: A Review after Two Years*, vol. II, *Italy* (Geneva, 1922), 62.

[20] The related effect of the rise of money supply on the total supply of means of payment and, particularly, on the increase of 'extended bank credits' used as means of payments was noticed by Gustav Cassel in his *Memorandum on the World's Monetary Problems* (London, 1920), published by the League of Nations for the International Financial Conference at Brussels (quotation at pp. 7–8).

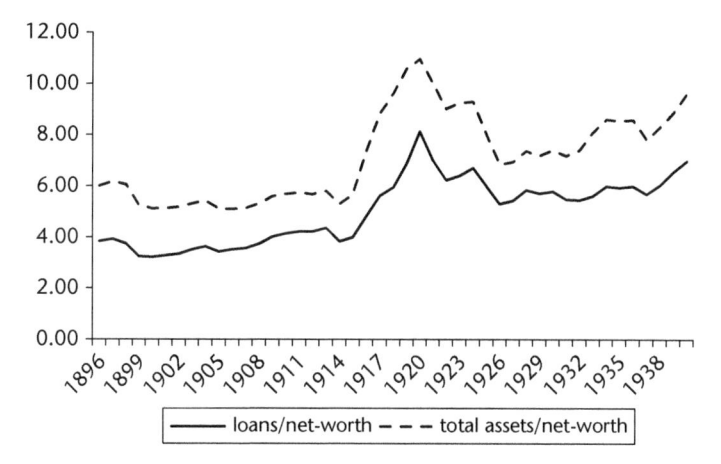

Figure 3.1. Aggregate total assets and loans on net-worth of the banking system as a whole, 1896–1940

Source: R. De Bonis, F. Farabullini, M. Rocchelli, and A. Slavio, 'Nuove serie storiche sulle attività di banche e altre istituzioni finanziarie dal 1861 al 2011: che cosa ci dicono?', Banca d'Italia, *Quaderni di Storia economica* 26 (2012) (our calculations).

On the whole, this empirical evidence suggests a sharp rise of levels of volatility, and hence of instability, throughout the first post-war decade with some pronounced upward and downward movements in the early 1920s. As the largest joint-stock banks, and particularly the German-style mixed banks, had a 'rising relative importance' within the Italian banking system during the 1920s,[21] as well as the banks of issue in accordance to the thoroughly accommodating monetary policies pursued in wartime, it may be worth considering how top banks behaved and their capital adequacy and profitability ratios varied in the interwar period. For this purpose, some capital adequacy and profitability ratios have been calculated for an open sample of the four largest banks ranked by total assets from 1919 to 1939,[22] adding to this sample the three banks of issue (Bank of Italy, Bank of Naples, and Bank of Sicily) up to 1926 and the sole Bank of Italy afterwards.[23]

---

[21] See Toniolo, 'Italian Banking, 1919–1936', 301, Table 10.1. See also Harold James and Kevin H. O'Rourke, 'Italy and the First Age of Globalization, 1861–1940', in Gianni Toniolo (ed.), *The Oxford Handbook of the Italian Economy since Unification* (Oxford, 2013), 54.

[22] The open sample comprises: (i) the three major mixed banks in the entire period (Banca Commerciale Italiana, Credito Italiano, Banco di Roma) plus the fourth ailing mixed bank, Banca Italiana di Sconto (1919) and Banca Nazionale di Credito (1924–9) up to its merger with Credito Italiano in 1930; (ii) a major regional bank, Banca Popolare di Novara in eleven years (1920–3, 1931, 1934–7); (iii) finally, two emerging public banks in the 1930s, Monte dei Paschi di Siena (1930, 1932–3) and Banca Nazionale del Lavoro (BNL) (1938–9).

[23] The Bank of Naples had a share of 20–25 per cent of the total amount of money circulating in these years, whilst the Bank of Sicily was responsible for a mere 5–8 per cent.

Table 3.1. The four largest Italian banks (C4) and banks of issue: volatility (standard deviation) of indicators of capital adequacy and profitability, 1919–1939

	1919–1939	1919–1929	1930–1939
total assets/equity capital			
C4	3.394	4.522	2.214
C4+banks of issue	13.713	14.011	3.058
total assets/net-worth			
C4	2.792	3.426	2.007
C4+banks of issue	3.835	3.714	1.833
loans/equity capital			
C4	3.366	4.5	2.175
C4+banks of issue	13.224	13.659	3.034
loans/liabilities			
C4	0.073	0.048	0.092
C4+banks of issue	0.834	0.774	0.103
ROE			
C4	3.529	1.5	1.779
C4+banks of issue	4.574	4.317	0.912

Source: Credito Italiano (until 1926) and Associazione fra le società italiane per azioni (Assonime) (from 1928), *Società italiane per azioni. Notizie Statistiche, ad annos* (our calculations).

Table 3.1 shows the standard deviation as a measure of volatility for the average values of three ratios of capital requirements (total assets on equity capital, total assets on net-worth, loans on equity capital), of possible funding gap (loans on liabilities), and of profitability (return on equity [ROE]) for the four largest banks (C4) and for an ampler sample including the banks of issue (C4+banks of issue) for the whole period as well as for two sub-periods (1919–29 and 1930–9). The data suggest a remarkable high volatility for the extended sample (C4+banks of issue) due to an acute under-capitalization of the banks of issue in the 1920s as a consequence of previous and current inflationary pressures depending upon unrestrained public spending. To a lesser degree this tendency could be observed even for the smaller sample of the top banks, as a measure of relative rigidity in adjusting their equity capital component to a higher level of prices. In both cases such phenomena appear mitigated when considering not the equity capital component but the net-worth, that usually follows prices in a more easy way. The volatility of all ratios is clearly generally much higher during the first sub-period by comparison with the 1930s levels, although differences are relevant for single ratios and samples as well.[24]

Thus, as these data imply, the increased volatility in the banking system was largely related to monetary instability phenomena deriving from soaring

---

[24] These findings are consistent with those provided by Riccardo De Bonis and Andrea Silvestrini, 'The Italian Financial Cycle: 1861–2011', *Cliometrica* 2014 (8.3): 301–34.

inflation, currency inconvertibility, and sovereign debt overhang. In fact, the recurrent banking crises of the 1920s emphasized the international dimension of central banking as an institutional response to financial instability in which the lending of last resort function was to be subordinated to major macroeconomic objectives of adjustment.[25] After the First World War this meant that a central bank as a lender of last resort had necessarily to deal with the international context in domestic credit creation, that is the lending of last resort, in essence, was in the main dependent on monetary policies allowed or coherent with the stabilization programmes that were adopted at international level.[26] Since the early 1920s the programmes devised to restore national macroeconomic stability and multilateralism in international markets were centred upon the return to the Gold Standard, a condition which called for credibility and cooperation and subject to constrained choices between competing macroeconomic objectives described, by Obstfeld and Taylor, as a trilemma of policy choices.[27] In view of a return to the Gold Standard regime it was therefore a natural corollary to adjust to wartime fiscal overhang and high inflation by adopting deflationary measures whose outcomes in terms of growth were bound to be negative. In other terms, as experienced in the deflationary juncture of 1921, instability as much as volatility within the banking system was a function of choices amongst competing monetary policies whose sign and intensity was to be defined internationally. In fact, the quest for stabilization was essentially an international achievement and implied the restoration of cooperation and credibility by settling a set of financial imbalances, such as reparations and inter-allied debts, disturbingly affecting monetary policies and, hence, volatility in the banking sector. After the Paris Conference the quest for stabilization was pursued as a first attempt to recreate an adequate international context for reconstruction in the wake of a total war. The international community had inherited an informal private structure of cooperation from the pre-war world and wartime,[28] but the lack of a previous serious experience in reconstructing an international economic and financial system after a total war was likewise obvious: in short, at the outset there was no feasible blueprint to adopt in a world in which international cooperation—one of the linchpins of the faded Gold Standard regime—was seriously in jeopardy.[29]

---

[25] As to the distinction between macroeconomic and microeconomic functions of a central bank see Charles A. E. Goodhart, *The Evolution of Central Banks* (Cambridge, MA, 1988).

[26] Cf. Charles Pigou, *Memorandum on Credit, Currency and Exchange Fluctuations* (London, 1920), 7–9 (in the same series of Cassel's memorandum published by the League of Nations).

[27] See Maurice Obstfeld and Alan M. Taylor, *Global Capital Markets: Integration, Crisis, and Growth* (Cambridge, 2004).

[28] See Michael J. Hogan, *Informal Entente: The Private Structure Cooperation in Anglo-American Economic Diplomacy, 1918–1928* (Columbia, MO, 1977 [1991]), 39.

[29] As Barry Eichengreen has stated, credibility and cooperation were actually the factors functioning in the pre-war Gold Standard, hardly on offer in the post-war period (cf. Eichengreen, *Golden Fetters*, 3–28).

The arduous quest for stabilization severely put financial elites on trial as the institutional arrangements and economic policies entailed a profound redefinition of their own traits and boundaries, in the end promoting processes of professionalization of bankers and financiers with an impact on the private and cosmopolitan character of this high-ranking group: at the end of the process in the 1930s, at least in Italy, the highest ranks of the financial system largely shifted from the private sector to the public sector.

3.3 The Quest for Stabilization: Inter-Allied Debts and International Cooperation

In the early 1920s financial elites around Europe had to address international imbalances and largely related domestic crises at the same time. The stabilization strategies to be outlined and adopted were to be of paramount importance, as they would condition monetary policies and affect internal stability in turn. Thus, the ability of national financial elites to foster arguments and negotiate policies at international level would define their internal horizon of action and economic chances of growth as well. From 1920 to 1925 a new scheme of formal coordination emerged accompanying the idea that the Gold Standard should be reinstated to promote stability as a prerequisite of future growth. This scheme of international cooperation had three institutional pillars—the Economic and Financial Organization promoted by the League of Nations, the two economic and financial conferences at Brussels and Genoa, and the club of the central banks in the making—and two fundamental principles as to macroeconomic policies—the return to the Gold Standard and central banking.[30]

Such a scheme was not per se in contrast, or incompatible, with the private structure of domestic and international cooperation prevailing at the time. On the contrary, it could emphasize its strengths in any attempt to get the world economy as a global system of mutual interdependence on track to recovery. In fact, as a tentative experiment in international economic relations, it gathered together a plurality of interests, expertise, and views as its construction was dependent on a plurality of actors, both public and private. The hybrid structure of international cooperation built up at the end of the war, as a result of a rising awareness of the importance of a global approach to stabilization and reconstruction, presented overlapping interests between public and private spheres, as both of them had become increasingly conscious that a war-torn world needed a joint effort to which only public authorities

---

[30] Cf. Patricia Clavin, *Securing the World Economy: The Reinvention of the League of Nations, 1920–1946* (Oxford, 2013).

could make the difference.[31] A first attempt to define feasible macroeconomic policies able to restore stability in Europe, and around the world, was pursued by the League of Nations by adopting a different perspective on how to address single domestic economies and international relations.[32] Being a first experience of its kind in international economic relations, this attempt typically combined a wide range of expertise and competences from the private financial world and from the civil service, along a relatively novel pattern which emerged during the war within the inter-allied cooperation organizations.[33] The first experiment in 'financial diplomacy', the International Financial Conference held in Brussels in 1920, promoted by the League of Nations as an intergovernmental organization, was encouraged as a conference of 'experts' by the national state founders of the League.[34] Coherently, the delegates to the conference at Brussels were appointed by their governments 'as experts and not as spokesmen of official policy',[35] a quite peculiar formula that reduced the political content of individual stances and overall resolutions by promoting international cooperation essentially on a technical basis along the informal structure prevailing before the Great War.[36] At this occasion, the Italian financial elite displayed its composite character from the very start. As a member of the organizing committee, chaired by Jean Monnet, the Italian government appointed Alberto Beneduce, a rather hybrid emerging figure: a statistician by training, a senior official at the Ministry of Agriculture, Commerce and Industry at the beginning of his career, a close collaborator of the director general of the Bank of Italy, Bonaldo Stringher, and a prominent MP at the time.[37] In a way, Beneduce embodied the composite nature

---

[31] This became apparent in January 1920 when, after Geard Vissering and Ter C. E. Meulen promoted two meetings in Amsterdam in October and November 1919, a call for an international conference, inspired by J. M. Keynes, was issued by more than fifty senior bankers, such as J. P. Morgan, Paul Warburg, Charles Addis, Robert Brand, Reginald MacKenna, and Richard Vassar Vassar-Smith. The call appeared in *The New York Times*, 15 January 1920 (cf. Michel Fior, *Institution globale et marchés financiers: la Société des Nations face à la reconstruction de l'Europe, 1918–1931* (Bern and Oxford, 2008), 121–6). Even the most prominent Italian banker, Giuseppe Toeplitz, managing director of the Banca Commerciale, called for an international conference in November 1919. Cf. Archivio Storico della Banca d'Italia, Rome (ASBI), Rapporti con l'estero, cart. 9, letter from Toeplitz to Arrigo Rossi, Milan, 12 November 1919.

[32] See Yann Decorzant, *La Société des Nations et la naissance d'une conception de la regulation économique internationale* (Brussels, 2011), 21.

[33] See Martin Hill, *The Economic and Financial Organization of the League of Nations: A Survey of Twenty-Five Years' Experience* (Washington, 1946), 14–18; Decorzant, *La Société des Nations*, 110–61.

[34] Cf. Yann Decorzant, 'Internationalisation in the Economic and Financial Organisation of the League of Nations', in Daniel Laqua (ed.), *Internationalism Reconfigured: Transnational Ideas and Movements between the World Wars* (London and New York, 2011), 129.

[35] League of Nations, *International Financial Conference*, vol. I, *Report of the Conference* (Brussels, 1920), 4.

[36] See Decorzant, *La Société des Nations*, 182–3 and 233–50.

[37] See Franco Bonelli, 'Alberto Beneduce (1877–1944)', in Alberto Mortara (ed.), *Protagonisti dell'intervento pubblico* (Milan, 1984), 329–56; Mimmo Franzinelli and Marco Magnani, *Beneduce. Il finanziere di Mussolini* (Milan, 2009).

of the organizing committee itself, composed of businessmen and bankers as well as government representatives and officials of the League of Nations, like Jean Monnet and Walter Layton, whilst the composition of the Italian delegation at the Brussels Conference was even more multi-faceted including civil servants, manufacturers, and bankers. The leading figure was undoubtedly Beneduce himself who was flanked by two prominent bankers, both close to the Bank of Italy, inside the Financial and Economic Committees constituted by the League of Nations after the conference: Federico Ettore Balzarotti, the authoritative managing director of Credito Italiano, who joined the Financial Committee, and Luigi Della Torre, an eminent Milanese private banker who had sustained the Bank of Italy's action in crucial events such as the 1907 crisis, who joined the Economic Committee.[38]

It was probably not coincidental that, in 1920, at the Brussels Conference Italy was represented by Alberto Beneduce, who was shaping his professional profile as a competent 'expert' and as a politician as well. His close collaboration with Stringher at the Bank of Italy in redefining the insurance sector, by assigning to the state the monopoly on life insurance as a way to manage a large share of the national savings, was coherent with his considerations on how to achieve a form of development finance which could guarantee macroeconomic stability in the long term. In different terms, since 1915 Beneduce had been laying down the intellectual foundations for a model of financial intermediation radically alternative to the model based on the German-style mixed banks, understood as an irredeemable factor of systemic instability that put pressure on the reserves of the Bank of Italy, an unbearable condition when in a Gold Standard regime. The alternative model gradually constructed by Beneduce, substantially in accordance with the wider macroeconomic model of adjustment to the Gold Standard devised by Stringher, entailed a specialization of intermediaries according to the maturity of their liabilities and assets thus separating commercial banking from investment banking. This model had its concrete starting test in 1919, when Beneduce established the first of a series of specialized credit institutions, Crediop (Consorzio di Credito per le Opere Pubbliche): by issuing state-guaranteed bonds to raise funds, Crediop perfectly matched the maturity of its liabilities and assets, the latter represented by mortgages financing long-term investments in infrastructural networks. Overcoming the maturity mismatching of liabilities and assets underlying universal banking, the ultimate aim of the model worked out by Beneduce and Stringher was to stabilize the national financial system as

---

[38] Both Balzarotti and Della Torre were usually rather sensitive to the Bank of Italy's orientation. Traditionally, the Bank of Italy had a series of relations with the representatives of Credito Italiano from its foundation in 1895, from Giacomo Castelbolognesi to Ettore Levi della Vida, whilst Banca Commerciale Italiana had a more independent stance vis-à-vis the preferences of the major bank of issue.

a whole, sheltering it from the exogenous shocks experienced in the pre-war world, typically in relation to the Kuznets cycles, by substituting a thin and ineffective stock market with a state-backed bond market.[39]

Thus, it was not trivial who composed the Italian delegation at the Brussels Conference where a first sketch of stabilization programmes was drawn in respect to monetary standards and exchange rates. In fact, the monetary standard would dictate the degrees of freedom which policy-makers and central bankers would have in case of financial instability and bank failures. Post-war instability was related to hitherto never experienced large budget deficits, high inflation, and floating exchange rates whose negative impulses required, as commonly assumed amongst governments and central authorities, a final restoration of the international Gold Standard.[40] Yet, as underscored in late 1919 in a joint statement setting the agenda for the International Financial Conference to be held in Brussels, stabilization was conditional upon choices of how to subdue budget deficits in order to reduce inflation so that exchange rates could be effectively stabilized.[41] The main points, therefore, were mainly how to stabilize and according to which principles resolutions were to be adopted and programmes implemented, and how to settle inter-allied debts and promote international cooperation in a global economy in which balance-of-payments deficits persisted largely unbalanced and price misalignments remained unsolved. Since stabilization policies were yet to be defined, even if expectations of a return to the Gold Standard were high from the Cunliffe Committee Report in 1919,[42] entering such uncharted waters meant that the probability of gaining a safe haven relied upon an effective selection of masters and pursers.[43] The difficult adjustment processes ahead needed an adequate helmsman, and a steering elite able to define

---

[39] The National Insurance Institute (INA) created in 1911, in fact, took part in the equity capital of the specialized credit institutions designed by Beneduce in the 1920s as well as subscribed a significant share of their bonds along with Treasury bonds. On the overall rationale of the model see Giandomenico Piluso, 'L'Italia e il gold standard: genesi e razionalità del modello Beneduce', *Imprese e storia* 2012 (21.41/42): 13–33. On the Kuznets cycles and the Italian economy see Stefano Fenoaltea, *The Reinterpretation of Italian Economic History: From Unification to the Great War* (Cambridge, 2011).

[40] Cf. Eichengreen, *Golden Fetters*, 100–7.

[41] The joint statement was presented by Gustav Cassel (Sweden), Arthur Cecil Pigou (UK), Charles Gide (France), G. W. J. Bruins (the Netherlands), and Maffeo Pantaleoni (Italy). See Eichengreen, *Golden Fetters*, 154–6.

[42] See R. W. D. Boyce, *British Capitalism at the Crossroads, 1919–1932: A Study in Politics, Economics, and International Relations* (Cambridge, 1987), 33–78. For France see Kenneth Mouré, *The Gold Standard Illusion: France, the Bank of France, and the International Gold Standard, 1914–1939* (Oxford, 2002), 40–51.

[43] At the time the metaphor was largely adopted. For instance, in December 1918 Robert H. Brand, who had just joined the London merchant bank Lazard Brothers and would have served as vice-president of the Public Finance Commission at Brussels, wrote: 'under the inexorable pressure of war we have [. . .] been swept from our old financial moorings and [. . .] we have under compulsion embarked on an uncharted sea' (see Robert H. Brand, *The Financial and Economic Future* (London, 1919), 9).

realistic objectives and fitting tactics within the international community, an elite able to define their own rationale and negotiate conditions at conferences in relation to internal stability and external interdependence. According to the informal structure of cooperation then prevailing in these provinces, this steering elite appeared largely as a result of self-selection within the broader financial community. Within the emerging group of top civil servants and bankers Beneduce proved to be the most politically connected and intellectually fitted for the task as a leading figure in the Italian delegation at Brussels from the very inception of its undertakings.[44] In his first moves, as a member of the organizing committee, Beneduce tried to draw a sort of 'nautical chart' for a successful conference and agreement on monetary standards and exchange rates in terms acceptable to the Italian economy.[45] Being sceptical of the effectiveness of a large summit, in April 1920 Beneduce proposed to organize a meeting between the ministers of Finance, or Treasury, and central bankers from France, Italy, and the UK in the Italian Riviera in order to define a common stance on exchange rates in view of the Brussels Conference itself.[46] The underlying thought, originally suggested by Luigi Luzzati before the war, was that cooperation between central bankers could have improved significantly their chances of success in fixing the unstable system of floating exchange rates.[47] These personal stances and prospects show how widespread was the idea that central banks should foster international cooperation as a means of financial and monetary stabilization.[48]

Although appointed by the Italian government, Beneduce was quite conscious that his role was to convey also private sector positions, and to some extent even interests, by virtue of the mixed nature of the 'diplomacy of expertise' at work at Brussels. In September 1920, as a delegate to the Commission on Currency and Exchange Rates, Beneduce received a report from the four largest banks advising the return to 'sound finance' as to budget deficits and a relatively soft landing as to inflation, even though they were

---

[44] In this sense Beneduce could be included in the category of the emerging 'diplomacy of expertise' represented by technocrats, or would-be such, which shaped the typical forms of internationalism related to nation-state interests of the interwar period. See Patricia Clavin, 'Conceptualising Internationalism between the World Wars', in Laqua (ed.), *Internationalism Reconfigured*, 1–14.

[45] In those years Nittians usually assumed a pro-British stance, as noted in Carole Fink, *The Genoa Conference: European Diplomacy, 1921–1922* (Chapel Hill and London, 1984), 48. Between February and May 1920 the Italian Prime Minister Francesco Saverio Nitti vainly tried to obtain an extra £25 million loan on the London market through Hambro as Lloyd George opposed his attempts (cf. Giancarlo Falco, *L'Italia e la politica finanziaria degli alleati* (Pisa, 1983), 101).

[46] See ASBI, Beneduce, cart. 110, 'Commissione dei cambi, Conferenza di Bruxelles', manuscript memo.

[47] The Minister of Treasury Luigi Luzzatti proposed to organize forms of international cooperation between central banks firstly in 1908 and, again, in 1915–16. See his introduction, 'Histoire d'une idée', in Luigi Luzzatti, *La paix monétaire à la Conférence de Gênes* (Rome, 1922).

[48] In his memo Beneduce used the expression 'Banks of issue'.

aware that a restrictive adjustment in liquidity would have an impact on the banking sector determining a string of crises and failures. The memo by the largest banks was rather sceptical as to innovative projects, such as the creation of an international fiat currency or international loans to stabilize national currencies and exchange rates according to the Ter Meulen scheme.[49] The stance assumed by the Italian top bankers was, thus, a mixture of pragmatic approaches and cautious conservativeness.[50]

As a matter of fact, at Brussels Beneduce sustained an intermediate position between the hard-line programmes of an immediate return to the Gold Standard at pre-war values, as solicited by the Bank of England, and programmes aiming at stabilizing currencies and exchange rates by adopting gradual measures in order to prevent a severe and disruptive deflation. At Brussels Beneduce advocated for free trade, free movement of capital, and international cooperation, asserting that the most important thing was to address economic disequilibria by fostering growth more than restoring pre-war parities in a Gold Standard regime which should have provoked deflation.[51] In this regard, Beneduce's stance was not far from Keynes's and from that of some other representatives of the City of London, such as Robert H. Brand of Lazard Brothers, who at Brussels acted as vice-president of the Public Finance Commission.[52] A gradual adjustment essentially meant a monetary stabilization at current levels, albeit the Italian government agreed with British and French official positions on the return to the Gold Standard in principle. In the end, at Brussels, as is well known, there emerged a rather tempered version of the Gold Standard and not the full-fledged restoration at pre-war parities passionately promoted by Montagu Norman and Benjamin Strong.[53] The conference's recommendations stressed that, whilst inflation should be curbed as it had negative effects on markets and business, it was 'useless to attempt to fix the ratio of the existing fiduciary currencies to their normal gold value'. Thus, as the 'reversion [...] to an effective gold standard' would demand 'enormous deflation', 'such deflation' was to be 'carried out gradually and with great

---

[49] Cf. League of Nations, *International Credits (the 'Ter Meulen' Scheme)* (London, 1921).

[50] See ASBI, Beneduce, f. 109, 'Commissione dei cambi, Conferenza di Bruxelles', typewritten memo, 'Promemoria', Rome, September 1920, transmitted by A. Rossi on 15 September 1920.

[51] See League of Nations, *International Financial Conference*, vol. II, *Verbatim Record of the Debates* (Brussels, 1920), 73–6.

[52] Cf. Robert H. Brand, *War and National Finance* (London, 1921), 262–3. In his address as vice-president of the Public Finance Commission Brand was a proponent of 'sound finance' but in a rather nuanced way and measure (278). On Brand's career as one of 'the great and the good' who 'used the skills acquired in and the financial security provided by merchant banking, in carrying out a number of political responsibilities' see Kathleen Burk, 'Brand, Robert Henry, Baron Brand (1878–1963)', *Oxford Dictionary of National Biography* (Oxford, 2004).

[53] Cf. R. S. Sayers, *The Bank of England 1891–1944* (Cambridge, 1976), vol. I, 110–11. A critical résumé of the proceedings of the Commission's activities was published by H. A. Siepmann, 'The International Financial Conference at Brussels', *The Economic Journal* 1920 (30.120): 447–9.

caution'. That was, by and large, the Italian stance advocated by Beneduce, even though Lord Cullen, formerly Sir Brien Cockayne and governor of the Bank of England, succeeded in emending the first draft sketched by Gerard Vissering of the Netherlands Bank from supporting a 'cheap money' strategy to sponsoring a 'more or less dear money' policy.[54] Besides, the conference recommended the adoption of a *'central* bank of issue' and, if needed, the 'assistance of foreign capital' through 'some form of international control' to countries without one. The sketched principle of central banking was instead in line with the idea advocated by the governor of the Bank of England, Montagu Norman, who was then elaborating the concept.[55] The financial assistance was however subordinated to the acceptance of mutual cooperation in implementing the conference's recommendations, that is, accepting fiscal discipline and long-term deflationary programmes centred on central banking.[56]

One of the main results of the Brussels Conference as 'the first effort of international cooperation', aside from stating the opportunity for a gradual deflationary strategy as a means of stabilization through cooperating 'central banks of issue', was the establishment of an Economic Committee and a Financial Committee within the League of Nations. In the former committee Italy appointed Federico Ettore Balzarotti, the influential managing director of Credito Italiano, and in the latter Luigi Della Torre, a Milanese private banker rather close to Stringher and the Bank of Italy. The Italian move to appoint private sector representatives was quite different from that adopted by other governments, such as France's and the UK's, which preferred to rely upon civil servants.[57] Thus, at this stage the Italian elites facing the international challenge in which new principles and rules were in the process of being defined preserved their mixed contours, as would be the case at the ensuing Conference at Genoa and in the settling of inter-allied debts in 1925–6. At Genoa governments tended to reassume a certain degree of control over discussions and negotiations, but they had to rely, nonetheless, on experts in financial matters in the technical content of many issues so that experts were actually

[54] So Lord Cullen in a letter to Norman of October 1920 quoted in Sayers, *The Bank of England*, vol. I, 154.
[55] The principles of central banking, which Norman was defining in winter 1920–1, was stated *in nuce* at Brussels, but unequivocally clearly referred to in its general and fundamental terms: 'central banks of issue', as they were presented in the Conference's recommendations, were to be 'freed from political pressure', as précised in the third resolution unanimously adopted by the Commission on Currency and Exchange Rates (cf. League of Nations, *International Financial Conference*, vol. I, *Report of the Conference*, 18). Differently on Brussels resolutions as to central banking Philip L. Cottrell, 'Norman, Strakosch, and the Development of Central Banking: From Conception to Practice, 1919–1924', in Philip L. Cottrell (ed.), *Rebuilding the Financial System in Central and Eastern Europe, 1918–1994* (London, 1994), 33.
[56] Cf. League of Nations, *International Financial Conference*, vol. I, *Report of the Conference*, 8–11.
[57] See Decorzant, *La Société des Nations*, 312–13. Balzarotti resigned in 1921 and was substituted by Giuseppe Bianchini, general director of the Italian Banking Association (ABI) (cf. Sergio Cardarelli, 'Giuseppe Bianchini', in *Dizionario biografico degli Italiani* (Rome, 1988), vol. 34, *ad vocem*).

in a position to orientate the negotiations and their outcomes.[58] In this regard, the Italian delegation at Genoa maintained its previous mixed character in the technical component of experts and advisers, as Beneduce, Bianchini, Della Torre, Nathan, Rossi, and Stringher were present informally or officially in various capacities, as were private sector entrepreneurs like Alberto Pirelli, Guido Jung, and Oscar Sinigaglia.[59]

At Genoa the Italian stance was confirmed, as the result of a compromise between competing positions: in fact, the conference approved the principle of an international, but not deflationary, monetary cooperation centred upon independent central banks as the cornerstone of stabilization programmes in Europe.[60] Accordingly, in the mid-1920s Mario Alberti, a central director at Credito Italiano and adviser to the Treasury, was appointed chairman of the Central Bank of Albania, whilst Carlo Feltrinelli, a polyglot entrepreneur and a prominent banker (Banca Feltrinelli & Co and Credito Italiano), joined the international board of the German Reichsbank.[61] This was a typical combination of private sector and public sector representatives as delegated experts within international institutions created in the wake of the conferences held at Brussels and Genoa. Following the same pattern, Alberti and Beneduce as advisers to the Treasury by then headed by Giuseppe Volpi, a financier, played a significant part in the American–Italian negotiations conducted for the settlement of inter-allied debts in 1925–6, whilst in 1925, in three missions, Alberto Pirelli, accompanied by Alberti, discussed with Otto Niemeyer in London the settlement of inter-allied debts owed to Britain.[62] The settlement of inter-allied debts was at last reached in the winter of 1925–6 paving the way for a monetary stabilization in the ensuing months. A crucial role was played by a relatively cohesive set of technocrats, bankers, and financiers acting as advisers to the Treasury and ranging from Beneduce and Alberti to Pirelli and Volpi, the latter as the Minister of Finance.[63]

In the late 1920s, however, this composite set was largely substituted by a more homogeneous group of civil servants from the Bank of Italy, such as the new governor Vincenzo Azzolini (since 1931), or trustees directly reporting to Mussolini, like Beneduce. From the first Hague Conference (1929) onwards, characteristically, the complex negotiations related to central bank

---

[58] Cf. Decorzant, *La Société des Nations*, 355.
[59] Cf. Giuseppe Bianchini, 'Questioni monetarie alla Conferenza di Genova', *Rivista Bancaria* 1922 (3.7).
[60] Cf. Ralph G. Hawtrey, *Monetary Reconstruction* (London, 1923), 131–47. See also AS BI, Beneduce, f. 284, 'Conferenza di Genova', Doc. L 9, 'Questioni finanziarie', London, March 1922.
[61] See Fondazione Feltrinelli, Milan, Archivi Famiglia Feltrinelli, IV.12 'Reichsbank', f. 29. Cf. also Luciano Segreto, *I Feltrinelli* (Milan, 2011), 306–8.
[62] Cf. Alberto Pirelli, *Dopoguerra 1919–1932. Note ed esperienze* (Milan, 1961), 124–6, 128.
[63] Cf. Mario Alberti, *La guerra delle monete* (Como, 1937), vol. I, 142–9; vol. II, 108–15; Alberto Pirelli, *Taccuini, 1922/1943* (Bologna, 1984), 70–80; Franzinelli and Magnani, *Beneduce*, 162–3; Sergio Romano, *Giuseppe Volpi, industria e finanza tra Giolitti e Mussolini* (Milan, 1979), 142–54.

cooperation saw Beneduce as the influential Italian representative involved at every stage of the process, from creating the Bank for International Settlements to the unsuccessful London Conference in 1933. In the 1930s, as the most prominent Italian representative, Beneduce asserted his role and views in all the international conferences and committees, as well as being a prominent member of the BIS, defending the national interests and maintaining an increasingly pro-Gold Standard stance.[64]

3.4 The Return to the Gold: Central Banking and Financial Regulation

The Genoa Conference was pivotal to the definition of central banking as a crucial institutional structure of international cooperation for the decade. Benjamin Strong and, above all, Montagu Norman had the main part in defining and organizing central banking as a response to instability in Europe. The adoption of the central banking model as defined in the early 1920s required the acceptance and implementation of an entire array of economic policies and institutional devices available at the time. In this regard central banking was then intimately entangled with the idea that stability was related to the restoration of the Gold Standard by rebuilding an international monetary system centred upon fixed exchange rates.[65] Even though the measure of external stabilization was not passively accepted along strictly orthodox lines, as expressed at Brussels and Genoa, it was plain that Italy had to realign its macroeconomic position to the international macroeconomic environment. Yet, the adherence to central banking as outlined by Norman was an ongoing and uncertain process before the return to gold by Britain in April 1925. The Bank of Italy, formally, joined the 'circle of cooperating Central Banks' in a relatively short time, by participating coherently in fiscal and monetary stabilization programmes in Europe, although maintaining an accommodating stance as to monetary policies and exchange rates at least up to 1924. As observed by Beneduce in 1921, London hegemony and related deflationary options could have had a negative impact on employment and production levels as well as on national sovereignty.[66] Thus, according to Genoa's arrangements, monetary policies had to be implemented according to nationally specific economic conditions in order to avoid deflation. However, in January 1925 the sentiment started changing and the return to the Gold Standard

---

[64] Cf. Gianni Toniolo, *Central Bank Cooperation at the Bank for International Settlements, 1930–1973* (Cambridge, 2005), 39–44, 127–31, 144–57; Franzinelli and Magnani, *Beneduce*, 170–87.
[65] Cf. Stephen V. O. Clarke, *Central Bank Cooperation: 1924–31* (New York, 1967), 27–44.
[66] See AS BI, Carte Beneduce, box 209, folder 1, 'Il Credito Internazionale e il Convegno di Parigi', a typewritten note by Beneduce, 19 January 1921.

gradually emerged as a priority on the European financial agenda as set by Norman and Strong.[67]

From February 1925 onwards, the restoration of the Gold Standard forced the Italian central authorities to opt for an adaptive strategy. Yet, such a strategy was enormously complicated by the choices made by the fascist government during the previous year in contrast with the principle of central bank independence. The Bank of Italy's autonomy was significantly constrained by the fascist government when it offered to take part in the currency rehabilitation of Central Europe (Gold-Diskonto Bank in Germany, the Dawes Plan, and the Greek refugees loan). In March 1924 Banca Commerciale Italiana launched a loan for the stabilization of Poland, previously refused by JPMorgan, amounting to 400 million lire. Banca Commerciale, supported by Mussolini, acted in sharp contrast with the Bank of Italy's positions without informing Stringher either. Stringher was rather, and rightly, reluctant as he was well aware of the underlying risks threatening the exchange rate of lira to the French franc, historically a 'twin currency', then under speculative attack.[68] Indeed, from August 1924 to May 1925 the Italian lira was the object of major speculation and devalued from about 90 up to 153 against sterling. The strategies and techniques adopted by Stringher to sustain the currency, ineffectively despite a short-term loan in January 1925 ($5 million) and a longer-term loan ($50 million) in June by JPMorgan (both backed by Strong), attracted severe criticisms by Alberti as an adviser to the Treasury.[69]

Speculative attacks and Britain's return to gold were matters of great concern and induced a reaction to the changing international environment by overlapping—and substantially inconsistent—institutional choices. On the one hand, since February 1925 a regulatory cycle tried to offset financial speculation intervening on stock market functioning by banning short-selling: to this end measures were promoted by Alberto De Stefani, Minister of Finance, to dwarf speculation (namely, to curb naked short-selling), but they had a profoundly negative impact on the stock market, as stock capitalization consistently declined with a deflationary effect which seriously affected mixed banks' assets. On the other hand, since June 1925 the new Minister of Finance, Giuseppe Volpi, adopted a managed currency policy by law and from August 1925 to May 1926, under the aegis of Volpi himself, Banca Commerciale took over the management of the currency crisis. After

---

[67] This point was expressed by Alberto De Stefani, Minister of Finance, to Thomas J. Lamont (JPMorgan) in April 1925. Cf. Thomas W. Lamont Collection, Baker Library, Harvard Business School, box 103, folder 11, letter from Lamont to Russell Cornell Leffingwell, Florence, 20 April 1925, in De Cecco (ed.), *L'Italia e il sistema finanziario internazionale*, 168.

[68] Cf. AS BI, Carte Stringher, 401/3.01/43, letter from Stringher to De Stefani, Rome, 8 March 1924, in De Cecco (ed.), *L'Italia e il sistema finanziario internazionale*, 755.

[69] Cf. AS BI, Carte Stringher, 405/1.01/31, Mario Alberti, 'Progetto di un'azione tattica per la difesa della lira', 13 August 1925, in De Cecco (ed.), *L'Italia e il sistema finanziario internazionale*, 954–7.

the settlement of inter-allied debts, from which Stringher was substantially ousted, lira stabilized around 120 against the British pound. Still, such a result was obtained at a cost to international financial circles: writing to Norman, Volpi was adamant about the merely instrumental role to which the Bank of Italy was diminished by the fascist government. As a result, negatively impressed by Volpi's stance, Norman became increasingly sceptical about the actual independence of the Italian central bank.[70]

In May 1926 a major strategic change modified drastically the position of the Italian central bank vis-à-vis the government. Whilst Norman remained still sceptical about the independence of the Bank of Italy, Benjamin Strong and JPMorgan decided to support the Italian attempt to stabilize the lira within the gold exchange standard system by allowing both for assistance and for a fresh loan ($100 million). In the last week of May 1926 Strong had a series of conversations with Mussolini, Volpi, and Stringher in Rome finding that they were 'determined to adopt a sound program with courage as soon as they can be certain of eventual success'. But a sound programme required that Italy comply with a crucial condition for acceding to central bank credits—the independence of the central bank—as Norman continued to be reluctant 'to have much to do with the Bank', at least 'so long as the Finance Minister [Volpi] persists and glories in dominating the Governor [Stringher]'.[71] Thus the return to the Gold Standard implied a sea change in the status of the central bank. At this point in early May 1926 a new law on the banks of issue was approved conferring to the Bank of Italy the monopoly of issue (R.D.L. 6 May 1926, no. 812). In effect, the new banking law was a key act as to the compliance with the prerequisites on which Norman and Strong had been insisting since 1920. This law, studied and perfected by the Bank of Italy's technocracy, had been promoted by Stringher and Beneduce allowing the bank to get a better control on money supply and reserves, i.e. on exchange rates. The law represented clear-cut evidence that the Italian government was shifting towards the Genoa model of central banking. The law assigned the monopoly of issue to the Bank of Italy declaring the end of a semi-free banking regime by excluding Bank of Naples and Bank of Sicily from the money supply function. In September 1926 a new banking 'law on the protection of savings' (R.D.L. 9 September 1926, no. 1511), again designed by Beneduce and Stringher, first introduced minimum capital requirements for

---

[70] In February 1926 Volpi said to Norman that 'he himself was going to direct Central Bank policy which should not be separated at all from general policy'. See Archive of the Bank of England, London, G14/95, 'Italy', letter from Norman to Strong, 4 March 1926 (also quoted in Lester V. Chandler, *Benjamin Strong, Central Banker* (Washington, 1958), 382, and Sayers, *The Bank of England*, 193).

[71] Respectively, Strong to JPMorgan's on 30 May 1926 and Norman to Strong on 20 May 1926 as quoted in Chandler, *Benjamin Strong*, 383 and 384. See also Richard H. Meyer, *Bankers' Diplomacy: Monetary Stabilization in the Twenties* (New York and London, 1970), 42–57.

banks and reinforced the ability of the Bank of Italy to supervise banks and financial intermediaries. Actually, in this way there was something more concrete than mere reputation that allowed Stringher to demonstrate himself to be 'a thoroughgoing central banker' who ' "talks the language" in orthodox style', as Strong wrote to Harrison in May.[72]

These two banking laws were a coherent evolution of the first measures adopted by De Stefani to rein in naked short-selling which had inflationary effects through refinancing operations and increased instability by amplifying stock market volatility.[73] Yet, the monetary stabilization, in the medium term, needed international cooperation and a different status for the Bank of Italy. In fact, a stronger and independent central bank constituted the consistent goal of this first regulation package which culminated with the official recognition of the Bank of Italy as 'a free and independent company' by law in December 1927. But to this point Italy had evolved progressively through the intense persuasion of Norman and Strong. If Strong was convinced that Italy could stabilize since spring 1926, Norman remained doubtful about the actual independence of the Bank of Italy. In October and November Stringher, Beneduce ('Signor Beneducci', according to Norman's diaries), Nathan, and Alberti had a series of talks with Norman and Siepmann in London. Despite protracted discussions, Beneduce and Stringher were not able to break a lasting stalemate as Norman remained unconvinced about Italy's real adherence to central banking and international cooperation principles. The deadlock was at last overcome in December as Beneduce and Stringher succeeded in getting Strong involved in the negotiations. Strong, who convincingly supported Stringher as an accomplished central banker, ended the stalemate and induced Norman to concede his *placet* to the Italian stabilization.[74] Two points were crucial in this regard: (i) Norman took into account that a stabilization without the Bank of England could have menaced the Anglo-American relationship and (ii) the ongoing regulation in Italy had been positively modifying the Bank of Italy's status as an independent institution since September 1926. Under those circumstances the Bank of Italy 'enter[ed] into absolute possession of the reserves' and 'assume[d] the responsibility of

---

[72] As in a letter from Strong to George Harrison, Rome, 26 May 1926, published in De Cecco (ed.), *L'Italia e il sistema finanziario internazionale*, 218.

[73] Cf. Giangiacomo Nardozzi and Giandomenico Piluso, *Il sistema finanziario e la borsa* (Rome and Bari, 2010), 24–6.

[74] Norman, before meeting the Italian delegation in November, received Beneduce ('Beneducci') and Fummi, JPMorgan's man in Italy, at the Bank on Wednesday 19 October 1927 ('general talk as to Italy stabilisation'), whilst Stringher was introduced later by Nathan, on Tuesday 25 October (see Norman's diaries). On the talks at the Bank of England in London see Archive of the Bank of England, London, G14/95, 'Italy' (particularly, the 'Extracts from the Minutes of the Committee of Treasury').

maintaining the gold value of the lira', as Stringher had assured Norman.[75] Eventually, the Italian lira was stabilized de jure at 'quota novanta', that is actually at 92.5 lire against British sterling or 19 lire against the US dollar, on 21 December 1927 by relying upon credit lines provided by major central banks and private credits provided by an international syndicate organized by JPMorgan in New York ($25 million) and London (£5 million).[76]

The stabilization within the gold exchange standard regime entailed a severe deflation, the burden of being in golden fetters. Deflationary effects on the banking sector were particularly acute as the restrictive monetary stabilization at 'quota novanta' badly overlapped with a poor performing stock market as a consequence of the tightening measures adopted in 1925 to curb speculation. Thus, the Italian mixed banks had to cope with a restrictive monetary policy in conjunction with an illiquid stock market, whilst they were forced to roll over almost unconditionally firms' debts. This implied that they had to deal with an increasing mass of non-performing loans and losses within their own portfolio as they could not transfer maturing loans and risks to the stock market, depressed by a tight monetary policy. In fact, the new regulation had cut off mixed banks from the stock market igniting a liquidity crisis as longer-term maturity assets mismatched systemically with short-term liabilities (deposits). The regulation adopted in 1925 and 1926 was primarily intended to counter external instability and focused on promoting central banking in order to favour macroeconomic stabilization through an adaptive strategy to changes in the international environment. Yet, the related restrictive monetary policy deflated both production and banking assets triggering an internal financial instability as soon as the international capital market entered a major crisis after 1929. The ephemeral return to the gold exchange standard was seriously threatened by the increase of interest rates by the Federal Reserve in 1928, a choice which exerted a 'real strain upon European exchange rates'.[77] In the end, the attempts to stabilize international financial and currency markets centred upon the Gold Standard option proved to be ineffective and deflationary policies were unable to balance severe shocks[78] in the presence of multiple conflicting objectives.[79]

---

[75] AS BI, Baffi, 2–II A, letter from Stringher to Norman, London, 18 December 1927, in De Cecco (ed.), *L'Italia e il sistema finanziario internazionale*, 361–2.

[76] See Chandler, *Benjamin Strong*, 381–90; Sayers, *The Bank of England*, 193–5; M. De Cecco, 'Introduzione', in De Cecco (ed.), *L'Italia e il sistema finanziario internazionale*, 70–83.

[77] See AS BI, Rapporti con l'estero, f. 22, confidential letter from Norman to Stringher, London, 21 February 1929.

[78] Cf. Eichengreen, *Golden Fetters*, 222–30; Filippo Cesarano, *Monetary Theory and Bretton Woods* (Cambridge, 2006), 100–12.

[79] Cf. Obstfeld and Taylor, *Global Capital Markets*, 126–45.

In the Italian case the financial instability addressed by strict monetary policies—a condition imposed by the adherence to the gold exchange standard—was dealt with by forging an alternative regulatory model, partially tested in the 1920s by supporting the growth of a bond market for special credit institutions such as Crediop. The model was realized by Beneduce himself in the early 1930s, by then depicted as the 'dictator of the Italian economy', as an institutional response to the crisis of the mixed banks. This model, consistent with the external constraints related to the Gold Standard, entailed: (i) the separation of investment banking from commercial banking to realign the maturity and related risks of assets and liabilities; (ii) the creation of public special credit institutions, such as Crediop and Istituto Mobiliare Italiano-IMI (1931), funded through bond issuance to overcome maturity mismatch problems for long-term industrial and infrastructural investments; and (iii) the development of a bond market backed by the state guarantee to bridge effectively savings and investments in a condition of macroeconomic stability. The model created by Beneduce in the 1920s and achieved in the early 1930s was, at the end of the process, sanctioned by the Banking Law of 1936–7, even materially written by Beneduce and a few close collaborators such as Menichella, and it lasted, at least formally, up to the early 1990s.[80]

The return to the Gold Standard implied a long regulatory cycle, appearing in 1925 and mainly related to the currency instability, culminating with the Banking Law approved in 1936. The stabilization strategy pursued by Stringher and Beneduce in the mid-1920s stemmed from the necessity to cope with external constraints, a currency crisis, but eventually contributed to define and organize a model of financial intermediation centred on special credit institutions and a thick bond market backed by the state alternative to universal banking. In the process Beneduce emerged as the mighty plenipotentiary of the Italian government in financial matters, both as to regulatory questions and financial diplomacy. From the early 1930s this concentration of influence in one man as Mussolini's trustee in financial affairs made clear the relationship between the strategies pursued to cope with the external constraints and the policy choices in terms of financial regulation. The ascent of Beneduce as the financial *dominus* in Italy embodied the shift from a semi-private structure of policy to a financial structure and economic policies largely centred upon state primacy, as the changing composition of Italian delegations at international conferences in the 1930s visibly demonstrated.

---

[80] Cf. Nardozzi and Piluso, *Il sistema finanziario e la borsa*, 49–52.

3.5 A Tale of Two Delegations: The Italian Financial Elites at Brussels and London

From the second half of the 1920s a clear shift in the composition of the Italian financial elites is observable when restrictive macroeconomic policies were adopted after 'quota novanta' was launched in August 1926. The contours and boundaries of financial elites can be traced by using a simple prosopography approach and identifying the group which could represent as a proxy the rather elusive concept of 'financial elite'. This very small group is constituted by the Italian delegates at the two economic and financial conferences held in Brussels (1920) and London (1933) at a distance of thirteen years and, above all, separated by the watershed of the 1929 financial shock. This group is particularly revealing as a sample of what a financial elite could be at a precise point in time, for it was the limited choice operated by governments that looked for both expertise and representativeness amongst national practitioners and civil servants, a mix of professional competence, political power, intellectual influence, and bargaining abilities. This modest sample was the result of a complex selection process in which several powerful forces were at work. It was the outcome partly of a self-selection process and partly of an external choice by government and central authorities (ministries and the central bank). The two samples, whose figures are presented in Tables 3.2 and 3.3, provide unambiguous evidence of the major shifts which intervened in the period. Approximately, the two samples have the same size (respectively, 21 and 24 individuals), a fact even more apparent if we consider the relative weight of the diplomatic service within each of them (respectively, 5 and 8 individuals): in this case, the two groups are perfectly equals, amounting to 16 individuals each.[81] From Brussels to London only two representatives maintained their position as delegates and undoubtedly in key, albeit different, positions: Alberto Beneduce, as a government representative at large, and Joe Nathan, as an influential and expert representative of the Bank of Italy (Beneduce and Nathan were also present at the Genoa Conference in 1922, the latter with the same important role). The main feature of the first group of delegates is its semi-private character, as 11 out of 16 delegates (mainly advisers) were from the private sector (banks and manufacturing firms), whilst the second group is overwhelmingly the expression of the state and its agencies, from ministries to state-owned enterprises

---

[81] Even the rise of the diplomatic service component could be considered as the result of the general shift from a semi-private structure to a largely public framework. As providers of mere technical services all the diplomats, independently of their hierarchical level, commonly took part in a single conference.

Table 3.2. Italian delegates at the International Financial Conference at Brussels, 1920

	Profession	Sector*	Title	Delegation	Commission	Genoa Conference
Maggiorino Ferraris	Senator [publisher]	P	Doctor	President	International Credits	
Vittorio Rolandi Ricci	Senator [corporate lawyer]	P	Doctor	Delegate	Public Finance	
Alberto Beneduce	MP	S	Professor	Delegate	Currency and Exchange	*
Ferdinando Quartieri	Manufacturer	P		Deputy Delegate	International Trade	*
Emilio Pagliano	Councillor of Embassy	S		Adviser		
Icilio Rossi Fortunati	Chief Inspector to the Italian Treasury	S		Adviser		*
Francesco Giannini	Commercial Attaché to the Italian Embassy**	S		Adviser		*
Arrigo Rossi	General Sub-Manager to the Bank of Italy***	CB		Adviser		*
Alberto D'Agostino	Manufacturer	P		Adviser		
Leo Goldschmied	Vice-Director of the Banca Commerciale Italiana	P		Adviser		
Carlito Rosa	Banco di Roma	P		Adviser		
Mario Solza	Manager of the Credito Italiano	P		Adviser		
Emilio de Benedetti	Manufacturer	P		Adviser		
Raimondo Targetti	Manufacturer	P		Adviser		
Riccardo Falco	Manufacturer	P		Adviser		
Joe Nathan	Delegate of the Bank of Italy in London***	CB		Adviser		*
Pietro Giovanni Lazzerini	[diplomatic service]	[D]		Chief Secretary		*
Liberato Bruti Liberati	[diplomatic service]	[D]	Marquis	Secretary		
Marino Mariotti	[diplomatic service]	[D]		Secretary		
Ettore Perrone di San Martino	[diplomatic service]	D	Earl	Secretary		
Guglielmo Ventimiglia	Commercial Attaché in Brussels	D		Secretary		

* Prevailing sector.
** Also Chief of the Economic Mission in England.
*** Although the Bank of Italy was formally a private joint-stock company at the time it is here assumed as a public institution in consideration of its prevailing role.
CB: central bank; D: diplomatic service ([D]: attributed); P: private sector; S: public sector or ministries.

Source: International Financial Conference, Official Guide and List of Members of Delegations, Brussels, 1920 (second edition, 4 October 1920), p. 10; Conferenza Internazionale Economica di Genova, Elenco dei Membri delle Delegazioni, Genova, 1922 (seconda edizione), pp. 57–67.

Table 3.3. Italian delegates at the Monetary and Economic Conference, London 1933

	Profession	Sector*	Title	Delegation	Brussels Conference	Genoa Conference
Guido Jung	Minister of Finance	S		Head of the delegation		*
Fulvio Suvich	Under Secretary of State, Ministry of Foreign Affairs	S		Delegate		
Alberto Asquini	Under Secretary of State, Ministry of Corporations	S	Professor	Delegate	*	
Alberto Beneduce		S	Professor	Delegate		*
Alberto Pirelli	Manufacturer	P	Doctor	Delegate		*
Bonifacio Ciancarelli	Minister Plenipotentiary	S		Delegate		
Galeazzo Ciano di Cortellazzo	Minister Plenipotentiary	S	Earl	Delegate		
Eugenio Anzilotti	General Director, Ministry of Corporations	S		Expert		
Mario Mariani	General Director, Ministry of Agriculture	S				
Giuseppe Del Vecchio	Chief of Section, Ministry of Finance	S				
Felice Guarneri	General Director, Confindustria	EO/P				*
Giuseppe Cerutti	Confederation of Commerce	EO/P				
Fernando Pagani	Conferation of Agriculturists	EO/P				
Giuseppe Dall'Oglio	Vice-Director of the National Exportation Institute	S				*
Joe Nathan	Delegate of the Bank of Italy and INCE	CB			*	*
Paride Formentini	Vice-President of IMI	S				
Falletti di Villa Falletto	[diplomatic service]	[D]	Earl			
G. Piserchia	[diplomatic service]	[D]				
Pietro Rallo	[diplomatic service]	D				
Umberto Grazzi	First Secretary of Legation	D		Secretariat		
Cristoforo Fracassi Ratti Mentone	Consul	D	Earl	Secretariat		
Aubrey Casardi	Vice-Consul	D		Secretariat		
Egidio Ortona	[diplomatic service]	D		Secretariat		
Gino Pazzaglia	[diplomatic service]	D		Secretariat		

* Prevailing sector.
CB: central bank; D: diplomatic service ([D]: attributed); EO: employers' lobbying organizations; P: private sector; S: public sector, including SOEs, or ministries.
Source: Monetary and Economic Conference, London, Secretariat List, 17 July 1933, p. 16 (University of Oxford, Nuffield College Library, X LN 18); Conferenza Internazionale Economica di Genova, Elenco dei Membri delle Delegazioni, Genova, 1922 (seconda edizione), pp. 57–67.

and only the cosmopolitan and authoritative Alberto Pirelli represents the private sector (see Tables 3.2 and 3.3).[82]

As Table 3.2 clearly shows, the delegation of experts designated by the Italian government at the Brussels Conference in 1920 was in line with the wartime experiences of coordination between civil servants and private entrepreneurs. The four Italian delegates—Beneduce, Ferraris, Quartieri, and Rolandi Ricci—were representatives of the government and three of them were senators or member of Parliament and only one a private sector manufacturer (Quartieri). However, they actually were a much more balanced set as in most of them the boundaries between public and private sector tended to blur to a significant extent: although formally a senator, Ferraris owned a publishing house and used to move between politics and business;[83] Rolandi Ricci, a corporate lawyer, had an intense political career in the 1920s and 1930s under the fascist regime;[84] Beneduce is even more difficult to categorize as a former civil servant and then an MP and a Labour minister who was rapidly moving up the political and economic ladder as a prominent expert in financial and monetary issues, from contributing to implement the first national life insurance scheme to the creation of a string of public-endowed special credit institutions;[85] Ferdinando Quartieri was a successful businessman in the chemical industry, a manufacturer and engineer who had been a technical expert at the Peace Conference in Paris for the Italian government.[86] The private sector advisers to the delegation were the majority (7 out of 12) within this group of experts: four manufacturers and three high-ranking managers from the three largest universal banks (Banca Commerciale, Credito Italiano, and Banco di Roma). Yet to be confirmed in their role two years after, at the Genoa Conference in 1922, were the two technical experts from the Bank of Italy, then formally a private joint-stock company, and the one from the Treasury.[87]

A completely different group emerges at the Monetary and Economic Conference held in London in 1933. A sharp contrast is apparent when considering

---

[82] In the Italian delegation the proportion between private and public sector representatives is overwhelmingly marked by the prevalence of the former component over the latter one, in much higher measure in comparison with the overall professional distribution at Brussels (cf. Fior, *Institution globale et marchés financiers*, 127–8; Decorzant, 'Internationalisation in the Economic and Financial Organisation of the League of Nations', 121–4).

[83] See Rosanna De Longis, 'Maggiorino Ferraris', in *Dizionario biografico degli Italiani* (Rome, 1996), vol. 46, *ad vocem*.

[84] Cf. Archivio Storico del Senato della Repubblica Italiana, Rome, personal file 'Vittorio Rolandi Ricci'.

[85] See Bonelli, 'Alberto Beneduce', 329–56.

[86] Quartieri was made a senator in 1921. Cf. Archivio Storico del Senato della Repubblica Italiana, Rome, personal file 'Ferdinando Quartieri'.

[87] At the Genoa Conference, even if not as an official member of the Italian delegation, Bonaldo Stringher was equally present as a central banker (cf. John Saxon Mills, *The Genoa Conference* (London, 1922), 142–3).

the relative weight of the public and private sectors: at the London Conference Alberto Pirelli was the only representative, as such, of the private sector in the Italian delegation, since Felice Guarneri, Giuseppe Cerutti, and Fernando Pagani were designated as technical experts for their respective employers' organizations then subsumed under the corporative state recently introduced by the fascist regime, a role hardly comparable with that offered to private manufacturers at Brussels. In such a group Guido Jung, Minister of Finance, and Alberto Beneduce had a prominent position unmatched by any other delegate or expert, regardless of their appointment or formal position (see Table 3.3).[88] The ailing major mixed banks were in no condition to obtain a place in the delegation so as to influence the Italian stance at the conference and even the expert from the Bank of Italy, Nathan, probably owed his appointment to his role as chief of the London branch and to the fact that he was very knowledgeable about the British financial scene and somewhat of an insider within the Bank of England itself.[89] Such a composition marked a major shift from the semi-private framework of cooperation and coordination of the wartime and post-war experiences to a full-fledged public structure in which ministers and civil servants wholly dominated the scene, relegating private bankers and entrepreneurs, if any, to a minor or merely complementary position by reason of individual competences or reputation, such as in the case of Alberto Pirelli.[90] These major changes are consistent with general trends within the overall economic institutional architecture as it emerged in the early 1930s. As the failure of the major universal banks caused difficulties to an entire group of financiers who had prominent positions in the previous decade, a new elite of financial technocrats emerged and substituted the former at the very helm of the banking system by imposing a different regulatory scheme, introducing a more rational style of risk management, and preferring technical competences deriving from a formal education and training.[91] In other words, these two

---

[88] In the 'Secretariat List', a rather curious and revealing detail, Beneduce's name is not followed by a specific role but by a blank space (cf. University of Oxford, Nuffield College Library, X LN 18, Monetary and Economic Conference, London, 'Secretariat List', 17 July 1933, p. 16, typescript).

[89] As the London representative of the Bank of Italy Joe Nathan was particularly appreciated by Norman and Siepmann and often admitted to discussions at the Bank of England (see the correspondence in Archive of the Bank of England, London, OV36 'Overseas Department: Italy'; ADM 1/1 and 1/5 'Commonwealth Central Bank Letters'). There, for instance, a highly critical Nathan discussed with John M. Keynes ('Prof. Keynes') the position of British sterling after leaving the gold in September 1931 (see AS BI, *Segreteria Particolare*, prat. 6, fasc. 1, 'confidential' letter from Nathan to Vincenzo Azzolini, London, 10 September 1931). Keynes met 'Signor Nathan' in Nice in 1915 when at the Treasury (cf. Roy F. Harrod, *The Life of John Maynard Keynes* (London, 1951), 202).

[90] Significantly, Alberto Pirelli emerges as a 'big linker' within the Italian corporate networks as studied by Alberto Rinaldi and Michelangelo Vasta, in Chapter 4 in this book, through the specific lens provided by the network analysis approach to interlocking directorates.

[91] See Douglas J. Forsyth and Ton Notermans, 'Macroeconomic Policy Regimes and Financial Regulation in Europe, 1931–1994', in Douglas J. Forsyth and Ton Notermans (eds.), *Regime Changes* (Providence and Oxford, 1997), 17–68.

samples are more representative of the general trends occurring at the apex of the financial system than a professional or social group in terms of positions, income, and wealth: in a sense, this was the reason why the new technocratic elite actually constituted the financial elite as it emerged from the string of instability phenomena and related adjustments of the previous decade.

In fact, although these two groups of delegates at international conferences could be regarded as too limited to be properly representative of the Italian financial elites as a whole, the two underlying tales provide a measure of the dramatic changes that intervened within the institutional framework throughout the first post-war decade. In the first post-war years bankers were an essential, if not the foremost, part of the Italian financial elites cooperating and sometimes even competing with the central monetary authorities. As a result, they were largely recognized as an influential part of policy-making and represented as such in their delegation to the international financial conferences held in Brussels and Genoa. Such a mixed group of bankers and civil servants was the typical expression of the informal and essentially private structure of cooperation, also within the single nation states, mirroring their sizeable influence in political institutions usually exerted by private financiers in pre-war capitalism. The shift to a formal structure of cooperation or intervention reflects a wider transformation in institutional and regulatory patterns. The relatively long regulatory cycle started in early 1925, and which culminated a decade later with a new banking law in 1936, entailed an analogous change in the contours and traits of the financial elites reflected in the group at the Conference in London, where the Italian delegation was represented almost exclusively by technocrats and civil servants. This new financial elite was the result of adjustment strategies that substantially reduced the relative weight and influence of private bankers, the state taking over their banks in the wake of bailouts and replacing them at the helm with public managers. In the mid-1930s the Italian financial elites were, by that time, 'nationalized' under a technocratic umbrella, as they were constituted by technocrats and managers operating in public-controlled institutions. In a way, such a result mirrors a more general tendency within European elites, where 'gentlemen' were more and more frequently substituted by 'players' since the 1920s, as well as income and wealth by competences in defining elites and allocating responsibilities.[92] This form of institutionalization of banking expertise replaced semi-private informal structures of cooperation and imposed a long-term regulatory arrangement that was due to last up to the early 1990s when privatizations were gradually undertaken under the pressure of a fiscal crisis.

---

[92] This change was parallel to that occurring in the big business in the 1920s and 1930s, when managers took over the control of large corporations (cf. James Burnham, *The Managerial Revolution: What is Happening in the World*, New York, 1941).

3.6 Conclusion

In the 1920s the Italian financial elites changed significantly their contours and a technocracy eventually emerged. The Italian financial elites shifted from the pre-war 'cooperation model' still at work in the 1920s, in which public sector representatives and private sector elites intermingled and cooperated, to a 'technocratic model', in which public sector officials tended to prevail promoting state-led regulation in antithesis to club-style auto-regulating markets. Characteristically, quintessentially cosmopolitan financiers such as Feltrinelli, Pirelli, and Toeplitz, all of them perfectly polyglot, were an expression of the pre-war 'cooperation model'. The 'technocratic model' was mostly embodied by Beneduce, the technocrat par excellence, and later by his close collaborator Menichella, the governor of the Bank of Italy in the 1950s. In the process, from the mid-1920s, a new breed of technocrats regulated the domestic financial system largely in response to external constraints. Such a rationale, which reshaped the financial sector and had a long-term impact on markets and intermediaries, evidenced deeper relationships than is commonly understood within the complex array of international constraints.[93] Specifically, this approach provides insights quite different from a literature assuming that financial regulation should essentially respond to domestic instability and crises.[94]

On the whole in the interwar period central banking evolved and financial innovation took place as an institutional response to the intertwined domestic and international financial instability factors, stabilizing prices, exchange rates, and intermediaries. Since the early 1920s recurrent instability phenomena within the banking sector imposed major interventions by the bank of issue during two crucial junctures, in the early 1920s and in the early 1930s. Between those junctures the international pressure for monetary stabilization altered the overall picture by favouring a key selection process within the national financial elites that imposed a sea change in the nature of the public intervention promoting the reorganization of the whole system along new regulatory principles. As empirical evidence from the major banks' balance sheets implies, the increased volatility in main banking indicators during the 1920s mostly depended on monetary instability deriving from inflation, currency inconvertibility, and unsustainable sovereign debt.

---

[93] On this topic see Olivier Feiertag and Michel Margairaz (eds.), *Les banques centrales à l'échelle du monde/Central Banks at World Scale* (Paris, 2012).

[94] See Alfredo Gigliobianco, Claire Giordano, and Gianni Toniolo, 'Innovation and Regulation in the Wake of Financial Crises in Italy (1880s–1930s)', in Alfredo Gigliobianco and Gianni Toniolo (eds.), *Financial Market Regulation in the Wake of Financial Crises: The Historical Experience* (Rome, 2009).

The institutional response to financial instability promoted a different elite, constituted by professionals and civil servants, particularly aware of the international dimensions of central banking. This elite reshaped both regulation and the banking system so as to realize a successful macroeconomic adjustment by introducing forms of financial innovation and reducing banking instability as the data suggest.

4

Financial Elites and the Italian Corporate Network, 1913–2001

Alberto Rinaldi and Michelangelo Vasta

4.1 Introduction

The issue of financial elites, with the analysis of the structure of their networks, has been studied by several different strands of literature, which have introduced a plurality of approaches and methodologies.[1] Sociologists and political scientists have tackled the issue by studying the power of dominant groups and their effects on the institutional set-up of a country.[2] Economic and business historians have analysed the influence of business elites in different contexts and their responsibilities in financial crises.[3] The interest in the topic, after a boom in the 1970s and in the 1980s, vanished in the 'roaring nineties', when it disappeared from the research agenda of social scientists. It returned to the centre of attention in the last few years due to the resilience of the recent financial crisis and the consequent growth of inequality, which, for instance,

---

[1] This work has relied on the use of Imita.db, a large dataset funded by Miur, the Italian Ministry for University and Scientific Research, on Infocamere, the large dataset of Unioncamere, the Association of the Italian Chambers of Commerce, and on R&S Mediobanca dataset on the Italian top companies. We thank the Camera di Commercio of Modena for letting us have access to Infocamere and R&S Mediobanca for providing precious information on balance sheets of the Italian firms. Special thanks is due to Fulvio Coltorti, former Head of R&S-Mediobanca, for his valuable and generous help. A previous version of this work has been presented at the European University Institute (EUI) in the Conference Financial Elites in Historical Perspective (Fiesole, May 2013).

[2] Charles W. Mills, *The Power Elite* (New York, 1956); Robert D. Putnam, *The Comparative Study of Political Elites* (Englewood Cliffs, NJ, 1976).

[3] Youssef Cassis, 'Financial Elites in Three European Centres: London, Paris, Berlin, 1880s–1930s', *Business History* 1991 (33.3): 53–71; Youssef Cassis, 'Financial Elites Revisited', in Ranald Michie and Philip Williamson (eds.), *The British Government and the City of London in the Twentieth Century* (Cambridge, 2004), 76–95; Marc Flandreau, 'The Vanishing Banker', *Financial History Review* 2012 (19.1): 1–19.

contributed to the worldwide success of the 2014 book by Thomas Piketty, *Capital in the Twenty-First Century*.[4] As to methodologies, financial elites have been studied in several perspectives. Qualitative analysis, based on the prosopographic approach, largely dominated the scene with many works, mainly from the perspective of political scientists and business historians. At the same time, the quantitative approach—largely based on network analysis—introduced by sociologists, gained popularity amongst all social scientists, particularly economists but also economic historians.

The role of financial elites can be traced back to Hilferding's theory of the hegemony of finance capital.[5] According to this view, there is a stage of capitalism in which financial capital controlled by banks and industrial capital controlled by stock corporations merged and formed powerful groups of companies or trusts. The theory of finance capital was pushed a step further by Kotz who maintained that banks are on top of the decision-making hierarchy within a group of companies and use this power in their own interest, so that a banking elite is at the top of the financial elite.[6] Along this stream of literature, some authors, by adopting a Marxist approach, argued instead that bank dominance was a transient stage in the evolution of modern capitalism. Sweezy claimed that a later stage would be characterized by reciprocal relationships between banks and industry, where coordination, rather than bank dominance, is the prevalent mode of interaction.[7]

In recent years, some approaches have developed theoretical tools to analyse the structure of corporate systems. The 'law and finance' approach suggests that legal protection of investors is the crucial determinant of capital market development, ownership concentration, and organizational structures, and argues that legal protection is ultimately a by-product of a country's legal origin which includes culture and ideologies.[8] An alternative approach, known as 'political economy', has resulted from observing that the structure of financial systems is not uniform over time. Proponents of this view maintain that a country's financial system and governance structure are not determined by unchanging institutional factors, but mainly by the behaviour and structure of interest groups that change over time. One prediction of these theorists is that ownership is more concentrated in countries where the state plays a bigger

---

[4] Thomas Piketty, *Capital in the Twenty-First Century* (Cambridge, MA, 2014).
[5] Rudolf Hilferding, *Finance Capital: A Study in the Latest Phase of Capitalist Development* (London, 1981 [1910]).
[6] David M. Kotz, *Bank Control of Large Corporations in the United States* (Berkeley, CA, 1978).
[7] Paul Sweezy, 'The Illusion of the "Managerial Revolution"', *Science and Society* 1942 (6.1): 1–23.
[8] Rafael La Porta, Florencio Lopez de Silanes, Andrei Shleifer, and Robert W. Vishny, 'Law and Finance', *Journal of Political Economy* 1998 (106.6): 1113–55; Rafael La Porta, Florencio Lopez de Silanes, and Andrei Shleifer, 'Corporate Ownership around the World', *Journal of Finance* 1999 (54.2): 471–517; Rafael La Porta; Florencio Lopez-de-Silanes, and Andrei Shleifer, 'The Economic Consequences of Legal Origins', *Journal of Economic Literature* 2008 (46.2): 285–332.

role in the economy.[9] By referring to these streams of literature, which provide different emphasis on the role of financial elites, and by using both quantitative and qualitative approaches, this chapter focuses on Italian financial elites by adopting a long run perspective and using network analysis as its main tool of investigation.

In the framework of the literature on 'varieties of capitalism', Italy does not fit well with either the 'Liberal Market Economy' or the 'Coordinated Market Economy' model. In the former, as in the case of the United States and the United Kingdom, firms coordinate their activities primarily via hierarchies and competitive market mechanisms. In the latter, which include Germany, Japan, and the Scandinavian countries, inter-firm coordination takes place by resorting to a large extent to non-market collaborative relationships, such as exchange of information inside networks.[10] However, Latin countries are in a more ambiguous position. Thus, a third variety of capitalism has been distinguished to account for these countries: 'state-influenced market economies'. This encompasses those nations—especially Italy and France—in which the state plays a crucial role, intervenes more, and differently, in the economy than in the two other models, and retains a higher influence over business and the labour market.[11] Following the most recent approaches, Aganin and Volpin stress that low legal protection of investors curbed the development of financial markets in Italy. This led to high ownership concentration (there are no American-style public companies in Italy) and the emergence of pyramidal groups to allow for the separation of ownership and control.[12] A recent research study has shown that the formation of business groups seems therefore the 'only way to grow' for Italian firms or, at least, as the easiest way to reach a reasonable size.[13]

Actually, the Italian banking and financial history in the twentieth century could be divided into two main periods since it has been characterized by two major institutional breakups. The first one occurred in the 1930s when, to deal with the Great Depression, the fascist government created in 1933 the Istituto per la Ricostruzione Industriale (IRI), a big state-owned conglomerate, which took over the ailing universal banks and their industrial securities. In 1936, a

---

[9] Marco Pagano and Paolo Volpin, 'The Political Economy of Finance', *Oxford Review of Economic Policy* 2001 (17.4): 502–19; Raghuram Rajan and Luigi Zingales, 'The Great Reversals: The Politics of Financial Development in the 20th Century', *Journal of Finance Economics* 2003 (69.1): 5–50.

[10] Peter A. Hall and David Soskice (eds.), *Varieties of Capitalism: The Institutional Foundation of Comparative Advantage* (Oxford, 2001).

[11] Vivien A. Schmidt, 'European Political Economy: Labor Out, State Back In, Firm to the Fore', *West European Politics* 2008 (31.1/2): 302–20.

[12] Alexander Aganin and Paolo Volpin, 'History of Corporate Ownership in Italy', in Randall K. Morck (ed.), *A History of Corporate Governance around the World: Family Business Groups to Professional Managers* (Chicago, 2005), 325–61.

[13] Andrea Colli, Alberto Rinaldi, and Michelangelo Vasta, 'The Only Way to Grow? Italian Business Groups in Historical Perspective', *Business History* 2016 (58.1): 30–48.

Banking Reform Law forbade universal banking. In fact, banks could provide only short-term credit to the industrial sector and were prohibited to own shares of industrial companies. Long- and medium-term credit could be provided only by special institutes, most of them state-owned. The second major institutional breakup was in the 1990s, when a massive privatization programme reduced the state-owned sector of the economy.[14] At the same time, in 1993 a new Banking Reform Law was passed, which allows banks to provide both short-, medium-, and long-term credit and to acquire shares in non-financial firms, thereby paving the way to a return of universal banking.[15]

The crucial role of the state, jointly with that of banks, has been emphasized as a 'substitution factor' for the financial markets in the process of Italian industrialization by the seminal work by Gerschenkron.[16] Indeed, Gerschenkron singled out the main universal banks as the major drivers of industrial spurts in the pre-First World War years. In his view, these banks functioned as a 'substitution factor' for otherwise missing prerequisites of industrialization, i.e. substantial capital accumulation and a willingness to invest it in industry, which enabled Italy to catch up to the technological paradigm of the Second Industrial Revolution. However, the role of universal banks has been reconsidered by a more recent 'revisionist' historiography. In particular, Fohlin found evidence that these banks had a limited impact on capital mobilization, industrial investment, and economic growth. However, she finds that universal banks were at the centre of an entangled network with large and established companies.[17] A study by Vasta and Baccini—using a large sample of more than 4,000 Italian joint-stock companies and the interlocking directorates (IDs) technique[18]—held that the Italian corporate network does not seem to have been characterized by such a strong centrality of banks as it was commonly believed.[19] The location of banks at the centre of the network could be detected in 1911 and even more in 1927, but this was no longer the case in 1936, after the collapse of the universal banks. By that time, insurance companies and utility companies had replaced banks at the centre of the system.[20] Recently, Vasta and his co-authors have confirmed that the

---

[14] Emilio Barucci and Federico Pierobon, *Le privatizzazioni in Italia* (Rome, 2007).
[15] Salvatore La Francesca, *Storia del sistema bancario italiano* (Bologna, 2004).
[16] Alexander Gerschenkron, *Economic Backwardness in Historical Perspective* (Cambridge, MA, 1962).
[17] Caroline Fohlin, 'Fiduciari and Firm Liquidity Constraint: The Italian Experience with German-Style Universal Banking', *Explorations in Economic History* 1998 (35.1): 83–107; Caroline Fohlin, 'Capital Mobilisation and Utilisation in Latecomer Economies: Germany and Italy Compared', *European Review of Economic History* 1999 (3.2): 139–74.
[18] An interlock is the link between two companies when a person is a director of both.
[19] Michelangelo Vasta and Alberto Baccini, 'Banks and Industry in Italy, 1911–36: New Evidence Using the Interlocking Directorates Technique', *Financial History Review* 1997 (4.2): 139–59.
[20] Alberto Baccini and Michelangelo Vasta, 'Una tecnica ritrovata: "interlocking directorates" nei rapporti tra banca e industria in Italia (1911–36)', *Rivista di storia economica* 1995 (12.2): 219–51.

centrality of the universal banks in the Italian corporate system varied over time.[21] At the same time, they have shown that Italian capitalism seems to be structured to a remarkable extent on a sizeable and stable system of corporate interlocks that exist in parallel to that centred on the universal banks. These authors also showed that the influence of financial capital was abundant but not limited to a few large banks. Its influence played a crucial role, at least in Lombardy and in some other most developed areas of the North, involving many local banks which in turn developed a dense web of ties with industrial firms.

For the period after the Second World War, Chiesi analysed the top 250 Italian joint-stock companies in 1976 and noticed the absence of the larger banks from the centre of the network.[22] He attributed this fact to the effects of the 1936 Banking Law which, by separating the function of the collection of deposits from industrial credit, had rendered it impossible to re-establish those close relations between banks and industry that had distinguished the period prior to the Great Depression. Instead, a subsequent study by Ferri and Trento arrived at substantially different conclusions: basing themselves on a reduced sample of companies, they observed that, in spite of the implicit prohibitions in the Banking Law, a dense web of interlocks between banks and industrial firms existed throughout the twentieth century and represented a permanent trait of Italian capitalism. In the presence of legislation which strongly limited banks' participations in non-financial companies (and vice versa) cross-board memberships played a crucial role as substitutes for share relationships.[23] Rinaldi and Vasta analysed the structure of the Italian corporate network from 1952 to 1972 using a large sample of about 25,000 companies.[24] They showed that in 1952 and 1960 the network, centred on the larger electrical companies, showed the highest cohesion. This centre dissolved after the nationalization of the electricity industry in 1962 and in 1972 had been replaced by a new and less cohesive one hinged on financial intermediaries: banks, insurance, and finance companies.

This chapter adds to the previous research by analysing the structure of the Italian corporate network over a long time span from 1913 to 2001.

---

[21] Michelangelo Vasta, Carlo Drago, Roberto Ricciuti, and Alberto Rinaldi, 'Reassessing the Bank Industry Relationship in Italy, 1913–1936: a Counterfactual Analysis', *Cliometrica* 2017 (11.2): 183–216.

[22] Antonio M. Chiesi, 'L'élite finanziaria italiana', *Rassegna italiana di sociologia* 1982 (23): 571–95; Antonio M. Chiesi, 'Property, Capital and Network Structure in Italy', in Frans N. Stokman, Rolf Ziegler, and John Scott (eds.), *Networks of Corporate Power* (Cambridge, 1985), 199–214.

[23] Giovanni Ferri and Sandro Trento, 'La dirigenza delle grandi banche e delle grandi imprese: ricambio e legami', in Fabrizio Barca (ed.), *Storia del capitalismo italiano dal dopoguerra a oggi* (Rome, 1997), 405–27.

[24] Alberto Rinaldi and Michelangelo Vasta, 'The Structure of Italian Capitalism, 1952–72: New Evidence Using the Interlocking Directorates Technique', *Financial History Review* 2005 (12.2): 173–98.

Financial Elites and the Italian Corporate Network

For comparative purposes, we use a smaller sample of the top 250 companies by total assets in seven benchmark years. Network connectivity analysis is integrated by a prosopographic study of the *big linkers*, defined as those directors who had the highest number of board positions in each benchmark year. Big linkers were the central actors who assured the cohesion of the system of corporate interlocks and we consider them as a representative sample of the nation's corporate elite. We also assume that those big linkers who held directorships in both banks and industrial firms functioned as the financial elite. This seems a promising approach as it allows us to show the interactions between structure and agency, that is, between the evolution of the structure of the corporate network and the profile of business leaders. This chapter is organized as follows: Section 4.2 describes the source utilized for this study. Section 4.3 provides some descriptive statistics of the network. Section 4.4 analyses the structure of the network through the use of several indicators of network analysis. Section 4.5 presents a prosopographic analysis of the central actors of the system, the big linkers. At the end of the chapter we draw some conclusions.

4.2 The Source

The source we used in this work for the benchmark years from 1913 to 1983 is *Notizie statistiche sulle principali società italiane per azioni*, edited by the Associazione fra le Società Italiane per Azioni (Assonime). The Imita.db database is an electronic version of this source.[25] This dataset contains information regarding companies, boards of directors, and balance sheets of a large sample of Italian joint-stock companies for several benchmark years.[26] The source includes all the joint-stock companies listed on one of the Italian stock exchanges, together with those companies located in Italy whose share capital at the closure of the last balance was higher than a set threshold, which varied from year to year.[27] On the whole, the dataset contains data on more than 38,000 companies, almost 300,000 directors, and more than 100,000 balance

---

[25] Imita.db is one of the largest datasets on joint-stock companies in historical perspective in the world. For details on the database, see Michelangelo Vasta, 'Appendix: The Source and the Imita.db Dataset', in Renato Giannetti and Michelangelo Vasta (eds.), *Evolution of Italian Enterprises in the 20th Century* (Heidelberg and New York, 2006), 269–73. The database is available online: <http://imitadb.unisi.it>.

[26] Data for companies and boards of directors are available for 1911, 1913, 1921, 1927, 1936, 1952, 1960, 1972, and 1983; for balance sheets, time series are available for the span from 1900 to 1971 and for 1982 and 1983.

[27] The threshold was set at 1 million Italian lire until 1940, with the sole exception of 1914, when it amounted to 500,000 lire. In 1952, the threshold was raised to 10 million, then to 25 million in 1956, 50 million in 1961, and 100 million from 1964 through 1972. Finally, for the benchmark year 1983 the threshold was further raised to 2 billion lire.

sheets. Representativeness, in terms of share capital, is very high as the sample covers over 90 per cent of the total field in all but the first two benchmark years (1911 and 1913) and the last one (1983), for which the proportion is around 85 per cent.

For the benchmark year 2001 we selected the top 250 companies from *Le principali società italiane*, the annual report on Italian joint-stock companies edited by R&S-Mediobanca. As this source does not report the names of the board members, we extracted them from Infocamere, a large dataset of Unioncamere, the association of the Italian chambers of commerce.

This chapter focuses on seven benchmark years: 1913, 1927, 1936, 1960, 1972, 1983, and 2001. In compliance with the guidelines of the international comparative research project *The Power of Corporate Networks: A Comparative and Historical Perspective*,[28] for each benchmark year we have selected the top 250 companies (50 financials and 200 non-financials) by total assets. As to directors, we used only data for members of a board of directors in the strict sense, leaving out the members of *Collegi sindacali*.[29] We have carefully standardized the names of the directors to make them as homogeneous as possible.[30]

4.3 Descriptive Statistics of the Network

An interlock, as anticipated, is the link formed between two companies when a person is a director of both. In this work, we have used primary interlocks without taking into account either the directionality or the strength of the links.[31]

Table 4.1 gives a summary of the general statistics of the sample. The number of total seats was highest in 1927 with 3,024 board positions and an average of 12.1 members per board. The average size remained stable until 1972 at

---

[28] Thomas David and Gerarda Westerhuis (eds.), *The Power of Corporate Networks: A Comparative and Historical Analysis* (New York, 2014).

[29] *Collegi sindacali* are special committees of auditors for firms and their function does not coincide with that of the supervisory board in the German system. Thus, similarly to what was done in the two major international research projects on corporate networks in comparative perspective, for our analysis we have selected only members of the board of directors. See Stokman, Ziegler, and Scott, *Networks*; David and Westerhuis, *The Power*.

[30] We estimate that the information on boards of directors contained in Imita.db has a margin of error of about 1 per cent, as is the case with other similar databases. See Beth A. Mintz and Michael Schwarz, *The Power Structure of American Business* (Chicago, 1985). These errors are mainly due to cases of homonymy, misprints, or shortcomings in the source.

[31] In the case of directionality, it is assumed that the direction of the interlock goes from the company in which a director has a more important position to that in which the position is of lesser importance. In the case of strength, the connections between two companies are weighted by taking into account the number of directors who sit on both boards of directors. See Johannes M. Pennings, *Interlocking Directorates* (San Francisco and London, 1980); Stanley Wasserman and Katherine Faust (eds.), *Social Network Analysis: Methods and Applications* (Cambridge, MA, 1994).

Financial Elites and the Italian Corporate Network

about 11–12 members per board, but then it decreased to a minimum of 9.1 members in 2001.

An important measure in the description of the system is the *cumulation ratio* (CR), that is, the average number of positions held by a single director. This, too, reached a maximum in 1927. Then it decreased: slightly in 1936 and 1960, but then substantially since 1972.

Table 4.2 classifies the 250 companies of each benchmark year into several industries. The weight of the different industries varies over the time. Manufacturing firms were always the most represented industry. Their number dropped from 101 to 85 between 1913 and 1927, but then it increased and reached a peak of 148 in 1972. Their numbers remained stable in 1983, but then they dropped to 111 in 2001. However, the biggest change concerned the public utilities companies. These were highly represented from 1913 to 1960 when they accounted for about one-quarter of all non-financial companies. Then they nearly disappeared in 1972 and 1983 as a consequence of the

Table 4.1. Descriptive statistics of the network

	1913	1927	1936	1960	1972	1983	2001
A: Number of non-financial firms	200	200	200	200	200	200	200
Total number of seats	1,781	2,236	1,841	2,150	2,106	1,813	1,536
Average size of the board	8.9	11.2	9.2	10.8	10.5	9.1	7.7
Total number of directors	1,166	1,356	1,371	1,457	1,641	1,456	1,307
B: Number of financial firms	50	50	50	50	50	50	50
Total number of seats	611	788	705	783	909	865	727
Average size of the board	12.2	15.8	14.1	15.7	18.2	17.3	14.5
Total number of directors	554	668	592	653	761	752	602
A+B: Total number of firms	250	250	250	250	250	250	250
Total number of seats	2,392	3,024	2,546	2,933	3,015	2,678	2,263
Average size of the board	9.6	12.1	10.2	11.7	12.1	10.7	9.1
Total number of directors	1,571	1,827	1,618	1,932	2,230	2,108	1,850
CR: Cumulation Ratio	1.52	1.66	1.57	1.52	1.35	1.27	1.22

Table 4.2. Firms by sector

	Total	1	3	4	5	6	7	8	9	10	11	12	13
1913	250	50	8	37	4	101	9	–	8	21	7	4	–
1927	250	50	10	62	8	85	10	–	13	6	3	3	–
1936	250	50	5	66	4	98	7	–	2	9	3	4	2
1960	250	50	4	46	6	118	9	–	8	2	2	–	5
1972	250	50	5	5	5	148	6	–	10	–	1	3	17
1983	250	50	15	7	9	142	2	–	8	–	1	7	9
2001	250	50	10	41	11	111	1	–	2	3	–	11	9

Legend: 1: Financials; 3: Service industry; 4: Electric utility. Water, Telephone, and Gas; 5: Trade companies; 6: Manufacturing companies; 7: Mining industry; 8: Oil companies; 9: Shipping industry; 10: Railway companies; 11: Tramway companies; 12: Building companies; 13: Transport, Warehousing, and Communication.

nationalization of the electricity industry in 1962. Finally, they showed a staggering increase (from 7 to 41) in 2001 after the massive wave of privatizations of state-owned and municipal enterprises that was carried out in the 1990s.

4.4 The Structure of the Network

The most common indicator to analyse the structure of the network is the density index, defined as the ratio between the number of links between pairs of units and the number of possible connections:

$$D = L(r)/L(p)$$

where $L(r)$ is the number of real connections and $L(p)$, defined as $n(n-1)/2$, indicates the number of all possible connections. The density indicates the degree of overlap between the companies in the system. Given the same number of companies, a greater density means tighter relations between the sub-systems. It is possible to notice that an increase in the number of companies causes a decrease in the density index: with the same number of links, the increase in the number of companies determines a decrease in the density. The index D varies between 0 and 1, i.e. for $L(r) = 0$ and $L(r) = n(n-1)/2$, respectively. These refer, respectively, to the extreme cases of a total absence of any link and to that of the realization of all possible links.[32]

Figure 4.1 shows that the density peaked in 1927, when the German-type universal banks had a pre-eminent position in the system. Then, in 1936 and 1960 it returned to values only slightly higher than those of 1913. In 1972 the density started to decline and it further dropped in 1983 and in 2001.

A dynamics similar to that of the density is shown by isolated and marginal firms.[33] In fact, their overall proportion remained quite stable around 19 per cent prior to the Second World War; it dropped to 15 per cent in 1960 but then it began to rise and reached a maximum of 56 per cent in 2001.

Thus, the overall picture that emerges is a strong reduction in the cohesion of the Italian corporate network. This seems to have started after the major institutional breakup of the nationalization of the electricity industry in 1962, then it became more substantial between 1972 and 1983—that is, during the crisis that followed the end of the 'Golden Age' and the start of the transition from the technological regime of the second to that of the third industrial revolution based on ICT—and even sharper between 1983 and 2001, after the

---

[32] John Scott, *Social Network Analysis: A Handbook* (London, Newbury Park, and New Delhi, 1991).
[33] Isolated firms are firms that have no ties to other firms, whereas marginal firms are firms that are interlocked to no more than another two firms.

Financial Elites and the Italian Corporate Network

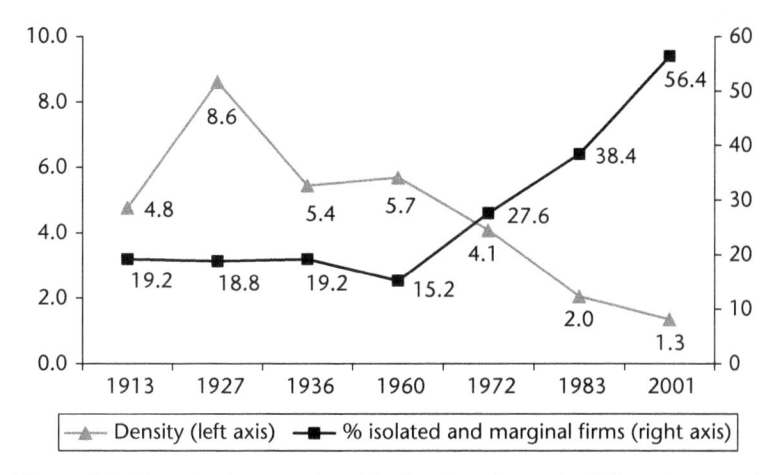

Figure 4.1. Density (per cent) and isolated and marginal firms (per cent)

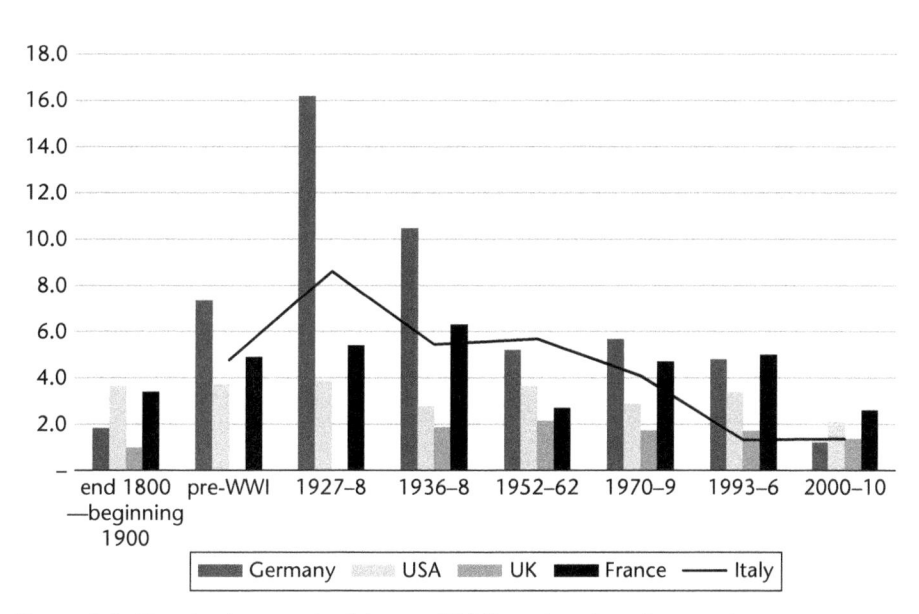

Figure 4.2. Density (per cent) of the top 250 firms in selected countries

Sources: David and Westerhuis, *The Power*, Appendix 1; Majka Patuzzi, 'The German Corporate Network during the Golden Age (1950–1970)', Master's thesis, University of Siena, 2012, for Germany in 1952 and 1970; and Paul Windolf, 'Corporate Networks in the 20th Century: Germany, United States, and France in Comparison', paper presented at the conference 'The Power of Corporate Networks: A Comparative and Historical Perspective', Lausanne, August 2012, for the USA in 1900, 1914, 1928, and 1938.

massive privatizations of state-owned enterprises (SOEs) that occurred in Italy in the 1990s.

In comparative perspective, Figure 4.2 shows that in the period prior to the Second World War the density index in Italy seems to have followed the same trend as in Germany, even if at lower values. Then Italy seems to have experienced a sharper and earlier decline of its corporate network than other major advanced economies.

The analysis of the top twenty firms graded by number of interlocks enables us to develop several further considerations (see Table 4.3). In fact, it is presumed that actors that are more connected have better opportunities to access and spread information, and play a central role in coordinating the whole network.

In 1913 the electricity sector was the most represented among the most central firms, with eight presences out of twenty. However, the three larger universal banks (Banca Commerciale Italiana, Società Bancaria Italiana, and Credito Italiano) and the Bank of Italy (at that time a privately-owned joint-stock company) seemed to play a central role in the system. In fact, they occupied four of the first ten positions, with Banca Commerciale Italiana and Società Bancaria Italiana placed in the top two positions.

In 1927 the centre appeared to have been enlarged and reached its highest connectivity. The two larger universal banks had further strengthened their links with industry, especially with the electrical companies which now accounted for ten of the top twenty. A paramount role at the centre of the network was now played by the Società Italiana per le Strade Ferrate Meridionali, a former railway company which, after the nationalization of the Italian railways in 1905, had turned into a finance company that invested the sums it had received from the state, in compensation for the railway nationalization, mainly in securities of the major electrical companies.

As we have seen, the Great Depression pushed the government to create, in 1933, the big state-owned holding IRI that took over the universal banks and

Table 4.3. Top twenty firms by number of interlocks and sector of activity

Sector of activity	1913	1927	1936	1960	1972	1983	2001
Manufacturing	3	2	2	3	7	11	3
Electrical power	8	10	6	7	–	–	4
Energy	–	–	–	–	1	1	–
Constructions	1	–	–	–	–	1	–
Railways	3	1	–	–	–	–	–
Motorways	–	–	1	–	–	–	1
Telecommunications	–	2	2	–	1	–	4
Banking	4	3	2	3	3	1	4
Finance	–	2	5	6	6	4	1
Insurance	1	–	2	1	1	2	3
Real estate	–	–	–	–	1	–	–
Total	20	20	20	20	20	20	20

their industrial securities. In 1936 a new Banking Law imposed a clear-cut separation between banks and industry. Banks were allowed to practise only short-term credit, while their share participations in non-financial companies were strictly limited. At the same time, industrial credit was entrusted to newly-created specialized medium-term credit institutes.

These changes had profound effects on the structure of the Italian corporate network and resulted in a remarkable decrease in the cohesion of the system. In 1936, the most central companies had little more than one-half of the links of their counterparts in 1927. The former universal banks had lost their pre-eminent position, even though three banks remained among the top twenty but at a lower rank than in 1927. Electrical companies were still the most represented among the top twenty, although their number fell from ten to six. The two largest insurance companies (Ras and Assicurazioni Generali) and a number of finance companies had surged to a central position. The latter included, in addition to the Società Italiana per le Strade Ferrate Meridionali, some state-owned medium-term credit institutes to underscore the role that the state had assumed in the financing of industry (especially of big business). Overall, SOEs were present amongst the most central companies with seven firms out of twenty.

The situation little changed in 1960. The nationalization of the electricity industry in 1962 led to a dissolving of the old centre of the network and to the formation of a new, less cohesive one. In fact, in 1972 electrical companies had disappeared from the top twenty, which now included a higher proportion of manufacturing companies (seven out of twenty) than ever before. SOEs reached their maximum influence with nine of the top twenty. Finance companies and banks remained stable at six and three respectively. However, both Banca Commerciale Italiana and Credito Italiano had significantly reduced their connections with other firms and had now disappeared from the top twenty. The three banks included in the centre were now the Banco di Roma—the smaller ex-universal bank—and two small Lombard private banks.

The year 1983 saw a dramatic decrease in the number of interlocks of the most central companies, which halved with regard to 1972. The central role of manufacturing companies was further strengthened as now these peaked at eleven of the top twenty. The centre of the system seems to have been reshaped around the pivotal role of Mediobanca, the only merchant bank in Italy at that time. Mediobanca did not appear amongst the more central companies in that year. However, eleven of the top twenty firms, especially those belonging to the Fiat and Montedison groups, were closely tied to it through credit relations, cross-participations, and Mediobanca's presence in their controlling syndicates.

The massive wave of privatizations of SOEs in the 1990s marked another major institutional breakup. As a result, in 2001 the Italian corporate network had become more disentangled with all the connectivity indicators showing their lowest values. Nonetheless, SOEs remained present with seven of the top twenty firms and confirmed the resilience of the state at the centre of Italian capitalism.[34] The major change involved the sectoral composition of the most central companies. Manufacturing firms dropped from eleven to two, whereas the most represented sectors were now telecommunications, electrical power, and banks with four presences each. If the surge of telecommunication firms was a consequence of the advent of the technological regime of the third industrial revolution, the presence of electrical firms and banks seems to mark a return of sectors that had been pivotal in Italy's first wave of industrialization. Once privatized in the 1990s, these firms returned to play a central role as connectors of the now weaker corporate network.

4.5 The Big Linkers

An analysis of the 'big linkers' (henceforth BLs)—that is, the individuals who held the largest number of directorships in joint-stock companies—can be very useful for interpretative purposes. In capitalist countries, the BLs perform an extremely important function in ensuring the cohesion of the economic system, for they are usually the business community's opinion leaders, the vehicle through which information is collected and spread among companies, as well as the principal channel connecting the business world and the political domain.[35]

They can therefore be considered as a representative sample of the nation's corporate elite and an analysis of their behaviour can help to shed light on what makes possible the agglomeration of firms into a more or less coherent social structure, and what determines the resulting kind of structure.[36] In particular, the study of the BLs can be very insightful to the analysis of inter-sectoral relations, and especially of those existing between banks, other financial intermediaries, and industry.

To that end, we considered a sample of the top twenty BLs, those who in each benchmark year accumulated the largest number of board positions in Italian joint-stock companies.[37] Table 4.4 shows that in each benchmark year

---

[34] Alberto Rinaldi and Michelangelo Vasta, 'Persistent and Stubborn: The State in Italian Capitalism, 1913–2001', David and Westerhuis, *The Power*, 169–88.
[35] John Scott, 'Theoretical Framework and Research Design', in Stokman, Ziegler, and Scott, *Networks*, 1–19.
[36] Mark Granovetter, 'The Nature of Economic Relationship', in Richard Swedberg (ed.), *Explorations in Economic Sociology* (New York, 1993), 3–41.
[37] In six out of seven benchmark years several individuals proved to be matched up in twentieth place with the same number of seats. In these cases, we included some of these individuals—selected in alphabetical order—so as to have a comparable sample of twenty BLs for each benchmark year.

Table 4.4. IDs generated by the top twenty BLs

	1913	1927	1936	1960	1972	1983	2001
(1) Total IDs	1,924	4,029	2,479	2,702	1,741	925	701
(2) IDs by the BLs	761	2,022	1,121	1,299	727	297	303
2/1 (%)	39.6	50.2	45.2	48.1	41.8	32.1	43.2

Table 4.5. BLs by age

Age	1913	1927	1936	1960	1972	1983	2001
Minimum	42	46	40	39	48	43	38
Mean	59	54	60	61	64	59	58
Maximum	76	67	72	83	77	76	74

BLs accounted for a very high proportion of total IDs, ranging from 32 per cent in 1983 to little more than 50 per cent in 1927. That is, the Italian corporate network was formed to a large extent by the links generated by a handful of individuals, a restricted corporate elite who played a paramount role in assuring the cohesion of the whole system.

Three BLs reappeared in three separate benchmark years, and another twelve reappeared twice.[38] Thus, the 140 positions available overall were covered by 122 persons. The highest continuity—with five permanencies out of twenty places—occurred between 1927 and 1936, despite the reshuffling of the network due to the collapse of the German-style universal banks and the creation of the IRI. Conversely, the most marked discontinuity is observable between 1983 and 2001, with no permanency in the time interval, to underscore that the disentangling of the network was accompanied by a total renewal of the nation's corporate elite.

Table 4.5 reports information regarding the age of BLs. In 1913, the mean age of these individuals was 59 years; in 1927 it diminished to 54 and then in 1936 it increased to 60. The following benchmark year did not register any substantial variation, but in 1972 it peaked at 64 years. The dynamics of the BL age in the first three benchmark years is not easy to interpret. This is especially the case of the 1927–36 interval, when the collapse of the universal banks and the advent of a big state-owned sector of the economy could have left room for a rejuvenated corporate elite. One could surmise that in the first two decades of the twentieth century—in a nation only recently industrialized as was Italy at that time—the entrepreneurial class, especially in newer industries such as electricity, was made up mainly of relatively *new men*. Subsequently, owing also to the increased complexity of corporate organizations as Italy

---

[38] The list of the top twenty BLs for each benchmark year is reported in the Appendix.

succeeded in catching up in the technological regime of the second industrial revolution, it is possible that business careers became longer and slower, and that a greater number of years were required to reach the top positions.[39]

In the 1972–83 interval BL turnover was marked by a pronounced rejuvenation, which amounted to a real generational change. In fact, the mean age of BLs diminished from 64 to 59 years, and then it further decreased at 58 in 2001. This might have been the consequence of the transition from one technological regime to another, which prompted relatively *new men* to top positions in the nation's corporate elite.

Table 4.6 reports the distribution of BLs according to their region of birth. Lombardy stands out among the regions represented. Overall, there was a prevalence of BLs born in the North-Western regions of most ancient industrialization—the so-called *industrial triangle* made up of the regions of Piedmont, Lombardy, and Liguria—which was particularly strong in the first two benchmarks. Then, the formation of the SOE sector (many SOEs were headquartered in Rome) seems to have widened the space for BLs born in other regions. Perhaps not by chance, the lowest proportion of BLs born outside of the North-West can be observed in 1972, the year that exhibits the highest proportion of SOEs among the most central firms. The surge of the Centre in 2001—that for the first time equals the North-West with eight BLs—is also principally due to the presence of several BLs who held their directorships in SOEs.

The analysis of the level of education and the type of university degree obtained can serve as a proxy for the personal qualification of the BLs. This type of close examination appears to be very useful, for the literature has indicated the existence of a connection between the latter and the management models of the firms in which these figures served as directors.[40] More specifically, though referring to chairmen and general managers, rather than to board members in general, it has been held that there is a correlation between the qualifications and the duties (in production, sales, or administration) performed prior to taking on management responsibilities, and the policies of firms, such as the pursuit of diversification strategies in related or unrelated sectors.[41]

Table 4.7 presents the distribution of the BLs by the level of education achieved. BLs were highly educated. The majority of BLs were university

---

[39] From a different, but complementary, perspective, it has been shown that in the interwar years the Italian financial elite shifted from a pre-war 'cooperation model' still at work in the 1920s, in which public sector officials and private sector leaders intermingled and cooperated, to a 'technocratic model' in which the former prevailed promoting state-led regulation in antithesis with club-style auto-regulating markets. See Giandomenico Piluso, Chapter 3, this volume.

[40] Francesca Ferratini Tosi et al., 'Il ceto imprenditoriale nel primo decennio repubblicano. Anticipazioni su un campione di ricerca', *Italia contemporanea* 1983 (153): 165–81.

[41] Neil Fligstein, *The Transformation of Corporate Control* (Cambridge, MA, 1990).

Table 4.6. BLs by region of birth

Region	1913	1927	1936	1960	1972	1983	2001
Piedmont	3	5	3	3	1	6	–
Lombardy	6	7	4	8	5	4	6
Liguria	1	1	–	–	–	1	2
Total North-West	*10*	*13*	*7*	*11*	*6*	*11*	*8*
Trentino-Alto Adige	1	–	–	–	–	–	–
Veneto	1	1	3	–	–	–	2
Friuli-Venezia Giulia	1	–	1	–	–	2	–
Emilia-Romagna	1	–	1	–	1	2	1
Total North-East	*4*	*1*	*5*	–	*1*	*4*	*3*
Tuscany	–	–	1	–	4	–	4
Marche	–	–	1	–	–	–	–
Umbria	–	–	–	2	–	–	1
Latium	–	–	–	1	2	4	3
Total Centre	–	*1*	*2*	*3*	*6*	*4*	*8*
Abruzzo	–	–	–	1	1	–	–
Apulia	–	–	–	–	2	–	–
Campania	–	1	3	1	1	–	–
Calabria	–	–	–	–	–	–	1
Sicily	–	–	1	1	–	–	–
Sardinia	–	–	–	1	1	–	–
Total South & Isles	–	*1*	*4*	*4*	*5*	–	*1*
Overseas	2	1	1	–	–	–	–
Total	16	16	19	18	18	19	20
Unknown	4	4	1	2	2	1	–

graduates. Only in 1913 were university graduates fewer than a half of BLs (nine out of twenty). University graduates jumped to fourteen in 1927 and in the following benchmarks they further rose up to a peak of eighteen in 1960, which was repeated in 1983. In 2001, sixteen BLs were university graduates.

There was a significant change in the type of university degree held. From 1913 to 1936 engineers prevailed, but in 1960 and in 1972 they were superseded by graduates in law. In 1983 graduates in engineering returned to prevail (ten BLs out of ten) probably as a consequence of the fact that the emerging new technological regime of the third industrial revolution required more sophisticated technical skills for business success. By contrast, in 2001 engineers plummeted to one, graduates in law were just two, while graduates in economics and business administration[42] by far prevail with nine of the sixteen graduates. This change probably reflected the increased importance of finance in the strategies of the largest Italian corporate groups.

As we have anticipated, the study of the BLs can be very insightful to the analysis of the relationship between banks and industry. The BLs who held

---

[42] The term 'Economics and Business Administration' is used in this chapter to refer to the following Italian university degrees: Scienze economiche e commerciali, Economia e commercio, and Amministrazione aziendale.

Table 4.7. BLs by level of education

	1913	1927	1936	1960	1972	1983	2001
University degree	9	14	15	18	17	18	16
– Engineering	4	10	9	6	6	10	1
– Law	3	2	4	8	7	3	2
– Economics & Bus. Adm.	1	1	1	3	4	5	9
– Agriculture	1	–	–	–	–	–	–
– Mathematics	–	1	1	1	–	–	–
– Chemistry	–	–	–	–	–	–	1
– Philosophy	–	–	–	–	–	–	1
– Physics	–	–	–	–	–	–	1
– Statistics	–	–	–	–	–	–	1
Diploma	2	5	3	2	2	1	1
– Classical school	1	1	2	–	–	–	1
– Accountancy	1	4	1	1	1	1	–
– Normal school	–	–	–	1	1	–	–
Other or not indicated	9	1	2	–	1	1	3
Total	20	20	20	20	20	20	12

directorships in both banks and industrial firms can be considered as a proxy of the nation's financial elite, or at least of its top.

Table 4.8 shows that in the first two benchmark years these individuals constituted a high proportion (60 per cent or more) of all BLs and accounted for nearly two-thirds of total IDs generated by BLs. These figures decreased after the collapse of the universal banks. Nonetheless, in 1960 still eleven BLs sat in at least one bank and one industrial firm and they accounted for nearly a half of the IDs generated by BLs. In 1972 the corresponding figures were nine BLs and 66 per cent of interlocks.[43]

This evidence seems to support Ferri and Trento's claim that, despite the 1936 Banking Law forbidding universal banking, banks and industrial firms recreated their cooperative ties through the sharing of board members, especially BLs, at least until the early 1970s.[44] Moreover, the financial elite constituted a large chunk of the corporate elite.

Links between banks and industry seem to have dramatically weakened only in 1983 as a consequence of the sharp decline of the Italian corporate network as a whole. Thus, the massive BL turnover between 1972 and 1983 seems to have been characterized by the advent of a new generation of BLs much less connected to both banks and industry, that is, by a dramatic weakening of the financial elite and a reduction of its overlap with the corporate elite. However, in 2001, in the face of a further disentangling of the network, there was a resurgence of the ties between banks and industry

---

[43] This result was principally due to the exceptional position of Massimo Spada, a financier strongly tied to the Vatican, who in 1972 generated 190 of the 727 IDs created by BLs (26 per cent of the total).

[44] Ferri and Trento, 'La dirigenza'.

Table 4.8. BLs with seats in at least one bank and one industrial firm

Year	BLs N.	BLs %	IDs N.	IDs %
1913	14	70	476	62.6
1927	12	60	1,308	64.5
1936	11	55	637	56.8
1960	11	55	622	47.9
1972	9	45	481	66.2
1983	5	25	46	15.5
2001	7	35	87	28.7

generated by BLs and increase of the weight of the financial elite in the corporate elite.

An analysis of the directionality of interlocks provides us some further insights about the structure of the financial elite. If a BL has an executive position (chairman and/or managing director) in a bank and no executive position in any non-financial firm, we call this person a banker and his IDs outdegree-interlocks of the bank. These individuals constitute a proxy of a banking elite. Conversely, if a BL has an executive position in an industrial firm and sits just as director on the board of one or more banks, we call this person an industrialist and his IDs indegree-interlocks of the bank.[45] Finally, if a BL is chairman and/or managing director of at least one bank and one industrial firm or he has an executive position in neither a bank nor an industrial firm, we say that his IDs are undirected and call him a financier.

Table 4.9 shows that, contrary to what is commonly believed, the banking elite was a minority of Italy's financial elite in the age of the universal banks. In 1913, bankers were just two of the eleven BLs who generated IDs between banks and industry, and dropped to none in 1927. The financial elite was instead made up principally of industrialists who had been co-opted onto boards of a bank and of financiers who functioned as zipper-figures between banks and industry. Among the former, the top executives of Edison—Italy's largest electricity firms—stood out: Carlo Esterle, managing director from 1896 to 1918, who combined company expansion with the safeguarding of the interests of the principal financing bank, the Banca Commerciale Italiana;

---

[45] Thus, if there is an executive director of a bank who has 10 positions in the network (one in the bank and nine as a non-executive director in as many industrial firms) he creates (10*9)/2 = 45 ties in the network. Of these, nine are interlocks between banks and industrial firms while the remaining 36 are links between industrial firms. In our analysis we consider all his 45 IDs as outdegree-interlocks of the bank as the whole sub-network created by this individual is an indicator of the influence of this bank on the industrial firms in which he holds his directorships. Vice versa, if there is an executive director of an industrial firm who has been co-opted to the board of a bank, and has board position in other eight industrial firms, we consider his IDs as indegree-interlocks of the bank.

Table 4.9. Financial elite by type of BLs

	Bank-outdegree				Bank-indegree				Undirected			
Year	BLs (1)	%	IDs	%	BLs (2)	%	IDs	%	BLs (3)	%	IDs	%
1913	2	14.3	49	10.3	5	35.7	173	36.3	7	50.0	254	53.4
1927	–	–	–	–	6	50.0	780	59.6	6	50.0	528	40.4
1936	1	9.1	55	8.6	7	63.3	490	76.9	3	27.3	92	14.4
1960	1	9.1	21	3.4	7	63.3	364	58.5	3	27.3	237	38.1
1972	–	–	–	–	4	44.4	106	22.0	5	55.6	369	76.7
1983	–	–	–	–	2	40.0	16	34.8	3	60.0	30	65.2
2001	4	57.1	28	32.2	–	–	–	–	3	42.9	59	67.8

(1) Bankers; (2) Industrialists; (3) Financiers

and his successor, Giacinto Motta, managing director from 1918 to 1942, who steered the company away from the Banca Commerciale Italiana's influence and over to the Credito Italiano in the early 1920s. Among the latter, the most prominent figure was Lodovico Mazzotti Biancinelli. Born in 1870 to a Lombard landlord family, after graduating in law he started to operate as a broker for the Banca Commerciale Italiana. In 1909 he became the president of Milan's Stock Exchange and in 1913 sat on the board of two banks (the Società Bancaria Italiana and the Banca Bergamasca di Depositi e Conti Correnti), eight industrial firms, and one real estate company. In the 1920s he strengthened his position as a financier and a zipper-figure between several entrepreneurial groups.

The prevalence of industrialists and financiers in the Italian financial elite was probably a consequence of a failure of corporate governance institutions. In fact, particularly after the First World War, Italian universal banks entered into close and long-run relationships with financed firms that favoured the elimination of prudential constraints, and increased the potential for conflicts of interest as borrowing industrialists were co-opted among their controlling owners. Poor corporate governance limited information disclosure by borrowing firms; this led to higher grades of opacity for investment projects' quality and industrial undertaking performances, and to higher risk for investment by universal banks.[46] The appointment of financiers to boards of directors also served to strengthen the long-run relationship between banks and industrial firms.

The collapse of the universal banks in the early 1930s led to a reshuffling of the financial elite in which industrialists—especially those at the head of the larger concerns operating in the capital-intensive sectors of the second industrial revolution—had an even higher weight. As a result, from the 1930s to the 1960s many top executives of Italy's largest companies sat on the boards of banks. Thus, Vittorio Valletta, chairman of Fiat from 1946 to 1966, and Carlo

---

[46] Stefano Battilossi, 'Did Governance Fail Universal Banks? Moral Hazard, Risk Taking, and Banking Crises in Interwar Italy', *Economic History Review* 2009 (62 special issue): 101–34; Carlo Brambilla, 'Miscarried Innovation? The Rise and Fall of Investment Banking in Italy, 1860s–1930s', *Entreprises et Histoire* 2012 (67): 97–117.

Faina, chairman of Italy's largest chemical firm Montecatini from 1946 to 1964, were also directors of the Credito Italiano, while Carlo Pesenti, managing director of Italy's largest cement firm Italcementi, sat also on the boards of two Lombard local banks and of one medium-term credit institute. Bankers retained the marginal position they formerly had (with about 10 per cent of the interlocks generated by the financial elite), while the major consequence of the end of universal banking was a reduction of the weight of financiers in the nation's financial and corporate elites.

In 1972, the nationalization of the electricity industry and the first signs of the crisis of Italian big business led to turnaround, with financiers gaining now a prominent position. Industrialists fell to a marginal position while bankers even disappeared from the elite.

The privatizations of the 1990s marked another turning point in the structure of the financial elite. The return of banks to a central position in the now weaker network was accompanied by the surge for the first time of bankers to a prominent position in the nation's financial elite. In 2001 bankers account for the majority of the financial elite (even though their interlocks were nearly one-third of the total), from which industrialists disappeared, the remainder being constituted by financiers.

The most prominent case of the surge of a banker at the top of Italy's financial elite was Giovanni Bazoli. He is the descendant of a Catholic family involved in politics since the early twentieth century, as his grandfather was one of the founders of the Italian People's Party (the Catholic inspired party) in 1919 and his father was a member of the Constituent Assembly for the Christian Democratic Party after the Second World War. Born in Brescia in 1932, and a graduate in Law, Bazoli was Professor of Administrative Law and Public Law at the Catholic University in Milan. While serving as director of the Banca San Paolo in Brescia, he was called by the government to contribute to the bailout of Banco Ambrosiano, Italy's second largest private bank that went bankrupt in 1982. Bazoli became the chairman of the Nuovo Banco Ambrosiano and in 1990 merged this bank with Banca Cattolica del Veneto, forming the Banco Ambrosiano Veneto. In 1997, the merger of this latter bank with Cariplo led to the creation of Banca Intesa, of which Bazoli became chairman. In 1999, Banca Intesa merged with Banca Commerciale Italiana establishing itself as Italy's largest bank, always with Bazoli as its chairman.

4.6 Conclusion

This chapter has analysed the structure of the Italian corporate network from 1913 to 2001 by considering a sample of the top 250 companies by total assets for seven benchmark years and using network analysis techniques.

The chapter has shown that the system was very cohesive from 1913 to 1960. The connectivity indexes remained substantially stable for the first four benchmark years; the highest values were observed in 1927, when the influence of the larger German-type universal banks reached its apex. The cohesion of the system declined starting from 1972, after the nationalization of the electricity industry. The disentangling of the network became even sharper in 1983 and 2001, probably as a consequence of the full emergence of the new technological trajectory of the third industrial revolution.

In a comparative perspective, in the period prior to the Second World War the structure of the Italian corporate network seems to have followed the same trend as Germany, even if at lower density values. Then Italy seems to have experienced an earlier and sharper decline of its network than the other major advanced economies. One major consequence of the massive privatizations that occurred in the 1990s was a return of banks to a central position in the now weaker network from which they had disappeared in the 1930s.

This chapter then analysed the BLs, defined as twenty individuals who in each benchmark year held the largest number of directorships in the Italian joint-stock companies—who can be considered as a proxy of the nation's corporate elite. These individuals accounted for a very high proportion of total IDs, ranging from 32 per cent in 1983 to little more than 50 per cent in 1927. There was a long-standing prevalence of BLs with origins from the North-Western regions of Italy, which was particularly strong in the first two benchmark years. Then, this situation underwent readjustment starting from the 1930s, as the formation of a large SOE sector widened the space for BLs born in other parts of the country. Already fairly high in 1913 with nearly one-half of the BLs being university graduates, the BL level of education increased in the years that followed. Significant changes took place regarding the field of study. In fact, while engineers prevailed in the beginning, over time there was a gradual turn towards graduates in law and in economics and business administration.

The BLs who held directorships in both banks and industrial firms can be considered as a proxy of the nation's financial elite. This chapter has shown that from 1913 to 1960 such a financial elite accounted for one-half or more of the whole corporate elite. Its weight fell slightly in 1972 after the nationalization of the electricity industry and then substantially in 1983 as a result of the sharp decline of the Italian corporate network. The financial elite rose again in 2001 following the return of banks to a central position in the network after the 1993 Banking Reform Law paved the way to a reintroduction of universal banking in Italy. Links between banks and industry were assured for a long time principally by industrialists and financiers, whereas bankers surged to a prominent position in the financial elite only in 2001.

Appendix: Top Twenty Big Linkers

1913

Surname and name	Age	Region of birth	Education	Seats
1. Esterle Carlo	60	Trentino-A.A.	BA: Engineering	17
2. Mazzotti Biancinelli Lodovico	43	Lombardy	BA: Law	11
2. Da Zara Giuseppe	58	Veneto	Not indicated	11
4. Belloni Gaetano	–	Lombardy	Not indicated	10
4. Mangili Cesare	63	Lombardy	SSD: Accountancy	10
6. Baragiola Pietro	59	Lombardy	BA: Agriculture	9
6. Conti Ettore	42	Lombardy	BA: Engineering	9
6. Della Torre Luigi	52	Piedmont	BA: Economics & Bus. Adm.	9
6. Falcone Giacomo	–	–	BA: Law	9
6. Pollone Eugenio	64	Piedmont	Not indicated	9
11. Joel Otto	57	Germany (overseas)	Not indicated	8
11. Mazzoni Cesare	–	–	BA: Law	8
11. Raggio Armando	58	Liguria	Not indicated	8
11. Toeplitz Giuseppe	47	Poland (overseas)	SSD: Classical school	8
11. Zander Carlo	–	–	BA: Engineering	8
16. Bertarelli Tommaso	76	Lombardy	Not indicated	7
16. Besso Marco	70	Friuli-V.G.	Not indicated	7
16. Castelbolognesi Giacomo	69	Emilia-Romagna	Not indicated	7
16. Ceriana Francesco	65	Piedmont	BA: Engineering	7
16. De Castro Osvaldo	–	–	Not indicated	7

Legend: BA Bachelor of Arts, Bus. Adm. Business Administration, SSD Secondary School Diploma.

1927

Surname and name	Age	Region of birth	Education	Seats
1. Panzarasa Rinaldo	50	Piedmont	BA: Law	19
1. Toeplitz Giuseppe	61	Poland (overseas)	SSD: Classical school	19
3. Conti Ettore	56	Lombardy	BA: Engineering	18
3. Lodolo Alberto	54	Piedmont	BA: Engineering	18
3. Mazzotti Biancinelli Lodovico	57	Lombardy	BA: Law	18
3. Ponti Gian Giacomo	49	Lombardy	BA: Engineering	18
7. Feltrinelli Carlo	46	Lombardy	SSD: Classical school	17
8. Garbagni Mario	49	Lombardy	BA: Engineering	16
8. Rossello Mario	50	–	SSD: Accountancy	16
10. Gaggia Achille	54	Veneto	BA: Engineering	15
11. Bocciardo Arturo	51	Liguria	BA: Engineering	13
11. Borletti Senatore	47	Lombardy	SSD: Accountancy	13
13. Motta Giacinto	57	Lombardy	BA: Engineering	12
14. Barberis Giovanni	–	–	BA: Engineering	11
14. Beneduce Alberto	50	Campania	BA: Mathematics	11
14. Benni Antonio Stefano	47	Piedmont	Not indicated	11
14. Covi Adolfo	–	–	BA: Engineering	11
14. Solza Mario	–	–	SSD: Accountancy	11
19. Besozzi Giuseppe	67	Piedmont	BA: Engineering	10
19. Della Torre Luigi	66	Piedmont	BA: Economics & Bus. Adm.	10

Legend: BA Bachelor of Arts, Bus. Adm. Business Administration, SSD Secondary School Diploma.

Financial Elites and European Banking

1936

Surname and name	Age	Region of birth	Education	Seats
1. Motta Giacinto	66	Lombardy	BA: Engineering	18
1. Beneduce Alberto	59	Campania	BA: Mathematics	15
3. Agnelli Giovanni	70	Piedmont	SSD: Classical school	13
3. Cenzato Giuseppe	54	Veneto	BA: Engineering	13
5. Cartesegna Francesco	54	Emilia-Romagna	BA: Engineering	12
5. Donegani Guido	59	Tuscany	BA: Engineering	12
5. Parisi Enrico	60	Sicily	Not indicated	12
8. Broglia Giuseppe	67	Veneto	BA: Economics & Bus. Adm.	11
8. Morpurgo Edgardo	70	Friuli-V.G.	SSD: Classical school	11
10. Bruno Luigi	40	Campania	BA: Law	10
10. Gaggia Achille	63	Veneto	BA: Engineering	10
10. Pirelli Alberto	54	Lombardy	BA: Law	10
13. Conti Ettore	65	Lombardy	BA: Engineering	9
13. Ferrerio Piero	54	Lombardy	BA: Engineering	9
13. Nizzola Agostino	67	Switzerland (overseas)	BA: Engineering	9
13. Rebaudengo Eugenio	72	Piedmont	BA: Law	9
13. Rossello Mario	59	–	SSD: Accountancy	9
18. Asinari Demetrio	58	Piedmont	Not indicated	8
18. Grassi Paolo	57	Marche	BA: Law	8
18. Maglione Girolamo	59	Campania	BA: Engineering	8

Legend: BA Bachelor of Arts, Bus. Adm. Business Administration, SSD Secondary School Diploma.

1960

Surname and name	Age	Region of birth	Education	Seats
1. Spada Massimo	55	Latium	BA: Law	19
1. Valerio Giorgio	56	Lombardy	BA: Engineering	19
3. De Biasi Vittorio	65	Lombardy	BA: Engineering	18
4. Torchiani Tullio	59	Sardinia	BA: Law	14
5. Bobbio Carlo	74	Lombardy	BA: Law	13
5. Marchesano Enrico	66	Sicily	BA: Law	13
5. Pesenti Carlo	53	Lombardy	BA: Engineering	13
5. Rossello Mario	83	–	SSD: Accountancy	13
9. Bruno Luigi	64	Campania	BA: Law	11
10. Falck Giovanni	60	Lombardy	BA: Engineering	10
10. Motta Galileo	54	Lombardy	BA: Law	10
10. Ricaldone Paolo	75	Piedmont	BA: Mathematics	10
13. Agnelli Giovanni (Gianni)	39	Piedmont	BA: Law	9
14. Bianchi Bruno	59	Umbria	BA: Engineering	8
14. Capanna Alberto	50	Abruzzo	BA: Economics & Bus. Adm.	8
14. Faina Carlo	66	Umbria	BA: Economics & Bus. Adm.	8
14. Prinetti Castelletti Ignazio	–	Lombardy	BA: Engineering	8
18. Arcaini Giuseppe	59	Lombardy	SSD: Normal school	7
18. Basola Enrico	–	–	BA: Law	7
18. Bazan Carlo	60	Piedmont	BA: Economics & Bus. Adm.	7

Legend: BA Bachelor of Arts, Bus. Adm. Business Administration, SSD Secondary School Diploma.

1972

Surname and name	Age	Region of birth	Education	Seats
1. Spada Massimo	67	Latium	BA: Law	20
2. Pesenti Carlo	65	Lombardy	BA: Engineering	13
3. Torchiani Tullio	71	Sardinia	BA: Law	10
3. Capanna Alberto	62	Abruzzo	BA: Economics & Bus. Adm.	10
5. Grandi Alberto	48	Lombardy	BA: Engineering	9
5. Lolli Ettore	64	Emilia-Romagna	BA: Engineering	9
7. Arcaini Giuseppe	71	Lombardy	SSD: Normal school	8
7. Calabria Fausto	50	Latium	BA: Law	8
7. Corsi Giorgio	49	Tuscany	BA: Law	8
10. Baldini Riccardo	62	Tuscany	BA: Engineering	7
10. Borletti Senatore jr.	–	Lombardy	Not indicated	7
10. Chiomenti Pasquale	58	Apulia	BA: Law	7
10. Destefanis Giovanni		Piedmont	SSD: Accountancy	7
10. Falck Bruno	70	Lombardy	BA: Engineering	7
10. Masturzo Tullio	–	–	BA: Engineering	7
10. Micchi Luigi	–	–	BA: Economics & Bus. Adm.	7
10. Tino Adolfo	72	Campania	BA: Law	7
18. Borri Silvio	77	Tuscany	BA: Economics & Bus. Adm.	6
18. Cesaroni Alberto	61	Tuscany	BA: Economics & Bus. Adm.	6
18. Dosi Mario	69	Apulia	BA: Law	6

Legend: BA Bachelor of Arts, Bus. Adm. Business Administration, SSD Secondary School Diploma.

1983

Surname and name	Age	Region of birth	Education	Seats
1. Garuzzo Giorgio	45	Piedmont	BA: Engineering	8
1. Mattioli Francesco Paolo	43	Latium	BA: Law	8
1. Romiti Cesare	60	Latium	BA: Economics & Bus. Adm.	8
4. Badile Didimo	62	Friuli-V.G.	BA: Engineering	7
4. Costa Giovanni Mario	–	–	BA: Engineering	7
6. Garrino Gian Luigi	48	Piedmont	BA: Economics & Bus. Adm.	6
6. Barbaglia Enzo	60	Lombardy	BA: Engineering	6
6. Pesenti Carlo	76	Lombardy	BA: Engineering	6
6. Pesenti Giampiero	52	Lombardy	BA: Engineering	6
6. Vezzalini Giancarlo	51	Emilia-Romagna	BA: Engineering	6
11. Cassaro Renato	43	Lombardy	BA: Economics & Bus. Adm.	5
11. Clavarino Giobatta	56	Liguria	BA: Engineering	5
11. Conciato Alvise	63	Friuli-V.G.	BA: Economics & Bus. Adm.	5
11. Cortesi Gaetano	71	Latium	BA: Economics & Bus. Adm.	5
11. Liberati Tommaso	60	Latium	BA: Engineering	5
11. Ortona Egidio	73	Piedmont	BA: Law	5
11. Rastelli Pietro	60	Emilia-Romagna	Not indicated	5
11. Rossi Carlo Eugenio	54	Piedmont	BA: Engineering	5
11. Venini Lino	74	Piedmont	SSD: Accountancy	5
20. Agnelli Giovanni (Gianni)	62	Piedmont	BA: Law	4

Legend: BA Bachelor of Arts, Bus. Adm. Business Administration, SSD Secondary School Diploma.

Financial Elites and European Banking

2001

Surname and name	Age	Region of birth	Education	Seats
1. Conti Fulvio	54	Latium	BA: Economics & Bus. Adm.	10
2. Barozzi Mario	38	Emilia-Romagna	BA: Economics & Bus. Adm.	9
3. Mion Gianni	58	Veneto	BA: Economics & Bus. Adm.	8
3. Tatò Francesco	69	Lombardy	BA: Philosophy	8
5. Benetton Gilberto	60	Veneto	Not indicated	7
5. Jaquinto Roberto	59	Latium	BA: Economics & Bus. Adm.	7
5. Moroni Alfredo	64	Umbria	BA: Statistics	7
8. Delfino Angelo	61	Liguria	Not indicated	6
9. Cerchiai Fabio	57	Tuscany	BA: Economics & Bus. Adm.	5
9. Profumo Alessandro	44	Liguria	BA: Economics & Bus. Adm.	5
9. Ripa di Meana Vittorio	74	Latium	BA: Law	5
9. Rocca Gianfelice	53	Lombardy	BA: Physics	5
13. Bazoli Giovanni	69	Lombardy	BA. Law	4
13. Berlusconi Piersilvio	32	Lombardy	SSD: Classical school	4
13. Bondi Enrico	67	Tuscany	BA: Chemistry	4
13. Cannatelli Pasquale	54	Calabria	BA: Economics & Bus. Adm.	4
13. Cirla Giorgio	61	Lombardy	Not indicated	4
13. Colombo Achille	62	Tuscany	BA: Engineering	4
13. Fabrizi Pier Luigi	53	Tuscany	BA: Economics & Bus. Adm.	4
13. Falck Alberto	63	Lombardy	BA: Economics & Bus. Adm.	4

Legend: BA Bachelor of Arts, Bus. Adm. Business Administration, SSD Secondary School Diploma.

5

French Bankers and the Transformation of the Financial System in the Second Half of the Twentieth Century

Laure Quennouëlle-Corre

5.1 Introduction: The Legendary Conservatism of the French Financial Elites

Historically, the French financial system is considered as representative of a state-oriented type of capitalism, and, from the end of the Second World War to the 1980s, as one of the most strictly regulated amongst European countries.[1] The traditional accusation of 'Malthusianism' (favouring well-established companies over new firms), which had been laid against French bankers and more generally against the French *patronat* since the beginning of the twentieth century, resurfaced after the Second World War. Policy-makers were able to make use of this wide consensus in order to legitimize an increased level of state intervention in financial affairs.

During the 1960s and 1970s, while capital markets and the banking system were kept under tight supervision, the financial system enabled France to remain one of the fast-growing European countries, with annual growth consistently reaching 5 per cent during three decades. From this perspective, financial leaders, state officials, and politicians did not consider it necessary to reform the financial system. Acceptance by the French banking elite of a strong regulatory regime was thus quite logical, and actually fairly widespread. French leading bankers felt at ease with the prevailing system, including working

---

[1] Laure Quennouëlle and André Straus, 'The State in the French Financial System during the Twentieth Century: A Specific Case?', in Stefano Battilossi and Jaime Reis (eds.), *State and Financial Systems in Europe and the USA* (Farnham, 2010), 97–121.

in state-owned banks—as evidenced by the network of former senior civil servants heading the country's large banks.

However, this reconstruction does not seem totally convincing in its simplistic assumptions. The purpose of this chapter is to reassess the role of French financial elites, especially bankers, in the context of a 'regulatory dialectic' proposed as a theoretical framework for this book. In fact, the position of financial elites has to be qualified. Several strategies have been set up by financial elites to face the regulatory system: they tried to benefit from regulations, but at the same time attempted to modify them; they were also able to bypass domestic rules by expanding banking activities beyond national boundaries, mainly through innovations. All three weapons were sometimes used simultaneously.

The chapter is divided into two parts. The first examines in more detail the above mentioned strategies (benefiting from regulation, lobbying for modification, and expanding abroad), concentrating on the three decades following the Second Word War. The second part considers the post-1981 period, marked by a double economic and financial change, first when the Socialists came to power, before being displaced by the Right in 1986. These upheavals had a direct impact on the financial sector and raise the question of the role of the financial elites: how did they react to the nationalizations and then the liberalization of the financial system? Was their position enhanced or diminished?

5.2 Financial Elites and the Regulated Financial System, 1945–1970s

This section analyses the means used by elite bankers to ease the effects of financial regulation or simply to avoid them—through think tanks and official institutions and through their individual networks within the body of the *inspecteurs des finances*. My purpose is to explain how they tried to benefit from the regulation. We will then see how they tried to bypass domestic rules before considering the way they attempted to modify the rules through targeted lobbying.

5.2.1 *Elites and the State: A Post-War Co-Management of Regulation*

Who were the French financial elites spanning the twentieth century? In this study, I will focus on bankers—the dominant group within the French financial word. Stockbrokers and other financial intermediaries were not considered as members of the upper class and did not really belong to the elites.

The first question concerns bankers' socio-professional recruitment. During the nineteenth century, internal or family recruitment for bank managers was a common practice in Western Europe. However, since the beginning of the twentieth century, the typical feature of the banking and financial industry was the development of external recruitment for that kind of appointment. From then on, career patterns of the banking elite changed. As a matter of fact, because of the growth of the banking industry and the development of financial services, new needs for managerial, commercial, technical, and legal competences appeared in the banking business: banks were looking more and more for external skills, and in Western Europe as a whole, family recruitment was generally on the decline, and even vanished, whereas in-house trained salaried managers competed with highly educated outsiders.

In France, external recruitment in the banking industry was quite specific compared to other countries. Since the late nineteenth century, top managers had been recruited from former high-ranking civil servants. It seems that the trend was actually reinforced after the Second World War, following the growth of state-owned and semi-public banking, and the nationalization of two-thirds of the stock market capitalization. Within the banking industry, senior managers[2] stemmed from several kinds of external recruitment: civil servants from the Ministry of Finance (*inspecteurs des finances*), engineers from the Ecole Polytechnique, business school graduates, in particular from HEC (Ecole des Hautes Etudes Commerciales de Paris), and graduates from Science Po and the Faculty of Law, whereas self-taught managers were in a minority. The *inspecteurs des finances* were considered as the government elite and were recruited by commercial banks as chairmen, except in the case of Paribas, an investment bank, where the appointment of well-known civil servants did not start before the end of the 1960s, with Jacques de Fouchier (1969–78, 1981–2) and Pierre Moussa (1978–81).

Apparently, the regulatory system put in place and developed after 1945 met with a consensus among financial elites, including the autarkic financial and monetary policy, since they could find their own interest through a state-controlled financial architecture. On the one hand, at the head of the big banks, they took advantage from the regulation to dominate the credit and financial system. The main example is given by the cartelization of credit and issuing protected by the state, which began during the interwar period. By 1929, a formal agreement between the six big commercial banks was signed in order to distribute the management of new issues on the financial market. After the Second World War, the cartel was maintained until the 1970s and developed on the credit market.

---

[2] The posts include: chairman, managing director, managing director assistant, and chairman advisers.

Table 5.1. Lead management and co-lead management of capital raising by the first hundred ranked French firms in 1963—credit and issuing

Lead or co-lead management	Crédit Lyonnais*	Société Générale*	CNEP*	Paribas	BNCI*	CCF	BUP	UEIF	Total*
Credit	28	19	13	8	5	5	3	5	94
Bonds	24	21	8	10	9	5	3	5	105
Stocks	17	13	5	7	6	7	6	4	93

The sum is different from 100 because not all the lead managers are named or some firms have several lead managers.
* State-owned banks.
Source: Archives Crédit Lyonnais, DAF 2067, 1962.

When looking at the details given in Table 5.1, it appears that the four state-owned banks were the lead managers for funds' raising by all state-owned companies (except Paribas which was in private hands). In 1975 the public banks[3] still accounted for 90 per cent of the co-lead issues. So it is obvious that the concentration of financing in a few banks was favoured by a cartel and vice versa. Moreover, since 1967, a conciliation procedure between the banks and the Treasury was set up, on the volume and the calendar of issuing. This support by the state reinforced the cartel, especially as the five largest banks were the only ones allowed to negotiate with the state for their own issues. The cartel was maintained very late. In 1975, when Banque de Suez and Crédit du Nord asked to enter the cartel, they were rejected.

The banking industry supported the segmented credit and the direct interest rate policy. It agreed to help declining industries as well as the 'national champions' when the Ministry of Finance asked it to do so. By supporting new industries and by subsidizing 'lame ducks', it is clear that this complacency succeeded in promoting social stability.[4] But on the other hand, financial elites maintained a system based on risk aversion and lack of innovation. During the three decades following the war, the majority of bankers and brokers were wary of liberalization and modernization because their guaranteed incomes inside the command system did not encourage innovation.

5.2.2 Avoiding Regulation and Implementing Innovations

The thinking process of dominant financial elites was probably based on a real attachment to the state's role, a French consensus legitimated by necessary economic reconstruction after the war. But senior civil servants from the Ministry of Finance could also change their mind when moving to the banking sector

---

[3] Public banks only numbered three because of BNCI and CNEP's merger and the creation of the Banque nationale de Paris (BNP) in 1966.
[4] Michael Maurice Loriaux, *France after Hegemony* (New York, 1991).

and from then on, they tried to avoid regulation. This is best illustrated by two examples: the creation of mutual funds and the internationalization of banks.

One of the main innovations launched by the banks is the creation of the Undertakings for Collective Investment in Transferable Securities (UCITS), called SICAV in France (Sociétés d'investissements à capital variable). For a long time collective investments were not allowed in France because of resistance from both the Ministry of Finance and stockbrokers.[5] Thanks to lobbying by some persevering bankers,[6] the law was changed in 1963. From 1964, numerous SICAVs were created thanks to a partnership between investment banks and deposit banks: Sogevar, Epargne-Valeur, Epargne mobilière, Optima, Soginter, and others. Crédit Lyonnais was the most dynamic bank and launched three SICAVs on its own. By 1975, thanks to the SICAVs, the number of investors on the stock market had reached one million (Table 5.2).

To avoid the regulatory system set up for domestic purposes, banks began developing international activities towards the end of the 1960s. At the time, the euro–dollar market played a major role in the reopening of European financial systems and the globalization of banking activities.[7] Influenced by American banks, established mainly in London, but also in the rest of Europe, European banks learnt new practices, launched new financial instruments such as swaps and roll-over credits, expanded branches around the world, and participated in international consortia in the euro-credit and the euro-bond markets. The more the domestic capital markets were controlled, the

Table 5.2. Funds raised by the SICAV of the three big deposit banks (millions of francs)

	1964	1965	1966	1967	1968	1969	Total
Crédit Lyonnais Slivam Slivafrance Slivarente	135	145.2	108.4	127.4	578.3	578.4	1921.5
Société Générale Sogevar Soginter Sogepargne	89.6	109	67.5	80.8	530.7	582.6	1654.6
BNP Epargne Valeur (Unival) Epargne Obligations	71.6	89.3	78.5	61.7	645.9	848.8	2095.5

Source: Archives Crédit Lyonnais, 135 AH 42, 16/09/1970.

---

[5] I developed this point in a recent book, *La place financière de Paris. Des ambitions contrariées* (Paris, 2015), 217–20.
[6] Jacques de Fouchier for instance.
[7] Catherine Schenk, 'The Origins of the Eurodollar Market in London: 1955–1963', *Explorations in Economic History* 1999 (35.2): 221–38.

more the French banks tried to encourage business beyond the frontiers. Some dynamic banks, such as Paribas, established subsidiaries in New York and London in order to profit from capital markets' developments. The investment bank became one of the top ten lead managers and co-lead managers of international issues between 1963 and 1972, just behind Deutsche Bank, Warburg, and White Weld.[8] By 1973, Crédit Lyonnais had created Europartners Securities Corporation in New York, while Société Générale continued its international development throughout the world, according to Altamura.[9]

This paradoxical situation, which led to a 'double life' of the French banking system in the 1970s, resulted from the ambiguous attitude of the government's financial elites, who maintained a strong regulation of the domestic credit, while allowing banks to develop their international operations. Herein lies the question of relationships between public and private financial elites.

5.2.3 Lobbying and Networks

The first advantage of recruiting a former high-ranking civil servant is what is called 'social capital'. Generally, these civil servants belonged to the economic elite, with an upper-class social background. Thanks to their social status, they were close to industrial managers, government officials, and political leaders. Above all, they conveyed to the bank an 'information capital', which is essential for its very survival. In order to evaluate the risks when making loans, commercial banks and merchant banks need to get information regarding the activities of each industry or business, the financial situation of a company, technical innovations, upcoming political decisions, and so on. This precious information was easily passed on by *inspecteurs des finances*, thanks to their social capital and their relationships with former and current civil servants—because every financial state institution, every regulatory authority used to appoint one of them as chairman or secretary general. They were present in all the domestic financial centres of influence, as the recent *Dictionnaire historique des inspecteurs des finances* forcefully demonstrates.[10]

Specifically, they formed the major part of the think tanks in charge of financial reflection. At the time, the most dynamic were the Commissariat général au Plan, the Monetary Studies Department of the Banque de France, and the Conseil économique et social. Except for the Banque de France, where economists were the main experts, these institutions comprised officials, bankers, and businessmen. Within the group, many *inspecteurs des finances*

---

[8] Archives BNP-Paribas, DOFI, 233–6, 29 September 1972.
[9] Eduardo Altamura, *European Banks and the Rise of International Finance: The Post-Bretton Woods Era* (London and New York, 2017).
[10] Fabien Cardoni, Nathalie Carré de Malberg, and Michel Margairaz (eds.), *Dictionnaire historique des inspecteurs des finances, 1801–2009* (Paris, 2012).

actively strived at modernizing the French financial system. The role of the planning institution is particularly interesting. Since the 1960s, the Commissariat Général au Plan had been one of the leading reformers—and that is an irony of history.[11] It repeated its recommendations in 1978-9, claiming that the French financial system was too highly compartmentalized and recommended a suppression of the 'encadrement du crédit' (credit tightening), segmented credit and specialized finance circuits.

An example of their influence can be pointed out when, at the end of the 1970s, most of the experts from the Plan, the Banque de France,[12] and the INSEE (the economic studies department of the Ministry of Finance) suddenly became aware of the asphyxia of firms (heavy indebtedness) and of the need for funds from the state (rise of deficit spending). As a matter of fact, the 'overdraft economy' appeared to be an obstacle to pulling out of the crisis, in the context of an inflationary period and floating exchange rates. In order to stop inflation, it appeared necessary to adapt the French economy to the new international environment. Financial elites began to press for a modernization of the financial market, for instance the quoting and trading system on the Stock Exchange. For the first time, the whole financial architecture set up since the war was challenged. And for once, as the situation became more dramatic, they began to be heard by policy-makers.

However, the behaviour of the various components of the financial elites cannot be assessed on the same basis. The corporation of the *inspecteurs des finances* can be considered as a whole. The senior civil servants, who were appointed by banks at the beginning of their career, did not have the same expertise and the same skills as those who had been trained as civil servants for decades. They didn't even have the same state of mind. The former turned out to be good entrepreneurs, whereas the latter were filled with interventionist ideology and a state-controlled attitude. This could be an explanation for their different attitudes towards innovation, since at the time, in France, innovation was often confused with liberalization. At the eve of the second globalization, a divide could then be identified between innovators and conservative elite bankers in France, a divide that tended to overlap the traditional distinction between investment and deposit bankers, as well as between elites from the private sector and senior civil servants. The best example is that of Jacques Mayoux (*inspecteur des finances*, managing director of Crédit Agricole between

---

[11] In 1946, the CGP was created to plan economic recovery and created then a restrictive frame for industrial and financial sectors. At the end of the war the Plan became an original institution where high civil servants, businessmen, and trade unionists met regularly to discuss the economic and social situation. The Reports of the CGP were read with attention by policy-makers although they did not often follow their recommendations.

[12] Eric Monnet, 'La politique de la Banque de France au sortir des Trente Glorieuses: un tournant monétariste? / The Policy of the Banque de France in the 1970s: A Monetarist Turn?', *Revue d'histoire moderne et contemporaine* 2015 (62.1): 147–74; Loriaux, *France after Hegemony*.

1963 and 1975), who upset the recruitment of managers at the mutual bank in the 1960s: as the new managers were high civil servants from the Ministry of Finance, they appeared as more efficient and modern managers than the traditional agrarian notables.[13]

We can classify the body of financial elites of the post-war generation into four categories:

(1) *Managers or administrators*. This major group aggregates the main corps of the Treasury's senior civil servants: they entered a commercial bank after ten or fifteen years spent in the civil service. So they kept close links with the controlling authority and were not entirely independent from the government. They were present in every kind of bank, of any size. They served the company thanks to their social capital, relations and information networks in business and government. They were not regarded as pioneers but could play a role in the financial change of the 1980s. The best example is that of Dominique Chatillon, who had a long-standing career in the banking industry: CFO at the Caisse des dépôts et consignations (1967–74), and CEO of Credit industriel et commercial (1978–82) and then of Compagnie La Hénin (1983–90). He took an active part in the think tanks that were emerging at the time within the banking system.

(2) *Financiers and builders*. This group is formed by a minority of bankers who can be considered as entrepreneurs. They entered early in the banking industry where they were trained from the inside by climbing the corporate ladder from managerial posts. They expanded the bank's activities and favoured financing modernization, but were not implicated in policy-making. They launched innovations like consumer credit (Jacques de Fouchier at Paribas). They built financial empires such as the quartet of managers at group Suez: Jacques Georges-Picot, Michel Caplain, Dominique de Grièges, and Jack Francès. This group of bankers was very independent from the government. Their priority was to serve the firm, but thanks to their good standing connections they were able to have an influence over the entire banking system in order to modernize it.

(3) *'Policy-makers'*. This very small group of bankers was close to political power and had a direct influence on its decisions. They worked at the Minister's cabinet and thus became very close to the political staff. They were appointed directly at the top of the firm. They benefited from an important social and political capital, almost since the beginning of the Fifth Republic in 1958. They could facilitate the Minister's control of the

---

[13] Hubert Bonin, 'Les inspecteurs des finances et la modernisation de la firme bancaire depuis la fin du XIXe siècle', in Cardoni, Carré de Malberg, and Margairaz (eds.), *Dictionnaire historique*, 335.

banking industry if they belonged to the same political party. They constituted a real vector for the government's influence over the financial system. Crédit Lyonnais inherited most of these types of profile: François Bloch-Lainé, Jean Saint-Geours, Jean-Yves Haberer. That group also includes bankers who helped the Minister of Finance to reform the French banking system. The iconic leader from this perspective is certainly Maurice Lorain, an *inspecteur des finances* who entered the Société Générale very early and became its CEO in 1967. He became the president of the Investment Commission which engaged a decisive reform of the banking system in the 1960s. He wrote the *Conseil économique et social* report on mutual funds in 1968.

(4) *International bankers*. A minority, the international bankers were an exception before 1980. They presented a very interesting profile, because of their ability to put some pressure on the government thanks to their relationships and their receptivity to innovation. Most of them have been appointed at Paribas, like Pierre Moussa and Bernard de Margerie, but Marc Viénot at the Société Générale also belonged to that small group of pioneers.

To sum up, a minor part of *inspecteurs des finances* played a crucial role in trying to reform the financial market, but as a whole, financial elites seemed to have had an ambiguous attitude: on the one hand, some of them advocated liberalization; on the other hand, at the head of the banks, most of them did not act in favour of internationalization and competition and preferred to maintain a profitable autarkic system.

5.3 A Changing Attitude toward Innovation since the 1980s?

After the 1980s, internationalization became a survival issue for banks and that is why most of the financial elites converted to liberalization and deregulation. How did this change occur so rapidly? Several factors played a role, but it is difficult to hierarchize them. Undoubtedly, the international context played a major role, from monetary constraint to the pressure of other countries or institutions. But the financial elites, at least some of them, also played the game.

5.3.1 *The International Context as a Booster of Financial Reform*

The liberalization process in the United States and the United Kingdom put pressure on other developed countries. The Thatcher government's measures of deregulation and privatization were certainly considered with attention by Paris. The London Big Bang, planned for October 1986, opened the

Stock Exchange to competition. But it was not the only model. The Canadian computer assisted trading system was adopted in Paris. Although the creation of the European Options Exchange in 1978 was rejected by the Treasury, some French stockbrokers decided to become dealers on this market. On the other hand, the EEC stimulated innovation by ordering several reports on technological connection between European members. In particular, the SEA (Single European Act), signed in Luxembourg on 17 February 1986, accelerated the process of financial harmonization between European partners.

5.3.2 *Financial Asphyxia and the Changing Attitude of Financial Elites*

By the eve of the 1980s, the French economic and financial situation could not continue much longer. Undoubtedly the development of financial markets was linked to an increasing need for funds from governments and the wish of firms to raise capital at a less expensive cost on the markets. As outlined above, interest rates reached a dramatic level between 1979 and 1984. The rationed credit policy showed its limits and led to 'asphyxia' in firms.

Banks became aware of the great benefits that market activities could grant. After the debt crisis of 1982, which brought about severe losses to European banks, their strategies consisted in a reorientation of the banking trade towards financial activities or market operations to the detriment of their traditional role of credit intermediaries. Therefore, the main banks' activities shifted towards financial operations in the beginning of the 1980s, favouring disintermediation. On the other hand, the monopoly of stockbrokers on the Paris Bourse had been in existence since 1816. Only forty-five brokerage houses were operating on the Paris Bourse, and these ran into difficulties when the volume of trading was booming at the end of 1970s. Faced with the increasing development of dealing and the futures markets' project, they had no other choice than to accept the end of monopoly and the alliance with their traditional enemy, the banks. Furthermore, French brokers had to face traditional competition with the London Stock Exchange. The two financial centres had been rivals since the middle of the nineteenth century, despite the City's continued predominance. As the United Kingdom joined the EEC in 1972, and capital flows began circulating more freely throughout developed countries throughout the 1970s, competition became stronger and stronger. London brokers directly approached smaller French firms in order to convince them, with some success, to be quoted in London. The London Stock Exchange (LSE) developed a modern technical system for computing, quoting, and clearing. The know-how of the City was growing and producing innovations, including the futures market established in 1982 (LIFFE). Starting on 26 October 1986, all British and foreign banks were allowed to take a stake in the capital of the major City stockbroking firms. This was the beginning of the

British Big Bang. It encouraged French brokers to accept the Stock Exchange reform law of January 1988. Moreover, to avoid the risk of being completely rejected from the futures market, brokers needed to be backed by French or foreign banks. The big banks quickly seized the opportunity to do what they had claimed for decades: entering the financial market and developing trading activities all over the world. They followed up with modernization and became important actors of the internationalization of the French economy. Since then, they have developed new products and services, expanded abroad, and become more exposed to competition and risk. During that period of liberalization, financial elites obviously supported change and innovation.

Despite the dramatic political change of 1981 to the left wing, the will to reform the financial system did not really stop at that moment and liberal reforms began to take place a few years later. The political context changed radically and forced financial elites to adapt to new economic policies.

When François Mitterrand came to power in 1981, state interventionism reached a peak with the increase of deficit spending, the reinforcement of a credit squeeze and of exchange controls, the nationalization of a wide range of banks[14] and industrial firms, and the reinforcement of selective credit policy in favour of nationalized industries. The 1981–2 period appears as a short parenthesis while the financial reforms, which were more or less engaged at the end of 1970s, marked time. The innovation moved towards the side of economic and social Keynesian policies more than towards the financial one.[15]

Policy-makers intended to tightly control the allocation of credit in order to establish their economic programme, which gave a priority to the investments of nationalized firms. In fact, nationalization did not mean a reinforcement of business control and Prime Minister Pierre Mauroy declared that the government would not interfere with the banks' management and even allow them to expand beyond the borders. As a whole, government intervention was limited to domestic financing.

Although the governance of the banks was completely transformed and the boards of directors entirely changed, bank management remained basically the same. In fact, after the access of the Socialists to the government in 1981, the managerial elite based on *grand corps* membership did not change in the big banks. Albeit the nationalization of banks led to the appointment of new managers, the latter still belonged to the *inspection des finances*, except Jean

---

[14] Thirty-nine banks and two financial companies passed under state control (100 per cent of the capital owned by the state).
[15] See Serge Berstein, Pierre Milza, and Jean-Louis Bianco (eds.), *Les années Mitterrand, les années du changement 1981–1984* (Paris, 2001); David R. Cameron, 'The Colors of a Rose: On the Ambiguous Record of French Socialism', *Center for European Studies, Working Papers*, 1988, no. 12, 1–70.

Deflassieux (Law degree) at the head of Crédit Lyonnais and Jean Peyrelevade (Polytechnique) at Suez. New managers were chosen because of their expertise and their political affinities, or their acceptable neutrality.[16] When the Right came back to power in 1986 and privatized the banks between 1986 and 1995, the same phenomenon occurred: the recruitment of top banking managers was based on the same criteria as *inspection des finances'* membership.

As the power of policy-makers became dominant, did the financial elites in both private and public banks still play an influential role in financial policy, in terms of regulation for example? The nationalization of Paribas appears as an emblematic event in order to evaluate bankers' attitude in the face change, through the role of three *inspecteurs des finances* who were named successively at the head of the bank in less than two years. From confrontation to accommodation, they showed different ways of overcoming what appeared as adversity. Pierre Moussa, Chairman of the bank in 1981, decided to resist nationalization by selling unofficially the banks' assets to a foreign firm located in Switzerland. When the plot was discovered, the big scandal forced Moussa to resign. Jacques de Fouchier, former Chairman of Cofimer and Suez, founder of the Compagnie bancaire in 1959, and former CEO of Paribas from 1968 to 1978, replaced Moussa in October 1981. In total opposition to his predecessor, he tried to alleviate political pressure thanks to his personal network within the Socialist Party and recommended the recruitment of the Directeur du Trésor, Jean-Yves Haberer, as Chairman of the public group. His suggestion, finally accepted by the President of the Republic himself, is indicative of his level of influence. Thanks to his reputation and stature, Jean-Yves Haberer succeeded in restricting the state's hold by maintaining Paribas's international position and avoiding political interference in its management.[17] At different levels, each of these three financiers played a specific role in Paribas's nationalization. One chose confrontation, the two others preferred accommodation. Although they did not agree with the nationalization, they tried to circumvent the political rule, while the government actually proved less directive than it declared itself to be.

At the beginning of 1982, the French economic and monetary situation had seriously deteriorated, forcing the government to change its policy. From an international point of view, the American restrictive monetary policy since 1979 increased the balance of payments deficit and indirectly the cost of credit. The evolution of the dollar directly affected the franc–mark parity—in a

---

[16] Vivien Ann Schmidt, *From State to Market? The Transformation of French Business and Government* (Cambridge, 1996).

[17] Laure Quennouëlle-Corre, 'Paribas et le monde: les enjeux d'une nationalisation', in Florence Descamps, Roger Nougaret, and Laure Quennouëlle-Corre (eds.), *Idendités croisées. Banques et sociétés aux XIX–XXIe siècles. Hommages à Pierre de Longuemar* (Brussels, 2016).

negative sense for the French currency, which was devalued three times in less than two years. Moreover, the fight against inflation, decided in the United States and Germany, created a gap with the French Keynesian policy. France was isolated. If the government wanted to maintain its international position, it had to change its monetary and economic policy. This occurred at the beginning of 1983, when the inflation rate reached 14 per cent and the position of the franc became unsustainable, and the crucial question became whether to leave the EEC or to completely change the economic policy. By March 1983, François Mitterrand chose to stay in the European Union, devalued the franc once more, and established a rigorous plan to reduce deficit spending and inflation. The so-called *tournant de la rigueur* (the turn towards austerity) meant that an austerity policy was gradually replacing the initial stimulus plan. At the same time, the financial and banking reforms, which had been postponed in 1981, came back to the agenda.

After the austerity plan of 1983, a series of measures were taken in favour of savings, in order to revitalize domestic investment. The aim of Jacques Delors, Minister of Economy and Finance, was to direct savings towards firms' financing, possibly through the financial markets. Symbol of the beginning of a supply policy in favour of firms, new savings instruments were introduced, such as the 'Livret d'épargne populaire', 'Compte d'épargne en actions', and CODEVI which were much appreciated. As for the financial markets' development, the second market for unlisted securities was finally created in February 1983. Certificates of participation (*titres participatifs*) and investment certificates (*certificats d'investissements*) offered new opportunities for firms to raise funds on the market. In January 1984, a Banking Act, decided by the Ministry of Economy and Finance, began to modernize the banking industry.[18] Once more, the decision was in the hands of the government. But the main reforms of the capital markets were to come.

5.3.3 *1984–1986: The Big Leap Forward*

In 1984, a new government was formed, presenting a more realistic programme. The new Minister of Economy and Finance, Pierre Bérégovoy, an autodidact and pragmatic socialist, decided to fight against the privileges held by banks and to reduce the cost of financing for both private firms and the

---

[18] The decompartmentalization of the banking sector was effective in the late 1990s. Pierre-Henri Cassou, 'Seize ans de réorganisation bancaire en France', *Revue d'économie financière* 2001 (61): 13–30.

state. He intended to radically change the financial landscape within eighteen months, before the parliamentary elections. So he imposed a fast rhythm to his financial reform and forced officials and operators to cooperate. The main examples of this profound change were the creation of the futures market (MATIF) in 1985 and the negotiable options market (MONEP) in 1987, and of a Treasury bond market. From then on, every investor, individual or non-financial firm, or bank, could buy and sell financial products on a wide capital market which extended from short term to long term. That was the end of the subdivision of finance and credit.

Disintermediation was underway with the dramatic growth of capital markets. The volume of new securities issues multiplied by five between 1982 and 1986, from 65.5 to 346 billion francs. With 26 million contracts negotiated in 1989, the outstanding success of the new MATIF, which was soon to become one of the leading futures markets in the world, looked very impressive.

As for banks, their involvement in market activities changed their business, now operating from the monetary market to the futures market. The end of the stockbrokers' monopoly had arrived. The major deposit and investment banks bought out the majority of the French brokers' firms. The banks' raid over capital markets enlarged the market's liquidity, which could not be provided by brokers alone. Fees and banking commissions were reduced, and, from then on, bonds became freely negotiable. The introduction of negotiable bank certificates of deposit (*certificats de dépôts*) increased the banks' resources and reduced their dependence on the central bank's discounting. As of 1985, a series of measures liberalized the banking system: the *encadrement du crédit* was progressively abolished, the majority of subsidized loans were suppressed, and partial monopolies over deposits and lending were dismantled.

5.3.4 *The Decisive Political Impulse*

In fact, the political approach appears to have been decisive. Many of the reforms introduced between 1983 and 1988, such as the second market and the futures markets, were ready to be voted on. The role of 'public financial elites' has to be underlined here. During the previous two decades, economists of the Banque de France and experts from the Commissariat au Plan alerted policy-makers to the necessary reforms of the financial system. But due to the cautious attitude of the Treasury, the unwillingness of policy-makers, and the reluctance of financial intermediaries, no decision was made. From this perspective, the role of Pierre Bérégovoy and his close circle of advisers must be emphasized. The Minister of Finance was determined to suppress traditionally protected and strictly regulated capital markets. In order to do this, he was helped by two iconoclast civil servants: Jean-Charles Naouri, a brilliant mathematician, and Claude Rubinowicz, a physicist who had a good experience of capital markets.[19] The two scientists did not apply any economic theory, but a mathematical logic to reduce the cost of financing. Moreover, they were free of attachment within the civil service and were indifferent to any lobby. To make their decision, the trio combined three assets: power, legitimacy, and skill. Often reforms fail to succeed because one of these qualities is lacking. But in 1984, this exceptional configuration came into being and thus allowed France to enter globalization. For that part of the story, financial elites were not in the limelight.

5.3.5 The Liberal Programme of 1986: The Beginning of Privatizations

When the Right came back to power in 1986 for only two years, its programme was based on the liberalization of the French economy. The programme, established by Edouard Balladur, the Minister of Economy and Finance, was based on the suppression of prices and exchange controls, the development of competition inside the economy thanks to deregulation, especially through an ambitious programme of privatization according to which no less than sixty-five firms were supposed to be privatized, including forty-one banks and insurance companies.[20] In two years, it succeeded in reforming large parts of the economy, but the 1988 elections were won by the Socialists who delayed liberalization reforms until the 1990s. Yet similarities between the financial policy pursued by the Socialists after 1984 and the one pursued by the Right in 1986–8 tend to put into perspective the so-called 'dramatic changes' which occurred during the decade. Since then, the state continuously lost its intervention's tools in the economic area, while the reinforcement of the European Union's power reduced its policy space.

From this perspective, privatizations, which insidiously began between 1983 and 1986, clearly exemplify the political continuity, in terms of state ruling, that marked the period.[21] First of all, the general philosophy of the French privatization's programme was quite original: the operation primarily aimed at developing economic democracy, which could be achieved by the access of small savers to the capital of French big firms; the second aim was to allow employees to partake in a firm's management and benefits.[22]

Secondly, decision-making belonged entirely to the government, especially to the Minister of Economy and Finance, Edouard Balladur. Banks were not

---

[19] Both were also *inspecteurs des finances*, but they studied at Princeton and experienced American financial deregulation. They entered the Ministry of Finance after several years of external professional experience and had a different mind-set compared to that of the civil servants.

[20] Only five banks were privatized in 1986–8, one in 1993, and the rest of the banks during the last decade of the twentieth century.

[21] Michel Durupty, *Les privatisations en France* (Paris, 1988).

[22] 'Vers la liberté. La réforme économique 1986' (Paris: La Documentation française, 1987). This was a concern of the Gaullist party in the 1960s.

consulted, nor were other firms. With the help of a committee of senior civil servants (Commission de privatization) and of the Treasury Department (Philippe Jaffré), he decided in last resort the whole process, the list of firms to privatize, the list of advisory banks, the schedule of privatizations, even the price of shares. But the most important issue lies in the creation of *noyaux durs*, which can be defined as a hard core of cross-shareholdings between the major players in banks and industry. Balladur wanted to protect the capital of French firms and to avoid hostile takeover bids or major foreign shareholders. The consequence was that banks became significant shareholders of the industrial firms as well as active investors in the industrial sector.

As for the management of privatized banks, as with the Socialists in 1982, the right-wing government changed the heads of the major banks in 1987–8 and again in 1993–5. Once more, the *inspection des finances* was in the front row in banks and insurance companies, but new profiles appeared amongst the chairmen of the big banks.[23] According to Vivien Schmidt,[24] these new managers were quite different: they were younger, with a dynamic approach to management—'business friendly', as we would say today. They accompanied the development of business in a new deregulated environment and their power was reinforced by interlocking directorships: corporate governance was profoundly modified and managers became more and more powerful. According to Morin, the 'hard core' created a systemic break in the heart of the financial system, by dismantling the public pole and creating a model of corporate governance based on particular property rights called 'circular property'.[25]

From this perspective, on the eve of the twenty-first century, private financial elites seemed to have become more and more independent from the state. But this issue needs further discussion, as relationships between government and business are still intricate in terms of the new French capitalism.[26]

5.4 Conclusion

To conclude, two points have to be made regarding the dialectical relationship between regulation and innovation. For fifty years, the traditional appointment of senior civil servants from the Ministry of Finance at the top of the

---

[23] For instance the new CEO of Paribas in 1986, Michel François-Poncet was not a former civil servant (Harvard and Science-Po) and his successor in 1992, André Lévy-Lang, was trained at a Polytechnique.
[24] Schmidt, *From State to Market?*
[25] François Morin, 'Privatisation et dévolution des pouvoirs: le modèle français du gouvernement d'entreprise', *Revue économique* 1996 (47.6): 1262.
[26] See for instance Stéphane Denis, *Le roman de l'argent. Une histoire secrète des rapports entre le pouvoir financier et le pouvoir politique sous le premier septennat de François Mitterrand* (Paris, 1988) and Nazanine Ravai, *La République des vanités. Petits et grands secrets du capitalisme français* (Paris, 1997).

banking industry maintained the domination of the same elite on the financial system. In terms of financial regulation and innovation, such a situation led to different consequences. First of all, the elite played a crucial role in establishing a state-based system in France, almost until the 1970s. For their own benefit, bankers accommodated to state intervention and regulation or circumvented them when possible. Finally, at the beginning of the 1980s, a minority of the financial elite helped to reform the strongly regulated system inherited from the war by riding the liberal wave coming across the Atlantic, considered as a good opportunity for profits. Some of them played a special role in the reopening of the French economy and the modernization of its financial and banking systems.

They all belonged to the same upper class, benefited from the same education and training, and yet, as we outlined, they displayed a variety of attitudes and a plurality of roles. Their relationships with policy-makers were based on a community of views, of language, and an exchange of courtesies (give-and-take relationships). Financial elites cannot be just perceived as a ruling elite capable of directing economic policy, they also happen to be a more or less powerful lobby depending on different periods.

This short study offers an opportunity to discuss a broader question: the nature of French capitalism and its evolution since the end of the Second World War. After a period characterized by 'state capitalism', when government was interventionist, a new era of French capitalism, a 'state-enhanced capitalism' has come into being since the 1990s, in which the state still plays an active, albeit much reduced, role.[27] Recent publications have already underlined this particular feature (Schmidt, Monnet) but most academic studies continue to refer to the advent of a so-called neoliberalism in France (Denord, Orléan, Théret) as a dramatic break, which set France on the road to financialization and led the country towards the Anglo-American model. The issue opens up a vast debate that cannot be discussed here, but that deserves to be studied more specifically.[28]

---

[27] According to Vivien Ann Schmidt, 'French Capitalism Transformed, Yet a Third Variety of Capitalism', *Economy and Society* 2003 (32.4): 526–54. See also Elisabetta Gualmini and Vivien Ann Schmidt, 'State Transformation in Italy and France: Technocratic versus Political Leadership on the Road from Non-Liberalism to Neo-Liberalism', in Vivien Ann Schmidt and Mark Thatcher (eds.), *Resilient Liberalism in Europe's Political Economy* (Cambridge, 2013).

[28] See, for instance, Florence Descamps and Laure Quennouëlle-Corre (eds.), 'Le tournant de mars 1983 a-t-il été libéral?', Dossier, *Vingtième siècle. Revue d'histoire*, Numéro 138, April–June 2018.

6

Trust and Regulation in Corporate Capital Markets before 1914

Leslie Hannah

6.1 Introduction

The nations of the pre-1914 world were united internally and also internationally linked by railways, shipping lines, and cable communications, most (whether owned by governments or capitalists) financed by equities and (corporate or government) bonds. The majority of these—and industrial and financial sector securities—were listed on the stock exchanges of Europe, notably London, Paris, Berlin, Amsterdam, Brussels, Vienna, and St Petersburg. The New York Stock Exchange (NYSE) was the only non-European exchange to rival them in size,[1] but—unlike most major European exchanges and like smaller exchanges elsewhere—was largely domestically orientated; and many of its securities were also listed in Europe (about a fifth of NYSE-listed corporate securities by value were European-owned).[2] This globalized world is commonly pictured as the heyday of free market capitalism, though the trust essential for international securities issuance was arguably at least as much derived from confidence in governments.[3] Of the securities (by values at par) listed on the London Stock Exchange 46 per cent were (British, colonial, or foreign) government securities; and on some other exchanges the government portion was

---

[1] The NYSE was (by par values of all listed securities, a measure which flatters it, because US—but not European—securities were generally quoted below par) about half the size of the LSE, equal in size to Paris, Berlin, or Amsterdam and about twice the size of the others or of Manchester, a British provincial exchange.

[2] In 1914 only 16 per cent of NYSE securities were foreign or colonial. Of the European exchanges mentioned, only St Petersburg (which was legally limited to domestic securities) was less internationally orientated.

[3] Leslie Hannah, 'Leading Stock Exchanges before 1914: States, Bonds and Equities' (forthcoming).

even higher: 60 per cent on Berlin, 64 per cent on Paris, and 76 per cent on St Petersburg.[4] If we added corporate securities guaranteed by national or colonial governments—such as Russian, French, Argentine, or Indian railways—the portions that were government-backed would be even higher. We have gained some understanding of the political mechanisms which promoted domestic trust in state borrowing[5] and also the methods by which empires or financial intermediaries—notably the Rothschilds, Barings, and HSBC—enabled some distant governments to gain the confidence of European investors,[6] at least until their world was undermined by the First World War. There is, however, much less consensus on how capitalist corporations had been able to gain the trust of national and international investors, in most cases without government guarantees. That is the problem addressed here.

6.2 The Agency Problem: and Solutions

Why should investors trust the managers of the purely private-sector companies whose shares (or bonds) they own? Modern writings on corporate governance focus on the difficulties that shareholders (the 'principals') encounter with company directors (their 'agents'). This 'agency' problem—deriving from unequal information and misaligned incentives—is viewed as a critical barrier to the development of the modern managerial corporation in which ownership is divorced from control. At least as old as Adam Smith, this view is still surprisingly resilient even after it has apparently been proved wrong by the rise of the corporate economy in the nineteenth century and its reinforcement in the twentieth. Today discussion by financial economists routinely assumes that directors of public companies wish to feather their

---

[4] Again the NYSE was an outlier among large exchanges, with only 12 per cent of listed par values being government securities.

[5] Douglass C. North, John Joseph Wallis, and Barry R. Weingast, *Violence and Social Orders: A Conceptual Framework for Interpreting Recorded Human History* (New York, 2009); Timothy Besley and Torsten Persson, 'The Origins of State Capacity: Property Rights, Taxation and Politics', *American Economic Review* 2009 (99.4): 1218–44.

[6] Marc Flandreau, 'Collective Action Clauses before they had Airplanes: Bondholder Committees and the London Stock Exchange in the 19th Century (1827–1868)', Graduate Institute of International Studies and Development, Geneva, January 2013 working paper; Marc Flandreau and Juan Z. Flores, 'Bonds and Brands: Foundations of Sovereign Debt Markets, 1820–1830', *Journal of Economic History* 2009 (69.3): 646–84; Marc Flandreau and Juan Z. Flores, 'Bondholders versus Bond-Sellers: Investment Banks and Conditionality Lending in the London Market for Foreign Government Debt, 1815–1913', *European Review of Economic History* 2012 (16.4): 356–83; Marc Flandreau, Juan Z. Flores, Norbert Gaillard, and Sebastián Nieto-Parra, 'The End of Gatekeeping: Underwriters and the Quality of Sovereign Bond Markets, 1815–2007', NBER working paper 15128, July 2009; Niall Ferguson, 'Political Risk and the International Bond Market between the 1848 Revolution and the Outbreak of the First World War', *Economic History Review* 2006 (59.1): 70–112; Niall Ferguson and Moritz Schularick, 'The Empire Effect: The Determinants of Country Risk in the First Age of Globalization, 1880–1913', *Journal of Economic History* 2006 (66.2): 283–312.

own nests: their natural instinct is to loot the companies they run for all they can get for themselves (though mechanisms exist to constrain them to serve the owners' interests).[7] This picture of rapacious managers—though recently amply confirmed in companies like Enron, Lehman, or Parmalat (not to speak of many earlier examples)—has not gone unchallenged. Some critics point to the undesirable consequences of teaching based on such models as the reflexive root of the problem: managers may behave according to the simplistic, amoral norms presented to them in the routine misuse of such models in MBA courses.[8]

The crude version of the agency model—though it usefully fixes attention on one critical aspect of the governance problem—is, in a broader sense, plainly absurd. We underestimate the power of obliquity.[9] Business leaders are people, not 'rationally' maximizing black boxes, and many are fundamentally driven by pride in their job. Many inherently want to behave well, and others see advantage in being perceived by others as doing so, so the inherent satisfaction of ethical behaviour and the pressure of peers (more than fear of the policeman's knock) keep most directors reasonably honest most of the time. One suspects the numbers of managers who wake up in the morning thinking either 'How can I defraud my shareholders today?' or 'How can I maximize shareholder value today?' are tiny compared with those who think about their product or service and how they and their staff will deliver it. Yet it is the ones who successfully target the latter objectives who win large markets and (coincidentally) pay large dividends to their owners. That is why we respect Bill Gates and Steve Jobs more than Al Dunlap and Fred Goodwin, Lord Leverhulme, and Lord Nuffield more than Lord Kylsant and Whittaker Wright. Managers enjoy salaries and bonuses (sometimes more than they should), but they also crave social esteem and professional recognition and those who win shareholder trust are in the long run likely to be given more resources (and be more loved by their neighbours) than the rogues.

Interaction between investors and directors in a public company is a repeated game in which cooperative, mutually beneficial solutions become more likely than short-term personal maximization to the detriment of shareholders.[10] Thus stable, modern economies had a sporting chance of developing some

---

[7] Harold Demsetz, 'The Structure of Ownership and the Theory of the Firm', *Journal of Law and Economics* 1983 (26.2): 375–90.

[8] Rakesh Khurana, *From Higher Aims to Hired Hands* (Princeton, NJ, 2007). Historians can be forgiven for being sceptical, since the actions he condemns had many historical precursors, most of whom lacked the benefit of an MBA education. However, they were more likely to commit suicide on being found out, while their modern heirs loudly, if implausibly, protest their innocence, so the modern innovation may be the capacity to educate MBAs in self-deception.

[9] John A. Kay, *Obliquity* (London, 2010).

[10] David M. Kreps and Robert Wilson, 'Reputation and Imperfect Information', *Journal of Economic Theory* 1982 (27.2): 253–79.

trust between investors and corporate boards conducive to the development of the corporate securities market. Trust could be enhanced by more than experience of cooperative outcomes in the repeated game scenario. Rules for the division of benefits and standards of transparency and behaviour in business could be made and enforced (by legislatures and in the courts, and/or in corporate charters and in annual general meetings); some information asymmetries could be mitigated (by accounting standards and by directors self-dealing disclosure rules); incentives could be aligned (directors may be required to hold shares, compensated by bonuses related to profits, or offered equity options). Directors who purloined shareholders' funds surreptitiously— whether by egregious slacking or fraudulent conversion—were indulging in what will usually be a zero- or even negative-sum game. Yet those who attracted more shareholders by transparently good governance and honest behaviour were likely to raise the profitability of the firm, so both principals and their agents may both have gained considerably.[11] The business world was competitive and often ruthless (so we ignore roguish motivation and rubbish the agency problem at our peril) and business probably attracted more of the greedy than, say, nursing, but it was often a long way from the caricatures of human motivation implicit in agency theory.

The problems exposed in the current global financial crisis, of short-termism and high financial sector profits and salaries rewarding shockingly poor performance, impressively outlined in the recent Kay review of UK capital markets,[12] were not without parallels in Victorian England. Yet such indicators as we have suggest that similar depredations were then on a smaller scale. Perhaps the most outrageous nineteenth-century financial crook, Gregor MacGregor (who actually issued bonds for a non-existent country, sending migrants there in the 1820s), defrauded bond investors of only £1.3 million: even in real terms only a fraction of the $65 billion recent depredations of Bernard Madoff.[13] Legitimate businessmen have also increased their (legal) depredations. Financial intermediaries such as investment trusts then charged lower fees for better performance than their modern counterparts[14] and there was arguably less portfolio churning and momentum-chasing

---

[11] At a time when private business sales were at a p/e of perhaps six and stock exchange IPOs could command a p/e of 12 or more, and many vendors wanted to retain a stake in the business, it might be argued that the agreements on governance and cash flows between vendors and investors at IPO (or propositions put to them by their financial intermediaries) would have to be extraordinarily poorly designed to leave both of them worse off than they otherwise would have been.

[12] John Kay, *The Kay Review of Capital Markets and Long-Term Decision Making: Final Report*, July 2012, <http://www.bis.gov.uk/kayreview>.

[13] *Economist*, 22 December 2012, 103–6.

[14] David Chambers and Rui Esteves, 'The First Global Emerging Markets Investor: Foreign and Colonial Investment 1880–1913', *Explorations in Economic History* 2014 (52): 1–21.

herd behaviour in nineteenth-century markets, leading to lower costs and better chances of the evolution of trust and reciprocity in investor–firm relationships.[15]

6.3 Britain: The Leading Corporate Issuer

Yet many historians note that corporate governance standards enforced by the law, by stock exchange listing rules, or by private contract were then inadequate.[16] There is little sign in this literature of Britain diverging from the global norm of minimal investor protection by government regulators, as its unusually high ratio of corporate securities to GDP might suggest.[17] It is, of course, possible that Britain's precocity in divorcing ownership from control was a burden and that countries like the United States, France, and Germany, which relied more than the United Kingdom on financing by alternatives to stock markets—banks (which may have had better information than public investors), or families (where direct ownership avoided agency problems)— were more efficient. However, it requires quite an imaginative leap to picture the British economy as in collapse from over-financialization before 1914: Britain then had living standards similar to Australia's and the United States' and well above those of Germany or France. Having only the industrializing world's seventh largest workforce and third largest GDP, Britain remained the world's largest manufacturing exporter, multinational investor, and global power. Despite the managerial failures that economic historians have detected in a few sectors,[18] it beggars belief that all this was achieved if Britain's major quoted corporations had developed totally dysfunctional ownership and governance structures. Pursuing further a recent trend of revisionism, I argue here that the ownership structures of companies and their governance rules were not exogenous shocks doled out by capricious Clio from which British capitalism found it difficult to recover, but, rather, the endogenous outcome of an evolutionary, maximizing process in which managers and shareholders were

---

[15] Although we do not have accurate measures of the turnover of quoted stocks annually before 1914, it is clear from shareholder's registers that ownership was then typically long-term.

[16] Brian R. Cheffins, *Corporate Ownership and Control: British Business Transformed* (Oxford, 2008); Philip Cottrell, *Industrial Finance, 1830–1914* (Abingdon, 1980), 39–79; Timothy W. Guinnane, Ron Harris, and Naomi R. Lamoreaux, 'Contractual Freedom and the Evolution of Corporate Control in Britain, 1862 to 1929', NBER working paper 20481 (2014); Paul Johnson, *Making the Market: Victorian Origins of Corporate Capitalism* (Cambridge, 2010); William Paca Kennedy, Industrial *Structure, Capital Markets and the Origins of British Industrial Decline* (Cambridge, 1987), 126.

[17] Leslie Hannah, 'Rethinking Corporate Finance Fables: Did the US Lag Europe before 1914?', University of Tokyo CIRJE working paper F-994, October 2015.

[18] E.g. John Dodgson, 'New, Disaggregated, British Railway Total Factor Productivity Growth Estimates, 1875 to 1912', *Economic History Review* 2011 (64.2): 621–43.

informed actors feeling their way to workable options by an iterative process of experimentation with effective feedback loops. I suspect that the solutions adopted to address agency problems before 1914, albeit not perfect, at least did a workmanlike job in aligning shareholders' and directors' interests.[19] There was nothing inevitable in this development, but rather a large element of contingency: not all that we find in British capital markets had to be, nor was it necessarily designed in the name of good governance (though it sometimes was).

Economists puzzling over why British shareholders were willing to trust their money to quoted, public companies have recently begun to come up with some plausible answers. Franks et al. suggest that the early dispersion of ownership in the United Kingdom was possible 'on the basis of informal relations of trust rather than formal systems of regulation. Shareholders had little recourse in courts but much influence in the communities and local markets of which they and their firms were a part. Even as it became dispersed, ownership remained geographically concentrated, and directors were concerned to maintain their reputations among local investors... Eventually (from 1948), as local relations of trust became harder to sustain, formal investor protection emerged to substitute for them.'[20] This basic argument is plausible, well-supported by their UK evidence on the regional concentration of shareholdings, and chimes well with some contemporary comment.[21] The burgeoning literature attempting to measure modern levels of trust also confirms the contemporary intuition of John Stuart Mill and others that general levels of trust in the United Kingdom were unusually high by international standards.[22] Such trust in the markets for business capital and trade credit had long existed in the provinces: 'This was a social market for credit and capital based largely upon face-to-face relationships, personal knowledge, reputation, esteem and trust, all of which were aided by conventions and common understandings and by accepted, often ritualised, modes of self-presentation,

---

[19] James Foreman-Peck and Leslie Hannah, 'Some Consequences of the Early Twentieth-Century British Divorce of Ownership from Control', *Business History* 2013 (55.4): 543–64; Graeme G. Acheson, Gareth Campbell, John D. Turner, and Nadia Vanteeva, 'Corporate Ownership and Control in Victorian Britain', *Economic History Review* 2015 (68.3): 911–36.

[20] Julian Franks, Colin Mayer, and Stefano Rossi, 'Ownership: Evolution and Regulation', *Review of Financial Studies* 2009 (22.10): 4009–56 at p. 4046 (my brackets); see also Janette Rutterford, Dimitris P. Sotiropoulos, and Carry van Lieshout, 'Individual Investors and Local Bias in the UK: 1870–1935', Open University working paper 2015. Similar points have been made by historians, e.g. Cottrell, *Industrial Finance*, 91–4.

[21] E.g. Frederick Lavington, *The English Capital Market* (London, 1921).

[22] John Stuart Mill, *Principles of Political Economy* (London, 1848), 132; Paul J. Zak and Stephen Knack, 'Trust and Growth', *Economic Journal* 2001 (111.470): 295–321. Yann Algan and Pierre Cahuc, 'Inherited Trust and Growth', *American Economic Review* 2010 (100.5): 2060–92 at p. 2066 estimate levels of trust in 1935 shown as 'inherited' by different immigrant groups by modern US survey evidence.

hospitality and communication.'[23] Of course, such local markets existed elsewhere (indeed regional markets were arguably stronger in America).[24] However, it may be that Britain—longer industrialized and urbanized than France and Germany and more homogeneous than a restless America still absorbing many culturally dissimilar immigrants—had developed higher levels of trust among the experienced investing classes.

One cannot, however, rely too much on generalized arguments about local trust. There were many larger UK companies than the sixty (modestly-sized, domestic manufacturing and distribution) companies in the Franks et al. sample and these had already before 1914 dispersed shareholdings more widely than the levels which these authors describe as later creating difficulties in sustaining trust.[25] Campbell and Turner agree on the importance of local trust but point out that as early as 1883, only just over a third of quoted companies were headquartered in a provincial city where their stock also traded.[26] Before 1914 there were at least sixty UK companies with more than 10,000 shareholders and some had many more,[27] most of them headquartered in London, distant from provincial trust networks. Indeed two-fifths of the largest British-owned companies mainly operated overseas so even their UK directors were substantially dependent on information generated by managers thousands of miles away.[28] Many shareholders were in British cities a hundred or more miles distant from the boardroom and some were from overseas.[29] They all clearly needed alternative forms of reassurance. This could not come from the local bourgeoisie having personal trust in and knowledge of the

---

[23] Pat Hudson, 'Industrial Organisation and Structure', in Roderick Floud and Paul Johnson (eds.), *Cambridge Economic History of Modern Britain*, vol. 1 (Cambridge, 2004), 28–56 at p. 53. See also Mark Freeman, Robin Pearson, and James Taylor, *Shareholder Democracies? Corporate Governance in Britain and Ireland before 1850* (Chicago, 2012), 245 and *passim*, for the effectiveness of supervision by local urban proprietaries before 1850, though they see that already eroding by mid-century.

[24] Naomi Lamoreaux, Margaret Levenstein, and Kenneth Sokoloff, 'Financing Innovation in the Second Industrial Revolution: Cleveland, Ohio, 1870–1920', in Naomi Lamoreaux and Kenneth Sokoloff (eds.), *Financing Innovation in the United States, 1870 to Present* (Cambridge, MA, 2007), 39–84; Hannah, 'Rethinking'.

[25] They note a mean of 943 shareholders in their 1920 sample. The mean for 337 large UK-owned companies in 1911 (James Foreman-Peck and Leslie Hannah, 'Extreme Divorce: The Managerial Revolution in UK Companies before 1914', *Economic History Review* 2012 (65.4): 1207–38) is 6,241 shareholders.

[26] Gareth Campbell and John D. Turner, 'Substitutes for Legal Protection: Corporate Governance and Dividends in Victorian Britain', *Economic History Review* 2011 (64.2): 571–97 at p. 578. Moreover, comparison with Essex-Crosby's *Stock Exchange Official Intelligence* (*SEOI*) data for 1884 suggests their *Investors' Monthly Manual* sample probably excluded most provincially quoted companies, albeit generally small ones.

[27] *Investors Year Book* (London, 1915), with allowance for the omission of the *SEOI* mining sector.

[28] Proportion based on the 337 firms analysed in Foreman-Peck and Hannah ('Extreme Divorce') and the 60 overseas mining firms that they omit.

[29] Cottrell, *Industrial Finance*, 93–4 shows in a sample of 78 1885 registrations that 24 per cent of shareholders were from overseas, though they are probably not representative; see also T. A. B. Corley, 'British Overseas Investment in 1914 Revisited', *Business History* 1994 (36.1): 71–88.

people who directly managed what was going on in the local brewery, engineering factory, or electric utility, so there were many dozens of companies before 1914 for which it is quite implausible that traditional local 'trust through propinquity' mechanisms proposed by Mayer et al. as the pre-1948 norm worked effectively.

6.4 Intermediaries and the Financial Elite

If local networks of trust can be ruled out for many of the larger companies—which already accounted for most corporate capital on pre-1914 exchanges—what is left? To a modest extent, the bankers who were active in providing quality certification in the sovereign bond market also did so for corporate IPOs. For example, a few leading companies (including Shell, Burma Ruby Mines, Manchester Ship Canal, Vickers, Guinness, Rio Tinto, and Cunard) used Barings and Rothschilds as financial advisers. It is clear that the Rothschilds sponsored securities issues for some firms (parallel to their underwriting government securities internationally, though on a smaller scale) and Lopez-Morell and O'Kean have suggested that they concentrated their own and favoured clients' investments on large companies with market power, over whose boards they could exercise some control, even with minority interests.[30] Competitor merchant banks—like Hambros—also underwrote both sovereign debt and corporate equity issues for generally lower fees and retail (clearing) banks also dabbled in the business: among the pioneering 1880s brewery IPOs, for example, London & Westminster issued Allsopps and a smaller bank, Sir Samuel Scott Bart & Co, issued Bass. However, most intermediated issues in London were rather sponsored and/or underwritten by stockbrokers, investment trusts, or issuing houses.[31] One of the largest promoters, H. Osborne O'Hagan and his City of London Contract Corporation, sometimes collaborating with the stockbrokers, Phillips & Drew, and the accountant, John Ellerman, offered an effective and widely-used IPO service. The '69 Old Broad Street' group of investment trusts—led from 1891 by the lawyer John Philipps (Lord St Davids), leveraging wealth he had inherited from his wife's family—founded and reconstructed companies in Latin America and Britain, using its shareholdings to affect corporate policies.[32]

---

[30] Miguel A. López-Morel and José M. O'Kean, 'The Rothschilds' Strategies in International Nonferrous Metals Markets, 1830–1940', *Economic History Review* 2014 (67.3): 720–49.
[31] Carsten Burhop, David Chambers, and Brian R. Cheffins, 'Regulating IPOs: Evidence from Going Public in London, 1900–1913', *Explorations in Economic History* 2014 (51): 60–76.
[32] John P. Scott, 'John Wynford Philipps', in David J. Jeremy (ed.), *Dictionary of Business Biography*, vol. 4 (London, 1985), 662–7.

The records of some important intermediaries have largely been lost. The largest British estate recorded at death before 1914 amounted to £10.9 million ($53 million): that of Charles Morrison, a Geneva-, Edinburgh-, and Cambridge-educated bachelor private banker, who died at the age of 91 in 1909.[33] In 1864 Morrison, his family fortune already well internationally diversified with infrastructure investments in France, the United States, and United Kingdom, had, while still in his forties, sold outright London's Fore Street Warehouse, the leading textile dealership built up by his (self-educated and self-made) merchant prince father. Already rich, and with an academic education, extensive management experience, and cosmopolitan outlook, he focused on his role as a financier. Leaving the established sovereign loan business to major players like the Barings and Rothschilds, Morrison instead concentrated on the corporate sector, which was expanding rapidly at home and internationally after the general UK limited liability law of 1856. Morrison closely supervised the entrepreneurial investments he financed from his office, at 53 Coleman Street in the financial district. His dealings at the time were quiet and unostentatious, and his business records were later destroyed in the Blitz, leaving only scattered historical traces of his many corporate involvements in Britain and abroad. At various stages he was chairman, president, deputy chairman, or director of North British & Mercantile Insurance, the Hounslow & Metropolitan Railway (an extension into the expanding western suburbs of what we now know as the Underground's Piccadilly line), Netherlands Land Enclosure (a Dutch company that reclaimed land from the Scheldt estuary), the Swedish Central Railway (an English-registered enterprise, reconstructing a late-developing railway), and Trust & Loan Company of Canada (a mortgage provider); and he was also the direct owner of Scottish island ferries that later became Caledonian MacBrayne and a major shareholder in Argentine enterprises, though he appears to have been represented on the latter boards by relatives and by the solicitors Ashurst, Morris, Crisp.[34] We have no way of knowing what portion of his (by British standards) enormous wealth at the end of his life derived from his being, variously, a trusted venture capitalist, company doctor, and financial intermediary for such enterprises or from less admirable insider dealings. It may, like that of his transatlantic counterpart, J. P. Morgan, have involved both; the two Anglo-Saxon multi-millionaires

---

[33] William D. Rubinstein, *Wealth and the Wealthy in the Modern World* (London, 1980), 55. UK probate inventories only measure personalty not realty and Morrison also owned many acres, but the richest Briton was probably the Duke of Westminster, widely believed to have inherited £14 million ($68 million), substantially in land, from his father in 1899, making him as rich as J. P. Morgan.

[34] *Directory of Directors*, 1880, 1890, 1900, 1908.

also resembled each other in having chosen their fathers well.[35] Morrison appears to have taken large positions in both innovative and troubled companies, to have adopted a contrarian investment strategy (investing in stock market downturns, when others were selling), to have sustained an optimistic liberal faith that, given capital and people, Argentina and Canada would develop impressively as prosperous mini-USAs, and to have had a following among some small investors. His wealth was invested in his own private bank, old masters, landed estates in Berkshire and Scotland (though firmly London-based, he remembered his Scottish ancestry), and a portfolio of internationally and sectorally diversified securities, many of which he had himself floated on the Victorian world of entrepreneurial capitalism. We will not know the ultimate composition of his portfolio, until his full probate inventory is released to the public domain, a date still some years in the future. His largest known corporate connection was North British & Mercantile Insurance, which conducted fire, marine, accident, life, and annuity business on five continents. He served on its board from its formation as a merger of two leading London and Edinburgh companies in 1862 until shortly before his death. Its directors were required to own only 40 shares and the votes of any holdings beyond 100 shares were restricted to only one-tenth that of small shareholders, so, if he did own a large block, it was for investment, not control, purposes.[36]

Descendants of Scottish immigrants like the Morrison family were not the only incomers to make good in the vigorously competitive Victorian City. Possibly already as rich as Morrison in 1909 and developing a similar City venture capital and company promoter profile, John Ellerman (though his German-born immigrant father was only a modest Hull merchant) was to leave Britain's largest-ever estate of £36.7 million ($179 million) in 1933. Already by 1911, he had a preponderant personal shareholding in Ellerman Lines (a shipping company he had set up in 1901) and in Brewery & General Investment Trust: the latter (betting creatively in troubled sectors) was invested in many companies and his core eponymous shipping holding accounted for only a fraction of his wealth. Diversified share portfolios thus already appear to have had a major, but not exclusive, role in the wealth management strategies of Britain's—old and new—super-rich entrepreneurs. The London Stock Exchange (LSE) rules barred stockbrokers from becoming bankers (and vice versa) but this was held not to include the business of securities issuance or underwriting: both now considered a major component

---

[35] Morrison had inherited $5 million at the age of 40; J. P. Morgan $10 million at the age of 53.
[36] Anon, *North British & Mercantile Insurance: Centenary 1809–1909* (Edinburgh, 1909), 54–5.

of investment banking.[37] Wagg (stockbrokers to the Rothschilds) had conducted their own issuing business for decades, with successful IPOs for Lipton's Tea, Furness (ships), the Elysée Palace Hotel (Paris), and Imperial Paper (Canada) to their name, when in 1912 they resigned from the stock exchange to specialize as an issuing house, dropping share trading in the secondary market of their own volition.[38] The stockbrokers Rowe & Pitman could raise and underwrite a modest sum (£100,000) for Rolls-Royce for a total fee of less than 5 per cent.[39] Another leading London brokerage, Foster & Braithwaite, charged 1–1.25 per cent commission for issues, with an optional extra 2.5–5 per cent for underwriting, handling domestic and overseas share issues for hotels, electrical companies, waterworks, and Lever Brothers.[40] Such stockbrokers were modestly capitalized, but leveraged this through banking relationships (trusted intermediaries could raise significant sums from large retail banks to finance temporary acquisitions prior to issue) and underwriting syndicates (in which banks, insurers, trusts, other brokers, and wealthy individuals participated). Stockbrokers also had excellent facilities for securities distribution, through their own and their underwriting syndicates' clients, to whom they sometimes offered preferential allotments to foster loyalty.

6.5 The Free ('Do-It-Yourself') Market

It was thus *possible* to hire financiers as full-service intermediaries in London, but not at all *necessary*. Many firms with a high public reputation—including J & P Coats (the leading global manufacturer of sewing thread), Boots (the largest UK pharmaceutical manufacturer and pharmacy chain), and many railways and banks—chose to issue their own capital, without *any* underwriting or major financial intermediation.[41] Most business owners or company secretaries knew how to place a newspaper advertisement (or send circulars to existing shareholders) and most investors could read a prospectus. The price–earnings ratios of comparable listed firms (obvious guidelines to setting the issue price) were not well-guarded professional secrets, but published daily.[42]

---

[37] Ranald C. Michie, 'Dunn, Fischer and Co. in the City of London, 1906–14', *Business History* 1988 (30.2): 195–218 at p. 201.

[38] Richard Roberts, *Schroders: Merchants and Bankers* (Basingstoke, 1992), 358–64. See also David Kynaston, *Cazenove & Co: A History* (London, 1991), 83–5.

[39] Ian Lloyd, *Rolls-Royce: The Growth of a Firm* (London, 1978), 41.

[40] William Joseph Reader, *A House in the City: A Study of the City and the Stock Exchange Based on the Records of Foster & Braithwaite* (London, 1978), 94 and 108.

[41] This was rare in highly regulated Germany, but a common practice also in France and the Netherlands.

[42] Moreover, fixing the issuing price oneself eliminated the moral hazard of intermediaries, who might fix it low enough to remove underwriters' liabilities or ensure their own insider post-issue 'stagging' gains. Boots was the most unorthodox of these issuers: selling its securities literally 'over

Hence shareholders and vendors alike were often reluctant to pay elevated fees for elementary advice on new issues which appeared—for an attractive issue for which investor demand in the world's largest securities market was assured—quite unnecessary.[43] In fact, most domestic issues at this time were not underwritten at all, though this was already becoming standard on Berlin (partly through the effect of government regulation) and the NYSE (where a banking oligopoly increasingly dominated issues).[44] British vendors with no stockbroker-underwriter (if they wanted their shares to be traded on the LSE) were *required* to pay a modest fee to a stockbroker to present their application (for official listing or special settlement) to the listing committee, and they also often *chose* to offer a small commission to brokers forwarding prospective investors' applications. Some other routine functions were often subcontracted: subscription processing and share allocations to a retail bank, or, if they wished to appeal beyond their existing stakeholders, advertising and prospectus distribution to a specialist marketing firm (London had several direct mail firms offering lists of hundreds of thousands of prospective shareholders).[45] Solicitors were usually hired to draft the prospectus (and the articles of association if a new company was formed), perhaps consulting a broker to give advance assurance that these conformed to stock exchange listing requirements, and an auditor (and, where appropriate, a mining consultant, patent agent, or consulting engineer) for authentication of the financial (or other) data. For those who wanted to offer debenture holders extra reassurance through professional trustees, the Debenture Corporation (and others) offered that specialist service. In such cases the prospectus would bear the names of an impressive list of City professionals (banker, broker, auditor, solicitor, etc.), but the main emphasis was on the assets, brand, and reputation of the *issuer* (which mainly concerned long-term investors), not the *intermediaries* (whose short-term liabilities to the firm or its investors were confined to their own specifically contracted or legally mandated professional

---

the counter' at its pharmacies, and listing only a minority of its securities on the Sheffield exchange.

[43] See J. Walker and R. M. Watson, Investor's and Shareholder's (Edinburgh, 1894), 83, 86, and 103–5 for contemporary advice to avoid underwritten issues, in order to avoid value dilution.

[44] Alan Ross Hall, *The London Capital Market and Australia* (Canberra, 1968), 79; Burhop, Chambers, and Cheffins, 'Regulating IPOs'; Carsten Burhop, David Chambers, and Brian R. Cheffins, 'Law, Politics and the Rise and Fall of German Stock Market Development, 1870–1938', University of Cambridge Faculty of Law, working paper 283/2015, January 2015.

[45] British companies were required to update lists of their shareholders (with shares held, addresses, and occupations) annually in a central companies registry at Somerset House in London (or equivalents in Dublin and Edinburgh), enabling marketing firms to assemble comprehensive mailing lists, weeded of duplicate names and classified by current investment interests. When it was suggested that the United States should adopt this practice, many state legislators considered it an outrageous affront to personal privacy.

responsibilities).[46] The total expenses (without underwriting) might be no more than 1–2 per cent of the amount raised and could be less for large issues.

It might seem daunting to some industrialists unfamiliar with the City to put together such a package: that, and the certainty of an underwritten issue, explains why full-service issuing houses, stockbrokers, and bankers had a market, even at higher fees of 4–10 per cent, though they, too, used the same City networks to outsource much of the work in much the same way: given contemporary data-processing technology, few firms had enough resources to do all the work. For example, in 1890, after it took 200 clerks three weeks to process the 15,000 applications for the £5.75 million IPO of J & P Coats, the job of receiving the called capital from 8,000 successful allottees was subcontracted to two retail banks.[47] In *retail* financial services for the general public, there were substantial *internal* economies of scale (from risk-diversification, leveraging brand reputation, and routinized and inspected clerical processing), so some UK banks and insurance companies had *national* staffs of many thousands, who could fit such work into their routines. On the other hand, the competitive advantages of the, more specialist, London business services of stockbrokers, investment trusts, merchant bankers, and issuing houses derived from divisions of labour, professional networks, and *external* economies of scale among the 50,000 financial service workers in the City.[48] Like other 'industrial districts' identified at the time by Marshall, the City's specialist, clustered, small to medium-sized enterprises enjoyed the flexibility, innovativeness, and high incomes typical of such territorial clusters when they work effectively.[49] Even the leading City firms of lawyers, brokers, accountants, and merchant bankers were only modestly sized (a few dozen employees could be very effective, and it was rare to have more than a hundred) and the corporate form was rare (though Barings and O'Hagan's

---

[46] Tellingly, while in the United States it was J. P. Morgan who dipped into his own pocket to enable International Mercantile Marine to avoid default on scheduled interest payments, in the United Kingdom, it was the eponymous entrepreneur, Lord Leverhulme, not the issuer, who did the same for Lever Brothers (Charles Wilson, *History of Unilever* (London, 1954), 265–6). Both gestures showed an untypically high level of commitment to past (and clearly conditional) promises.

[47] This was near to the modern instantaneous IPO with public subscription. On the NYSE, by contrast, J. P. Morgan & Co, which did not have retail distribution capacity, made many large issues with underwriting from a dozen or more networked financiers, releasing stock post-issue on the market or to underwriters or wholesalers.

[48] Sarah Cochrane ('Explaining London's Dominance in International Financial Services, 1870–1913', University of Oxford Department of Economics working paper 455, October 2009) and Simon Mollan and Ranald Michie ('The City of London as an International Commercial and Financial Center since 1900', *Enterprise and Society* 2012 (13.3): 538–87, at pp. 557–61) demonstrate the importance of network externalities and financial clusters in London. For the number of workers see Corporation of London, *City of London Day Census Report* (London, 1911).

[49] Jonathan Zeitlin, 'Industrial Districts and Regional Clusters', in Geoffrey G. Jones and Jonathan Zeitlin (eds.), *The Oxford Handbook of Business History* (Oxford, 2008), 219–43.

CLCC had already adopted it). Even the largest, international, interlocking unlimited financial partnerships (like Wernher Beit, J. P. Morgan, and Rothschild) directly employed, at most, only a few hundred staff worldwide.

Such networked, clustered, competing, and cooperating business services required high levels of trust among professional participants, issuers, and investors, but there were mechanisms—law, custom, reputation, information dissemination, reciprocity, collective snobbery, socializing and charitable activity in clubs and livery companies, corporate incentive structures, knowledge flows generated by close proximity—reinforcing that and raising the costs of opportunistic behaviour.[50] The robust attitude of a later president of JPMorgan Chase, who defended some of its more dubious deals on the grounds that 'There's a big difference between committing a fraud and knowing the committer of a fraud', would have spelled social and business death in early twentieth-century London.[51] The City had its share of fraudsters (indeed probably more than its share: it is in the nature of finance that fraud is hard to detect and money could be made by sailing close to the wind while preserving reputation), but, for identical reasons, it was also a world in which ethics and behaviour were necessarily monitored and misrepresentation and dubious associations punished.

Vendors of British businesses, organizing their own IPOs, might be supposed to have incurred hidden costs, if their lack of credibility and expertise led to their setting the IPO price too low, thus leaving money 'on the table' that professional intermediaries would have more competently obtained. The long-run record of IPOs examined by David Chambers and his collaborators suggests scepticism on that score. UK IPO under-pricing in this era was *below* what later became the norm in both the United Kingdom and the United States, when investment bankers developed stronger control of the new issue market, and, possibly, levels of trust had declined and tolerance of profitable

---

[50] On the basis of high-trust relationships in this period, see Leslie Hannah, 'Pioneering Modern Corporate Governance: A View from London in 1900', *Enterprise and Society* 2007 (8.3): 642–86, and Cochrane, 'Explaining'.

[51] Many in the City before 1914, of course, encountered multiple fraudsters, and some bankers, like Lord Farquhar, sailed close to the wind themselves without being exposed. Nonetheless most financiers were quick to dissociate themselves when suspicion of others spread on their network, and, post-exposure, preferred silence, apology, and/or suicide to such feeble excuses (as, for example, in the cases of Ernest Hooley or Whittaker Wright). The literature on this question bobs around from seeing a glass half full to one half empty and both are right. For the effective criminal prosecution of securities fraudsters, see James Taylor, *Boardroom Scandals: The Criminalization of Company Fraud in Nineteenth Century Britain* (Oxford, 2013). For a more sceptical view, see Paul Johnson, 'Civilizing Mammon: Laws, Morals and the City in Nineteenth Century England', in Peter Burke, Brian Harrison, and Paul Slack (eds.), *Civil Histories: Essays presented to Sir Keith Thomas* (Oxford, 2000), 301–20, and his *Making the Market*. For increasingly favourable public opinion of City morality, though with regression to the mean in the 1890s, see Ranald C. Michie, *Guilty Money* (London, 2015).

opportunism had increased.[52] In the nineteenth century a UK business proprietor might fall victim to (respectable) Barings and pay an outrageous 10 per cent of the amount raised for an IPO as badly *under*-priced as investment bankers later contrived to achieve (as did Guinness in 1886), or pay 12 per cent to an (unscrupulous and corrupt) share-pusher like Sir Ernest Hooley to conjure an *over*-priced issue that later alienated the duped shareholders (as did Dunlop, Schweppes, and Bovril in the 1890s); but many issuers before 1914 paid fees around a third of these levels to honest, reasonably-priced, capable, and fair-dealing intermediaries. It required really serious incompetence in London to be milked of fees sometimes as high as 20 per cent, charged by J. P. Morgan and others for NYSE (and even occasional UK) issues. One of the reasons why the LSE was then so attractive to UK businessmen (and to some US ones, like George Eastman, who in 1898 floated Kodak there, without underwriting, in preference to New York) was that the LSE was cheaper for new issues. That competitive London financial world has since disappeared: British corporations now pay high fees to investment bankers in the belief that they are paying for quality, when they have, arguably, been manoeuvred by dominant suppliers into an undesirable equilibrium.[53]

Colonial millionaires (like the 'Randlords', Sir Julius Wernher and Sir Alfred Beit) were also involved in some domestic financing, as were some foreign ones such as the Morgans and the Speyers. None of these were pussycats and at the time insider trading and other sins which would meet the disapproval of modern regulators were no doubt rife, but such people generally had an interest in limiting their depredations: all were conscious that industrialists who made issues and investors who subscribed to them were very attractive geese laying golden eggs for each other, from which bankers and brokers might also profit. They wanted their share of the gold (there is no evidence their already fabulous wealth moderated their taste for more), but a competitive market placed limits on all of them and none wanted to kill the geese that laid these golden eggs by being more openly predatory than the market norm. Not all were so restrained, but those who were not risked ostracism, public disgrace, or, in extreme cases, jail. J. P. Morgan was too greedy with the IMM issue of 1902 and found it more difficult to win corporate finance business in the United Kingdom after its debacle (though he developed a deservedly excellent reputation on the backward but rapidly developing NYSE).[54]

---

[52] David Chambers and Elroy Dimson, 'IPO Underpricing Over the Very Long-Run', *Journal of Finance* 2009 (64.3): 1407–43. For similar evidence of the recent demise of quality control by investment bankers in sovereign debt markets, see Flandreau et al., 'End'.

[53] Though they still have low fees relative to the United States, see Mark Abrahamson, Tim Jenkinson, and Howard Jones, 'Why Don't U.S. Issuers Demand European Fees for IPOs?', Oxford Saïd Business School working paper, November 2009.

[54] Leslie Hannah, 'J. P. Morgan in London and New York before 1914', *Business History Review* 2011 (85.1): 113–50.

Promoters who were plainly dishonest such as Sir Ernest Hooley and Horatio Bottomley MP served time in jail. Whittaker Wright was a flamboyant and popular financier who fled to the United States via France when public outcry against his personal depredations revealed by corporate bankruptcy proceedings became difficult for government law officers to ignore. He was extradited and convicted, taking cyanide at the conclusion of his 1904 fraud trial, in preference to living through his seven-year jail sentence. However, sailing close to the wind by the rich and well-connected could pay off and was not always found out. The 'Randlord' Sir Joseph Robinson brazenly defrauded shareholders[55] and Lord Farquhar, of Parr's Bank, was close to bankruptcy when he died,[56] rather than the rich, influential socialite he seemed. Both managed to preserve a reputation of sorts before the war.

6.6 Listing Rules

One institution whose natural monopoly characteristics did give it some market power to enforce rules[57] was the LSE, which dominated the market for larger UK corporate issues. The LSE was certainly not in the business of judging the investment quality of quoted shares—*caveat emptor* was its watchword—but its listing committee did impose minimal standards beyond what the law required. It checked that the corporate and financial documentation complied with the law and listing rules and (well before the NYSE) insisted that listed companies give shareholders balance sheets (before that was legally required in the United Kingdom in 1900) and profit and loss accounts (before that was legally required in 1929). The LSE also required that at least two-thirds of any officially listed security be initially sold to the general public rather than held by the vendors (to encourage liquid markets and discourage ramps and corners). Other requirements were that the articles

---

[55] In 1905 Joseph Robinson defrauded the shareholders of Randfontein Estates by personally buying some mines, then selling them to the company (which he then controlled) at a massive (undisclosed) mark-up. In 1915, its new owners sued him and he was ordered by the South African High Court to repay more than £500,000, a civil judgment upheld on appeal to the judicial committee of the UK Privy Council. His actions—judged 'wholly inconsistent with the obligation of good faith'—did not provoke criminal prosecution, and, before he was exposed, his Boer friends in South Africa successfully proposed him for a baronetcy, though his attempt to buy a peerage for £30,000 in 1922 pushed his luck even further than the House of Lords could tolerate. When he died, he was reviled for leaving nothing to charity (in marked contrast to other 'Randlords': Rhodes, Beit, and Wernher).

[56] Farquhar married into Parr's Bank money and traded influence in royal and party circles, but, on his death in 1923, was revealed to be bankrupt.

[57] Flandreau ('Collective Action Clauses') persuasively argues that it was the LSE's use of its market power to compel (quasi-statutory) arbitration rather than the voluntary activity of the Corporation of Foreign Bondholders that devised the Victorian system of collective action to discipline sovereign defaulters.

of listed companies contain provisions for directors personally to own shares,[58] provisions that directors abstain from voting on (and disclose any personal interest in) any contract with the company, and from the 1870s a clause preventing companies buying back their own shares (a common enough occurrence today, but then considered detrimental to the market's transparency and price discovery role).[59] Although such conditions were explicit in the published listing rules, there were also some unwritten rules. The directors of the furniture company, Maple & Co, for example, loudly mocked the listing committee's 'antiquated rules' in 1897, but it is clear that what led the committee initially to refuse Maple an official listing was the company's grossly inequitable rules entrenching directors, not one of the published listing requirements.[60]

It has been argued that NYSE listing rules were tougher and more meticulously applied, but that may reasonably be doubted.[61] Many NYSE requirements—such as that to publish accounts—had been enforced in London longer or—like the NYSE's certificate engraving requirements—were of negligible (indeed possibly negative) value.[62] The one clear difference was that the NYSE listing committee disliked small issues. This aimed—by a different route—at the same objective as the distinctive London 'two-thirds' rule. This rule enabled the admission of smaller companies than the de facto £1 million ($5 million) NYSE minimum, provided at least two-thirds of the issue was issued to the public rather than retained by the vendors, to ensure market liquidity. This alternative may have improved (appropriately diversified) investor returns, at least judging by the higher market/par ratios of such small, officially listed companies.[63]

The official listing requirements affected only a minority of quoted companies but these accounted for most of the market by value. By 1914 there

---

[58] Campbell and Turner ('Substitutes', 582) report that of the 791 quoted companies of 1883 for which they found data, 654 had directors' share qualifications. Presumably the remainder were provincially quoted, subsidiaries, or had IPOs before the LSE requirement took effect. By 1911 all large independent UK companies had such requirements (Foreman-Peck and Hannah, 'Extreme Divorce').

[59] Campbell and Turner, 'Substitutes'. The House of Lords ruled it out more generally in 1887 (*Trevor v. Whitworth* 12 App Cos. 409). Earlier bank deeds authorized directors to repurchase shares using bank funds, and there is evidence that they availed themselves of this provision (Graeme J. Acheson and John D. Turner, 'The Secondary Market for Bank Shares in Nineteenth-Century Britain', *Financial History Review* 2008 (15.2): 123–51, at pp. 146–8).

[60] *Economist*, 27 February 1897, 317–18.

[61] Mary O'Sullivan, 'Yankee Doodle Went to London: Anglo-American Breweries and the London Securities Market, 1888–92', *Economic History Review* 2015 (68.4): 1365–87.

[62] Security printing of certificates was sensible, but requiring it to be by one firm (allegedly controlled by insider interests at the NYSE) was not clearly better than the more competitive London securities printing market.

[63] I am indebted to Richard Grossman (email, 9 October 2009) for this information on market-par ratios for the securities reported in his 'New Indices of British Equity Prices, 1870–1913', *Journal of Economic History* 2002 (62.1): 121–46.

were 1,852 companies officially listed on the LSE, with an average nominal capital (shares and debentures) of £3.4 million. However, many of these were not UK companies (London had become a global market, with extensive listings of companies operating, registered, sometimes mainly owned, and/or also listed in Africa, America, continental Europe, Asia, and Australasia). Probably around a thousand of them were British (more or less, depending on whether one includes UK-headquartered and registered companies mainly operating abroad), with a somewhat lower average value (the official list concentrated on larger overseas issues, but listed more medium-sized domestic ones). The LSE had also developed a distinction between firms formally admitted to the official list and those merely traded, which included some admitted to the LSE's less fussy 'special settlement' status—the equivalent to today's London Alternative Investment Market (AIM) or the contemporary New York curb or NYSE unlisted status—plus some listed in the provinces or with markets made in London commodity markets and merchant banks (but also sometimes dealt in by LSE brokers) There were, in fact, some 6,500 UK firms (whose securities had an average par value of £700,000) listed in the *Stock Exchange Official Intelligence* and thus 'known on London', so a substantial majority by number had *not* met the requirements for official listing. However, firm size distributions are highly skewed (the largest ten companies—all officially listed—accounted for 20 per cent of securities values at par) and UK listed companies alone probably accounted for more than three-quarters of the par values of the securities of all UK companies known on London.[64]

Very few IPOs that applied for official listing were turned down, though more than two-thirds did not even bother to apply, opting for 'special settlement' status instead. If the listing requirements filtered out poorer quality issues and signalled this to investors, then, it must have been by unwritten rules and self-exclusion by potential candidates advised they would not succeed, not (as at the NYSE) by refusals of listing. Burhop et al. are sceptical of the London listing process, but their results show that, while unlisted London IPOs performed poorly,[65] those that were officially approved by the LSE listing committee did about as well as Berlin IPOs in the same period. The latter were subject to intense government regulation, whose restrictive terms also ensured that they were largely sponsored and underwritten by leading German banks (unlisted public trading—which prospered in the United States and United Kingdom—was forbidden). There remains, however, an unresolved mystery in

---

[64] Author's estimates at par values based on the ten largest companies and sampling of the rest. The share of officially listed companies in 1900–13 IPOs was only half of values (Burhop et al., 'Regulating IPOs', Table 1). The official list was of course dominated by mature companies admitted long ago.

[65] Burhop et al., 'Regulating IPOs', though for doubts about the representativeness of their unlisted companies see Hannah, 'Rethinking', 40–4.

the Burhop et al. article about the alchemy by which London listing produced such favourable results, though there are several possible candidates.

No British financial institution could match the quality of investment research offered by the 500-strong team of investment analysts at Crédit Lyonnais in Paris and it was the American John Moody who pioneered the letter-graded bond credit ratings in 1909 that were widely used in the United States and Europe. On the other hand, the widespread implementation of professional external auditing was primarily a British achievement,[66] and the most comprehensive contemporary securities index was the global monthly index of the (British) *Bankers Magazine*, available from the 1880s.[67] None of these innovations were perfect, but they were improvements on the tools investors would have enjoyed in their absence. While such innovations by the private sector helped the development of markets, the criminal law could also be used to protect investors. James Taylor has recently convincingly argued that prosecution of securities fraud in Victorian Britain has been severely underestimated, yet was remarkably effective.[68]

6.7 The Rule of Corporate Laws

In the case of corporate laws, also, the professionals who serviced the London IPO market were not short of nudges towards good corporate governance practices that are recommended and more widely implemented today. Indeed in the case of UK statutory companies (that is those created by private act of parliament or provisional order rather than simply registered at the Board of Trade), strong anti-director rights were legally required in their corporate charters under the terms of the 1845 Companies Clauses Consolidation Act (CCCA).[69] This required, for example, that shareholders should have proxy voting rights, pre-emption rights to new issues, and that holders of 10 per cent of the share capital should be able to requisition a general meeting without the consent of the board. Its provisions have been largely ignored by legal historians, even though most LSE-listed corporate securities at par until around

---

[66] Hannah, 'Pioneering'. It was already well-established when required by law (the 1900 Companies Act required that auditors could not be directors; independent audits were only required by the NYSE from 1928 (Carol J. Simon, 'The Effect of the 1933 Securities Act on Investor Information and the Performance of New Issues', *American Economic Review* 1989 (79.3), 295–318, at p. 298).

[67] Arthur Ellis, 'The "Quantitation" of Stock Exchange Values', *Journal of the Royal Statistical Society* 1888 (51.3): 567–98. Charles Dow introduced a daily index slightly earlier but it included only 20 US securities and so was not much use to global investors.

[68] Taylor, *Boardroom Scandals*.

[69] James Foreman-Peck and Leslie Hannah, 'UK Corporate Law and Corporate Governance before 1914: A Re-interpretation', in Matthew Hollow, Folarin Akinbami, and Ranald Michie (eds.), *Complexity and Crisis in the Financial System* (Cheltenham, 2016), 183–213.

1890 were subject to that law (and its revisions), not to the Companies Acts of 1856–1907, which figure so prominently in legal histories. Even after that date, when non-statutory companies (those merely registered at the Board of Trade) came to dominate LSE listings, such companies contemplating IPOs and their advisers were not operating in a vacuum, but had very similar default provisions in a schedule to the ordinary Companies Acts. Although, unlike with CCCA companies, their adoption was voluntary, most large listed companies adopted most of the recommended anti-director rights, with only minor modifications (in some cases even strengthening them). It is true that these provisions could be avoided either by convincing the listing committee they would nonetheless be well-governed or by accepting a special settlement, but there was a price to be paid for poor governance. Listed companies enjoyed greater liquidity and thus higher valuations than unlisted ones. Professional standards and networks among the banker and broker elite had a life of their own, but they operated within a framework of legal guidance and resultant economic incentives. By contemporary international standards, British corporate governance was reckoned to be good around 1900. The *Economist* in 1902 felt that the protection of shareholder rights in the then-dominant New Jersey version of US corporate law (when Delaware had not yet driven modal corporate law standards even lower) was weaker than that in Britain.[70]

6.8 Conclusion: Were UK Shareholder Protections Unique?

British corporate law applied to companies that were mainly owned, managed, and registered in Britain, while the LSE was at this time a global stock exchange. Many listed stocks were firms operating abroad, most of them mainly owned by foreign shareholders and managed by foreign managers: companies such as US Steel, Hokkaido Tanko Kisen, or the Paris-Lyons-Méditerranée Railway. Although they were not subject to British corporate laws, some of the mechanisms identified above applied also to them. The potential for London's listing requirements to improve overseas corporate governance—in much the same way as an NYSE listing does today[71]—existed: indeed it was larger since London then dominated international listings and accounted for a higher proportion of them than the NYSE today. However, the LSE's influence on overseas governance was attenuated by its practice of requiring any listed foreign

---

[70] In the USA, benign regulation came from private order institutions (especially the NYSE) and federal regulation (especially, from 1934, the SEC), not from capaciously tolerant state-level corporate law.

[71] Craig Doidge, Andrew G. Kirby, and René M. Stulz, 'Why Do Countries Matter So Much for Corporate Governance?', *Journal of Financial Economics* 2007 (86.1): 1–39.

corporation to be quoted on its own national exchange first: the LSE then usually accepted listing on a *major* foreign exchange as a qualifier, without further requiring the application of its own (sometimes tougher) listing rules, though it did occasionally refuse foreign listings, while some foreign firms, as with British companies, chose to apply only for a special settlement.[72]

However, some companies mainly operating abroad chose to incorporate under British corporate law, thus committing to conform to both British investor protection laws and, if also applying for official listing, LSE listing rules. This road was taken, for example, by many Indian and Argentine railways and banks and some companies operating in the United States (Kodak, Pillsbury, the Alabama, New Orleans, Texas and Pacific Junction Railway), Germany (Liebig's Extract of Meat, Siemens Brothers, Sankt Pauli), Australasia (New Zealand & Australian Land, Dalgety & Co), Canada (Hudson's Bay, Canada Mortgage), and Brazil (London & Brazilian Bank, Rio de Janeiro City Improvements).[73]

Beyond such overseas, but UK-headquartered or UK-registered, companies, it is unclear how far the quite widespread anti-director rights and good governance on the LSE was paralleled in other countries before 1914. It is possible that there, too, companies voluntarily adopted charters which were more investor-friendly than the law required. Thus our evidence provides plausible explanations of why British companies were able to divorce ownership from control so early, but does not necessarily explain why other countries developed equity markets more slowly. If similar sampling of major American, German, or French[74] listed companies' charters showed similar public or private rules requiring, or nudging firms in the direction of good corporate governance, we would need to seek alternative explanations of differential development elsewhere. It is already clear that both Norway and Brazil adopted more shareholder-friendly charter terms than were legally required.[75]

---

[72] Some issues listed on the NYSE and automatically accepted by the LSE would not have qualified under its own rules, mainly because vendors retained more than one-third of some NYSE IPOs.

[73] Some (e.g. Kodak, Siemens) later transferred to home country majority control or adopted new corporate forms with dual legal status.

[74] Pierre-Cyrille Hautcoeur ('Asymétries d'information, coûts de mandat et financement des entreprises françaises (1890–1936)', *Revue Economique* 1999 (50.5): 1053–87) suggests corporate securities were encouraged by various methods of overcoming information asymmetries. He has little to say on actual charters and their anti-director rights, though his treatment (pp. 1063–6) makes clear that France's statutory provisions for the anti-director rights pre-dated England's for most companies and they generally placed France somewhere between the UK's CCCA and the Companies Acts on the anti-director rights index. Burhop et al. ('Law') suggest legal requirements for listing in Germany were stringent, but did not principally operate via charters.

[75] Aldo Musacchio, *Experiments in Financial Democracy: Corporate Governance and Financial Development in Brazil, 1882–1950* (Cambridge, 2009); Charlotte Ostergaard and David C. Smith, 'Corporate Governance before there was Corporate Law', *Norwegian School of Management working paper 3*, 2011.

London's developing role in spreading good governance beyond British shores was essentially destroyed by the First World War. This not only limited London's global reach, but also began a long downward trend in the UK ratio of domestic stock exchange capitalization to GDP, part of a general 'great reversal' to which Rajan and Zingales have drawn attention.[76] No amount of good corporate governance rules was proof against the global military and economic disasters and political changes which lay behind that decline. In financial markets the work of generations can be undone in a very short time. Meanwhile, whether or not they had achieved something voluntarily earlier, some countries' governments moved to catch up in regulatory terms. The NYSE was already putting its house in order with the closure of its unlisted department in 1910, but the broader spread of good practice in the United States depended on decisive federal intervention in 1933, with the creation of the Securities and Exchange Commission.[77] Since then in most countries the balance has again moved towards governmental regulation, rather than private order institutions.[78]

Direct state supervision was not a pathway down which nineteenth-century Victorian politicians had wished to go very far. Even the development of statutory regulation under the 1845 CCCA had been predicated on giving shareholders the powers they needed to regulate their companies, not on massively extending Whitehall inspection and regulation. As the British government establishment then ran a global empire with only several hundred civil servants in Whitehall (a fraction of the staffing level required *by the SEC alone* today), they could initially hardly have chosen otherwise.[79] Any bureaucrats who wished to extend their reach and protect the public investor

---

[76] Raghuram G. Rajan and Luigi Zingales, 'The Great Reversal: The Politics of Financial Development in the 20th Century', *Journal of Financial Economics* 2003 (69.1): 5–50.

[77] On the value of the SEC, see Donald L. Kemmerer, 'American Financial Institutions: The Marketing of Securities, 1930–1952', *Journal of Economic History* 1952 (12.4), 454–68; Simon, 'Effect'; Thomas K. McCraw, *Prophets of Regulation* (Cambridge, MA, 1984), 153–4; Robert A. Prentice, 'The Inevitability of a Strong SEC', *Cornell Law Review* 2006 (91.4): 775–839; and B. Holmstrom and Steven N. Kaplan, 'The State of U.S. Corporate Governance: What's Right and What's Wrong?', NBER working paper 9613, 2003. There are some grounds for scepticism about the SEC. Its controls (and high investment banker fees) were bypassed in various ways (Simon, 'Effect'). Burhop et al. ('Regulating IPOs' and 'Law') suggest that the post-1933 US investor protection in IPOs was still not as good as London and Berlin pre-1914; while Susanne Espenlaub, Arif Khurshed, and Abdulkadir Mohamed ('IPO Survival in a Reputational Market', *Journal of Business Finance & Accounting* 2012 (39.3/4): 427–63) find London's modern—very lightly regulated—Alternative Investment Market (AIM) has as good a survival rate as SEC-regulated US exchanges.

[78] The fact that the quality of corporate governance today varies among firms mainly by country, rather than by firm characteristics such as the need to acquire external finance (Doidge et al., 'Why Do Countries Matter'), suggests that the quality of corporate governance is typically embedded in national laws and/or is a consequence of nationally specific culture or behaviours collectively reinforced by peak associations (like listing committees of major exchanges) or at least by shared values in the national financial community.

[79] Peter Jupp, *The Governing of Britain 1688–1848* (Abingdon, 2006), 137.

more directly from fraud received no encouragement.[80] Common law judges also buttressed the laissez-faire approach: making it clear they would not do the shareholders' job for them.[81] The purpose of nineteenth-century regulation was to give shareholders the tools they needed, requiring the adoption of good governance rules in statutory corporations, nudging them towards their adoption in registered ones, providing legal recourse if directors refused implementation, but avoiding the further expansion of the state into a regulatory job best undertaken by the wealthy bourgeoisie or their financial intermediaries conscious of their own and their clients' interests. To a modern mind this is an unrealistic expectation: apart from the financial incompetence of many investors, any activist investor or intermediary with the knowledge and time would encounter the problem of subsidizing free-riders. There were a succession of major frauds which seemed to underline the impotence of private action by shareholders, but the state maintained its stance of limiting direct intervention.[82] We should recall, by way of retrospective apologia, that the massive increase in state supervision in the second half of the twentieth century appears to have been equally ineffective in eliminating financial frauds and egregious unethical behaviour by bankers.

However, many investors did have enough 'skin in the game' to take some interest in monitoring management in the pre-1914 period and this was probably not confined to those—like the Rothschilds—about whose activities evidence has survived. Only the richest few per cent of the population invested in equities. The market value of the average shareholding of outsiders (i.e. excluding directors' holdings, which were larger and presumably well-tended) in 1911 was probably around £1,500, nearly ten times the £160 annual income threshold at which income tax was then payable.[83] With the average portfolio consisting of five shares,[84] in today's terms the mean shareholder perhaps had a portfolio worth in excess of half a million pounds,[85] though, since wealth distributions are highly skewed, most owned less and some much more.[86] Significant numbers of these are likely to have had enough

---

[80] Freeman et al., *Shareholder Democracies?*, 249.

[81] Notably in the much-cited 1843 case, *Foss v. Harbottle* (67 ER 189).

[82] The Board of Trade could appoint inspectors to investigate skulduggery in registered companies, but the hurdles were high and that provision was little used (for examples see the Board's *Annual Reports*). Senior Whitehall law officers were also notoriously slow in prosecuting the frauds of Whittaker Wright.

[83] The average non-director shareholding at par was £895 (Foreman-Peck and Hannah, 'Extreme Divorce', 1223–5). This is based on 337 companies with £1m+ share capital; smaller companies appear to have had smaller average shareholdings with proportionately more held by directors. The *Bankers Magazine* index suggests prices were 34 per cent above par in 1911, but Grossman's index suggests a rather higher uplift.

[84] Janette Rutterford, 'Democratisation of Shareholding in the US and UK' (forthcoming).

[85] Correcting by the consumer price index would uplift the figure by about 77 times, but much more if we allowed for rising stock exchange prices.

[86] Rutterford, 'Democratisation'.

'skin in the game', time, and financial experience for it to be worth monitoring carefully some investments, even if they were not directors. The less sophisticated widows, orphans, and adult male incompetents, if they had no personal trustees, might reliably trust a banker, a solicitor, or a broker recommended by family or friends to act for them, charging less rapacious fees or indulging less in hidden churning and kickbacks than their modern successors. It is arguable that this system was workably efficient: hardly perfect, though—confounding Whig perspectives which bedevil the literature—better than on the NYSE today. Consistent with this, the econometric evidence for a population of more than two hundred large UK firms of 1911 suggests that the business outcomes (as measured by accounting profit rates or equity share premiums) of divorcing ownership from control were not generally inimical to the interests of shareholders.[87]

---

[87] Foreman-Peck and Hannah, 'Some Consequences', 543–64.

7

Financial Elites, Law, and Regulation

A Historical Perspective

T. T. Arvind, Joanna Gray, and Sarah Wilson

7.1 Introduction: The Concept of a Financial Elite

Elite groups and clusters of power and influence can play a critical role in determining who gains and who loses within the financial system. This is borne out most starkly when losses occur and crystallize in times of financial crisis and shock. But it holds true too throughout the entire financial and economic cycle. For, far from being the products of some kind of entropic spontaneous ordering, the markets, products, and services that are the bones and lifeblood of the financial system itself are constituted and shaped by elites rather than by the ultimate users of the financial system.[1] Alexis Drach makes this point in Chapter 9 in this volume showing how the ultimate elite of banking supervision, the Basel Committee on Banking Regulation and Supervisory Practices constitutes the market itself as well as its supervision. The role of these elites, and their divergence from the interests of users of the financial system, came under intense scrutiny in the period immediately after the post-2008 financial crisis. The focus of that scrutiny was on those who occupy leadership and management roles at the apex of the financial system: the members of the governing bodies of financial institutions—be they mutual associations, partnerships, trusts, or proprietary corporations—and on the cadre of richly compensated individuals—traders, brokers, investment analysts—whose reckless risk-taking was seen as being the key cause of the crisis. This aetiology is not without basis. But these individuals are only the

---

[1] Katharina Pistor, 'Towards a Legal Theory of Finance', ECGI Working Paper Series in Law, working paper 196/2013, February 2013.

most visible part of the networks of elites who dominate the financial system. And although in the wake of many financial scandals it is the competence, integrity, and behaviour of bank boards and senior management that have been at the forefront of calls for accountability, and the focus of public anger and popular scorn, the influence of the other less visible elites in finance must not be overlooked.

The purpose of this chapter is to draw attention to one such less visible grouping of elites, namely, the community of lawyers—practitioners, judges, arbitrators, and academics—who play a vital role in structuring and maintaining the functioning of the financial system. Financial activity takes place within the framework of law and is enabled by the law, but it also claims *legitimacy* from the law. Financial transactions, at a private level, cloak themselves in the normative claims that underpin the private law concepts of contract, expectations, trust, fiduciary conduct, and shareholder responsibility. At a regulatory level, they claim legal legitimacy through their purportedly willing and voluntary engagement with regulatory standards—seen, most recently, in the eagerness of financial institutions suspected of misconduct to reach agreed settlements with regulators under which they undertake to reshape their future conduct, and to pay vast sums of money to atone for their past misdeeds.

Yet the law is not static: it is constantly being reshaped through processes in which elites are strongly implicated. It is often forgotten that the complex financial instruments that have been the target of so much opprobrium were legal documents—contracts, deeds, and other instruments of obligation—and that their creation involved *legal* innovation as much as it involved *financial* innovation.[2] It is also often forgotten that this pattern of legal innovation—a relentless drive to transmute and transform the legal framework of finance—is as old as modern finance. Legal history tells us of a constant trend, going back at least as far as the seventeenth century, of financial elites working through and with legal actors to reshape, extend, and repurpose legal concepts, categories, and understandings in ways that better serve the ends they seek to pursue.[3]

This makes it imperative that we consider who these legal actors are. Who are the individuals who advise and assist financial institutions? What role do they play within the broader networks of financial elites and the financial system? How do they influence understandings and outcomes in relation to what is and what is not permissible, possible, or profitable within the

---

[2] For a rare exception, see David Howarth, *Law as Engineering: Thinking about What Lawyers Do* (Cheltenham, 2013).

[3] See e.g. T. T. Arvind, 'Law, Creditors, and Crises: The Untold Story of Debt', in Abdul Karim Aldohni (ed.), *Law and Finance after the Financial Crisis: The Untold Stories of the UK Financial Market* (London, 2016).

framework of law? And is it possible for the law to be structured in a way that ameliorates the most deleterious effects of their influence? These questions, which are fundamental to any enquiry into the role, influence, and accountability of financial elites, are the subject of this chapter.

7.2 Financial Elites and Legal Elites: Mapping the Relationship

Insofar as an elite is an exclusive repository of specialist knowledge and privilege, the legal profession must surely be seen as being one. In the case of the financial sector and especially in the case of the large financial institutions that have come to dominate it from the late twentieth century to the present time there is now a core of global highly specialist professional advisory firms. A significant number of these have grown up in the United Kingdom and remain headquartered in the City of London. In the United Kingdom the term 'Magic Circle' is often used to refer to this elite group of legal advisers.

As with all elites, the elite status of this group of legal actors is enhanced by their relationship with the individuals and organizations which occupy the highest circles of state power. The contribution financial elites make to UK GDP and export earnings—and, thus, their overall importance to the British polity—is highlighted from time to time not just by the industry and profession themselves, but also by government ministers and other public authorities. Thus in 2011, the then Lord Chancellor and Secretary of State for Justice, Sir Kenneth Clarke, extolled what he termed a 'national genius' for legal services in the United Kingdom highlighting export earnings and contribution to UK GDP of law as a business sector.[4]

The relationship between these leading law firms and the financial industry is fundamental to their elite status. The Corporation of the City of London, in a report issued around much the same time as Sir Kenneth's comments noted above, singled out the contribution these law firms made to the financial industry, and their role (along with their counterparts in New York) in making the United Kingdom a key centre for financial, tax, and commercial law.[5]

---

[4] <https://www.gov.uk/government/news/kenneth-clarke-uk-should-be-lawyer-and-adviser-to-the-world> and see also Department of Justice Press release accompanying Action Plan for Legal Services Market reforms, <https://www.gov.uk/government/news/uk-cements-position-as-centre-of-legal-excellence> (16 May 2011).

[5] The report trumpeted the UK as 'a leading provider of many professional and support services associated with the financial services industry [and that] Legal services generated £20.9bn in 2011, 1.6% of GDP, and net exports of £3.3bn. The UK is one of two leading centres for international legal services, including corporate finance, corporate and commercial law and tax. Four of the ten largest global law firms are from the UK', *An Indispensable Industry: Financial Services in the UK*, report published by the City of London Corporation in 2011, <https://www.cityoflondon.gov.uk/business/economic-research-and-information/statistics/Documents/an-indispensable-idustry.pdf>.

Financial Elites, Law, and Regulation

Unsurprisingly, then, such firms inevitably identify closely with their client base of (equally global) financial institutions. This identification has profound implications for their activities and goals. Far from simply documenting financial transactions and deals after they have been struck, such lawyers are intimately involved with their financial sector client base. A revolving door of secondment of staff from law firms into their financial sector clients and back again, into their clients' regulatory bodies, and into government departments that shape financial sector policy, cements cultural ties and secures a congruence of perspective and world view from the earliest stages of a lawyer's career.

The close and symbiotic relationship between financial institutions and their lawyers exists at every level of the law firm. Taken together with the importance government and regulatory bodies attach to the symbolic capital built up by elite lawyers, it leads to a culture in which elite firms have both the opportunity and the motive to influence policy in their clients' interests. Junior lawyers in elite firms monitor legislative, regulatory, and policy developments that might affect their clients' interests, and identify areas on which mid-career lawyers can devote time to lobbying and advocacy with government on their clients' behalf. Senior and retired partners in the 'Magic Circle' law firms are in demand not only as non-executive board members of financial institutions, but to fulfil critical roles within regulatory bodies.[6] This is far from a purely modern phenomenon. The discussion in section 7.4 of the role of Standing Counsel at the Bank of England in the wake of a nineteenth-century banking scandal shows the facility with which the legal profession has long been able to stay close to and intertwined with the very core of finance and to influence its elites.

7.3 Financial Elites and the Courts: The Problem of Insulation

In addition to the legal profession, two other elite groups in the United Kingdom that are less visible than the directors and senior managers of

---

[6] For example in 2004, following an overhaul of its investigation and enforcement procedures and culture, the then lead regulator for the UK financial sector, the Financial Services Authority announced the appointment of a partner in Clifford Chance to chair its newly established Regulatory Decisions Committee, <http://www.fsac.org.uk/library/communication/pr/2004/098.html>. More recently, Charles Randell, previously a corporate finance law partner at Slaughter & May and lead adviser to HM Government on many of the key financial stability and restructuring arrangements during the height of the 2008 financial crisis, was appointed as an Independent Director to the Board of the Prudential Regulatory Organisation (the subsidiary of the Bank of England responsible for safety and soundness in prudential regulation of much of the finance sector), <http://www.bankofengland.co.uk/publications/Pages/news/2014/034.aspx>. Indeed the managing director of the IMF, Christine Lagarde, herself chaired key executive committees at one of the largest global law firms having been a corporate law partner at Baker & MacKenzie prior to assumption of a political career, <https://www.imf.org/external/np/omd/bios/cl.htm>.

banks are the judges tasked with adjudicating financial sector disputes and the regulatory bodies tasked with oversight of the financial sector. Adjudication by the judiciary of both private law disputes between parties to a financial transaction and public law challenges to regulatory action is constitutive of the way in which law and the legal process mediate competing interests in the financial system. The civil judiciary have, in particular, played a key role over the years in the allocation of property rights, and in determining the priority of the claims of different interest groups, in the aftermath of market collapses, financial shocks, or frauds.

In a common law system such as that of England and Wales,[7] however, the judiciary has a second, broader role, in that it is through the outcome of adjudication of specific disputes that common law behavioural standards and norms are set, as well as losses and gains apportioned. That prospective standard-setting characteristic of the common law occurs through the effect of the operation of the common law doctrine of precedent, according to which like cases are treated alike.[8] This means that the manner in which the courts dealt with a prior case influences the manner in which subsequent cases are decided, having a value that is either persuasive or even binding, depending on the position of the prior court within the judicial hierarchy. Judges' choice of different legal norms and concepts within which to frame and evaluate legal issues arising from complex factual matrices is therefore determinative not just of the outcome of any individual adjudication, but also of whose interests are privileged and advanced not just by the instant decision but by the future development of the financial system and the conduct of future financial business within it. Judges in England and Wales are, however, drawn from an extremely narrow pool not only with reference to society as a whole, but even with reference to the legal profession. Most judges are drawn from the bar, which constitutes less than 10 per cent of the legal profession in England and Wales, and almost exclusively from the most senior ranks of the bar, narrowing the pool even further.[9] It is, in other words, inherent in the nature of the English legal system that a

---

[7] The United Kingdom has three distinct legal systems: England and Wales, Northern Ireland, and Scotland. Northern Ireland is a common law jurisdiction, which means that its laws share core principles with the laws of England and Wales, but it is governed by a different set of precedents and statutes and often differs in particulars. The laws of Scotland are derived from the civil law tradition and Roman law, and differ fundamentally from the common law of England and Wales. Crucially for our purposes, each jurisdiction has its own independent community of lawyers, who are not automatically entitled to practise in the other jurisdictions.

[8] The alchemy of the workings of the common law doctrine of precedent are well explained to the lay reader (and to those from civilian legal systems) by former Law Lord Reid, 'The Judge as Law Maker', *Society of Public Teachers of Law* 1972–3 (12): 22–9.

[9] See Alan Paterson and Chris Paterson, 'Guarding the Guardians? Towards an Independent, Accountable and Diverse Senior Judiciary' (2012), <http://www.centreforum.org/assets/pubs/guarding-the-guardians.pdf> (accessed 1 February 2015).

narrow section of the legal elite are entrusted with important aspects of the law-making and norm-establishing functions.

This does not, of course, in and of itself mean that the law that emerges from the courts will reflect the interests of the financial sector. A notable characteristic of the early modern common law was that it was structurally insulated from being captured by elite groups, despite the elite composition of its institutions, because the legal system and legal institutions were strongly characterized by what Peter Evans has termed 'embedded autonomy'. A system or institution has embedded autonomy if it combines in itself the ability to make decisions that are *not* mere reflections of the interests of the class of persons with which its members identify (autonomy) with the presence (embeddedness) of 'a concrete set of social ties' that binds the institution in question to society, and provides 'institutionalized channels for the continual negotiation and renegotiation of goals and policies'.[10]

An institution will, typically, be embedded if officials responsible for its functioning have a close personal relationship with society, or if it has within it a set of feedback loops through which officials can gather information about the preferences or interests of a broad cross-section of society (and not just its best-connected members). It will be autonomous if there are formal or informal institutional constraints in place which insulate its officials from identifying too closely with any particular sector in society, whether through formal regulatory capture or more informally through subscribing to the 'thought styles' that are characteristic of any section of society.[11]

Historically, the fact that the common law evolved through litigation gave it a high degree of embeddedness. At the same time, the role of legal doctrine in adjudication before the latter half of the twentieth century, a time when legal thought saw the common law tradition as a repository of high wisdom,[12] ensured that the approach to adjudication remained largely autonomous of the competing interests of different classes and groups within society. Inherent in this approach was the view that if there was a conflict between merchant rationality and the rationality inherent in common law doctrine, then it was the rationality of the common law that should prevail. The history of the early modern common law is littered with cases in which the common law courts refused to give effect to novel instruments such as the promissory note,[13] on the basis that doing so would be contrary to the common law understanding of the nature of contract: the mere fact that a new instrument had been 'invented in Lombard Street' would not give it any special standing

---

[10] Peter Evans, *Embedded Autonomy: States and Industrial Transformation* (Princeton, NJ, 1995).
[11] See T. T. Arvind, *The Law of Obligations: A New Realist Approach* (Cambridge, 2016), chapter 3.
[12] On this, see Julia Rudolph, *Common Law and Enlightenment in England 1689–1750* (Martlesham, 2013).
[13] *Clerke v. Martin* (1702) 2 Ld. Raym. 758, 92 ER 6 (KB).

in the eyes of law, because Lombard Street did not 'give laws to Westminster Hall'.[14] As late as the 1930s, the fact that a particular rule was inconvenient to commerce, or even to finance, was not seen as an argument against the rule. It was, instead, seen as illustrating the need for commercial parties to write their contracts more carefully.[15]

None of this holds true today. Very little remains of the conventions and rules that served to insulate the judiciary so strongly from identifying with, or being captured by, the commercial and financial classes. Instead, modern judges in the superior courts identify closely with the elite interests of persons engaged in commerce and finance. The role of the courts, as they see it, is to put in place rules which support and further the needs of the commercial sector. Lord Goff, a leading commercial judge who did much to reshape commercial law in a more business-friendly direction in the 1980s and 1990s, put it in characteristically evocative language in a speech, originally delivered in a non-judicial capacity but subsequently adopted by the House of Lords:[16]

> We are there to help businessmen, not to hinder them; we are there to give effect to their transactions, not to frustrate them; we are there to oil the wheels of commerce, not to put a spanner in the works, or even grit in the oil.[17]

It is not our purpose here to argue that this is a change for the worse, although there is a powerful argument to be made that the law's role must, in fact, sometimes include putting a spanner in the works of the relentless pursuit by businessmen of their interests. It is, rather, to point out that the result is a profound shift, akin to what Philippe Nonet and Philip Selznick have characterized as a shift from 'autonomous' law to 'responsive' law,[18] wherein the courts see their role not as giving effect to the law's autonomous rationality, which is expressly insulated from the expectations of any individual section of society, but as being to fulfil the expectations of those who are primarily affected by it. The result is not just to challenge the law's traditional autonomy, but also to transform the basis of its embeddedness. Governing institutions, Evans pointed out, could be embedded in a broad cross-section of society, but they could equally be embedded in a much narrower section of society, such as the capital-owning classes. A narrowly embedded institution will still govern

---

[14] Ibid. (Holt CJ).
[15] See e.g. the observations of Scrutton LJ in *W.N. Hillas & Co Ltd v. Arcos Ltd* (1931) 40 Lloyds Rep 307, 310.
[16] See *The Starsin* [2003] UKHL 12, [2004] 1 AC 715, [57] (Lord Steyn).
[17] Lord Goff of Chieveley, 'Commercial Contracts and the Commercial Court' [1984] LMCLQ 382, 391.
[18] Philippe Nonet and Philip Selznick, *Law and Society in Transition: Toward Responsive Law* (New York, 1978).

effectively, but the outcomes it produces will reflect a much narrower range of interests and perspectives than a more broadly embedded institution.

Section 7.4 of this chapter will argue that this change has had the effect of entrenching and privileging the interests of global financial elites within the United Kingdom's legal system, but before getting to that argument it is useful to examine the common law courts' response to the last great financial crisis in Britain before the crisis that emerged in 2008, namely, the bank failures of the late nineteenth century. These came at a time when the case law emerging from the civil courts had begun to shift in a more overtly business-friendly direction, but before that shift would be institutionally entrenched by the effective abolition of the civil jury and the creation of the commercial court. Yet at the time of the Victorian banking failures, the law—particularly the criminal law—retained a strong sense that, notwithstanding the imperative of facilitating commerce, the legal system must enforce broader social standards of acceptable conduct.

There is a clear contrast to be made with the modern law. The new legal rules embodied in the Financial Services (Banking Reform) Act 2013 are illustrative. This package of statutory reforms was a response to the perceived absence of accountability for senior executives in financial institutions, particularly given the continued intensity of concerns expressed in the early post-crisis period. Reforms pursuant to this legislation include a new Senior Managers and Certification Regime[19] and a new criminal offence, which has become colloquially known as the 'reckless banking' offence. The character of this offence is of profound importance to analysing the significance of the financial elite in post-crisis discourse in the United Kingdom. The close alliances subsisting between the financial elite within the City of London and the UK legal elite can be illustrated by how, during the conception of the new law, it was proposed that incurring liability could be avoided. Interestingly, such consideration of the avoidance of liability arose notwithstanding that from the earliest stages of its conception, the new criminal offence was widely considered as a symbolic extension of criminal liability rather than one intended to be widely enforced.

It is this that highlights the contrast with the common law's attitude during its pre-elite, more socially embedded phase. Examining how these ideas worked themselves out in the course of the prosecutions and trials of leading bankers in the nineteenth century gives us a powerful insight into how a more socially embedded legal system responded to and dealt with financial elites. The manner in which the judiciary holds to account under criminal law those

---

[19] See HM Treasury (2012), *Senior Managers and Certification Regime: Extension to all FSMA Authorised Persons* (London, October 2015), <https://www.gov.uk/government/uploads/system/uploads/attachment_data/file/468328/SMCR_policy_paper_final_15102015.pdf>.

members of financial elites it deems responsible for egregious harm to the financial system or to particular groups of its customers (and indeed whether it does so at all) reveals something about our broader collective expectations of financial elites. And, even more fundamentally, exploring the opportunities generated for an increasingly identifiable and indeed metropolitan financial elite *through* a culture of heightening legal interest in banking during the nineteenth century sheds significant light on the nature of financial elites today, and the issues arising from their operation in the modern context.

7.4 Financial Elites and the Public Interest: Contrasting Nineteenth- and Twenty-First Century Criminal Law

The nineteenth century was a crucial time in terms of the financial elite's interactions with the legal elite. Legal change occurring from the middle years of the nineteenth century empowered the financial elite significantly, in an apparent inversion of the financial–legal elite alliances likely to arise from the operation of the new 'reckless banking' offence. The opportunities for the financial elite in actually scoping legal reforms relating to business broadly and banking specifically arose from how legal expertise in 'commercial law' was during that time burgeoning but also nascent. That this phenomenon from more than a century ago might be significant for analysing new law in the light of current policy trends and possible future directions flows in many ways from how the global financial crisis of 2007–8 has clearly concretized perceptions that new approaches are needed for how financial institutions are regulated.

From many highly profiled references to this from key regulators (who can themselves be configured as a specialist branch of the present-day financial elite), one appears to be particularly salient. In 2012 then head of Financial Stability of the Bank of England—and currently Executive Director Monetary Analysis & Statistics—Andy Haldane remarked that responding to the financial crisis would require nothing less than a radical departure from the regulatory path taken during the past fifty years. This alone would be capable of delivering change demanded by the 'once-in-a-lifetime crisis' represented by the events of 2007–8.[20] For Mr Haldane this radical departure would indeed require regulators to tread where they feared to go, rather than being led elsewhere by the market.[21] This reflected the need for fresh approaches, grounded in simplicity instead of 'feeding' the widely purported complexity

---

[20] Andrew G. Haldane and Vasileios Madouros, 'The Dog and the Frisbee', Federal Bank of Kansas Economic Policy Symposium, Wyoming, 31 August 2012.
[21] Ibid., 24–5.

of modern finance, and for brighter lines to separate commands of 'thou shalt' and 'thou shalt not'.[22]

Clearly the spirit of Mr Haldane's remarks in 2012 can be seen in earlier highly publicized policy critiques of financial institutions and particularly banks following the crisis, for example the FSA Report on Royal Bank of Scotland,[23] as well as subsequently for example in the publications of the Parliamentary Commission on Banking Standards appointed in the wake of the Libor-fixing revelations of June 2012. But for present purposes, attention is paid instead to how in making such aspirational statements, Mr Haldane adopted a long analytical time frame. Interestingly in drawing on times long predating the crisis as well as ones immediately doing so, Mr Haldane's remarks illustrate a more pervasive analytical trend within discourses on configuring new regulatory directions. Current references to the importance of history for configuring regulatory reform can be traced initially to the Treasury Select Committee's 2007–8 Report *The Run on the Rock*.[24] This report linked banking 'runs' from the nineteenth century to 'lessons' which must be learned from the collapse of Northern Rock in recognizing the importance of preventing the collapse of systemically important financial institutions in approaches adopted in future to promote systemic stability.[25] Subsequently, this can also be tracked through Bank of England references respectively to historical events and patterns,[26] and FSA allusion—prior to its demise—to the value of history,[27] and to then Governor of the Bank of England Mervyn King's lament in 2012 that too little attention had been paid to 'lessons' from history during the time which in retrospect was the antecedence of the crisis.[28]

Whilst regulators show no awareness of channelling 'historical awareness', these sentiments expressed by them are very much in the vein of historian John Tosh's representation of the present being part of an unfolding trajectory, whereby past and present are linked to one another and to the future through an understanding of the journey undertaken as societies pass from

---

[22] Ibid., 22–3.
[23] FSA Board, *The Failure of the Royal Bank of Scotland*, RBS Report (London: FSA, 2011).
[24] The House of Commons Treasury Committee Report on Northern Rock, *The Run on the Rock*, HC 2007–8, 56-1, see especially pp. 3 and 6–7.
[25] Captured in the acronym SIFI (systemically important financial institutions) with the prefix G-SIFI used to denote global importance. Banks specifically are also identified in the nomenclature (G) SIB to denote systemic importance: see e.g. Financial Stability Board publications from 2011 and 2013, <http://www.financialstabilityboard.org/publications/r_131111.htm>.
[26] As considered below in speeches from Andrew Haldane and Paul Tucker.
[27] See S. Dewar 'Tackling Financial Crime in the Current Economic Climate', Annual Financial Crime Conference, 27 April 2009, <http://webarchive.nationalarchives.gov.uk/*/http://www.fsa.gov.uk/>.
[28] Mervyn King, 'The *Today* Lecture 2012', 2 May 2012.

one point in time to another.[29] Even without reference to this intellectual underpinning for attaching significance to the past as responses to current societal challenges are being cast, in the regulatory aftermath of the crisis, it was recommended that the Bank of England should put in place measures which would in future promote its ability to learn from the past.[30] Prior to this, speeches from both Mr Haldane and then Bank of England Deputy Governor Paul Tucker,[31] had alluded to banking's operations during the nineteenth century, in presenting their visions for its future parameters in the wake of the crisis. Again, without reference to how historians and legal historians alike have identified the nineteenth century as a period of 'striking change' and 'pressure for change',[32] with this in turn mirroring contemporary reflections,[33] Mr Haldane and Mr Tucker's interest in this point of time provides an entreaty for analysing the significance of the nineteenth-century financial and legal elites. They also help to set out how important periods of financial instability—widely analysed as 'crises'—would be for consolidating their operations and actually their significance and power.

Very importantly, it appears that the basis of banking's traditional 'social contract'—that which permits bankers to pursue personal reward for undertaking risk inherent in providing services to the economy[34]—became forged as determined efforts were made to calibrate and then to embed a culture of responsibility and accountability. This reflected how banks would emerge as principal depositories of financial savings and primary allocators of credit and ultimately management of the nation's payment systems.[35] In turn, the development of such a discourse for banking would help to mark out 'commercial distress' experienced in Britain during the 1850s from a century-long pattern of 'economic uncertainty' with 'severe trade cycles and a stock market

---

[29] See John Tosh, *The Pursuit of History: Aims, Methods and New Directions in the Study of Modern History* (London, 2010), 40: see generally chapters 1 and 2 for Tosh's discussion of the uses of history.

[30] See its Final Report, 'Changing Banking For Good' (London, 2013).

[31] See for example Paul Tucker, 'Redrawing the Banking Social Contract', British Bankers Association Annual International Conference, 30 June 2009, p. 1, <http://www.bis.org/review/r090708d.pdf>, and Andrew Haldane, 'Credit is Trust', Association of Corporate Treasurers, Leeds, 14 September 2009, p. 4, <http://www.bankofengland.co.uk/archive/Documents/historicpubs/speeches/2009/speech400.pdf>.

[32] See respectively Jeremy Black and Donald McRaild, *Nineteenth-Century Britain* (Basingstoke, 2002), 17; and Chantal Stebbings, 'Benefits and Barriers: The Making of Victorian Legal History', in Anthony Musson and Chantal Stebbings (eds.), *Making Legal History: Approaches and Methodologies* (Cambridge, 2012), especially 72–3.

[33] See for example *A Century of Law Reform: Twelve Lectures on the Changes in the Law of England during the Nineteenth Century* (London, 1901), 1.

[34] And which Mr Tucker insisted must be rethought in the wake of the crisis: see Paul Tucker, 'Redrawing the Banking Social Contract', British Bankers Association Annual International Conference, 30 June 2009, p. 1, <http://www.bis.org/review/r090708d.pdf>.

[35] See Vincent P. Poliziatto, 'World Bank Prudential Regulation and Banking Supervision', background paper for the 1989 *World Development Report*, Washington DC 1989.

crash roughly every ten years'.[36] From this, by drawing on a strong tradition of 'banking history',[37] we can regard the 1850s as a decade of manifest importance for banking in becoming a matter of 'public concern', and not simply a 'matter of concern for shareholders', bringing about significant change for the contemporary elite.[38] During this decade generally industrial capitalism would become recognizably embedded in the world's first industrial nation, with this embeddedness increasingly manifested in the development of supporting legal and cultural frameworks, with this occurring within the setting of a nascent modern state which regarded itself as increasingly capable and confident. For banks specifically, structurally a growing preference for incorporation over the traditional partnership model would transform these business entities, with the trend towards incorporation having significant outward-looking effects. As increasing attention became fixed on the crucial links banks provided between business and the nation's pioneering capitalist economy, a growing discourse of responsibilizing the actions of bankers would become heightened by the instability of the 1850s.

More generally, this 'commercial crisis' had significant lasting impact from originating in turbulence experienced in US railway speculations,[39] and from the proximity of this with Britain's own railway crisis a decade earlier, which had shaken confidence in the new model of 'investor capitalism',[40] destabilized many banks, and even threatened the Bank of England's own ability to continue making payment.[41] The impact of this earlier turbulence on banking specifically would help to concretize a sense of the banking sector's increasing 'public utility' during the 1850s through the recognized importance of this financing sector across an increasingly broad section of society, and with this being increasingly reflected in the attraction of banks as investment prospects.

The responsibilizing effects of this trajectory can be seen readily in key mid-century developments spanning ones which are well known and ones which are less so. An example of the former lies in Palmerston's famous 1855 missive on the importance of distinguishing banks from other types of business, on account of recognizing their unique qualities arising from being underpinned

---

[36] Michael Lobban, 'Nineteenth-Century Frauds in Company Formation: *Derry v Peek* in Context', *Law Quarterly Review* 1996 (112): 287–8.

[37] See for example Youssef Cassis, *City Bankers 1890–1914* (Cambridge, 2009), and Youssef Cassis, 'Private Banks and the Onset of the Corporate Economy', in Youssef Cassis and Philip L. Cottrell (eds.), *The World of Private Banking* (Farnham, 1994), 43–61.

[38] See Lord Adair Turner; and indeed a matter of public concern: see FSA Press Notice 'FSA Board publishes report into the failure of the Royal Bank of Scotland', 12 December 2011.

[39] See David Morier Evans, *The Commercial Crisis 1857–1858* (New York, 1969 [1859]).

[40] See Sarah Wilson *The Origins of Modern Financial Crime: Historical Foundations and Current Problems in Britain* (London, 2014).

[41] Walter Eltis, 'Lord Overstone and the Establishment of British Nineteenth-Century Monetary Orthodoxy', *Discussion Papers in Economic and Social History* 2001 (42), University of Oxford.

by 'duty... of the nature of a trust'.[42] Drawing attention to this was necessary because banks, through the model of incorporation, were in many ways being required to behave as ordinary businesses in generating profit and appeasing shareholders. A less well-known illustration of this can be found in criminal cause célèbre trials dating from *c.*1850 when bankers predominated in accusations that businessmen had engaged in conduct so egregious that it should attract liability to reflect this: liability distinct from that arising from an institution's relationship with its customers and shareholders, and which instead acknowledged the impact of impropriety on society.

For pioneers of nineteenth-century criminal liability, responding to misconduct in business was a conscious reflection of harm believed to be inflicted by irresponsible conduct, and through a small cluster of 'financial crime history' far more is now understood about this. This has also been able to shed light on how banking became such a strong focal point within this generalized favour for engendering responsibilization through criminal culpability on account of its unique importance within the financial system and its corresponding unparalleled ability to scatter 'wide-spread ruin... over the whole of the country' ruining businesses and plunging families into poverty.[43] This setting appears to have its own parallels with current perspectives on how banking is capable of 'imposing unacceptable costs on the rest of society',[44] which new measures such as the Senior Managers and Certification Regime and the 'reckless banking' offence are seeking to remedy. But far too little is still known about how these attempts to responsibilize the activities of bankers through legal innovation and enforcement led to the empowerment of the nineteenth-century financial elite. This is a particularly interesting line of enquiry on account of how this occurred within, and consolidated the existence of, a distinctive 'space' in which the private sphere of business was able to influence a markedly special sphere of public activity. Indeed, even in the context of a dominant culture of private prosecution, criminal prosecution was recognized as responding to a public 'wrong'.[45]

More than a century later, in presenting the government's case for extending criminal liability for bankers, a Treasury Consultation in 2012 noted that the FSA's 2011 Report on the Royal Bank of Scotland had stimulated interest in new criminal sanctions as another way of 'shifting the balance between risk

---

[42] In the context of debates on making incorporation with limited liability generally available: HC Deb 27 July 1855, vol. 139, col. 1446, Viscount Palmerston.

[43] Sir Frederic Thesiger, Address for the prosecution in the trial of the Royal British Bank directors 1858, cited in David Morier Evans, *Facts, Failures & Frauds: Financial Mercantile Criminal* (New York, 1968 [1859]), 289.

[44] Bank of England, *The Role of Macroprudential Policy: A Discussion Paper* (Macroprudential Discussion Paper, 2009), 3. For general discussion see Eddy Wymeersch, Klaus J. Hopt, and Guido Ferrarini (eds.), *Financial Regulation and Supervision: A Post-Crisis Analysis* (Oxford, 2012).

[45] See extensive discussion of this in Wilson, *The Origins of Modern Financial Crime*.

and reward for bank directors'.[46] This emphasis was seen within a context of concern about the likely role played by excessive risk-taking in bringing about the crisis in 2007, and ensuring its effects would be widespread and prolonged. And although the Consultation endorsed earlier sentiments that extending criminal liability for reckless decision-making was intended to encourage care in decisions taken by institutions of 'vital national importance' through casting the 'shadow of prosecution' over their senior executives rather than being widely enforced,[47] it also envisaged that achieving this would require alliances between financial and legal communities. This was expressed through how determinations of liability arising for the 'Offence relating to a decision causing a financial institution to fail'[48] would involve discerning what would constitute 'normal or non-excessive risks' and in which a 'responsible bank board' was likely to seek 'legal advice about whether a decision could be considered reckless'.[49]

The significance which is being attached to *legal* assessments of *commercial* decision-making, and indeed the legitimation of the latter by the former speaks to how the consequences of conviction can be extremely grave, even if this measure is intended to be largely symbolic instead of widely enforced. Section 36 of the Financial Services (Banking Reform) Act 2013 carries a maximum sentence of imprisonment for seven years,[50] and in the course of targeting senior organizational figures, that those serving on bank boards intended to be subject to its reach might be configured as 'financial elite' can follow persuasively from emphasis within the discourse of SIFIs and 'institutions of vital national importance'. Moreover, that the legal advice envisioned is likely to be generated through legal services provided by the City's legal elite can be extrapolated from known alliances between these communities which transpired during the crisis. Indeed we need look no further than at the affairs of Northern Rock, coming to light in September 2007, and subsequently stimulating the Treasury Select Committee's interest in nineteenth-century bank runs. Whilst the popular sectors of the media diligently published the now iconic images of queues outside Northern Rock's branches as concerns about its continuing viability generated considerable public alarm, different sectors of the press explained how Northern

---

[46] HM Treasury, *Sanctions for the directors of failed banks*, HM Treasury, 2012, para. 4.1: see <https://www.gov.uk/government/uploads/system/uploads/attachment_data/file/81565/consult_sanctions_directors_banks.pdf>.
[47] Rt. Hon Matthew Hancock MP, 'The right are right to challenge rewards for failure', speech, 12 January 2012, <http://www.matthewhancock.co.uk/campaign/matthew-hancock-mp-right-are-right-challenge-rewards-failure>.
[48] See section 36 for conditions required for liability to arise, relating to institutional failure and seniority of those entrusted with decision-making.
[49] HM Treasury, *Sanctions for the directors of failed banks*, para. 4.11.
[50] By virtue of Financial Services (Banking Reform Act) section 36(4)(b).

Rock's difficulties had brought about a permanently changed relationship between City legal stalwarts Freshfields (Freshfield Bruckhaus Deringer), and its oldest and most famous client—the Bank of England.

Several years on from 2007, the banking community (elite?) itself continues to enthuse about how Freshfields is called upon regularly to advise the Bank of England,[51] but the position whereby the Bank sought legal advice from Freshfields exclusively, and which had subsisted since 1743, came to an end in 2007. This was when Freshfields commenced advising the stricken Northern Rock in relation to its restructuring, thereby creating a conflict of interest on account of the emergency assistance being provided by the Bank of England. The legal controversy created by Northern Rock's financial difficulties involving Freshfields also drew in two other key City law firms, as Clifford Chance advised the Bank of England and Allen & Overy provided guidance for Northern Rock in connection with its emergency assistance. These firms together with Linklaters and Slaughter & May embody the prowess and expertise associated with the 'Magic Circle', and they are thus particularly well placed to become prominent and influential players in the advice given to bank boards on avoiding decision-making which could be regarded as reckless. More than a century earlier, the firm known traditionally as Messers Freshfields played a central role in alliances forged between legal and financial elites during the nineteenth century. These were alliances which it is argued greatly empowered commercial interests in Victorian determinations of legal liability.

Through investigations into the history of financial crime it is possible to trace the emergence of a small elite of legal actors which occurred from the 1850s, who became experts in matters of 'financial crime'. This in turn tells a tale of how very bold and determined statements were made concerning the 'proper bounds' of conduct in business for the purposes of framing criminal liability in circumstances where law professed to know little about business matters,[52] and actually that it should not adjudicate on them, and instead leave such matters to business people.[53] Legal boldness in business matters can be seen in key statutory reform undertaken in the Punishment of Frauds Act 1857[54] and in courtroom statements made during criminal trials of businessmen for misconduct alleged to amount to 'high art' crime.[55] Both sought to communicate strong normative messages of propriety in the conducting of business affairs, and within this both placed particularly marked emphasis on

---

[51] See for example the British Banking Association's publicity on its key associates: <https://www.bba.org.uk/about-us/associates/freshfields-bruckhaus-deringer/>.

[52] As considered below herein.   [53] As stated seminally in *Foss v. Harbottle* (1843) 2 Hare, 461.

[54] 'An Act to make better Provision for the Punishment of Frauds committed by Trustees, Bankers, and other Persons intrusted with property', 20 and 21 Vict c 54.

[55] See Evans, *Facts, Failures & Frauds*, 1.

responding to indulgence in 'ill-considered' venturing[56] which then often precipitated secondary or collateral[57] wrongdoing manifested in misappropriations to try to make good losses, or misrepresentations designed to conceal them.[58]

Both these legislative and courtroom discourses, in their interest in the activities of the financial and wider commercial elites, often targeted bankers specifically. This professional grouping can be seen at the heart of the 'mischief' underpinning the 1857 Act,[59] and also as the subject of many of the criminal trials of the second half of the nineteenth century. And in terms of configuring the operations of nineteenth-century capitalist activities as ones occupied by an elite, it was of course so that through the onset and progression of the enterprise economy arising from embedding industrial capitalism the composition of the commercial elite would undergo significant change. Key actors would increasingly come from beyond the confines of the traditional elite embodying the 'City club'[60] as an influx of new participants and the decline in 'face-to-face' dealings resulting from increased transactional freedom precipitated a breakdown in traditional transactional governance.[61] But as the criminal proceedings show, those on trial either were from 'high office'[62] from the highest social echelons,[63] or 'respectable' 'gentlemen' from 'good family backgrounds',[64] who through their ability to penetrate such occupational circles were able to acquire elite credentials.[65]

In the context of courtroom addresses concerning those who stood accused and were convicted of misconduct in their business affairs, judicial pronouncements provide particularly fertile reference points for the importance being placed by mid-to-late nineteenth-century legal discourse upon the proper bounds of business. These show very clear statements on the expected

---

[56] Ibid., 128, considered by the author in respect of London bankers Strahan, Paul and Bates, tried at the Central Criminal Court in 1855 for embezzlement of property entrusted by customers.
[57] See David Nelken, 'White-Collar Crime', in Mike Maguire, Rod Morgan, and Robert Reiner (eds.), *The Oxford Handbook of Criminology* (Oxford, 1994), at 373–4.
[58] Both of which can be found provided for in the 1857 Act. [59] As evident in its long title.
[60] Per David Kynaston; see *The City of London* (in 4 volumes, London, 1994–2001), and indeed the titular significance evident in *The City of London Volume 4: Club No More, 1945–2000*.
[61] See discussion in Sarah Wilson, 'Tort Law, Actors in the "Enterprise Economy", and Articulations of Nineteenth-Century Capitalism with Law: The Fraudulent Trustees Act 1857 in Context', in T. T. Arvind and J. Steele (eds.), *Tort Law and the Legislature: Common Law, Statute and the Dynamics of Legal Change* (Oxford, 2012), 353.
[62] As expressed in Baron Alderson's concluding post-conviction remarks in the trial of Strahan, Paul and Bates in 1855, transcribed in Evans, *Facts, Failures & Frauds*, 145.
[63] As stressed in the Committal hearing for the trial of Strahan et al. before Bow Street Magistrates: see Evans, *Facts, Failures & Frauds*, 117.
[64] See the defence submissions made on behalf of John Stapleton in the trial of the Royal British Bank directors, the Central Criminal Court London, 1858 (reported (1858) F and F, 213), and fully transcribed in Evans, *Facts, Failures & Frauds*, 350.
[65] See the position of Bates in the firm of Strahan, Paul and Bates, as illuminated as background to their criminal trial in 1855 in Evans, *Facts, Failures & Frauds*, 110–11.

conduct of respectable businessmen regarded as being part of the elite. They also convey strongly the need to ensure that 'infamous' conduct—so called because of the harm it was considered capable of inflicting upon the economy and society—was severely punished, on account that failure to do so would amount to 'a disgrace to the law of any country'.[66] From this it might be asked how legal actors with little or no commercial expertise, and showing strong commitment to the autonomy of business interests in developing a framework for articulating law with industrial capitalism, could make such statements so confidently.

In the context of banking specifically from c.1850, it appears that increasingly the Bank of England became concerned to recruit those with expertise in criminal matters to the role of Standing Counsel. This office had existed since the eighteenth century,[67] but traditionally clustered around the largely chancery-oriented business of the Bank. Perceptions of change in the Bank's legal needs can be identified from exchanges between the Bank and its solicitor Freshfields, as illuminated in correspondence between the former and Charles Freshfield in the decade from 1849.[68] On a general level, Charles Freshfield regaled the importance of appointing persons who were most suitably qualified rather than those who might be the best connected,[69] thereby chiming into a more generalized social movement away from hierarchy towards meritocracy.[70] Beyond this, an identifiable legal elite can be seen to emerge from the triangulation of initial resource given to 'criminal matters'[71] and the expertise gleaned from involvement in the legal proceedings themselves with those who occupied key legal roles in the trials. Amongst those who were lead counsel in the iconic early phase 'financial crime' trials, were leading lights of the day—including Harry Bodkin Poland—who also held office as Bank of England Standing Counsel c.1850–80 during this critical time for criminalizing business activity.[72]

Beyond this, questions remain about how legal confidence in making pronouncements in conduct in business became formulated and entrenched. The early phase criminal trials abound with such clear and definite statements, insisting in turn that alleged misconduct amounted to 'infamous crime'

---

[66] Evans, *Facts, Failures & Frauds*, 110–11, see the transcription of Lord Campbell's closing remarks for the Royal British Bank trial, 384–5.

[67] This office had existed since the eighteenth century: see Judy Slinn, *A History of Freshfields* (London, 1994), 17.

[68] As documented in the Bank of England's Freshfield Papers Archive, B[ank] of E[ngland] Archives, F6/4.

[69] BE F6/4, Charles Freshfield to Deputy Governor, Letter, 25 June 1850.

[70] See Harold Perkin, *Origins of Modern English Society 1780–1880* (London, 1969).

[71] See discussion of this in S. Wilson, *The Origins of Modern Financial Crime: Historical Foundations and Current Problems in Britain* (London, 2014).

[72] The significance attached to this time frame is explored extensively in Wilson, *The Origins of Modern Financial Crime*.

which required severe punishment to avoid bringing disgrace upon the nation and its legal culture, and equally that (on different occasions) disgrace lay in that criminal proceedings were ever brought. The trials of the Royal British Bank directors in 1858 and of Overend Gurney's directors a decade later respectively illustrate these two positions, and also suggest that little factual difference appears to separate the cases.[73] Such divergent views do appear difficult to reconcile, save that contemporary reflection on the latter case points to how in the eyes of the City, the Overend Gurney directors were considered negligent and 'sanguine' in their approach to business, but that their conduct was not regarded as that which should be deemed criminal.[74]

From this, clarifying what underpinned judicial confidence in making such pronouncements in what was an entirely new context for criminal liability,[75] and where lack of expertise was professed alongside (equally strong) insistence that legal intervention in business affairs would be justified only in the most exceptional of circumstances,[76] is complex. However, this *does* appear to lie in significant attempts being made actively to involve City interests in framing criminal liability. This is certainly evident in the criminal trials, which point to a more generalized acknowledged importance of including City interests rather than alienating them in circumstances where commerce required external scrutiny. The perceived importance of constructive dialogue between legal and commercial interests—which would actively eschew accusations that crime flourished within the City's environs and culture, and stress the importance of channelling the power and expertise of business towards curbing its worst excesses—can be read into key criminal proceedings. These show considerable reliance being placed on businessmen as expert witnesses, and as jurors in testing the scope and limits of criminal liability, and correspondingly high levels of deference and gratitude for these valued inputs. It is also highly likely that sectors of the City community acted as private prosecutors, looking to ensure that malpractices deemed worthy of public exposure and public censure would receive this, and perhaps to try to keep ones deemed not to away from this scrutiny.[77]

In the trials themselves, that all courtroom interests—those of prosecutors, defence, and judges—appeared to look to men of commerce for guidance in the criminalization of business can be illustrated by reference to the trial of the Royal British Bank directors at the Central Criminal Court in 1858. Lord Campbell's regard for the qualifications and knowledge of the jurors is

---

[73] Ibid., especially 189–209.   [74] Ibid.
[75] See generally Wilson, *The Origins of Modern Financial Crime*.
[76] As embodied in *Foss v. Harbottle* (1843).
[77] Discussion of this specifically in the context of banking can be seen in Wilson, *The Origins of Modern Financial Crime*, 189–209.

manifest in his reference to them as 'proper judges of fact'.[78] This can be attributed to understandings arising ordinarily in jury trials,[79] but it also appears to recognize that judgement qualities could arise in more extraordinary ways. The value placed on expertise from business in determining the scope of criminal liability points to the importance of dominant mores and practices in determining which conduct would be considered 'acceptable' and what was to be regarded as damaging the 'high character...of mercantile transactions'[80] and thereby transgressive.

Within this limited evidence base,[81] what can be gleaned from it goes to some considerable lengths towards constructing a plausible narrative for responding to misconduct committed by the contemporary elite. And albeit that understandings of its composition and configuration were highly dynamic during this time, it was so that those standing accused of misconduct did not 'conform to the popular stereotype of "the criminal"',[82] and their actions would have lacked the 'immediate moral outrage' associated with many activities clothed with the label of crime.[83] Responding to these considerations was challenging and it might appear that legal support for City desire not to penalize carelessness or negligence demonstrates law's perception of its obligation to 'oil the wheels of commerce, not to put a spanner in the works, or even grit in the oil'.[84] Approaches taken might also appear to vindicate contemporary concern that rulings on lawfulness sought to reinforce dominant practices and the position of an established elite rather than respond to egregious conduct, reflecting concerns about intrusions from 'outsiders' and 'outlier' practices in a setting where capitalism's forces of disruption emerged alongside its ones of innovation (and indeed pressure to innovate).

Given a context where disruption sat uneasily alongside how innovation and economic prosperity held the key to wider societal progression, discerning the lawful limits for business activity became an imperative for contemporaries. And notwithstanding that what appear to be extremely fine distinctions *can* be found in nineteenth-century criminalizations—such as in the Royal British Bank and Overend Gurney trials—attempts to draw appropriate distinctions do appear to have been undertaken earnestly and robustly and

---

[78] Per Lord Campbell, trial of Royal British Bank directors 1858: see Evans, *Facts, Failures & Frauds*, 386.
[79] See for example Patrick Devlin, *Trial by Jury* (London, 1956).
[80] See Evans, *Facts, Failures & Frauds*, 214.
[81] See generally Wilson, *The Origins of Modern Financial Crime*.
[82] Edwin H. Sutherland, 'Is "White-Collar Crime" Crime?', *American Sociological Review* 1945 (10.2): 132–9 (137).
[83] Margaret Cole, 'The FSA's Approach to Insider Dealing', speech, American Bar Association, 4 October 2007.
[84] Lord Goff of Chieveley, 'Commercial Contracts and the Commercial Court' (1984) LMCLQ, 382; 391.

in good faith. In the setting of rapid financial evolution and limited developments in the legal framework for capitalism, discerning criminal liability was a particularly taxing task for contemporaries. This is notwithstanding that then, as now, concerns arose from whether determinations of legal accountability for conduct in business could be ones in the interest of ordinary financial citizens and wider society if their origins lie in the furtherance of the interests of business itself.

7.5 Conclusion: Financial Elites and the Legal System

Let us then conclude by considering the implications of the history of the mutual relationship between legal and financial elites for the modern day. As we have argued elsewhere, the relentless drive to prosecute financiers at the very highest levels presents a striking contrast with the approach to criminal prosecutions post-2008, which have invariably focused on foot soldiers rather than generals.[85] But there is also a more profound contrast between the approach of the criminal courts to the Victorian banking prosecutions, and the approach of the modern civil courts to banking cases. Much financial litigation occurs in the Commercial Court, which was created as an attempt by one set of legal elites to preserve their role in commerce against potential encroachment by another: the newly-formed City of London Chamber of Arbitration (now the London Court of International Arbitration), an organization which was 'to have all the virtues which the law lacks'. A series of poor decisions in the ordinary Court of Queen's Bench in commercial cases gave this particular impetus. Unsurprisingly, decision-making by the Commercial Court has since then been unashamedly rooted in traditions of freedom of contract and *caveat emptor*. It has therefore been reductionist in approach and effect. That means the Court has tended not to look beyond and behind contractual documentation. Indeed, in complex financial transactions that documentation tends to be standard form and drafted on terms that are designed to promote certainty and quick and easy payments rather than to allow for any enquiry into the underlying balance of fairness in the dispute. This echoes the point made by Mikael Wendschlag in Chapter 8 in this volume in relation to how economism came to dominate an increasingly technocratic international elite in central banking over the latter half of the last century. It has often been said that one reason for the Commercial Court's

---

[85] T. T. Arvind, J. Gray, and S. Wilson, 'From the Mid-19th Century Bank Failures in the UK to the 21st Century Financial Policy Committee: Changing Views of Responsibility for Systemic Stability', in Matthew Hollow, Folarin Akinbami, and Ranald Michie (eds.), *Complexity and Crisis in the Financial System: Critical Perspectives on the Evolution of American and British Banking* (Cheltenham, 2016), 261–86.

popularity as a forum for dispute resolution in global finance has been these concerns as to efficiency and speed of dispute resolution.[86] These concerns tend naturally to be favourable to frequent users and well advised financial elite users of the Court rather than to outsiders.

The Commercial Court has played a central and influential role in refereeing not just the United Kingdom but the entire global financial system.[87] Much of the financial sector work of the Commercial Court has been concerned with disputes between counterparties to what are known as 'Over the Counter' (OTC) derivative financial instruments—swaps, futures, contracts for differences, and the like. These technically complex contracts are very often concluded *within* financial elites—between financial institutions themselves to manage their own risk exposures. But non-financial corporate, public, and third-sector users also make use of such instruments from time to time in order to protect themselves from a range of risks which arise in the course of their core non-financial activities. They are therefore transacting with members of financial elites and, although obviously advised professionally, do not have the same familiarity or expertise with such complex instruments as do the financial institutions themselves who use them regularly, design and structure them, and, along with the core elite legal firms discussed above, set the parameters of the few Master Agreement templates of terms and conditions pursuant to which these OTC bargains are struck. The most ubiquitous of these Master Agreements is known as the 'ISDA Master Agreement' and consists of extensive sets of standard form yet highly differentiable contractual documentation produced and kept under a review by a wholly private global trade association—the International Swaps and Derivatives Association formed in 1985. ISDA's membership list reads like a roll call of the global financial elite drawn from financial institutions and their professional advisers in sixty-seven different countries and it describes its mission as being to provide safety and certainty to the global derivatives market.[88]

The ISDA Master Agreement has come before the Commercial Court (and also increasingly the Chancery Division of the High Court) on numerous occasions both before and after the 2008 crisis. These courts have almost invariably engaged in a robust application of the relevant terms and protocols of the ISDA Master Agreement to the disputes before it where attempts have

---

[86] Such as the praise for its work from Professor Sir Roy Goode Q.C. in his 1998 Hamlyn Lectures, *Commercial Law in the Next Millennium* (London, 1998).

[87] 'Three quarters of litigants in UK Commercial Court are foreign', *Financial Times*, 29 May 2014, <http://www.ft.com/cms/s/0/4c33f0c0-e716-11e3-88be-00144feabdc0.html#axzz3yun9nYns>.

[88] ISDA describes its key objectives as reduction of counterparty credit risk, increasing transparency, and improvement of the industry's operational infrastructure, <http://www2.isda.org/about-isda/>.

been made by parties from outside of the financial sector to advance legal arguments based on their lack of understanding, capacity, or real and genuine consent to the terms of these complex financial products. These types of argument, while they might once have won a fuller hearing from a Court of Equity, have largely fallen on deaf ears in the UK Commercial Court which has instead emphasized what is expressly provided within the four corners of the contract and highlighted the ubiquitous use of the Master Agreement and its commercial efficacy.[89] Although speaking in the Chancery Divison Mr Justice Briggs could easily have been summing up the approach of the Commercial Court when he commented: 'English law is one of the two systems of law most commonly chosen for the interpretation of the [ISDA] Master Agreement, the other being New York law. It is axiomatic that it should, so far as possible, be interpreted in a way that serves the objectives of clarity, certainty and predictability, so that the very large number of parties using it should know where they stand.'[90]

The work of the Commercial Court (and indeed other divisions of the High Court most notably Chancery) in interpreting and applying the ISDA Master Agreement to OTC derivatives business in the period following the 2008 financial crisis has won approval from some academic commentators.[91] Despite the financial sector's continuing preference to litigate its disputes in London, concerns have been voiced by others that try as they might, the judiciary have sometimes struggled to provide the certainty and predictability of decision-making in the resolution of complex financial transactions that international financial markets (and we would argue financial elites) require.[92] This has resulted in calls for specialist arbitral tribunals for the resolution of complex financial disputes and an initiative that began in 2010 known as PRIME Finance has now been established in The Hague as an expert and private dispute resolution service tailor made for the needs of efficient and low cost dispatch of disputes arising in complex financial transactions. It states its mission in terms that resonate in the public interest as being 'to foster a more stable global economy and financial marketplace by reducing

---

[89] Examples abound of the Commercial Court interpreting and applying the ISDA Master Agreement so as to thwart investor attempts to either imply terms beyond the ISDA standard form or otherwise agreement or invoke arguments from outside of contract law and include (inter alia) attempts to advance *Bankers Trust International plc v. PT Dharmala Sakti Sejahtera* [1996] CLC 518; *Credit Suisse v. Stichtung Vestia Groep* [2014] EWHC 3103 (COMM)]; *SNCB Holdings v. UBS AG* [2012] EWHC 2044 (Comm); *Standard Chartered Bank v. Ceylon Petroleum Corporation* [2011] EWHC 1785 (Comm).
[90] *Lomas and others v. JFB Firth Rixson, Inc and others* [2010] EWHC 3372 (Ch), [53].
[91] Joanne Braithwaite, 'OTC Derivatives, the Courts and Regulatory Reform', *Capital Markets Law Journal* 2012 (7.4): 364–85.
[92] Jeffrey Golden, 'Judges and Systemic Risk in the Financial Markets', *Fordham Journal of Corporate & Financial Law* (2012): 18 Article 4; Jonathan Ross, 'The Case for P.R.I.M.E. Finance', *Capital Markets Law Journal* 2012 (7): 221.

legal uncertainty and systemic risk, and, especially in emerging markets, promoting the rule of law'. And yet its description of itself is in terms that emphasize the elitism and specialism of its members and their closeness to the core of the financial industry:

> This carefully vetted international group includes sitting and retired judges, central bankers, regulators, academics, representatives from private legal practice and derivatives market participants. Many have first-hand experience structuring and executing transactions, as well as of the laws, regulation and standard documentation of the structured finance market, creating a combination of legal and market expertise that is both ideal to the task at hand and completely unprecedented.[93]

It is not hard to see this development in terms of one truly global and highly specialist legal elite close to and well versed in the ways of the more rarefied parts of the financial sector threatening the core business of another legal elite, namely the UK judiciary, which is also on record as seeing its role in terms of promotion of the rule of law around the globe and support of orderly financial markets.[94]

The response from the UK judiciary has been swift and interesting. In June 2015 the Lord Chief Justice of England and Wales announced the formal establishment within the UK court structure of what has been dubbed by some as a new 'Financial Super-Court' but is in actual fact a specialist list of the Commercial and Chancery Divisions of the High Court for financial claims of a value in excess of £50 million or that raise issues of concern to domestic and international financial markets.[95] In justifying the new list as enabling access to the expertise of London's financial markets lawyers and experienced judiciary, reducing costs and delays of litigation, and introducing a text case procedure by which to give fast, clear, and authoritative guidance to financial markets his Lordship could almost have been responding directly to the threat posed by PRIME Finance of loss of high value financial dispute resolution work to London's courtrooms and its attendant legal elites. 'Promotion of the rule of law' gains from the new Financial List come last on his list of justifications for it, almost as an afterthought.

The competition between different segments of the legal elite for a central position in hearing commercial disputes is, of course, precisely what prompted the creation of the Commercial Court in the first place, and its

---

[93] <http://primefinancedisputes.org/about-us/>.
[94] For example see comments of Mr Justice Geoffrey Vos in speech entitled 'The Role of UK Judges in the Success of UK PLC' (KPMG Lecture October 2011), <https://www.innertemplelibrary.com/2011/10/the-role-of-judges-in-the-success-of-uk-plc-speech-by-mr-justice-vos/>.
[95] Lord Thomas, Lord Chief Justice of England Wales speech to the Mansion House in the City of London June 2015.

recurrence at a time when the desirability of the continued autonomy of the financial sector had been called into question is unsurprising. Yet it instantiates, yet again, the key themes of this chapter, namely, the shift in the legal system's willingness and ability to respond robustly to wrongdoing by financial elites or harm caused by them; and the central role played in this shift by the mutually reinforcing interaction of legal and financial elites. The propensity of finance to do harm is a consequence not just of the socially irresponsible conduct of financial elites, but also of the willingness of legal elites to facilitate that conduct and even to reshape legal norms and institutions if that be necessary. Yet, as we have also sought to argue here, such an outcome is far from inevitable. The example of the nineteenth-century trials demonstrates that *even* a legal culture dominated by elites, and by a mutuality of relations between legal and financial elites, is capable of grappling earnestly and robustly with the problem of the socially irresponsible conduct of finance. Against this background, the failure to do so in the post-2008 crisis stands as a hallmark of the failure of legal and regulatory authorities to even begin to grapple with the ever-deepening role of financial elites in the everyday operation of the legal system.

8

Central Bankers in Twelve Countries between 1950 and 2000

The Making of a Global Elite

Mikael Wendschlag

8.1 Introduction

The central bank elite is an appointed elite empowered to lead the day-to-day work of the central banks and make decisions about monetary policy.[1] Their assessment of the economy, as individuals as well as spokespersons for the central banks, carries significant weight in society. This study is concerned with analysing the characteristics of this relatively small, yet influential elite in twelve developed economies between 1950 and 2000.[2]

The study focuses on the leaders, having the title of governor, director, chairman, or president depending on country (the title 'governor' will be used for the remainder of the chapter when not stated otherwise), assumed to be the most influential individuals within the central banks as well as in monetary policy-making. The powers of the central bank governor historically evolved from the general task of 'running the bank', but by the mid-twentieth century, the governorship had developed into a 'formally defined position of authority'.[3] The governor still has special influence over the organization of the central bank, for promotions, and the hiring of key staff. In addition,

---

[1] The work on this chapter began while I was a visiting researcher at the Department of History and Civilization at the European University Institute.
[2] Belgium, Canada, Denmark, Finland, France, Germany, Italy, Japan, the Netherlands, Sweden, UK, and USA.
[3] Anthony Giddens, 'Elites in the British Class Structure', in Philip Stanworth and Anthony Giddens (eds.), *Elites and Power in British Society* (Cambridge, 1974), 4.

formal statutes normally also grant the governor a stronger voting power in monetary policy-making. In monetary policy issues, the governor normally also has an agenda-setting prerogative and so can steers the focus of the bank's policy work.

Except for their formal powers, governors also have a number of less tangible ones. An important one is the convention of the majority voting in favour of the governor's position on policy matters. This custom is deeply rooted in the history of all central banks, and has become self-enforcing, not the least due to outside expectations from the market, media, academics, and other elites in society. Part of the explanation to this convention lies in the fact that the governor is the 'face and body' of the central bank, both in the eyes of the public, but also in the central bank's relations with the political elite, the media, and with the financial elites.

Given their powers and influence that can have significant effects on the economy and historical processes, the central bank elite is very interesting to study, and the academic literature on central banks and bankers is vast to say the least. But in addition to the research of central bankers' influence as agents, it is also possible to look at the central bank elite's personal characteristics and learn more about the power of the structure (to stay with Giddensian terminology).

The present chapter has taken some of this latter perspective to heart by accounting for the professional and educational background of the central bank governors, the 'elite among the elite' in central banking, and describes how these characteristics altered as the economic environment of central banks changed between 1950 and 2000.

To put it differently, the study will investigate *what has made for a credible central banker* at different points in history. The central bank elite is a bit different from business elites in that they are appointed, depending on the approval of another elite, the political one. This circumstance makes the membership in the central bank elite conditional on the political elite's approval, whose decisions in turn mainly are based on the performance of the economy. The central bank governors are thus appointed as much for their personal skills as their 'credibility' in the contemporary economic and political context. So, in general and in aggregate, the economic context seems to pick its particular kind of central bank elite. And economic recessions seem to speed up the turnover of governors and to trigger shifts in perceptions of central banker 'credibility'.

Changes in central bank practices, monetary policy, targets, and modes of operation appear to be closely connected to changes in leadership. Erik Buyst, for example, notes that the Belgian central bank's hard-headed focus on inflation fighting ended, and a more Keynesian monetary policy was adopted, only when governor Maurice Frere retired in 1957 and was replaced by Hubert Ansiaux.[4] The US Fed's attempts to fight inflation did not become credible until Paul Volcker was appointed.

Although the study emphasizes contextual factors, the assumption isn't that the central bank elite merely consists of a 'fairly ordinary executive entrusted with a certain degree of responsibility'[5] with no ability or discretion to take action. On the contrary, history is full of examples of individual central bankers who by their views and actions have played significant roles in financial history. Donald Kettl, for example, finds that 'the Fed's history—and the growth in its power—is largely the product of the leadership of its chairmen'.[6] For Richard Werner, the leaders of the Bank of Japan were very influential political actors during the last half of the last century.[7] David Marsh's study of the German Bundesbank to a large extent is concerned with the bank's leaders and their personal engagement in (quite successfully) defending the Bundesbank's autonomy in the face of political pressures.[8] Pierre Siklos is more sceptical as to the individual's impact on monetary policy but finds that individual central bank leaders may be particularly important at times when the central bank's institutional autonomy has been threatened.[9]

The *lack* of individual skills and characteristics of leading central bankers too can be of great importance. Milton Friedman and Anna Schwarz, for example, famously pointed to the incompetence of the leaders of the US Fed after the death of Benjamin Strong, head of the New York Fed, in 1928, as an important factor in the Fed's (in)action after the 1929 stock market crash.[10] Thus, this chapter recognizes the importance of the individual central banker, but since the focus here is the general trends of the central bank elite's characteristics between 1950 and 2000, most weight is given to the influence of the context, and more specifically, the economic environment, of this particular elite.

8.2 The Outline of the Study

The characteristics of the governors in office during the second half of the twentieth century have been studied by collecting information of their

---

[4] Erik Buyst, 'Why Was Belgium so Late in Adopting Keynesian Ideas and Devising Regional Development Policies', VIVES Discussion Paper No. 27, 2012.
[5] Youssef Cassis and Philip Cottrell, *Private Banking in Europe: Rise, Retreat and Resurgence* (Oxford, 2015), 85.
[6] Donald F. Kettl, *Leadership at the Fed* (New Haven and London, 1986), xi.
[7] Richard Werner, *Princes of the Yen: Japan's Central Bankers and the Transformation of the Economy* (New York, 2003).
[8] David Marsh, *The Bundesbank: The Bank That Rules Europe* (New York, 1992).
[9] Pierre Siklos, *The Changing Face of Central Banking: Evolutionary Trends Since World War II* (New York, 2002).
[10] Milton Friedman and Anna Jacobson Schwartz, *A Monetary History of the United States, 1867–1960* (Princeton, NJ, 1963).

individual professional and educational background, as well as the central bank elite's political ties. The empirical material on which this study is based has been collected from some of the large literature on the history of central banks and their leaders. In addition to financial history research, the study has also benefited from historical data now made available on many of the central banks' websites, including information on the central bank leaders. Separate archive studies on the central banks of our twelve countries have not been possible due to time and resource constraints. However, for the purpose of studying the overall trends in the central bank elite, it is believed that the sources used have been sufficient.

The social and family status of the governors is not surveyed, although these characteristics surely are of relevance also for this elite. The assumption is, however, that family status and connections primarily have played an important role in the early lives of the future governors, say by gaining entrance to prestigious schools. In taking the step up into the 'elite among elites' in central banking, having the types of professional and educational experiences that are 'credible' at the time have been more important. Countries differ in this regard, and this assumption will be contrasted with observations from some of the surveyed countries.

8.3 The Surveyed Governors

Table 8.1 details the central bank governors who were in office between 1950 and 2000. It should be noted that the averages and other calculations are based on the governors' whole term in office, even if it started before 1950 or ended after 2000. The information in the table will be discussed together with the professional background data in later sections of the chapter, but some points can be made already at this stage.

Eighty-five central bank governors led the central banks in the twelve surveyed countries during the period 1950–2000. Already from the basic information provided above, it is clear that there are differences between these countries. The Netherlands, for example, only had four governors during this period (stretching over a period of sixty-five years in fact), while Japan had eleven governors. We should note that the countries differ in terms of the governor's regulated term in office. In Japan, for example, the term is five years, while in the Netherlands it is seven years. In both countries the governor can sit one more term, although in the case of Japan this rarely has happened. In the United States the chairman is appointed for four years, but can sit for three terms.

Between 1950 and 2000, the average country had seven central bank governors who each stayed about nine years in office. This generally means that

Table 8.1. Central bank governors in twelve countries, in office 1950–2000

Country (term start–end)	Number of governors	Average term in office	Max	Min
Japan (1946–2003)	11	5.3	8	2
Germany (1948–2004)	9	6.2	11	2
Sweden (1948–2002)	8	6.75	18	3
France (1949–2003)	8	6.75	11	3
Finland (1945–2004)	8	7.4	14	1
Norway (1946–2010)	7	9.1	16	1
Belgium (1944–2011)	7	9.6	14	4
USA (1948–2006)	6	9.7	19	1
UK (1949–2003)	6	9	12	5
Canada (1934–2001)	6	11.2	20	6
Italy (1947–2005)	5	11.6	15	4
Netherlands (1946–2011)	4	16.3	21	14
Average, 12 countries	7	9.1	14.9	3.8

Note: Averages, max and min term in office calculations are based on the actual terms in office of the governors who were in office during the period 1950–2000.

the average governor sat two terms, thus being reappointed once. The average governor's term in office can be compared with the average head of government (president or prime minister) in the same countries who held office for half that time, 4.4 years. The average governor also stayed longer in office than the government-forming political party, which on average stayed in power for just under seven years.

We can see from the minimum and maximum terms that the averages in most countries come with considerable variation. Most countries, for example, had at least one governor who did not complete a full term (as indicated in the 'Min' column). One famous example is William Miller, who led the US Fed for just over a year (March 1978–August 1979). The two other governors who served just one year were Ahti Karjalainen, who led the Bank of Finland from 1982 to 1983, and the Norwegian governor Torstein Moland who served from 1994 to 1995.

Almost all the shortest serving governors were in office in the last quarter of the century, i.e. between 1975 and 2000, while most of the longest serving governors ('Max' in the table) served between 1950 and 1975.

During the fifty years surveyed, a number of central bank governors have resigned from office. The resignation of a governor can lead to increased market uncertainty about the future of monetary policy as well as regarding the political involvement in the central bank's work and in general damage the integrity of the central bank. Resignations have indeed often had their causes in the governor's tussles with the political leaders, either related to the government's fiscal discipline or decisions on devaluations by the political leaders. But in a few cases governors have also resigned due to 'affairs' that more or less directly have damaged their credibility.

In the former case of resignations we can count the two Belgian governors Ansiaux (1957–71) and de Strycker (1975–82), who both resigned due to considerable disagreement with the political elite. Yasuo Matsushita (Bank of Japan, 1994–8) resigned following the discovery of a case of bribery involving one of his closest staff.[11] Norwegian Torstein Moland was forced to resign after just one year due to an alleged 'tax affair' concerning his personal economy.[12] Italian governor Fazio (1993–2005) was forced to resign and later sentenced to jail after his involvement in a rigged takeover of an Italian commercial bank.[13]

While the turnover rate differs between the countries, it also differs somewhat over time. Of the governors appointed in the 1940s and 1950s, the average term in office was just above ten years, the highest for the fifty years surveyed. For appointees of the economically turbulent 1970s, the average term in office was at its lowest, 6.5 years. The highest turnover of governors is recorded for the turbulent years 1979 and 1993. In both these years five of the twelve surveyed countries replaced the head of the central bank. The early 1990s, when financial and economic crises hit several of the countries surveyed, was overall the period with the highest turnover in the central bank elite. Between 1990 and 1994, nine of twelve countries changed governors, and Germany twice.

Age will not be highlighted as a significant factor in the account of the central bank elite's characteristics. It can be noted, however, that this small group is very homogeneous in this regard. The average age for the incoming governor was just over 54 years (forty-one of the governors were aged 54 +/– five years at their appointment), while the average governor's term ended at the age of 63 (fifty-three of the governors were aged 63 +/– five years at term end). All governors in the survey are men with one exception—Sirkka Hämäläinen—who led the Bank of Finland between 1992 and 1998.

After this general introduction of the central bankers in the survey, the chapter will now proceed with an account of how the central bank elite transformed over the fifty years between 1950 and 2000. During this period, a number of transformations of the central bank elite have been identified: (1) the civil servant central banker of the 'golden age'; (2), the central bank politicians in the 1970s; (3) the market-oriented governors of the 1980s; and (4), the independent academic elite from the 1990s and onward. These four transformations will be presented in turn. Then a few long-term trends that have shaped the central bank elite over the period studied will be highlighted.

---

[11] 'Bank of Japan Governor to resign', *BBC News*, 12 March 1998.
[12] 'Minner om Moland-saken', *Avisa Nordland*, March 2007.
[13] 'Ex-Bank of Italy Chief Sentenced to 4 Years in Jail', *Thomson Reuters Markets*, 28 May 2011.

The chapter concludes with some thoughts on how and why the central bank elite appears to be transforming today.

8.4 The Central Bank Elite and Their Economic Environment between 1950 and 2000

After the Great Depression the central banks underwent significant reforms of their raison d'être and general function in the economic and political system. Most central banks went from having a relatively independent, technical, and sporadic role to play in the economy before the turbulent 1930s, to becoming much closer aligned with the political leadership and the overall economic policies of the political elite. With reforms in 1945 and 1946, the Banque de France for example was nationalized, and in 1946 the Bank of England's long history as a private institution ended and it became state-owned. In 1949, the Bank of Norway too was nationalized. In 1948 the Belgian state took a 50 per cent stake in the National Bank of Belgium and took over the appointment of its directors.[14]

The objectives of the central banks also increased in scope, going from primarily targeting exchange rate stability within the Gold Standard system and trying to avoid funding the government budget before the Great Depression era, to being tasked to do much more. Except for maintaining fixed exchange rates within the Bretton Woods system, established in 1944, central banks after the Second World War were tasked to enforce a strict financial regulatory regime, keep both inflation and unemployment down and productivity up, promote low but rationed credit to the export industry, and in other ways accommodate the Keynesian-style economic policies that were favoured in the decades following the war.[15] Many of these objectives took their most elaborate form some decades later, but already when this study takes its start, in 1950, institutional reforms set the rules that would enable the central banks' to move in this direction.

The educational backgrounds of central bankers were similar to those of the banking elite, not surprisingly since the former traditionally had been made up of the latter. In other words, those who led the central banks until the Second World War had in general started with a college degree or equivalent (at best), and then spent a long career with the bank, learning by doing, all the way from the menial services they had performed as entry level clerk assistants

---

[14] Buyst, 'Was Belgium so Late'.
[15] Douglas Forsyth and Ton Notermans (eds.), *Regime Changes: Macroeconomic Policy and Financial Regulation in Europe from the 1930s to the 1990s* (Providence and Oxford, 1993).

or similar.[16] However, with the transformation of the central banks into 'modern' institutions of the state, the need for central bank-specific competences increased. One such competence related to the growing need of collecting, processing, and analysing statistical data on the economy, and some central banks began to build and/or greatly expanded their in-house research capabilities in the first half of the twentieth century.[17]

These departments were often headed by a recognized expert in economic issues, but did not produce academic research in the modern sense, but rather assisted the central bank elite with statistical reports on the domestic economy and similar. In most countries, the research-producing departments emerged first in the last decades of the century.

Some of the US Federal Reserve Banks were comparatively early in facilitating in-house research and the hiring of academics; already in the interwar period, and after the Second World War the in-house research resources increased gradually and to all reserve banks. In Belgium too the central bank developed its research capacity during the interwar period and created a research department in 1948,[18] as did the Dutch central bank.[19] The central bankers' scepticism towards the academic economists was, however, strong in most other countries, and would remain so for a long time.

8.5 The 'Civil Servant' Central Bank Elite and the 'Golden Era' of the 1950s–1960s

In the first decades after the war, most of the developed economies experienced what has been termed a 'golden age' of economic growth and development. Economic growth was historically high, with the twelve surveyed countries experiencing average annual growth of 3 per cent or more each year from the early 1950s until the mid-1960s.[20] The quick post-war economic recovery in Europe was driven by the performance of key countries such as France, Italy, and Germany, who all had an average growth of over 5 per cent per year during this period. The global economy was further driven by the strong growth of the US economy and the rapid catch-up of the Japanese economy.

---

[16] Leslie Hannah, 'The Twentieth Century Transformation of Banking and its Effect on Management Training for Bankers', in Edwin Green and Monika Pohle Fraser (eds.), *The Human Factor in Banking History: Entrepreneurship, Organization, Management and Personnel* (Athens, 2008).
[17] Pablo Martin-Acena and Teresa Tortella, 'Regulation and Supervision: The Rise of Central Banks' Research Departments', in Stefano Battilossi and Jamie Reis (eds.), *State and Financial Systems in Europe and the USA: Historical Perspectives on Regulation and Supervision in the Nineteenth and Twentieth Century* (Farnham, 2002).
[18] Buyst, 'Was Belgium so Late'.
[19] Harro Maas, *Economic Methodology: A Historical Introduction* (London, 2014).
[20] Total Economy Database.

As mentioned above, Keynesian counter-cyclical economic policies and significant state interventions in the market came to influence most countries in the 1950s. The closer institutional alignment with the political elite made the objectives of the central banks more or less explicitly formulated by the political elite.[21] The idea that the monetary policy should accommodate the overall economic policies was made explicit by institutional reforms. The term of the governor, for example, was set to coincide with the political election cycle to enable the incoming government to appoint an accommodating governor.

The political influence over the central banks was, however, less profound in the 1950s than in later decades. In some countries the institutional framework ensured some minimum independence, such as in the case of Germany. In other countries individual central bank governor seem to have succeeded in keeping the political elite at bay, such as in Italy under the leadership of Menichella (1946–60),[22] and in the United States under the leadership of McChesney Martin (1951–60).[23] John Singleton defines the mid-century central banker as a 'civil servant', and by the backgrounds of the governors in office during the 1950s, this assessment seems to be quite right.[24] Figure 8.1 shows the surveyed governors' public sector background.

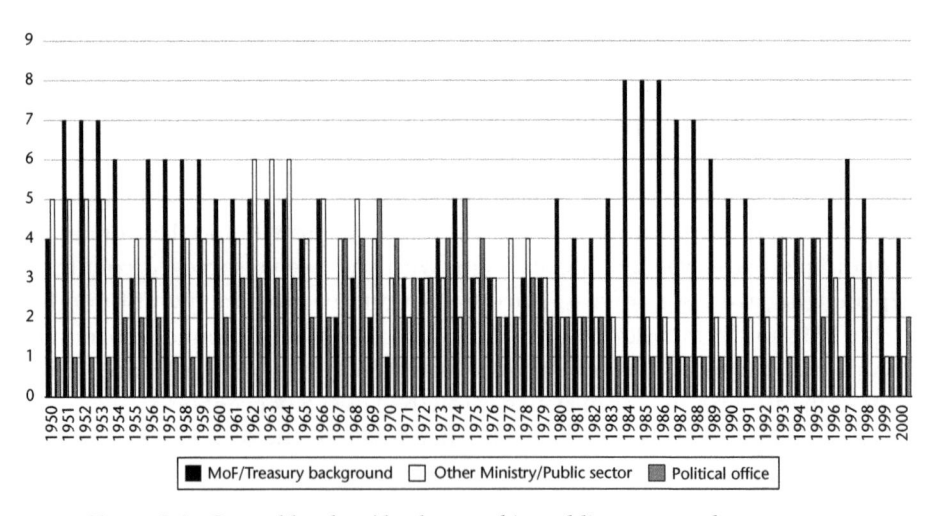

Figure 8.1. Central bankers' background in public sector and government

---

[21] See for example Gianni Toniolo (ed.), *Central Banks' Independence in Historical Perspective* (Berlin, 1988); Alan Meltzer, *A History of the Federal Reserve, Volume 2, Book 1, 1951–1969* (Chicago, 2009); Forrest Capie, *The Bank of England, 1950s to 1979* (Cambridge, 2010).

[22] Giangiacomo Nardozzi, 'A Central Bank between the Government and the Credit System: The Bank of Italy after World War II'; Toniolo, *Central Banks' Independence*.

[23] Kettl, *Leadership*.

[24] John Singleton, *Central Banking in the 20th Century* (Cambridge, 2010).

The figure shows the share of central bank governors in office in a year that had a background in the public sector, divided into three categories: a background in the Ministry of Finance; or the Treasury; and experience from other ministries or other public sector entities. The share of governors who had a background in their respective central banks is not included in the figure but was about one-quarter of the total in the 1950s.

For the whole fifty-year period, one of the most common backgrounds of the central bank elite was having served for some time at the Ministry of Finance (or similar ministry) (the white bars). Given the close institutional links, common policy interests, and similar human capital demand, this is not surprising. However, over the course of the 'golden age', the share of governors with a background in the Ministry of Finance fell every year, from four out of ten in 1953, to just one in 1969. Instead, governors who had served in other ministries or other public sector entities came to power (the dark grey bars), and by the mid-1960s the era of the 'civil servant' central banker can be interpreted to have reached its peak. Why the central bank elite came to consist of governors with quite diverse backgrounds in the public sector is not easy to answer. One can, however, note that this development coincides with the 1960s expansion of the objectives of central banking, which may have called for a wider variety of experiences among the policy-makers.

The black bars in Figure 8.1 show that only a handful of former treasurers made up part of the central bank elite for the whole period, and only in the 1950s and 1960s, and then again in the 1980s. Of these, three are Americans (Martin, Miller, and Volcker), and four French (Baumgartner, Brunet, Camdessus, and de Larosière). Central banks have always had a special relationship with the Treasury, since the former often have been expected but not always willing to help the latter fund public spending. So one motive for appointing former treasurers to lead the central bank may be to bridge any divides that may occur along these lines. Data on the government debt of France and the United States, however, show that such a simple connection does not hold. Government debt as share of GDP fell throughout the 'golden era', when the respective central banks were run by former Treasury officials (Martin in the United States, Baumgartner and Brunet in France).

Except for public sector backgrounds, some of the central bank elite of the 'golden age' had worked in the private sector too, at least in the 1950s. Marius Holtrop, for example, had spent a few years in the 1930s with the American arm of the Shell oil company, before eventually taking over the leadership of the Dutch central bank after the war (1947–60).[25] In Germany future governors Wilhelm Vocke and Karl Blessing in 1939 had been forced to leave the

---

[25] Jelle Zijlstra, 'Levensbericht M. W. Holtrop', *Huygens Institute Jaarboek* 1990: 136–49.

central bank by the Nazi regime and had taken up positions in corporate boards in the private sector.[26] Several of the incoming governors in the 1950s and 1960s had also proven themselves as leaders of various war-related state enterprises, such as Fed chairman McChesney Martin (1951–70), Bank of Italy's Donato Manichella (1947–60), and Belgium's Maurice Frère (1944–57). A number of governors had also spent some of their career in state-owned financial institutions, such as the Italian Guido Carli and Wilfrid Baubartner, head of the Bank of France (1949–60).

The turnover within the central bank elite was very low during these economically fortunate years. For a project like Bretton Woods, this may have been beneficial. In the international central bank world then, decade-long relations could develop among the governors that may have contributed to overcoming many hurdles on both low and high policy problems. The endurance of the Bretton Woods system was of course mainly related to the overall economic performance of the participating countries, but the personal relations may have played some part in smoothing the functioning of the system among the governors.

The 1950s central bank elite had very different educational backgrounds. The most common higher education was in law (four of twelve governors), and only one governor had studied economics (Holtrop of the Netherlands). Bank of England governors had less education compared to their international colleagues, but from the country's national perspective, they nevertheless were part of the educated 'high society'. Like their political and business elite peers, the UK governors in general started out at public schools, then went to Eton, and then spent one or more years at Oxford (Leigh-Pemberton) or Cambridge (Cobbold, Baring, Cromer, Richardson, George). In a similar national elite tradition, French governors for their part without exception studied at one of the renowned *grandes écoles*, just like most other members of the French public and private sector elite.

The academic field of economics expanded remarkably in the second half of the twentieth century.[27] But for a long time this expansion was not met with much enthusiasm in most central banks. The central bank elite was not trained in economics, and people like the Bank of England's governor Cameron Cobbold (1949–61) and the US Fed's chairman Martin (1951–70) saw little practical use for the theories and models thought up at the universities.[28]

The Keynesian approach to economics that was strongly represented in the academic world at the time nevertheless came to influence the economic

---

[26] Marsh, *The Bundesbank*.
[27] A. W Coats (ed.), *The Post-1945 Internationalization of Economics* (Durham, NC, 1997).
[28] Capie, *The Bank of England*; Meltzer, *A History of the Federal Reserve, Volume 2, Book 1*; Marsh, *The Bundesbank*.

policies that were implemented in the 1950s and 1960s, including the monetary policies of the central bank. Although economists still had a very limited job market outside academia at the time, their proclaimed expertise in economic policy matters had become in greater demand by governments following the extreme events of the preceding decades of wars and economic decline.[29] The main thrust of the economic policies was to counter and minimize the swings in the economic cycle with fiscal and monetary policies. Keynesian economists had developed more sophisticated theories and models that confirmed the belief that the business cycle could be controlled by adjustments of the interest rate, the credit growth, and other policy instruments.[30] The economics research thus to some extent went in favour of the central banks, by stressing the importance of monetary policy in balancing the business cycle. In many central banks, however, the economic theories of the time were not taken to heart so easily.

The central bank elite's acceptance of the economists came gradually in the 1960s. It may have been less out of conviction of the merit of the research and more about building a capacity for engaging with the academic critics that were becoming more and more influential as the economics departments grew. According to Forrest Capie, the Bank of England's incorporation of 'economics' into its organization was to ensure 'being able to defend themselves against economists rather than using them in the pursuit of improved policymaking'.[31] For central banks, the expansion of economics as a research field and as an independent discipline at the universities became too strong to ignore, although many central bankers themselves found the academic treatment of monetary policy issues as far from useful in practice.[32]

By the late 1960s, the 'golden age' of economic development was coming to an end in many countries. The expanded public sector, the increased welfare expenditures, and the efforts by the political elite to counter any downturn in the economic cycle, either by increased public expenditures or more elaborate interventions in the market, were taking their toll. Increased competition from fast developing countries such as Japan and South Korea too put pressures on the European economies and the United States.

To boost their own economies several countries engaged in competitive devaluations that undermined the credibility of the Bretton Woods system and also led to a return of high inflation. The devaluations were without

---

[29] Mary Morgan, 'Economics', in Theodore Porter and Dorothy Ross (eds.), *The Cambridge History of Science*, vol. 7 (Cambridge, 2003), 275–305.
[30] Rudolf Richter, 'German Monetary Policy as Reflected in the Academic Debate', in Deutsche Bundesbank (ed.), *Fifty Years of the Deutsche Mark* (Oxford, 1998), 525–72.
[31] Capie, *The Bank of England*, 33.
[32] See for example William White, 'Is Monetary Policy a Science? The Interaction of Theory and Practice Over the Last 50 Years', Federal Reserve Bank of Dallas, Globalization and Monetary Policy Institute, working paper 155 (2013).

exceptions decided by the political elite, and most often under protests by the central bank elite. Many of the resignations by governors during this fifty-year period occurred in connection with a devaluation. National Bank of Belgium's Cecil de Strycker, for example, chose to retire in 1982 when the government had decided to devalue the franc. After giving up their respective fixed exchange rates in 1992, the governors of the Bank of England and the Swedish Riksbank both retired in 1993.

Inflation would remain a crucial problem for all developed economies for the next two decades, a period that in the US context has been called 'the Great Inflation'.[33] As the anchor in the Bretton Woods system, the growing inflationary forces in the United States became a critical source of strain on the exchange rate system, and between 1971 (when President Nixon closed the gold window) and 1973, the system fell apart. The breakdown of the Bretton Woods system and the first oil price shock in 1974 serve as key events that marked the beginning of the second era of the post-war twentieth century.

8.6 The Politicized and Academic Central Bank Elite of the 1970s

From 1974 until the end of the century the economic growth in almost all developed economies was lower than in the previous decades. The 1970s were particularly turbulent with practically no economic indicator moving in the right direction. With the breakdown of the Bretton Woods system in 1973 and the oil price shock in 1974, inflation picked up from the already high rates of the 1960s. The increased production costs of the oil-dependent industries brought about major structural changes in developed economies. Unemployment rose while GDP growth fell. As prescribed by the Keynesian economics of the time, governments tried to meet the private sector demand glut by massive public spending and investment. But the economies did not recover and the government debt rose higher and higher.

Many of the developed economies experienced problems that the then conventional economic theories and models could not explain. Ben Bernanke and Frederic Mishkin made the observation that from the 1970s onward, central bankers tried to pursue a very wide spectrum of policy targets, while at the same time shifting attention to the one economic condition that was in most 'crisis' at any given time.[34] The evident failure of the policy-makers, both the political and central bank elite, came under severe criticism, not the least

---

[33] Allan Meltzer, 'Origins of the Great Inflation', *Federal Reserve Bank of St. Louis Review* 2005 (87.2, part 2): 145–75.

[34] Ben Bernanke and Frederic Mishkin, 'Central Bank Behavior and the Strategy of Monetary Policy: Observations from Six Industrialized Countries', NBER working paper 4082 (1992).

from a new generation of Keynes-sceptic economists such as monetarist Milton Friedman and Robert Lucas. The criticism was among other things that the central banks were pursuing too many targets, and that these were for the political elite to deal with rather than the central banks.[35]

By the look of the central bank elite's characteristics in the 1970s, the criticism seems to be well founded. During the 1970s, every third or fourth central bank in our sample was run by governors who had held prominent political offices (seats in parliament not included), a share much higher than at any other time between 1950 and 2000. The shift from civil servant governors to political governors had started in the late 1960s and continued to the very end of the 1970s.

Even among the central bank elite that did not have a political background many governors were closely aligned with the political elite, at least in the public's eye. Several commentators for example deemed Fed chairman Burns an 'accomplice' of President Nixon in accepting higher inflation by providing easy money in time for the 1972 election.[36] Karl Klassen led the Bundesbank between 1970 and 1977. He was a social democrat and according to Marsh probably the most political of all Bundesbank presidents.[37] In Nardozzi's account, Guido Carli's (1960–75) independence from the political elite of Italy was much weaker than his predecessor, Menichella's (1948–60).[38]

Another change in the elite composition in the 1970s was that the share of governors with an academic background (economics) increased (see the dark grey bars in Figure 8.2). Arthur Burns, who headed the Fed between 1970 and 1978, was a professor of economics, suitably specializing in economic cycles.[39] In the Netherlands the appointment of former academics had started already with Holtrop (1946–67), but continued with economics professor Jelle Zijlstra who became governor in 1967. Zijlstra also fits well into the 1970s central bank elite by his long prior career in politics. Paolo Baffi, who became governor of the Bank of Italy in 1975, had a PhD in economics with a special interest in statistics, and was one of the first governors to have come from the research department of a central bank.[40] From 1977 the German Bundesbank appointed presidents with at least some background at the influential Ifo Institute for Economic Research in Munich, (Emminger, Pöhl, and Schlesigner, who consecutively led the Bundesbank between 1977 and 1993).

---

[35] Richter, 'German Monetary Policy'.   [36] Kettl, *Leadership*, 136.
[37] Marsh, *The Bundesbank*, 47.   [38] Nardozzi, *The Bank of Italy*.
[39] Kettl, *Leadership*. Starting with Burns, most Fed leaders have had a background as chairperson of the president appointed Council of Economic Advisors (Miller, Greenspan, Bernanke, Yellen). The only exception is Paul Volcker.
[40] Kazuhiko Yago, Yoshio Asai, and Masanao Itoh (eds.), *History of the IMF: Organization, Policy, and Market* (Berlin, 2015).

The job of the central bank governor became harder as well as less secure. In 1979 alone, five out of twelve countries changed governor (France, Japan, Italy, Sweden, and the United States). This high turnover led to another transformation of the central bank elite. The credibility of the politicized central banker had been lost, and in its place came a more market-oriented elite. This transformation of course was occurring all over, not the least in the political elite.

In key economies such as the United States and the United Kingdom, new political elites under Reagan's and Thatcher's leadership started to pull back the state's role in the economy. The constraints put on the financial markets were gradually removed from the 1970s. The market now set the price of the pound and the dollar. In this process of deregulation, central banks were both actors and agents in the promotion of the new regime and the rejection of the old. Under the leadership of Cromer (Rowland Baring) and Leslie O'Brien in the 1960s, the Bank of England was for example promoting the revitalizing of London as a major financial centre for the Eurodollar market, something that required more leeway for its financial institutions.[41] While the 1970s saw the start of a long wave of financial market liberalizations in many countries, it was also the decade when international cooperation on regulatory matters began in earnest, such as in the Basel Committee on Banking Supervision (BCBS), formed in 1974. It is worth noting that the central banks preferred to send mid-level technical experts to these meetings rather than their governors (see Drach, Chapter 9 in this volume).[42] This was because substantial international cooperation on regulation and supervision appeared unlikely for the central bank leaders at the time, or even undesirable beyond some level of minimum engagement. But as history unravelled it is clear that the original assessment proved wrong and that the BCBS was to become one of the key forums for central banks and supervisory agencies to meet in the international arena.

The academic development of economics contributed to the transformation of the central bank elite by the end of the 1970s. The apparent failure of the interventionist state by the 1970s had brought bad-will both to the established political and the central bank elite of the time. The ideas of Friedman had become known in the mainstream, not the least after receiving the Nobel prize in economics from the Swedish Riksbank in 1976. Paul Volcker, chairman of the US Fed 1979–87, claimed himself to be a 'practical monetarist',[43] as did many other central bankers in the 1970s.[44] Although targeting

---

[41] Youssef Cassis, *Capitals of Capital* (Cambridge, 2006).
[42] Charles Goodhart, *The Basel Committee on Banking Supervision: A History of the Early Years, 1974–1997* (Cambridge, 2011).
[43] Meltzer, *A History of the Federal Reserve, Volume 2, Book 1*.
[44] Richter, 'German Monetary Policy'.

monetary growth turned out to be difficult to do in practice, the idea of reducing the number of targets for monetary policy stuck, as did the new economists' emphasis on reducing the use of 'discretionary' decision-making in favour of a more clear and predictable 'rule' based monetary policy.[45] The focus suggested, and practised by the central banker role models in the Bundesbank and the Fed, was price stability. Out of changed beliefs as well as competitive necessities other developed economies soon deregulated their financial markets as well. In this changed economic environment the central bank elite naturally changed also.

8.7 The Central Bank Elite and the Deregulations in the 1980s

By the 1980s the strict financial regulatory regime was in a process of being transformed into a much more market-oriented regime. For central banks, the new sentiment led to growing dissatisfaction with the political influence over central banks. In many countries institutional reforms were made to increase the political independence of central banks.[46] The changed views on the role of central banks also led to new perceptions of what the credible central bank elite would be. The independent conservative, inflation-targeting central banker became the ideal in new academic work,[47] with real-life examples in central banks such as the German Bundesbank and central bankers such as the Fed's Paul Volcker.

In the 1980s half of the surveyed governors had worked in the Ministry of Finance or similar ministry[48] (see Figure 8.2), and often had worked hands-on with the process of deregulating the financial markets. This type of experience and knowledge became sought after in the central banks as well, to better navigate in this new, market-oriented regime. The new generation of governors had not held political office to the same extent as their predecessors, and their public sector/government experience was more exclusively from the Ministry of Finance than from other parts of the state apparatus. Governors in the 1980s also had much more work experience from the private financial sector, a background that was much less common among their 1970s counterparts.

---

[45] Finn Kydland and Edward Prescott, 'Rules rather than Discretion: The Inconsistency of Optimal Plans', *Journal of Political Economy* 1977 (85.3): 473–91.
[46] Toniolo, *Central Banks' Independence*.
[47] See for example Kenneth Rogoff, 'The Optimal Degree of Commitment to an Intermediate Monetary Target', *Quarterly Journal of Economics* 1985 (100.4): 1169–89.
[48] In some countries and for some years, other ministry names were used, such as the Ministry of Monetary Affairs or of the Economy. In Table 8.1 and in the text these have been interpreted as similar or the same as the Ministry of Finance in their task of planning, analysing, and implementing the government's fiscal policies.

Financial Elites and European Banking

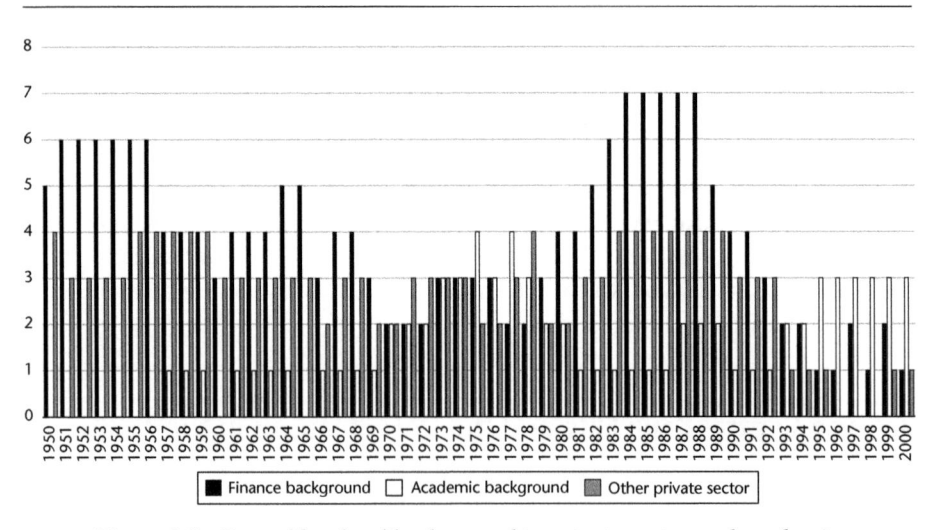

Figure 8.2. Central bankers' background in private sector and academia

A last notable shift was that the new generation of governors had not had a professional background in academia like their predecessors (the grey bars in Figure 8.2). This could have many explanations, but one might be that the economics discipline had lost some of its credibility since the 1970s and was marked by harsh intellectual debates between different theoretical camps. Keynesians had been criticized by the monetarists, who themselves by the 1980s came under criticism by a new generation of Keynesian economists.[49]

In Figure 8.2 the central bank governors' experience from the private sector and as professional academics is put together. Over the fifty years, this type of background has been more or less common, and has been of various kinds. In the 1950s and 1960s, a number of governors in office had worked part of their careers in the financial sector, as the black bars indicate. However, this was mainly in state-owned financial institutes. When the share of governors with experience from the financial sector rose again in the 1980s, all these governors had worked in the private sector. The countries differed in this regard as mentioned. In some countries, such as in the United States, Belgium, and the Netherlands, most central bank governors between 1950 and 2000 had spent at least some years in the private financial sector. But by the 1980s this background was found with governors of other countries as well, such as Belgium, Finland, and Germany.[50] Given the transformed view of the financial market in the 1980s, this development is hardly surprising. During the liberalization of the financial markets, the markets' and the policy-makers'

---

[49] Richter, 'German Monetary Policy'.
[50] In some countries such as Sweden, Norway, and Japan, practically no governor has worked in finance.

198

views became closer aligned, which made transitions from the market side to the central bank less challenged than had been the case one decade earlier.[51] It is more surprising that the reign of the financial market experienced central bank elite lasted so short a time.

8.8 The Independent Central Bank Elite and the Globalized Economy

Economic development remained turbulent until the end of the century, with a handful of the economies under scrutiny experiencing major financial crises in the early 1990s, namely Finland, Norway, Sweden, and Japan. Japan had experienced an extremely high and consistent rate of economic development since the middle of the century, but by the mid-1980s the development was replaced by speculative booms in the stock market and in real estate. The financial crisis that started in 1989–90 marked the beginning of a period of weak economic growth that characterizes the Japanese economy to this day. According to Richard Werner, the crisis was instigated in the 1980s by high-ranking civil servants in the Bank of Japan as a means to bring about large-scale structural reforms of the Japanese economy.[52]

The Nordic financial crises had both domestic and international causes, of which the implosion of the Soviet Union and the reunification of East and West Germany were the major international triggers.[53] The reunification of Germany was of course a critical event in the whole of Europe, as from many perspectives it set in motion the further development of the EU and the European Monetary Union. The implosion of the Eastern bloc of communist countries also had extreme economic effects, not least in those countries themselves.

The early 1990s, when financial and economic crises hit several of the countries under study, was overall the period with the highest turnover in the central bank elite. Between 1990 and 1994, nine of twelve countries changed governor, and Germany twice. The appointment of new governors in the 1990s led to a central bank elite with slightly more professional academic backgrounds (economics mostly) and with less experience from the private sector than their predecessors. Most had a longer background from within the central bank than their predecessors, but were just as experienced from work in the Ministry of Finance.

---

[51] For a more elaborate discussion on the links between regulators and the financial elite, see Arvind, Gray, and Wilson, Chapter 7 in this volume.
[52] Werner, *Princes of the Yen*.
[53] Lars Jonung, Jakko Kiander, and Pentti Vartia, *The Great Financial Crisis in Finland and Sweden: The Nordic Experience of Financial Liberalization* (Cheltenham, 2009).

Hartmut Berghoff and Ingo Köhler find that the globalization of banking and finance from the 1970s and 1980s appears to have called for new forms of human and social capital, such as international work experience, language skills, and academic training in economics, mathematics, and IT.[54] By the 1990s, it is fair to say that this human capital transformation occurred in central banks as well. International cooperation on monetary policy increased, especially within the EU in the process of constructing the European Monetary Union, and in forums such as the mentioned BCBS. By the effect of the Maastricht Treaty in 1993, the EMU countries among many other things committed to make their central banks more independent from political influence. In effect they adopted an institutional setting that mirrored the German Bundesbank's.

By the very end of the century, the mighty Bundesbank together with the other Euro-countries transferred their monetary powers to the European Central Bank, modelled after the German central bank as well.[55]

The globalization of financial markets, and the occurrence of more or less severe financial crises, also led to increased cooperation in the fields of financial regulation and supervision, such as in the BCBS that was created in the mid-1970s. With this development, experience of and from international negotiations and cooperation came to be a more important competence in the appointment of new governors.

By the 1990s, most developed country central banks had established research departments, staffed with academics with a PhD degree in economics, which produced independent research in areas of interest and relevance to central banking.[56] The central bankers' own accounts suggest that their background in economics has mattered little for their work and policy choices. In the individual case, and without a historical context, this may appear to be true. Furthermore, in their day-to-day work, central bankers have little time, or need, to take a broader perspective on their background's impact on their work.

However, the impact of economics during the second half of the twentieth century is undisputed when looking at the transformation of the central banks' human capital. From the top, more and more governors had a higher education in economics as shown in Figure 8.3. The black bars show the number of governors who had a higher education in economics, and we can see how the number of governors with this background rose from just one in 1950 (Holtrop, Netherlands), to practically all the end of the century. We can

---

[54] Hartmut Berghoff and Ingo Köhler, 'Redesigning a Class of Its Own: Social and Human Capital Formation in the German Banking Elite, 1870–1990', *Financial History Review* 2007 (14.1): 63–87.
[55] Singleton, *Central Banking*.
[56] Pierre St-Amant, Greg Tkacz, Annie Guérard-Langlois, and Louis Morel, 'Quantity, Quality, and Relevance: Central Bank Research, 1990–2003', Bank of Canada working paper 2005-37.

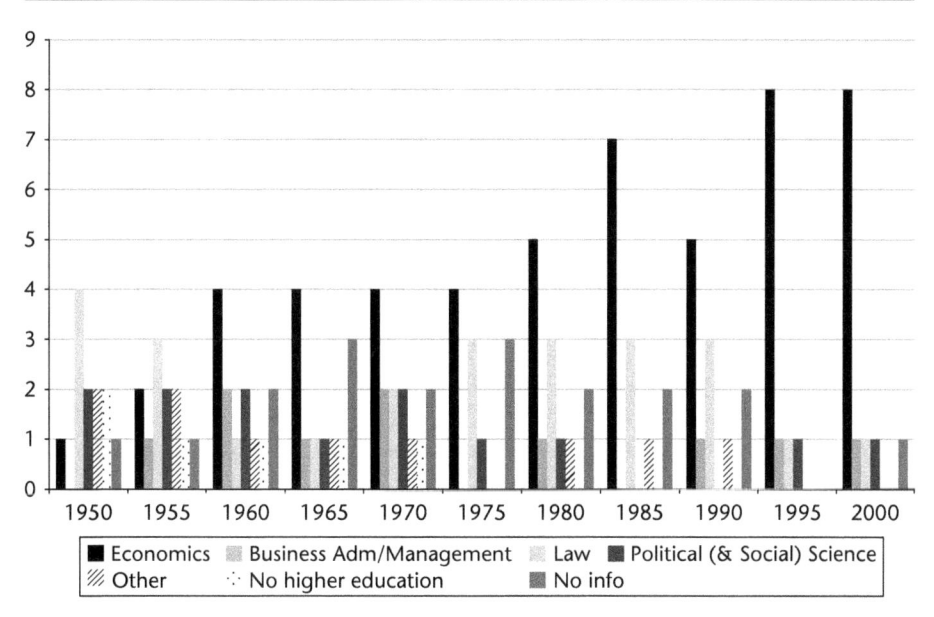

Figure 8.3. Academic background of central bank governors in office, 1950–2000

Note: In cases when a governor has held degrees in several academic disciplines, each discipline has been counted once. In some cases, biographical information indicates that a governor studied some economics while pursuing a degree in some other social science. In such cases the degree topic has been recorded.

also note that the economics background became particularly prevalent from the mid-1990s and onwards.

Overall, the human capital of central banks transformed significantly in the last decade of the century. The organization of central banks changed at this point too. Given their increased importance in the economy paired with their natural 'soft' budget constraints, central banks had grown in size throughout the twentieth century. However, with the political turn to deregulation, and privatization in the 1980s, pressures came to downsize the central banks as well.[57] With the advent of the large financial crises in the early 1990s, these plans came into effect in many countries. When the central banks shrunk in staff, more emphasis was put on the competence of those who remained with the central bank.

With the appointment of central bank governors with academic degrees in economics, many central banks in general became more 'academic' from the 1990s and onward. As a token of the rise of economics as a credibility-building science, internal research departments were created in many central banks, staffed with researchers from and in competition with academic institutions.

[57] Singleton, *Central Banking*.

The transformation into the 'academic' central bank continued into the new millennium, with support of the newer economic theories of the time. In contrast to the Keynesian economic thinking of the 1960s and 1970s, the new economic research was sceptical of market interventions in general and favoured simple 'rules' for monetary policy rather than politicized 'norms'. The work of the prior generation of central bankers to maintain fixed exchange rates, interest rate ceilings and floors, credit expansion controls and so on came to be seen as near impossible, and new economic research in general was in favour of central banks operating 'in' the market, rather than trying to control it.

The main arguments for central bank independence, narrow policy goals focusing on price stability and the use of short-term interest rates, open market operations and being transparent about the means and ends of its operations (not the least via more and more publications written by an increasingly academically trained staff), were all found in the mainstream economic thinking of the 1990s. The influence of economics over policy and practice continued into the new millennium, and probably reached its peak with the global financial crisis in 2007–9, which tarnished the credibility of the discipline, not the least since several of its most esteemed proponents had deemed deep economic recessions of Great Depression proportions a probability of the past.

It is difficult to assess how important the pre-crisis belief in modern economies having reached a new plateau of low volatility was in generating the financial crisis itself. But with hindsight it seems fair to assign some blame to an overconfidence among mainstream economists about having found the path to an era of 'Great Moderation' in economic development. The more stable economic development of the 1990s and early 2000s worked as confirmation that the theories and models used to understand the economy and the markets had developed. The 'academic' central bankers of course played a part in the promotion of these theories and models. Until the crisis they had little reason not to do so, since they succeeded in keeping inflation down just as their new, narrow, policy objectives required.

In sum, with the broad agreement among economists that major financial crises were a thing of the past, it is easy to see why the global financial crisis led to sharp criticism of them and the discipline as a whole. And since central banks were led by men (still mostly men) with a background in economics, it is also easy to see why central bankers received part of the blame as well.

It is an interesting fact that the academic pedigree among the central bank elite had never been higher than at the start of the global financial crisis. The central banks of Germany, the United Kingdom, and the United States were all led by former economics professors, Axel Weber, Mervyn King, and Ben Bernanke respectively, and so was the International Monetary Fund with managing director Dominique Strauss-Kahn at the helm. When the Bank of Japan got a new governor in 2008, it was the economics professor Masaaki Shirakawa.

8.9 The Harmonization of the Central Bank Elite

Aside from the transformations of the central bank elite that came about due to changed economic conditions, the fifty-year period studied here also displays some longer-term shifts in the central bank elite's characteristics. In many ways, the central bank leaders became more alike over the half-century that is our focus. It may in fact be reasonable to question if there even was an elite in 1950 in the form of a professionally and socially interconnected group of influential like-minded individuals within central banking. However, most studies on the matter do agree that such an elite, with international experience, developed over the course of the half-century under consideration, and especially during the last quarter of the twentieth century.[58] The harmonization of the central bankers' characteristics may have been one of the factors that enabled this particular elite to take form.

In the 1950s, the governor could have had a varied background from industry, the public sector, in law, in the financial sector, and/or in politics. By the year 2000, the average central bank governor almost always had a higher education in economics, a professional background in the Ministry of Finance and in the central bank, with some years in the financial sector and possibly also in academia. From our present point in time, it is worth emphasizing that the 1950 governor did *not* have a higher degree in economics, but rather in law, public administration, business administration, and the odd literature student. In 2000 you could be certain that the governor had a degree in economics, and possibly even a PhD.

The impact of economics came in no small part due to the changed composition of the central banks' human capital, especially from the 1990s and onward. On the one hand, the rising profile of the field of economics made economists credible candidates for posts at the top of the central banks. On the other hand, the demands for making the central banks more efficient as organizations, led to a reduction of the number of staff employed, and higher demands on the staff remaining. Many of the new employees had higher education in economics, just like the men at the top. From this perspective,

---

[58] See for example Amy Verdun, 'The Role of the Delors Committee in the Creation of EMU: An Epistemic Community?', *Journal of European Public Policy* 1999 (6.2): 308–28; Martin Marcussen, 'Central Bankers, the Ideational Life-Cycle and the Social Construction of EMU', RSC working paper 98/33 (1998).

the success of economics in infiltrating the central banks had as much to do with the educational transformation of the central bank elite and overall human capital, as with the persuasiveness of the arguments, problem formulations, and agendas put forward in academic circles. The effect was in any case a process of a gradual formation of what Verdun and Marcussen describe as an 'epistemic community', a shared set of world views within the central bank profession.[59]

Another clear trend over the five decades is the increased reliance on former central bank officials to take the position of governor. Of eighty-five governors, fifty had held some permanent position within the central bank prior to their governorship. There are, however, some interesting differences across time and between countries. In the early 1950s, one-quarter of the governors had worked at the central bank before becoming governor. By 1975 half of the governors had this background, and by 2000 the share had risen to three-quarters.

The late-century trend towards depoliticizing the central banks may be one explanation for the increased resort to civil servants already working in the central bank. It is worth noting, however, that the mid- and end-century governors differ in how long they had worked within the bank before taking office. The late-century governors usually had spent only part of their career within the central bank, while in the mid-century some governors worked their whole career in the bank. This shift could reflect the general trend of increased work-market mobility that marked the last quarter of the twentieth century, which also affected the private financial sector.[60]

Some countries relied more on in-house talents than others. In the case of Canada, for example, all governors were recruited from within the bank (except Graham Towers, 1934–54, who was the first governor of the Canadian central bank). In Belgium too, all governors had a long career within the central bank behind them. Of the German governors, only Karl Bernard (1948–57) was picked from outside the central banking community when he was appointed to lead the Bank Deutscher Länder together with Reichsbank veteran Wilhelm Vocke (1948–57). Italy too had governors who generally had had long careers at the Bank of Italy.

The Bank of England governors were by tradition often found within its own ranks and during the surveyed period Cobbold (1949–61), O'Brien (1966–73), and Edward George (1993–2003) were all career civil servants of the Bank. In the United States, Volcker (1979–87) had a background partly in the Federal Reserve System, as had his short-staying predecessor Miller,

---

[59] Verdun, 'The Role of the Delors Committee'; Marcussen, 'Central Bankers'.
[60] See, for example, Ron Chernow, *The Death of the Banker* (New York, 1997).

(1978–9). Martin (1951–70) had not worked at the Fed before his governorship, but had significant knowledge of the US central bank both from his own work on the 1951 Accord which structured the institutional relationship between the Treasury and the Fed, and certainly also from his father who was a member of the National Monetary Commission that wrote the 1913 Federal Reserve Act.[61]

Sweden on the other hand had no governor from within the Riksbank during the second half of the twentieth century (except for Klas Böök, 1948–51, who held an interim governorship after the early resignation of governor Ivar Rooth). The French case is similar in that six of eight governors were appointed from outside the Banque de France (the exceptions are Bernard Clappier and Renaud de La Genière). In post-war Japan, the tradition developed that every other governor was appointed from within the Bank of Japan, while the others were picked from the Ministry of Finance.[62] Of the four Dutch governors, only Arnout Wellink had made part of his career within the central bank.

One explanation for the increase in the appointment of in-house civil servants may be the mere fact that central banks grew in size over the course of the twentieth century, and especially after the Second World War.[63] There was thus simply more in-house talent to choose from. Another explanation is the increased political independence of central banks in the last decades of the century that may have reduced the range of possible external appointees.

The characteristics of the central bank elite transformed, by governor turnovers, when the economic conditions changed. In terms of economic growth, the most common assessment is that the decades before the 1970s were a 'golden era' of high growth and relatively stable financial markets (in no small part due to the strict regulatory regime). From then on, the last quarter century was characterized by low growth, small and big financial crises, and overall more dynamic financial markets. In these general trends, the central bank elite was affected in several ways. Job security, for example, was much higher in the 1950s and 1960s, compared to the 1970s and onwards. With the economic turbulence of the 1970s and the financial crises of the early 1990s, the turnover of central bank governors spiked and led to new transformations of the elite.

Institutionally, the central banks changed very much from 1950 to 2000. In 1950, recent institutional reforms had put central banks close to the political elite, and were expected to adapt monetary policy to accommodate the overall economic policies of the political elite. In 2000, central bank independence was seen as critical to the success of monetary policy.

---

[61] Allan Meltzer, *A History of the Federal Reserve, Volume 1: 1913–1951* (Chicago, 2004).
[62] Werner, *Princes of the Yen*.   [63] Singleton, *Central Banking*.

The multiple targets pursued by central banks during the 1950s and 1960s had by 2000 practically been boiled down to just one, price stability. Governments by the end of the century again aimed for balanced budgets, and rejected the Keynesian programmes of state-funded countercyclical interventions that were the norm after the war. In general, the fifty-year period went from a societal belief in the 1950s in the political elite's ability to harness the volatilities of the market by extensive regulatory and policy programmes, to a completely opposite conclusion by the end of the century. The discrediting of the political interventions in the economy affected the central banks through the institutional reforms of the 1990s, but also resulted in the changed characteristics of the central bank elite. While former ministers were appointed to head the central banks in the first decades after the war, this was practically impossible from the 1990s onward.

8.10 Conclusion

The central bank elite transformed several times during the fifty years studied here. The condition of the economy seems to have been the most important driver of change. Enduring weak economic performance and/or the occurrence of a financial crisis coincide with observable shifts in the characteristics of this elite. After financial crises, prolonged recessions, or other similar negative economic events, a new generation of central bank elite emerges, endowed with a different set of individual characteristics that were (seen as) more credible and/or appropriate in the new economic environment.

Consequently, we can also conclude that the characteristics of the central bank elite more or less stay the same as long as the economic environment is good. If anything, good times appear to lead to 'more of the same' in terms of central banker characteristics.

The 'civil servant' bankers of 1950 had become even more accommodating to the political elite by the late 1960s during the golden age growth. By the 1970s, the central bank elite had transformed into a more politicized group, comprising many former or active political elites. The poor economic development over the 1970s, however, discredited this type of central banker and in the 1980s the market-oriented central bankers took over. The trend of detaching central banks from political interference, which had been the norm in the 1950s, went further in the 1990s after a number of countries experienced severe financial crises that appeared to be partially due to weak central bank independence. From the late 1990s and onwards, the academic, internationally experienced central bankers gained in numbers and esteem, and probably reached 'peak professor' stage with the global financial crisis that started in 2007–8.

Given the apparent importance of economic and financial distress in the turnover rate among the central bank elite, as well as for changes in perception of *what makes for a credible central banker*, it is not surprising that the global financial crisis some ten years ago brought about a new transformation of central bank elites—and it is still in the making. It is hard to determine what the coming central bank elite will look like, but it is clear that the academically founded 'credibility' has come under question since the crisis.[64] Mandates and institutional set-ups still ensure formal political independence for central banks and central bankers, but this might change in the coming few years, not the least given the strong signals of a shift in the domestic and international political climate on central banks' role and responsibilities in the economy.[65]

If the coming central bank elite will not establish its credibility on academic pedigree, the question then is what kind of credibility it will base its elite status on. International experience (of crisis management, regulatory reform, and forms of cooperation) still appears to be a viable characteristic (examples are Mark Carney of the Bank of England and Haruhiko Kuroda of the Bank of Japan). This type of competence has been valued for the last few decades and will probably remain so *if* international policy and regulatory cooperation remain a common goal of the world community. As mentioned above, there are signs in national politics (the Brexit vote and the election of world trade-sceptic Trump in the United States) that this trend might not continue, which would make international experience less valuable than before.

Another apparent trend is a return of the politically vested central banker of the post-Second World War decades. Central bankers came under considerable critique after the global financial crisis because of their actions (and inactions). This has led to a call for more democratic accountability of the banks and of the elite that make the decisions. The idea that monetary policy is best left to the 'experts' that marked the 1990s and pre-crisis 2000s is being questioned more than ever, not least by political leaders elected on promises of major economic and structural reforms.

Institutionally, central banks still have the formal political independence established in the 1990s, but it is possible that political leaders will try to increase their influence over central banks and monetary policy by appointing an elite that is more accommodating to their political programmes. In 2017, the Trump administration for example had the opportunity to appoint three members of the Federal Open Market Committee, and so be able to pick members that share the economic policies of the President. Whatever their

---

[64] For a recent account of this development and some of its causes, see Sheila Dow, ' "People Have Had Enough of Experts" ', *Perspectives*, Institute for New Economic Thinking, 6 February, 2017, <http://www.ineteconomics.org/perspectives/blog/people-have-had-enough-of-experts>.

[65] 'Republican attack on Fed casts doubt over global bank rules', *Financial Times*, 3 February 2017.

academic merits, one might speculate that their 'weight' in the Committee is likely to be due more to their political ties than to their list of peer-reviewed journal publications.

It must be stressed that the transformation is an ongoing process that makes it hard to say what will characterize the central bank governors of tomorrow. If this study is anything to go by, however, we should expect that their human capital endowment will have a composition quite different from today.

9

Basel Banking Supervisors and the Construction of an International Standard-Setter Institution

Alexis Frédéric Drach

9.1 Introduction

The end of the twentieth century saw an increased role for expertise in both banking and banking regulation. New methods were devised in order to control better more internationalized and more complex banking practices. Who were the people in charge of establishing these new supervisory practices at the international level? The Basel Committee on Banking Regulation and Supervisory Practices, later called Basel Committee on Banking Supervision (hereafter BCBS), became the most important institution in this field. It was established in late 1974 after a series of banking failures in Germany, the United Kingdom, and the United States, as a reaction of the G10 central bank governors to the challenges of the post-Bretton Woods era.[1] They asked a group of senior officers in banking supervision to help them in their task of monitoring the international financial system. These supervisors became active first in the exchange of ideas to improve the control of international banking, and then in the production of common international standards in banking supervision. Varied networks were established and developed to support this process which both transformed the Committee into an institution in itself and contributed to the internationalization of national supervisory institutions.

---

[1] Catherine Schenk, 'Summer in the City: Banking Failures of 1974 and the Development of International Banking Supervision', *English Historical Review* 2014 (129.540): 1129–56.

Banking supervisors have a complex relationship with banks. They have daily contacts with bankers and in some cases are former bankers themselves, or have had a career in the private sector after experience in banking supervision. On the other hand, supervisors belong to the authorities, whether they come from central banks as in the United Kingdom, or from other separate institutions as in Germany. If they are now at the centre of interest in the field of banking regulation,[2] this was certainly not the case in the early 1970s. At that time, banking supervision differed radically from one country to another, and was linked to differences in the relationship between the state and the market within the Group of Ten.

The BCBS was a group of senior officers of banking supervision and foreign exchanges from twelve different countries (the G10 plus Luxembourg and Switzerland). They had real authority at home but played the role of experts for the central banks' governors when sitting on the Committee. In this capacity, they participated in the production of a new, more internationalized market. This chapter examines the characteristics and role of this group of senior officers in the establishment of a new institution, their relationships with banks, and their role in the shaping of a new post-Bretton Woods international financial market, between its creation in 1974 and its first agreement on a capital adequacy standard in 1988. More generally, it sheds light on the role of experts as historical actors in the field of financial regulation. It will examine the group of people who comprised the BCBS, the institutional evolution of the Committee between 1975 and 1988, and its influence within the field of regulation and supervisory practices.

This chapter states that the power of the Basel Committee members had various dimensions. On an individual basis, many members exerted influence. As a group, they were the only ones who could devise the rules for international banking supervision. As an institution, the BCBS acquired over time a legitimacy that gave it strong political power. Members of the Committee were empowered by their membership; a membership which placed them as key actors in the world of financial regulation. If they were not as powerful as central bank governors, their influence became undeniable, and as such they were part of the elite. The power of the BCBS was further reinforced by the fact that it favoured the development of a more unified profession of banking supervisors, and by the increased role of technocracy and expertise in financial regulation in the 1970s and 1980s. The relation between power and elites has been stressed by John Scott, a point that helps him distinguish elite from class.[3]

---

[2] Gianni Toniolo and Eugene N. White, 'The Evolution of the Financial Stability Mandate: From Its Origins to the Present Day', National Bureau of Economic Research working paper 20844 (2015).

[3] John Scott, 'Modes of Power and the Re-conceptualization of Elites', *Sociological Review* 2008 (56.1): 25–43.

Another approach is provided by Pierre Bourdieu and his followers, who stress the importance of various kinds of capital (economic, symbolic, social, cultural) in differentiating between types of elites, and the interrelations between structures and individuals.[4] This approach has been used to address topics, such as central bankers, from a comparative perspective,[5] or the characteristics of the elites of globalization.[6]

In this chapter, both perspectives will be taken into consideration. If Basel Committee members cannot be considered as representative of a 'class', their sociological properties provide us with important insights on the middle ranking elite of globalization and on its diversity. The Bourdieusian approach also stresses the resilience of national structures in the financial elites' profile, in spite of globalization forces. On the other hand, the increasing influence of the Basel Committee mirrors the growing power of a profession, that of banking supervisor, and the escalating importance of an activity, banking regulation, in the financial sector, at the end of the twentieth century. Therefore one can consider that a new type of financial regulatory elite emerged at that time, of which the Basel Committee and its members were a part: experts and senior officers in banking supervision and regulation. The growing field of banking regulation and supervision reflect the mutually reinforcing interaction of legal and financial elites stressed in Chapter 7 by Arvind, Gray, and Wilson. The newly acquired influence of regulatory and supervisory experts in international financial governance made them part of the elite in the sense of Scott.

Scholars have paid little attention to the members of the Basel Committee, despite an important literature on the question.[7] Only Charles Goodhart provides some biographical information, but only on important members.[8] More generally, the literature on central bank cooperation and internationalization, the Bank for International Settlements' (hereafter BIS) history, or banking regulation in historical perspective has not been particularly focused on the people and networks involved in the analysed changes, particularly

---

[4] Pierre Bourdieu, *Esquisse d'une théorie de la pratique, précédé de trois études d'ethnologie kabyle* (Paris, 2000); Pierre Bourdieu, *La Distinction. Critique sociale du jugement* (Paris, 1979).
[5] Frédéric Lebaron, 'European Central Bank leaders in the Global Space of Central Bankers: A Geometric Data Analysis Approach', *French Politics* 2010 (8.3): 294–320.
[6] Anne-Catherine Wagner, 'Les élites managériales de la mondialisation: angles d'approche et catégories d'analyse', *Entreprises et histoire* 2005 (41.4): 15–23; Yves Dezalay, 'Les courtiers de l'international', *Actes de la Recherche en Sciences Sociales* 2004 (151.152-1): 4–35.
[7] Ethan B. Kapstein, *Governing the Global Economy: International Finance and the State* (Cambridge, MA and London, 1994); Duncan R. Wood, *Governing Global Banking: The Basel Committee and the Politics of Financial Globalisation* (Aldershot, 2005); David A. Singer, *Regulating Capital: Setting Standards for the International Financial System* (Ithaca, 2010); Charles A. E. Goodhart, *The Basel Committee on Banking Supervision: A History of the Early Years, 1974–1997* (Cambridge, 2011); Emmanuel Mourlon-Druol, ' "Trust is good, control is better": The 1974 Herstatt Bank Crisis and its Implications for International Regulatory Reform', *Business History* 2015 (57.2): 311–34.
[8] Goodhart, *The Basel Committee*.

concerning the middle ranking elite.[9] However, several studies have been published on the role of experts and expert committees in international financial and monetary governance.[10] Enquiring into the Basel Committee members' characteristics helps us understand better the relationship between bankers and regulators, the relative importance of their national and international experience, the type of expertise on which their authority was based, and the networks to which they belonged. It thereby helps to comprehend the process of regulation, and not only its results. Newly available archival material from central banks and the BIS, as well as collective biographies of BCBS members, shed light on the role played by elites and institutions in the shaping of the post-Bretton Woods international financial system.

9.2 Collective Biography Analysis

If we follow the results of Goodhart's study, 127 people attended the Basel Committee between its first meeting in January 1975 and the last meeting of the year 1987, not counting those occasional members such as delegates from the European Commission. These 127 people included 120 national delegates and seven members from the BIS. Important variations existed between the representation of one country and another, because of the different turnover among delegates. For instance, four Canadian delegates came to the Committee during the period under study, but there were twenty-two from the United States and from Japan. Fifty biographies (39.4 per cent) have been found through various sources, such as the central banks' websites, online obituaries, archival material, and specialized websites or publications.[11] The main characteristics of these fifty members are indicated in the Appendix. Unfortunately, these biographies do not cover member countries equally. For example, all the French delegates have been found, but almost no Japanese.

---

[9] Gianni Toniolo, *Central Bank Cooperation at the Bank for International Settlements, 1930–1973* (New York, 2005); Kazuhiko Yago, *The Financial History of the Bank for International Settlements* (London and New York, 2012); Toniolo and White, 'The Evolution of the Financial Stability Mandate'; Olivier Feiertag and Michel Margairaz (eds.), *Les Banques centrales à l'échelle du monde: L'internationalisation des banques centrales des débuts du XXe siècle à nos jours* (Paris, 2012); John Singleton, *Central Banking in the Twentieth Century* (Cambridge, 2011); Emmanuel Mourlon-Druol, 'Banking Union in Historical Perspective: The Initiative of the European Commission in the 1960s–1970s', *JCMS: Journal of Common Market Studies* 2016 (54.4): 913–27.

[10] Robert Raymond, 'Le Rôle des Comités d'experts du Comité des Gouverneurs des Banques Centrales de la CEE', *Histoire, Économie & Société* 2011 (30.4): 101–5; Amy Verdun, 'The Role of the Delors Committee in the Creation of EMU: An Epistemic Community?', *Journal of European Public Policy* 1999 (6.2): 308–28; Ivo Maes, 'Alexandre Lamfalussy et les tentatives de la BRI pour éviter un endettement excessif en Amérique latine dans les années 1970', *Histoire, économie & société* 2011 (30.4): 59–77.

[11] Elizabeth Hennessy, *Who's Who in Central Banking* (London, 1997); Elizabeth Hennessy and Carola Gebhard, *Who's Who in Financial Regulation* (London, 1998).

Several other biases characterize this sample. For example, some members attended only one session whereas others attended more than fifty. Also, the biographical information found is not exactly identical from one person to another, and not always complete. Finally, the more high-ranking a member became during his life, the easier it is to find his biography. Therefore information found may not be representative, particularly when it is found online or in publications such as *Who's Who*. However, these biographies do help to assess the heterogeneity or homogeneity of the group, and understand better what kind of people sat on the Committee. Half the BCBS members came from supervisory departments in central banks or from supervisory institutions where there was one, and half from central banks' foreign exchange departments. Each country was supposed to send two delegates for each meeting, although on occasion some countries, such as the United States, sent more delegates.

A first distinctive feature of the members of the Committee is their diversity, between one country and another, but also within one and the same country. This variety stemmed both from national differences and from the fact that members were middle ranking elites, as opposed to central bank governors who represented the top level of each country's central banking profile.[12] In the French case, no delegate was a former Inspector of Finance, which was the traditional profile of the financial elite in France. Among the nine British delegates on which information is known for a total of eleven people over the period, four were Oxbridge graduates, among whom were the two chairs, George Blunden and Peter Cooke. Two British secretaries of the Committee, both from the Bank of England, attended the elitist public school, Eton. Out of five American delegates whose education is known, two were Harvard graduates. Three of the six known Swiss members were lawyers. Some members thus had a rather typical elitist profile of each country in terms of their education and earlier profession, but by no means all of them.

All members of the BCBS were senior officers in their home institution. However, while it is difficult to compare seniority from one country to another, it seems that some countries sent people who were more senior than others. For instance, in the case of the United States, David Willey was vice president of the Federal Reserve Bank of New York when he attended the Committee. Heimann and Bench were both Comptroller of the Currency, a position at the head of one of the three US regulatory institutions. On the other hand, the French delegates were less senior. They usually ranked just

---

[12] Youssef Cassis, 'La Communauté des Gouverneurs des Banques Centrales Européennes depuis la fin de la Seconde Guerre mondiale', in Olivier Feiertag and Michel Margairaz (eds.), *Politiques et Pratiques des Banques d'émission en Europe (XVIIe–XXe Siècle). Le Bicentenaire de la Banque de France dans la Perspective de l'Identité Monétaire Européenne* (Paris, 2003), 753–65.

below the head of the Banks' Control Commission, which was itself subordinated to the central bank. This was the case for Pierre Fanet and Jean Bonnardin, who held positions just below that of the secretary general of the Commission. In the Japanese case, career progression was linked to the frequency of transfers from one position to another at the Bank of Japan and the Ministry of Finance. Therefore, there was a rapid turnover of Japanese delegates.[13] Another G10-based committee, the Euro-currency Standing Committee was composed of more senior members than those in the BCBS, yet no hierarchical difference was ever expressed.

As an expert committee, the BCBS worked for the central bank's governors but still enjoyed relative independence. This was for two reasons: first, their expertise in banking practices and banking supervision and regulation gave them technical power, and second, some of the delegates were not coming from central banks but from other institutions: the Office of the Comptroller of the Currency (from 1978 onwards) and the Federal Deposit Insurance Corporation (from 1984 onwards) in the United States; the Ministry of Finance in Japan; the Federal Office of Supervision in Germany; and the Federal Banking Commission in Switzerland, for instance. Rivalries between these institutions and the central bank of these countries could be important. Several authors state that governors did not intervene much in the affairs of the Committee, partly because banking supervision was an esoteric topic.[14] However, governors did brief members at home and exerted considerable pressure on the capital convergence exercise which started in 1984. Governors' involvement depended on the kind of topic discussed and its policy implications, but in any case they could not write the reports on their own, and needed BCBS members to do so.

Almost all the members of the Committee were men, which reflected the predominantly male environment of central banking. Among the attendees only one was a woman: Mrs Lepoivre, from the National Bank of Belgium. According to Goodhart, she attended thirty-three meetings between 1984 and 1995.[15] Male predominance was particularly visible during international conferences or special meetings organized outside Basel, during which spouses were invited. This was the case for instance of a joint meeting of the Groupe de Contact and a working group of the Basel Committee in Copenhagen in May 1984,[16] or at the international conference of banking supervisors in Tokyo in

---

[13] Satoshi Watanabe, *The Origin and Development of International Cooperation for Financial Stability: International Cooperation at the Basel Committee on Banking Supervision* [translation from Japanese] (Tokyo, 2012).
[14] Richard J. Herring and Robert E. Litan, *Financial Regulation in a Global Economy* (Washington, DC, 1994), p. 9; Goodhart, *The Basel Committee*.
[15] Goodhart, *The Basel Committee*, p. 76.
[16] Bank of France Archives (hereafter BoF), 1749200912/263, Meeting of the Groupe de Contact in Copenhagen on 24 and 25 May 1984, 'Ladies programme'.

October 1988:[17] these events had a specific programme for spouses which included visits and shopping, in addition to common sociability practices such as buffets and dinners. These events thus illustrated a strong sexual division of roles in the society.

Was the BCBS a group of new transnational elites? The answer differs from one member to another, and within one and the same country. Even if many members had had an international experience, most of them had spent much of their career in their home country. Out of fifty people whose biographies have been found, twenty-four have had an international experience of one year or more in their career, or have been involved in several international groupings other than the BCBS. For example Gérard Aubanel, one of the first French delegates, was sent to the IMF between 1955 and 1958, and then to the European Commission between 1962 and 1963. Derrick Byatt, from the Bank of England, went to the BIS for fifteen months in 1955 and 1956. Motomichi Ikawa was an economist at the OECD between 1976 and 1979 before representing the Japanese Ministry of Finance on the Basel Committee, from 1982 on. However, some members have been more particularly involved in international activities during their career. This is the case for example of Albert Dondelinger, a delegate from Luxembourg at the Basel Committee. He was part of many other committees and institutions, such as the EEC committee of banking supervisors, known as the Groupe de Contact, the World Bank, the monetary committee of the EEC (between 1971 and 1976), and the interim committee of the IMF (between 1972 and 1976). John Heimann, Comptroller of the Currency and member of the Basel Committee between 1978 and 1980, was member and treasurer of the Group of Thirty and a president of the American Ditchley Foundation, among many other international groupings. Overall some members did have a very international profile and belonged to a vast network of committees and institutions, while others had a more domestic-centred career.

A comparison between British and French members sheds light on national differences concerning international profiles. There were seven French delegates and ten British delegates (excluding chairmen and secretaries) attending the Basel Committee between 1975 and 1987. Biographies of all the French members and of eight British members have been found. Of these eight British, three had experience in the former or then current British Empire: Derrick Byatt was seconded to the central bank of Zambia, and David Nendick to the central bank of Mauritius before going to work for the Hong Kong government to which Richard Farrant was also assigned. Conversely, most French delegates spent their career at the Bank of France or at the Banks'

---

[17] BoF, 1749200912/265, '1988 ICBS Tokyo. Programme'.

Control Commission. Some of them, however, did have a relatively extensive experience abroad, in Europe. For example, André Icard, member of the Basel Committee between 1982 and 1984, was deputy director-general of the BIS between 1996 and 2000, while Jean-Pierre Fèvre was seconded to the European Commission between 1989 and 1997 before going back to the Bank of France.

Were there bankers on the Committee? This question relates to the more general issue of the relationships the BCBS had with commercial banks. Goodhart states that there were few direct contacts between the BCBS and banks, because most of these contacts were established at a national level.[18] While being true on the whole, such a perspective establishes an artificial rupture between the BCBS and national authorities represented on the Committee. In addition, several members were indeed bankers themselves, before or after their time on the Committee. Of the fifty people whose biography has been found, thirteen had had some experience in the private sector. This experience ranged from consulting activities, sometimes after retirement, to an almost lifetime career as a banker. National variations were, here again, very important. Frederik Mush, a Dutch delegate between 1982 and 1992, had various positions in an investment bank and at PricewaterhouseCoopers before and after his experience at the Nederlandsche Bank. Two Swiss members, out of a total of six biographies collected (and a total of ten Swiss members between 1975 and 1987), ended their career in the private sector. This is also the case for two British members out of a total of seven biographies collected from a total of ten British members over the same period (excluding chairmen and secretaries). Additionally, Dondelinger (Luxembourg) was chairman of the Luxembourgian Banks and Bankers' Association between 1977 and 1978, member of the Overseas Bankers Club of London, and fellow of the International Bankers Association in Washington. French members had particularly little experience in the private sector, whether before or after their time on the Committee. Only André Icard, one of the seven French delegates between 1975 and 1987 (for whom all the biographies have been found), has been administrator at the Banque Française du Commerce Extérieur, established in 1946 to develop French exports, and closely linked to the French state.

American members seem to have had closer links with commercial banks or other private institutions, although information is missing. Four US members out of a total of seven biographies found (and a total of twenty-two people between 1975 and 1987) had experience in the private sector. David Willey, vice president of the Federal Reserve Bank of New York, worked at Morgan Stanley, while Robert Bench joined Price Waterhouse after twenty-two years spent at the Office of the Comptroller of the Currency. John Heimann worked

---

[18] Goodhart, *The Basel Committee*.

at Smith Barney & Co and E. M. Warburg Pincus & Co for about twenty years before becoming Comptroller of the Currency in 1977, until 1981. He returned to the private sector from 1982 onwards, working first at Becker Paribas Incorporated, then at Merrill Lynch, where he became chairman of Global Financial Institutions in 1991. In the same vein, Michael Patriarca spent most of his career in the private sector. US supervisors were more attracted to the private sector than in other countries, most notably France, a result that is confirmed by archival material.[19] These results hint that individual members' profiles reflected the overall relationship between the state and the market in each country.

What kind of expertise did the members have? If education gives insights into this question, it is also to be looked at carefully, as in some cases it could reflect a way of selecting the elite of a country. Two disciplines dominate the thirty-four cases whose educational background is known: law and economics. This reflects the different skill profiles of supervisors and central bankers already identified by Goodhart.[20] Twenty-two members out of thirty-four had studied law during their education, twenty members had studied economics. In addition, two French members had attended the Institut d'Etudes Politiques of Paris which could include a training in economics. Only three members had a proven PhD in economics. Helmut Mayer, secretary of the Committee and expert in euro-markets at the BIS had a PhD from Stanford. David Willey, from the Federal Reserve Bank of New York and member of the Committee between 1975 and 1982, had a PhD in economics from the University of Columbia. Motomichi Ikawa, from the Ministry of Finance and on the Committee between 1982 and 1984, had a PhD from Berkeley. Some members, such as Brian Quinn and Richard Farrant (Bank of England) had been economists at the IMF, but precise information on their education has not been ascertained. Gemmill from the Federal Reserve had a PhD from Harvard University, but the discipline has not been found, although economics is a most likely possibility. Law was particularly important in Switzerland (five out of the six members whose education is known had studied law, for a total of ten members over the period considered). Of the thirty-four cases known, seven members had studied both law and economics. The predominance of these two disciplines reflects the point stressed in Chapter 8 by Wendschlag about the central bank elites' education from 1950 to 2000, although the shorter time frame considered here does not allow us to identify the rise of economics.

---

[19] US National Archives and Records Administration (hereafter NARA), 101820027/20, 'Human resources issues for discussion by the Comptroller', 15 July 1977.
[20] Charles A. E. Goodhart, Dirk Schoenmaker, and Paolo Dasgupta, 'The Skill Profile of Central Bankers and Supervisors', *European Finance Review* 2002 (6.3): 397–427.

However, education was not the main source of expertise. There were relatively few members with a PhD, and professional experience and training within a home institution was important. Other fields of expertise such as accounting were also deemed important in the profession. Furthermore, knowledge of the market was a key element of members' skill profiles, and formed a sort of 'tacit knowledge', that is, a little formalized knowledge playing an important role in the exercising of their authority.[21] There was, however, little specific training in banking supervision at that time. To some extent the work of the BCBS was to produce a more formalized knowledge on banking supervision at the international level. Therefore, members' expertise was first and foremost based on their professional experience and authority.

The Basel Committee was well connected to a network of other committees and various institutions. It was in itself a network connecting central banks and supervisory institutions.[22] As Goodhart explains, connections were particularly important with EEC groupings, especially the Groupe de Contact and the Banking Advisory Committee of the EEC.[23] There was an important membership overlap between these two committees, both involved in banking regulation and supervision, and the BCBS. At least seven European members of the Basel Committee were also part of the Groupe de Contact, although not necessarily concurrently: Schmit (Luxembourg), Dondelinger (Luxembourg), Muller (Netherlands), Schneider (Germany), Baeyens (Beglium), Bonnardin (France), Coljé (Netherlands). Schneider became chairman of the Groupe de Contact in 1982,[24] and Bonnardin was chairman before him.[25] Furthermore, at least eight European members of the Basel Committee have been part of the Banking Advisory Committee: Muller (Netherlands), Musch (Netherlands), Schaus (Luxembourg), Farrant (United Kingdom), Schneider (Germany), Coljé (Netherlands), Lang (Germany), Cooke (United Kingdom).[26] Some members have thus been part of all three committees, though not always exactly at the same time. As a result, European members were particularly well involved in international networks of banking regulation, because of the European integration process.

Several members were also part of other transnational committees. The Eurocurrency Standing Committee (hereafter ECSC) of the BIS, another G10-based

---

[21] Michael Polanyi, *The Tacit Dimension* (Chicago, 2009).
[22] Martin Marcussen, 'The Basel Committee as a Transnational Governance Network', in Martin Marcussen and Jacob Torfing (eds.), *Democratic Network Governance in Europe* (Basingstoke, 2007), 214–32.
[23] Goodhart, *The Basel Committee*.
[24] BoF, 1749200912/305, Twenty-fourth meeting, 25 and 26 February 1982.
[25] Bank for International Settlements Archives (hereafter BISA), 1.3a(3) F, Seventeenth meeting, 8 and 9 November 1979.
[26] Hennessy, *Who's Who in Central Banking*; Hennessy and Gebhard, *Who's Who in Financial Regulation*; BoF, 1749200912/265, 'List of members of the Banking Advisory Committee', June 1986; <http://www3.tcmb.gov.tr/conference/cv/MuschCV.pdf> (accessed 5 May 2015).

expert committee working for the central bank governors, was working on international financial activities from a macroeconomic perspective. Both committees had had tense relationships at the turn of the 1980s because they worked on similar issues from a different perspective. Peter Cooke, chairman of the BCBS, represented the Basel Committee at the ECSC's meetings from 1980 on. Musch, a Dutch delegate at the BCBS between 1982 and 1992 was also a member of the ECSC, although the time of his membership is not known, and André, from the National Bank of Belgium, was probably a member of the ECSC for about ten years.[27] Musch and Mayer (secretary of the BCBS, BIS) participated respectively in a committee on financial services and a working group on banking regulation at the OECD.[28] Gutzwiller, a delegate from Switzerland, was member of the monetary law committee of the International Law Association while also being a member of the BCBS. In 1981, Peter Cooke participated in the sub-group of the Group of Thirty working on the question of international banking risk and supervision.[29] Some members were also part of various clubs such as the Rotary Club (Dondelinger,[30] Luxembourg; Hauri,[31] Switzerland), the Ditchley Foundation (Heimann, USA), and the City of London Club (Barnes, United Kingdom). Furthermore, some members participated in various groupings established by the BCBS itself together with other institutions: Willey (USA), Kloft (Germany), Dealtry (BIS, secretary of the Committee), Stahel (Switzerland), and Timmerman (Netherlands) were part of a joint working group with the Banking Commission of the International Chamber of Commerce.[32] Vachon (Canada), Pille (Belgium), Timmerman (Netherlands), Aubanel (France), Lanciotti (Italy), and Dealtry (BIS) formed a BIS group with other national delegates working on international maturity transformation.[33]

At national level, members were part of various committees and working groups, ensuring a connection with the international level. Bodmer, a Swiss delegate, was part of an expert group working on a report to the government on the improvement of the prudential system.[34] Danielsson, from Sweden,

---

[27] BISA, 1.3a(3) F, Eighth meeting, 28 and 29 October 1976.
[28] <http://www3.tcmb.gov.tr/conference/cv/MuschCV.pdf> (accessed 5 May 2015); BoF, 1749200912/304, Nineteenth meeting, 26 and 27 June 1980.
[29] BoF, 1749200912/305, Twenty-second meeting, 25 and 26 June 1981.
[30] <http://www3.tcmb.gov.tr/conference/cv/MuschCV.pdf> (accessed 5 May 2015).
[31] 'Base de données des élites suisses au XXe siècle', <http://www2.unil.ch/elitessuisses/index.php?page=detailPerso&idIdentite=60067> (accessed 5 May 2015).
[32] BISA, 1.3a(3) F, Tenth meeting, 30 June and 1 July 1977; BISA, 1.3a(3), 1979/9, BS/1979/2, 'Provisional report of Dr. Roesle's working party on the drafting of rules on outstanding forward foreign exchange contracts', 4 December 1978, annex 2.
[33] BISA, 1.3a(3) F, Fifteenth meeting, 2 and 3 March 1979; BISA, 1.3a(3) F, Eighteenth meeting, 28 and 29 February 1980.
[34] BISA, 1.3a(3) F, Fifth meeting, 11 and 12 December 1975.

Financial Elites and European Banking

was part of a committee examining banks' capital adequacy rules from 1976 on.[35] Müller (Switzerland) was part of a special commission created by the Swiss government to revise the banking law in 1977.[36] Fèvre, Fanet, and Bonnardin (France) were all part of the working group working for a new 'Plan Comptable' (accounting rules) between 1973 and 1976.[37] Heimann, Comptroller of the Currency between 1977 and 1981 and member of the Committee between 1978 and 1980, was the first chairman of the Federal Bank Examination Council, representing the three US federal regulatory institutions.[38] Wiley and Gemmill, US delegates, were both part of the System Steering Committee on International Banking Regulation established in early 1973 by the Federal Reserve.[39] The Basel Committee was thus well integrated in a national and international network of committees.

The BCBS was a heterogeneous network of senior officers who were differently connected to the private sector, and to international governance structures, even within one and the same country. However, some differences can be identified between countries: for instance, American members had closer links with commercial banks than French members. In addition, educational background reflects each country's traditions, a point also stressed in Chapter 8 by Wendschlag on central bank elites. Lastly, a majority of members had a rather 'national' career, despite their participation in the Basel Committee. Some members were already influential on an individual basis. This was particularly the case of the two chairmen, George Blunden and Peter Cooke, but also of several American members such as John Heimann. Over the period 1975–88 the evolution of the international context gave the BCBS a status which enabled it to shape the new international financial system of the late twentieth century.

9.3 From a Club to an Institution

The Basel Committee had first a club-like dimension and was supposed to bring together people who did not know each other very well. The objective was certainly not to harmonize banking regulations or supervisory practices, but to learn from each other, exchange ideas, and share information.[40]

---

[35] BISA, 1.3a(3) F, Eighth meeting, 28 and 29 October 1976.
[36] BISA, 1.3a(3) F, Eleventh meeting, 27 and 28 October 1977.
[37] BoF, 1749200912/166, '49ᵉ réunion du groupe de travail chargé de l'étude d'une réforme du règlement comptable des banques', 9 February 1976.
[38] BoF, 1749200912/304, Fifteenth meeting, 2 and 3 March 1979.
[39] Federal Reserve Bank of New York Archives (hereafter FRBNY), central files, box 615771, 'System Steering Committee on International Banking Regulation. Members of the Steering Committee', April 1974.
[40] BISA, 1.3a(3) F, First meeting, 6 and 7 February 1975.

This club-like dimension was maintained throughout the entire period: with dinners hosted by the chairman, meetings arranged outside Basel, and international conferences occurring every two years, all organized to foster trust and mutual understanding. Increasing international competition and risks in the international financial system placed the Committee in a key position within banking regulation. Over time, it gained a public authority that enabled it to issue common standards. This authority was reinforced by a context favouring more liberalized but more controlled international banking practices, thus empowering banking supervision in general. In close contact with bankers and various kinds of international experts, BCBS members helped shape a new international financial system.

From 1979 on, the BCBS organized international conferences of banking supervisors, gathering professionals from all over the world. Five conferences were organized between 1979 and 1988, in London, Washington, Rome, Amsterdam, and Tokyo. They soon acquired a role of circulating papers produced by the BCBS and obtaining endorsement on its proposed practices. They also reinforced a community feeling among supervisors. In October 1981, Cooke stated about these conferences that 'he believed that there was merit in allowing as many supervisors as possible to feel part of a larger "family" from time to time'.[41] Discussing the upcoming conference of 1988 in Tokyo after the Basel agreement on a common standard of capital adequacy, 'Mr. Musch [Netherlands] said that the conferences provided an ideal opportunity to obtain the endorsement of non-G-10 countries to policies adopted by Committee members. He hoped it might be possible to secure broad international agreement on the capital framework.'[42] These conferences usually gathered delegates from about a hundred countries over two days, and provided opportunities for developing and maintaining networks. High ranking officials such as central bank governors or ministers of finance made an opening speech. Some bankers were also invited, although not at the first conference.[43] Such conferences therefore considerably increased the Committee's visibility and authority in the field of banking regulation.

From 1979 on, the BCBS played a role in establishing other regional groupings of banking supervisors. The first one was the offshore group of supervisors, whose idea dated back to the first conference of 1979 in London.[44] It met several times with the BCBS or alone from 1980 on. By 1985, there were

---

[41] BoF, 1749200912/305, Twenty-third meeting, 29 and 30 October 1981, p. 3.
[42] BoF, 1749200912/265, BS/88/22 (extract from meeting of January 1988), 'd. Fifth ICBS in Tokyo', p. 3.
[43] BoF, 1749200912/355, 'International Conference of Banking Supervisors. London July 5–6 1979. Record of proceedings'.
[44] BoF, 1749200912/266, Issues in Bank Regulation, 'The Role of International Supervision in Banking', Bank Administration Institute, Summer 1984.

also groups of supervisors from the Gulf countries, from Latin America and the Caribbean, and from South East Asia, New Zealand, and Australia (SEANZA).[45] The BCBS, and first and foremost its chairman Peter Cooke, played a role in the establishment of these various groupings and members of the Committee attended their meetings. Thus the Basel Committee was soon at the centre of a network of banking supervisors' regional groupings. The BCBS was not in itself the oldest international supervisors committee—the Nordic group and the EEC Groupe de Contact were already in existence when it was created—but its geographic coverage included the biggest banking systems, and therefore its authority was the strongest.

The Committee itself changed between 1975 and 1988. Its second chairman, Peter Cooke, from June 1977 on,[46] played an active role in promoting international banking supervision, whereas George Blunden, the former chairman, had been more conservative in his role.[47] The international debt crisis of 1982 highlighted the risks of post-Bretton Woods international banking for the financial system taken as a whole. The failure of the BCBS to prevent this situation showed how difficult it was for authorities to control an international market due to strong accounting, legal, and economic differences between countries. From 1984 onwards, the BCBS came under strong political pressure as it became the key location for the construction of an international agreement on capital adequacy for international banks. While the detailed story of the agreement is outside the scope of this chapter, it is worth stressing how the capital convergence exercise changed the Committee. In 1984, at the initiative of Paul Volcker, chairman of the US Federal Reserve, the Committee was given a new mandate to work more thoroughly on capital adequacy convergence between the G10 countries.[48] At the same time, it was decided to give more power to Peter Cooke, and to allow him to make recommendations which were based on the Committee's discussions, but did not necessarily have the support of all of its members. The secretariat of the Committee was reshaped in order to introduce more supervisory expertise and to help cope with its increasing technical work pressure. During the following years, it became clear that the BCBS would be a key institution in the process of capital adequacy convergence, even though some countries, particularly Japan, France, and Germany, were opposed to the convergence

---

[45] BoF, 1749200912/266, International Conference of Banking Supervisors. Banca d'Italia—Rome, 13–14 September 1984, 'Report by S. Aoki, as the representative of SEANZA countries'; BoF, 1749200912/355, 'The Basle Supervisors Committee. Remarks by J. S. Beverly, May 24, 1985', Fifth Assembly of the Commission of Latin American and Caribbean Banking Supervisory and Inspection Authorities, Barbados, 23 and 24 May 1985.
[46] BISA, 1.3a(3) F, Tenth meeting, 30 June and 1 July 1977.
[47] Schenk, 'Summer in the City'.
[48] BoF, 1749200912/311, BS/84/31 revised: 'Text of Chairman's telex of 26th March 1984'.

exercise. As a result, by 1988, the Committee had gained an unprecedented role in the shaping of the international financial system.

The BCBS also played a role in the construction of an international authority facing multinational banking. Supervisors need some respectability in the eyes of banks in order to carry out their activities. At a time where banks' multinationalization and internationalization was a serious challenge to national authorities, the Basel Committee was used to reinforce this authority. In December 1975, George Blunden (chairman, Bank of England) stated that:

> if any member of the Committee used decisions reached, or recommendations made, by the Committee as a means of strengthening his hand in discussions with his country's banks, the Committee must, in his view, accept that such an approach was perfectly legitimate.[49]

Also part of the international construction of authority was the fact that members frequently circulated letters sent to their banks in order to discuss best practices and banks' reaction. For instance, at the June 1976 meeting, German delegates circulated papers sent by the Bundesbank and by the Federal Office of Supervision to other members to explain recent dispositions taken by German authorities in the field of internal audit requirement and foreign exchange transactions.[50] Exchanging views and ideas about supervisory practices was also meant to reinforce supervisors' authority at home. In the same vein, at the June 1981 meeting, the Belgian delegate Pille said that the Committee's questionnaire enquiring on banks' evaluation of country risk

> had been very useful in focusing the discussions the Banking Commission had had on this question with the Belgian banks, and the latter had expressed interest in the results of the Committee's exercise.[51]

Different representations of the role of supervisors existed, and discussions at the Basel Committee or during international conferences frequently initiated debates on the responsibilities and boundaries of the profession. For instance, the respective responsibilities of supervisors and bankers were difficult to delineate clearly. The discourses on the role of supervisors were often expressing a specific, market-oriented type of governance. For instance, Peter Cooke, chairman of the Committee, stated at the fifth international conference of banking supervisors in 1988 that:

---

[49] BISA, 1.3a(3) F, Fifth meeting, 11 and 12 December 1975, p. 9.
[50] BISA, 1.3a(3), 1976/5, Letter from the Bundesbank to the central associations of German banks, 20 May 1976; BISA, 1.3a(3) F, Seventh meeting, 17 and 18 June 1976.
[51] BoF, 1749200912/305, Twenty-first meeting, 26 and 27 February 1981, p. 35.

at the same time, as others have remarked, let us not assume that supervisors are omnipotent and all-seeing. Banks must fail and the disciplines of the market must play their proper part, even if, as a result, we as supervisors appear to have to shoulder the blame for problems when they occur.[52]

A blend of cultural representations and political ideas thus interwove to shape new practices of banking regulation, whereby a more liberal environment was counterbalanced by a reinforced supervision.

9.4 The Making of New Rules and Norms in Banking Supervision

The members of the Basel Committee wrote several reports to the governors between 1974 and 1988 in order to improve banking supervisory practices. A complete review of its activity is not possible in a few pages. However, a few examples can shed light on the role played by these experts in shaping the new international financial system. This section examines both the influence of the Committee and the role of its members in setting new rules for supervisory practices. The question of the influence of the BCBS is complex, because it was both direct and indirect, that is, involving official agreements or simply reflecting reciprocal influence between member countries. Most of the work of the Committee was about technical issues and exchange of ideas, which participated in the creation of a new method for international banking supervision. Some achievements of the Committee are already famous, such as the Concordat, established in 1975 and made public in 1979,[53] or the capital adequacy agreement of 1988, which has already received much academic attention.[54] Others, such as the consolidation of banks' balance sheets for supervisory purposes, have received less attention from researchers. The consolidation principle became integrated in the revised Concordat of 1983. Taken together, the Concordat and consolidation principle illustrate both technical and broader issues addressed by the Committee. They will be briefly explained in order to highlight its work until the early 1980s.

What was called the Concordat from 1979 on was initially a text written by Huib Muller, from the Nederlandsche Bank, on the division of responsibilities between G10 authorities in international banking supervision. The first meetings of the Basel Committee, in 1975, dedicated substantial time to discussing issues of prudential responsibilities of foreign branches and subsidiaries. These discussions resulted from the failure of the Israel-British Bank, an Israeli bank

---

[52] Ibid., P. Cooke, p. 207.   [53] Schenk, 'Summer in the City'; Goodhart, *The Basel Committee*.
[54] Kapstein, *Governing the Global Economy*; Wood, *Governing Global Banking*; Singer, *Regulating Capital*; Goodhart, *The Basel Committee*; Watanabe, *The Origin and Development of International Cooperation*.

Banking Supervisors and International Standard Setting

with a subsidiary in London and which had been involved in fraud, using a Swiss bank to hide part of its business.[55] In his paper, Huib Muller tried to clarify prudential responsibilities, suggesting a scheme to delineate them. Roughly speaking, the control of liquidity was mostly left to host authorities, while the supervision of solvency was the prime responsibility of home authorities.[56] The text was deliberately vague in order to state broad principles and avoid too lengthy negotiations, and was redrafted by the Committee to be sent as a report to the governors in October 1975.[57] It became public in 1979 after the London conference, and was revised in 1983 in order to include the consolidation principle and make clear that it did not cover lender-of-last-resort issues, a point that had always been too delicate for authorities when taking an official position.[58]

The nature of the 1975 agreement and its role for the Committee had several dimensions. In itself, the agreement was drawing on already existing though not formalized practices of banking supervisors. Nordic countries (Denmark, Sweden, Finland, Norway, Iceland) had long established cooperative practices to supervise their international banks.[59] The aim of the Concordat was to prevent gaps in banking supervision, making sure that all situations were covered by one or several supervisory authorities. In practice, it was difficult to implement, because of several obstacles such as lack of information, banking secrecy rules, absence of lender-of-last-resort responsibilities, and the diversity of situations in international banking. However, the Concordat and its successive refinements may also be seen as a progressive formalization of international cooperation between supervisory administrations. The agreement established between authorities formalized a network of supervisors and played a role in internationalizing national administrations.

The principle of the consolidation of banks' balance sheets for supervisory purposes is an interesting case of circulation between the EEC groupings and the Basel Committee. It was a direct consequence of banks' multinationalization,[60] and consisted of taking into account all the foreign establishments of a bank, including its foreign subsidiaries, when evaluating its

---

[55] Schenk, 'Summer in the City'.
[56] BISA, 1.3a(3), 1975/1, 'Paper for the BIS-Committee on banking regulations supervisory practices', H. J. Muller, 23 May 1975.
[57] BISA, 1.3a(3) F, Fourth meeting, 25 and 26 September 1975.
[58] BoF, 1749200912/263, BS/84/22, 'The Basel "Concordat" on the Supervision of Banks' Foreign Establishments', Text submitted by Peter Cooke to the Swiss Institute for International Economics, Regional Science and Market Research, for publication in its quarterly journal, *Aussenwirtschaft*, 15 February 1984.
[59] BISA, 1.3a(3), 1982/17, 'Reports to the governors on the supervision of banks' foreign establishments: extract from the replies received from non-Group of Ten central banks and supervisory authorities to whom the report was sent', March 1976.
[60] Geoffrey Jones (ed.), *Multinational and International Banking* (Aldershot, 1992).

Financial Elites and European Banking

liquidity and solvency.[61] The aim was both to be more informed of foreign subsidiaries' activities and to prevent banks from escaping regulation through subsidiaries established in less regulated countries. Legally independent, foreign subsidiaries were until then not included in the calculation of solvency ratios and could thus be used to bypass home regulations. At the October 1976 meeting, Hugo Coljé, from the Dutch central bank, explained that he was writing a paper for the EEC Groupe de Contact on consolidation and suggested also discussing this issue at the Basel Committee.[62] In fact, the Basel Committee addressed the topic only one year later, in October 1977, and most of the initial work was made by the EEC Groupe de Contact.[63]

The Basel Committee worked thoroughly on the topic of consolidation in late 1977 and 1978. When Coljé presented his paper in October 1977, he stressed the challenges of offshore centres for banking supervisors.[64] In this, he stated that home authorities had a moral responsibility not only to banks' foreign branches, but also to their foreign subsidiaries, and that subsidiaries could carry a risk superior to actual participation for parent banks. Countries were then at different stages of reflection on the question. The Netherlands and the United States were very favourable to the idea, whereas in Japan authorities had only just started to deliberate on it. In France, reaction to Coljé's paper had been very positive because it called attention to a problem which was still little considered.[65] During 1978, most members rapidly agreed on the desirability of consolidating banks' balance sheets. Debates centred around the technical details and on the importance and implementation of the method. The main technical problem concerned what to do with minority participations. Danielsson, a Swedish delegate, explained in June 1978 that he was unable to convince his colleagues in Sweden of the desirability of the method of consolidation, and therefore was in favour of a report to the governors in order to strengthen the idea.[66] Consolidation implied heavy technical work on the part of supervisors, and was difficult to apply in practice.[67] Despite these technical difficulties, the Basel Committee members were largely in favour of this technique which was meant to improve international banking supervision. They wrote a report advocating this method in 1978, and submitted it to the governors in September after several revisions.[68] In December, the governors strongly endorsed it and invited the

---

[61] BoF, 1749200912/295, 'Consolidation des comptes de banques', 19 January 1981.
[62] BISA, 1.3a(3) F, Eighth meeting, 28 and 29 October 1976.
[63] BISA, 1.3a(3) F, Eleventh meeting, 27 and 28 October 1977. [64] Ibid. [65] Ibid.
[66] BISA, 1.3a(3) F, Thirteenth meeting, 29 and 30 June 1978.
[67] BoF, 1749200912/305, Twenty-second meeting, 25 and 26 June 1981.
[68] BISA, 1.3a(3), 1982/17, 'Past circulation of Committee documents', 1982.

Committee to write another report stating progress made in the field and giving directives.[69]

The second report was sent to the governors on 22 March 1979.[70] This reaffirmed the desirability of consolidation for supervisory purposes and called for its implementation. Consolidation faced considerable resistance from banks in some cases, notably Switzerland, because it revealed the undercapitalization of several Swiss banks once their foreign subsidiaries were taken into account.[71] In practice, consolidation could not solve all the issues of international supervision, and needed cooperation of foreign authorities in order to obtain the necessary information. Some countries needed a change in the legislation in order to implement the principle of consolidation.[72] On the whole, the exercise showed an effort on the part of authorities to think more globally and take into account all the risks taken by international banks when evaluating their soundness, but it faced considerable delay with banking institutions which were already advanced in their multinational expansion.

The method of consolidation for supervisory purposes was disseminated both at the G10 level and beyond. Within the G10, implementation of the consolidation's principle was very uneven until the early 1980s. The countries that were particularly in favour of its adoption, such as the United States or the Netherlands, applied it quite early.[73] Japan reinforced its measures in 1978, and Canada extended consolidation to majority participations and important minority participations in 1980. In Germany, the legal framework for consolidation did not exist yet in 1981, but was strongly favoured by the Ministry of Finance. Meanwhile, German authorities had to rely on a gentlemen's agreement with banks from 1979.[74] In France, consolidation was possible, but not compulsory, from 1979 on. Outside the G10, the principle of consolidation was spread through direct correspondence with other authorities, through the G10 governors' statements, and through the London international conference of July 1979. The first report on consolidation was circulated in advance to the guests of the conference and many replies were received over the following months. The method of consolidation was further supported by the governors in a press communiqué of April 1980, where they stressed the importance of the work of the Basel Committee in this field.

---

[69] BISA, 1.3a(3), 1979/9, 'Consolidation: the next steps', 1979.
[70] BISA, 1.3a(3), 1982/17, 'Past circulation of Committee documents', 1982.
[71] BISA, 1.3a(3) F, Sixteenth meeting, 28 and 29 June 1979.
[72] BoF, 1749200912/305, Twenty-second meeting, 25 and 26 June 1981.
[73] BISA, 1.3a(3), 1980/11, 'Rapport aux gouverneurs sur les progrès accomplis par les pays membres dans l'application du principe de consolidation à l'échelle internationale', 26 January 1981.
[74] Ibid.

At that point the G10 governors' support for consolidation triggered an active agenda on the part of European institutions, in order to issue a new directive.[75] The idea behind this was part of a more ambitious project initiated by the 1977 directive on the coordination of banking regulations in member states. The Commission wished to make consolidation compulsory in all member states but also to harmonize periodical returns submitted by banks to authorities.[76] Consolidation was therefore included in a broader framework, including the improvement of the circulation of information between prudential authorities in member states, simplification of banks' declarations, and the harmonization of definitions of accounting categories. Several projects were subsequently submitted by the Commission to the Banking Advisory Committee from 1980 on. The discussion between the Commission, the Advisory Committee, and the Groupe de Contact lasted two years, until the directive was eventually issued in 1983.[77] Thus, a method of banking supervision initially put forward by a European expert committee (the EEC Groupe de Contact), was then discussed and endorsed by the Basel Committee and then went back to the EEC level. To some extent, the principle of consolidation was a simple administrative practice, but its use increased considerably through the influence of the Basel Committee, and its spread highlighted a global turn on the part of the authorities. This case study illustrates the international circulation and construction of supervisory practices through the Committee.

9.5 Conclusion

This chapter has shown how institution building, elites, and networks played a combined role in the transformation of the post-Bretton Woods financial system. If the context was favourable to the reinforcement of specific international committees such as the BCBS, its members played a crucial role in devising new rules for banking supervision and banking practices. This membership was quite diverse: some members were much more influential or had a more international career than others. The various networks they were part of, such as international committees, other international organizations, or national institutions, highlight the density of the regulatory field at the turn of the global era. Furthermore, the BCBS as a group gained much symbolic capital over the period considered, and evolved from a club to an institution. Its visibility and respectability increased over time, and so did its legitimacy.

[75] BoF, 1749200912/304, Nineteenth meeting, 26 and 27 June 1980.
[76] BoF, 1749200912/295, 'Coordination des information périodiques fournies par les banques à des fins de surveillance. Résumé des travaux effectués jusqu'à présent'.
[77] BoF, 1749200912/295, 'Proposition modifiée de directive du Conseil relative à la surveillance des établissements de crédits sur une base consolidée', 27 January 1983.

At the same time, the profession of banking supervision was on the rise and in many ways the BCBS looked like a body to reinforce it, in front of ongoing liberalization of the banking sector. As individuals, members of the BCBS were the elite of the banking supervisors. Its achievements were not just simple 'agreements' between them, but also collective constructions involving intellectual reflection and cultural representations of the market and of the supervisory role. Their influence culminated in the drawing of the first international standard in banking regulation, the capital adequacy agreement of 1988.

More generally, this chapter has shed light on the process by which banking supervision became international and gained importance within the broader field of regulation, thereby helping us to better understand some aspects of the origins of the recent global financial crisis. Banking supervision, which was supposed to control banks' daily activities, became an increasingly important part of the overall regulatory framework within which banks operated. Its internationalization and its increasing focus on capital adequacy issues transformed its role. However, as we have seen from the cases of offshore centres or other non-G10 countries, gaps in banking supervision could never be completely filled. Furthermore, regulatory power was not entirely in the hands of supervisors. Concerns about national competitiveness and financial liberalization, which are beyond the scope of this study, played an important role, and involved many other actors than just supervisors. Nonetheless, the roots of the global financial crisis are best understood by considering the new regulatory framework established in the aftermath of the collapse of the Bretton Woods system, a change epitomized by the story of the Basel Committee.

Appendix: Name and Background of BCBS Members Mentioned in Text

	Name	Country	Background	Attendance at Basel Committee meetings
1	Pierre André	Belgium	National Bank of Belgium, 1945–1981. 1968: Chief of Foreign Department. Education: sales engineering.	1975–1977
2	Willy Vanleeuw	Belgium	National Bank of Belgium, 1941–1984. 1974: Inspector General.	1978–1984
3	François Heyvaert	Belgium	National Bank of Belgium, 1941–1982. 1979–80: Head of Foreign Department. 1980: Deputy Director. Education: Business.	1982–1982
4	Françoise Massai née Lepoivre	Belgium	National Bank of Belgium, 1971–2014. 1973: International Agreements Department. 1988: Inspector General. Member of several international committees. Education: philosophy, law, economics.	1984–1995
5	Pierre Fanet	France	Banque de France from 1950 to retirement in 1985. General Inspector from 1976 on. Education: Law.	1975–1976
6	Gérard Aubanel	France	Banque de France from 1945 to retirement in 1983. Seconded to the IMF from 1955 to 1958, and to the Statistical Office of the European Communities from 1962 to 1963. Director of foreign services. Education: Law.	1975–1982
7	Jean Bonnardin	France	Banque de France and French Banking Commission, seconded to the Federal Reserve Bank of New York in 1974–1975. Education: law, economics.	1976–87
8	Jean Pierre Fevre	France	Banque de France from 1964 to retirement in 2001 (inspection). Seconded to the European Commission from 1989 to 1997. Education: HEC, Institut d'Etude Politique de Paris.	1978–86
9	André Icard	France	Banque de France and French Banking Commission, seconded to the Federal Reserve Bank of New York. Banque Française du Commerce extérieur. Deputy Director of the Bank for International Settlements (1996–2000).	1982–84

10	Alain Vienney	France	Banque de France, inspection (1968–1976), foreign services (1976–1985), seconded to New York in 1978–1979. Executive Director of various services at the Banque de France. Executive Director of various French overseas departments and institutions. Education: Institut d'Etude Politique de Paris, law.	1985–1989
11	Michel Lieuze	France	Banque de France and French banking commission 1951–1990, economic studies, and deputy secretary general of the French Banking Commisssion (1987–1990). Education: law, English, international economics.	1987–1990
12	Manfred Schneider	Germany	German Federal Banking Supervision Office. Education: Law, economics, history.	1975–1990
13	Carlo Santini	Italy	Banca d'Italia, 1961–2000. Economic Studies Department. Private career from 2000 on. Education: law.	1982–1984
14	Francesco Carbonnetti	Italy	Banca d'Italia, 1967–1986. Legal advice. Private career from 1989 on. Education: law.	1982
15	Fabrizio Saccomani	Italy	Banca d'Italia. Head of International research. Five years secondment to the IMF. Member of several European committees. Education: economics and business administration, Bocconi and Princeton.	1985–1987
16	Giovanni Carosio	Italy	Banca d'Italia, 1970. Research Department. 1985: Regulations and Supervision Department. 1993: Head of Banking Supervision Department. Member of several European and international committees. Education: economics, La Sapienza (Rome), Cambridge.	1987–1997
17	Akira Nagashima	Japan	Bank of Japan, 1962. 1972–1975: Representative in the Americas. 1975: Alternative Executive Director for Japan, IMF. 1976: seconded to the Banking Bureau, Ministry of Finance. 1978: Manager, International Department. Education: law, economics (Wharton School of Finance and Commerce).	1975–1975

(continued)

	Name	Country	Background	Attendance at Basel Committee meetings
18	Motomichi Ikawa	Japan	1976–1979: economist at the OECD. 1979–1985: various positions at the Ministry of Finance. Education: PhD in economics, Tokyo, Berkeley.	1982–1984
19	Albert Dondelinger	Luxembourg	Commissariat au contrôle des banques, 1959–1977. 1968–1976: commissioner. 1977: private career at the Banque Internationale du Luxembourg. Member of many EEC and international groupings. Education: law.	1975–1975
20	Pierre Jaans	Luxembourg	Deutsche Bundesbank, 1962–1972. Secretariat of the OECD, 1972–1974. Commissariat au contrôle des banques, from 1975 on. Member of several EEC groupings. Education: economics.	1975
21	Jean Nicolas Schaus	Luxembourg	1966–1969: lawyer. Commissariat au contrôle des banques, 1969–1983. Manager of the Institut Monétaire Luxembourgeois, 1983–1995. Member of the EEC Banking Advisory Committee. Education: law.	1978–1989
22	Huib Muller	Netherlands	Nederlandsche Bank, 1964–1991. Supervisory Department, 1968. Alternative Deputy Director, 1973–1976. Then member of the Bank's governing board, with a special brief for prudential supervision. 1977–1985: member, then chairman, of the EEC Banking Advisory Committee. Education: law, economics.	1975–1976 (as member), 1988–1991 (as chairman)
23	Frederick Musch	Netherlands	Private career at Pierson, Heldring & Pierson, 1970–1977. Nederlandsche Bank. Deputy Executive Director in charge of banking supervision, 1986–1992. After 2001: private career at PricewaterhouseCoopers. Member of EEC Banking Advisory Committee and OECD Financial Services Committee.	1982–1992

24	Ake Tornqvist	Sweden	Riksbank, 1976–1997 (then Ministry of Finance). Economist, department manager at the international department, monetary and exchange policy department. Education: business administration, economics.	1985–1990
25	Daniel Bodmer	Switzerland	1957–1980: Federal Department of Finance. 1980: Swiss Federal Banking Commission. Education: economics.	1975
26	Bernhard Müller	Switzerland	Swiss Federal Banking Commission, secretary, 1976–1986. 1990–1993: Banca del Gottardo. Education: law.	1976–1986
27	Paul Ehrsam	Switzerland	Federal Department of Finance, before 1967. Swiss National Bank, 1967–1970. Swiss Federal Banking Commission, from 1976 on. Education: law.	1980–1982
28	Daniel Zuberbühler	Switzerland	Swiss Federal Banking Commission. Head of legal service (1981–1985), Vice Director (1986–1987), Deputy Director (1988–1995), Director (1996–2008). Member of Working Party 3, IOSCO. Education: law, economics.	1986–1995
29	Peter Klauser	Switzerland	Lawyer. Swiss National Bank from 1974 on. Legal Service Department, study period at the Federal Reserve Bank of New York (1981), Deputy Head of Department I, in charge of the Legal and Administrative Division (1982). After 1997: private career at Orell Fussli Holding. Education: law.	1986–1995
30	Kurt Hauri	Switzerland	Swiss Federal Banking Commission. President, 1996–2000. Education: law	1986–1997
31	George Blunden (chairman)	United Kingdom	Bank of England, 1947–1990. Seconded to the International Monetary Fund, 1955–1958. Head of Banking Supervision, 1974–1976. Executive Director, 1974–1984. Deputy governor, 1986–1990. Education: Public school, Oxford.	1975–1977

(continued)

	Name	Country	Background	Attendance at Basel Committee meetings
32	Galpin	United Kingdom	Bank of England, 1952–1988. Deputy Chief Cashier, Banking and Money Market Supervision, 1974–1978. After 1988: private career at Standard Chartered. Education: Haileybury and imperial college service.	1975–1977
33	Derrick Byatt	United Kingdom	Bank of England, 1949–1986. Seconded to the BIS, 1954–1955. Chief Cashier at the Bank of Zambia, 1964–1967. Various positions in Foreign Exchange Division. Education: Whitgift school.	1975–1984
34	Anthony Laurie Coleby	United Kingdom	Bank of England, 1961–1994. Secondment to the IMF, 1964. Deputy Chief Cashier, 1973–1980. Education: Cambridge.	1977–1980
35	William Peter Cooke (member, chairman)	United Kingdom	Bank of England, 1955–1988. Seconded to the Bank for International Settlements, 1961–1965. Head of Banking Supervision, 1976. Associate Director, 1982–1988. Education: Oxford.	1977–1988
36	Roger Barnes	United Kingdom	Bank of England, 1961–1993. Head of Banking Supervision, 1988–1993. After 1993: private career at Hambros Bank Ltd. Education: Oxford.	1980–1993
37	David Allan Challoner Nendick	United Kingdom	Bank of England, 1953–1989. Seconded to the Bank of Mauritius, 1970–1972. Seconded to Hong Kong Government, 1985–1989. Secretary for Monetary Affairs, Hong Kong Government, 1989–1993. Education: Haileybury College.	1981–1993
38	Brian Quinn	United Kingdom	Economist at the IMF, 1964–1970. Bank of England, 1970–1996. Assistant Director, Banking Supervision (1982–1986), Head of Banking Supervision (1986–1988). Education: economics.	1983–1995

39	Richard Farrant	United Kingdom	Bank of England, joined in 1967. Period as Economist in the Central Banking Service, IMF. Seconded to the Isle of Man Government, 1982. Seconded to the Hong Kong Government as Advisor to the Hong Kong Banking Commissioner, 1984–1986. Deputy Head of Banking Supervision, 1990–1993. Several international committees. Education: economics.	1987–1993
40	Robert F. Gemmill	USA	Board of Governors the Federal Reserve. Adviser in the Division of International Finance. Education: PhD, Harvard University.	1975–1978
41	David Willey	USA	Federal Reserve Bank of New York, from 1964 on. 1972: Vice president, assigned to the loans and credits function. Has worked at Morgan Stanley. Education: law, PhD in economics, Columbia University.	1975–1982
42	John Heimann	USA	Career in private sector (Smith Barney & Co., E. M. Warburg Pincus & Co) from 1956 to 1975. Comptroller of the Currency from 1977 to 1981. Then came back to private sector: Warburg, Paribas Becker, Becker Paribas Incorporated, and Merrill Lynch. Education: economics, law.	1978–1980
43	Robert Bench	USA	Office of the Comptroller of the Currency. Assistant chief national bank examiner, then Deputy Comptroller of the Currency. Joined Price Waterhouse's Financial Services Practice after twenty-two years at the OCC. Education: Boston and Harvard Universities.	1978–1984
44	Sam Cross	USA	Prior to 1974: deputy assistant treasury secretary for International Monetary and Investment Affairs. 1974–1981: executive director at the IMF. 1975–1980: special assistant to the secretary of the Treasury. 1981: Federal Reserve Bank of New York, Head of Foreign Exchanges and Foreign Relations, then Vice President. Education: BS and MS, University of Tennessee.	1979–1982
45	Robert Clarke	USA	Joined the Office of the Comptroller of the Currency after a career in a law firm's banking section. 1985: Comptroller of the Currency. Education: law, Harvard Law School.	1983

(continued)

	Name	Country	Background	Attendance at Basel Committee meetings
46	Todd Conover	USA	Various positions in the private sector before joining the Office of the Comptroller of the Currency. 1981: Comptroller of the Currency. Education: MBA, Berkeley University.	1983
47	Michael Patriarca	USA	Office of the Comptroller of the Currency, then career in the private sector. Education: history, law.	1983–1985
48	Michael Dealtry (secretary of the BCBS)	United Kingdom	Bank of England, joined in 1951. 1954 to 1990: seconded to the BIS. Secretariat of the Group of Ten. Head of BIS' economic and monetary department. Education: Eton, Oxford (philosophy, economics, politics).	1975–1984
49	Helmut Mayer (secretary of the BCBS)	Austria	BIS, joined in 1963. Education: PhD in economics, Stanford University.	1975–1984
50	Charles Freeland (secretary of the BCBS)	United Kingdom	Bank of England, joined in 1964. BIS, 1975–2007. Seconded in 1975 at the BIS. Education: Eton, MA in economics, Saint Andrews University.	1978–1997

Index

69 Old Broad Street group 141

Abrahamson, M. 148n.53
Abruzzo 107, 114–15
academics 15, 159, 180, 183, 189, 195, 198, 200
accountability 15–16, 159–60, 165, 168, 177, 207
Acemoglu, D. 61n.2
Acharya, V. V. 19n.10
Acheson, G. J. 150n.59
acquisitions 27, 37, 48, 144
Adams, J. Q. 55
Addis, C. 71n.31
administrators 49, 124, 216
Africa 33n.64, 151
Aganin, A. 94
agencies 62–3, 84, 196
agency 49, 97
  model 136
  problems 135, 137–9
agents 6, 10n.28, 13, 30, 40, 44, 49–50, 53, 57, 135, 137, 145, 183, 196
agent theorists 10n.28, 14
Agnelli, G. 114–15
agriculture 5, 57, 108, 113
Alabama, New Orleans, Texas and Pacific Junction Railway 154
Alberti, M. 77, 79, 81
Alderson, Baron 173n.62
Algan, Y. 139n.22
Alien Sedition Act 55
Allen & Overy 172
Allsopps 141
Altamura, E. 122
Alternative Investment Market 151, 155n.77
America 24, 28, 40, 50, 140, 151, *see also* United States
American
  bankers 2, 18, 23, 33n.67, 34
  banks 121
  bonds 57
  clients 54–6, 59
  company charters 154
  conference delegates 213
  counterparts 25, 32n.60
  economy 29n.45, 34
  financial deregulation 131n.19
  financial regulations 19n.11
  legislation 19n.10
  merchants 51, 54–6
  monetary policy 128
  ports 53
  shipowner 53
  society 34
  trade 55
American–Italian negotiations 77
American-style public companies 94
American War of Independence 42, 55
Amsterdam 41, 49, 54, 56, 57n.38, 59, 71n.31, 134, 221
anarchism 17, 36
André, P. 219, 230
Angelides, P. 39
Angell, N. 30
Anglo-American
  model 133
  relationship 81
Anglo-Dutch War 43
Anglo-French
  bankers 47
  merchants 52
Anglo-Saxon
  bankers 2
  multi-millionaires 142
Angola Metropole Bank 36n.77
annuities 41–4, 57n.39, 59, 143
Ansiaux, H. 184, 187
anti-banker rhetoric 36
anti-finance tirades 18
anti-Semitic motives 30n.50
Anzilotti, E. 86
Apulia 107, 115
Arab Spring 33n.64
arbitration/arbitrators 15, 149n.57, 159, 177
Arcaini, G. 114–15
Argentina 143

Index

Argentine
 banks 154
 enterprises 142
 railways 135, 154
aristocracy 4–5, 10
Arnold, M. 39n.89
Arnold, P. 3
Arrighi, G. 31n.54
Arvind, T. T. 14
Ashenking, A. 36
Ashurst, Morris, Crisp 142
Asia 151, 222
Asinari, D. 114
Asquini, A. 86
assets 11, 13, 32n.58, 52, 60, 65, 72, 79, 82–3, 97–8, 111, 128, 145, *see also* total assets
Assicurazioni Generali 103
Associazione fra le Società Italiane per Azioni 68, 97
Atkinson, A. B. 1n.2
Atlantic Ocean 2, 31, 55, 133
Atlantic/transatlantic commerce/trade 53, 56, 142
attorneys/lawyers/solicitors 2, 15, 54, 56, 85, 87, 141–2, 145–6, 157, 159, 161, 162n.7, 174, 180, 213, 232–3, *see also* legal
Aubanel, G. 215, 219, 230
auditors 98n.29, 145, 152n.66
Australasia 151, 154
Australia 138, 222
Australian financial institutions 32n.60
Austria 43, 236
Austrian Credit-Anstalt 35
Austrian Empire 40
autonomy 5, 15–16, 79, 163–4, 174, 181, 184
Azzolini, V. 77, 88n.89

Baccini, A. 95
Badile, D. 115
Baffi, P. 82n.75, 195, 213
balance sheets 90, 92n.1, 97, 149, 224–6
Baldini, R. 115
Balladur, E. 131–2
Balls, E. 32n.62
Baltimore 55
Balzarotti, F. E. 72, 76
Banca Bergamasca di Depositi e Conti Correnti 110
Banca Cattolica del Veneto 111
Banca Commerciale Italiana 30, 67n.22, 71n.31, 72n.38, 79, 85, 87, 102–3, 109–11
Banca d'Italia, *see* Bank of Italy
Banca Feltrinelli & Co 77
Banca Intesa 111
Banca Italiana di Sconto 67n.22
Banca Nazionale del Lavoro 67n.22
Banca Nazionale di Credito 67n.22
Banca San Paolo 111
Banco Ambrosiano Veneto 111
Banco di Napoli, *see* Bank of Naples
Banco di Roma 67n.22, 85, 87, 103
Banco di Sicilia, *see* Bank of Sicily
Bank Deutscher Länder 204
Bankers' ramp 18, 35
Bankers Magazine 152, 156n.83
Bank for International Settlements (BIS) 62n.7, 63–5, 78, 211–12, 215–19, 230, 234, 236
Banking Act 129
Banking Advisory Committee 218, 228, 232
banking laws 80, 83, 89, 96, 103, 108, 220
Banking Reform Law 95, 112
banknotes 36n.77
Bank of America 38
Bank of England 3, 34–5, 75–6, 81, 88, 161, 166–9, 172, 174, 188, 192–4, 196, 204, 207, 213, 215, 217, 223, 233–6
Bank of Finland 186–7
Bank of France, *see* Banque de France
Bank of Italy (Banca d'Italia) 64, 65n.13, 67, 71–2, 76–81, 84–8, 90, 102, 187n.13, 192, 195, 204, 222n.45, 231
Bank of Japan 184, 187, 199, 203, 205, 207, 214, 231
Bank of Naples (Banco di Napoli) 67, 80
Bank of Sicily (Banco di Sicilia) 67, 80
Bank Recovery and Resolution Directive 19n.9
bankruptcy 18, 34, 39, 53, 57, 111, 149
banksters 33
Banque de France (Bank of France) 5n.16, 41, 53, 57n.38, 122–3, 130, 188, 192, 205, 215–16, 230–1
Banque de Paris et des Pays-Bas 25, 30
Banque de Suez 120
Banque Française du Commerce Extérieur 216, 230
Banque nationale de Paris (BNP) 120n.3, 121
Banque Oustric 29
Banque particulière dans les Pays Bas autrichiens (Private Bank in the Austrian Low Countries) 43
Baragiola, P. 113, 115
Barberis, G. 113
bargaining abilities 64, 84
Baring, G. R. S. 192, 196
Barings 25, 135, 141–2, 146, 148
Barnes, R. 219, 234
Barozzi, M. 116
Basel Committee on Banking Supervision (BCBS) 16, 158, 200, 209–16, 218–30, 232, 234, 236
Basola, E. 114
Bass 141
Batavian Republic (Kingdom of Holland) 56
Bazan, C. 114
Bazoli, G. 111, 116

Index

Bebchuk, L. 10n.28
Becker Paribas Incorporated 217, 235
Beit, W. 147–8, 149n.55
Belgian
  banks 183, 223
  governors 187
  state 188
Belgium 182n.2, 186, 188–9, 192, 194, 198, 204, 214, 218–19, 230
Belloni, G. 113
benchmark years 1, 13, 97–9, 104–8, 111–12
Bench, R. 213, 216, 235
Benedetti, E. de 85
Beneduce, A. 64, 71–8, 80–1, 83–8, 90, 113–14
Benetton, G. 116
Benni, A. 113
Bérard, T. S. 49–50
Bérégovoy, P. 129–30
Berenbrock, R. 57n.40
Berghoff, H. 200
Berlin 26, 134–5, 145, 151, 155n.77
Berlusconi, P. 116
Bernanke, B. 21n.16, 194, 202
Bernard, K. 204
Bertarelli, T. 113
Besozzi, G. 113
Besso, M. 113
Bianchi, B. 114
Bianchini, G. 76n.57, 77
Biancinelli, L. M. 110, 113
Big Bang 6, 125, 127
Big Five 3
big linkers (BLs) 13, 88n.90, 97, 104–10, 112–13
bills of exchange 55–6
Binham, C. 39n.89
Blankfein, L. 38–9
Bloch-Lainé, F. 125
Blunden, G. 213, 220, 222–3, 233
BNCI 120
Board of Trade 152–3, 156n.82
Bobbio, C. 114
Bocciardo, A. 113
Bodmer, D. 219, 233
Bonaparte, Louis 58
Bonaparte, Napoleon 41
Bondi, E. 116
bond market 31, 73, 83, 121, 130, 141
bonds 57–8, 72, 73n.39, 83, 120, 130, 134–5, 137, 141, 152
Bonnardin, J. 214, 218, 220, 230
bonuses 26–7, 136–7
Böök, K. 205
Boots 144
Borletti, S. 113, 115

Borri, S. 115
Borski, W. 57
Boston 55, 235
  merchants 56nn.35–6
Bottomley, H. 149
Bouchary, J. 42n.7, 43n.8
Bourbon monarchy 47
Bourdieu, J. 11–12, 47–52, 58–60
Bourdieu, P. 10–11, 58–9, 211
bourgeoisie 3–4, 17, 140, 156
Bourguignon, F. 1n.2
Bovril 148
Boyd & Ker & Co 43
Boyd, W. 11, 42–7, 49, 58–9
Brand, R. H. 71n.31, 73n.43, 75
Brandeis, L. 3, 31
Brazil 28n.43, 154
Brescia 111
Bretton Woods 8, 16, 188, 192–4, 209–10, 212, 222, 228–9
Brewery & General Investment Trust 143
brewery IPOs 141
Brexit 207
bribery 187
Brienne, L. de 45
Briggs, Mr Justice 179
Britain 3–4, 14, 16, 18, 19n.10, 24–9, 32n.62, 34, 51, 77–9, 138, 140–3, 152–3, 165, 168–9
  Labour Party 35
  National coalition government 35
  House of Commons 47
  House of Lords 149n.55, 150n.59, 164
  Labour government 18
  see also England, Northern Ireland, Scotland, Wales, United Kingdom
British
  bankers 34–5
  banking 30, 34–5
  banks 3, 34–5, 43, 126
  Big Bang 127
  borders 5
  bourgeoisie 3n.7
  businesses 147
  capital markets 139
  capitalism 138
  cities 140
  companies 140, 151, 154
  conference delegates 213, 215
  corporate governance 153
  corporate laws 153–4
  corporations 148
  economic history 4–5
  economy 29n.45, 138
  estate 142
  finances 42n.6
  financial elite 4
  financial institutions 3, 6, 32n.60, 152

239

Index

British (*cont.*)
  financial regulation 35
  financial scene 88
  government 155
  imperialism 4
  industrial decline 4
  investors 51
  landholding aristocracy 5
  navy 55
  northern industrialists 4
  polity 160
  pound 65–6, 80
  public opinion 35
  royal finances 43
  securities 134
  shareholders 139
  sterling 82
  stock market 43
  vendors 145
British Bankers Association 32n.62, 168n.31, 168n.34
British Empire 215
Broglia, G. 114
brokerage/brokering 42, 126, 144
brokers 37, 51, 110, 120, 126–7, 130, 141, 144–6, 148, 151, 153, 157–8, *see also* stockbrokers
Bruno, L. 114
Brussels 43, 49, 88
  stock exchange 134
Brussels International Financial Conference 12, 63, 66nn.19–20, 70–8, 84–7, 89
builders 124
Buist, M. G. 44n.11
Bundesbank 184, 195, 197, 200, 223, 232
BUP 120
bureaucrats/bureaucracies 7, 12, 63, 155
Burhop, C. 151–2, 154n.74, 155n.77
Burke, P. 147n.51
Burk, K. 75n.52
Burma Ruby Mines 141
Burnham, J. 89n.92
Burns, A. 195
business 11, 26, 30, 32, 37, 43, 51, 56, 58, 75, 87, 89n.92, 103, 111, 119, 122, 124, 130, 132, 141, 143, 162, 164, 166, 170, 172, 177, 179–80, 225
  activities 41, 174, 176
  administration 107–8, 112, 201, 203, 231, 233
  affairs 172–3, 175
  ambitions 12
  capital 139
  careers 106
  community 13, 57n.38, 104
  control 127

correspondences 42
  cycle 193
  development 24
  elites 3, 5, 92, 183, 192
  entities 169
  groups 94
  historians 1–2, 92–3
  interests 55, 174
  leaders 24, 97, 136
  outcomes 157
  owners 144
  plutocracy 1
  proprietor 148
  records 142
  relationships 12
  sector 160
  services 146–7
  world 13, 104, 137
businesses 50, 54, 58–9, 147, 170
businessmen 57, 72, 122, 123n.11, 137, 148, 164, 170, 172, 174–5
Buyst, E. 183
Byatt, D. 215, 234

Cahuc, P. 139n.22
Cain, P. 4
Caisse de l'Extraordinaire 51
Caisse des dépôts et consignations 124
Caisse d'Escompte 49
Calabria 107, 116
Calabria, F. 115
Caledonian MacBrayne 142
Calonne, C.-A. de 45–7
Campania 107, 113–15
Campbell, G. 140, 150nn.58–9
Campbell, Lord 174n.66, 175, 176n.78
Canada 142–4, 154, 182n.2, 186, 204, 219, 227
Canada Mortgage 154
Canadian
  central bank 204
  conference delegates 212
  financial institutions 32n.60
  trading system 126
Cannatelli, P. 116
Capanna, A. 114–15
Capie, F. 193
capital 9, 11, 18, 25, 27, 29nn. 43, 45, 30, 37, 41–2, 44, 47, 49–50, 52, 54–6, 58–9, 66, 73n.39, 75–6, 95–8, 110, 120, 126, 127n.14, 131–2, 139, 141, 143–4, 146, 151–2, 156n.83, 161, 164, 191, 200–1, 203, 210–11, 214, 228
  adequacy 16, 66–8, 210, 220–2, 224, 229
  controls 65, 93
  convergence 214, 222
  flows 25, 63, 126
  framework 221

240

Index

markets 31n.54, 41n.2, 62, 82, 117, 121–2, 129–31, 134, 137, 139
  mobility/mobilization 8, 95
  movements 34n.70
  requirements 68, 80
  see also human capital, social capital
capitalism 4–6, 12, 20, 24, 31, 89, 93–4, 96, 104, 117, 132–4, 138, 143, 169, 173–4, 176–7
capitalist 17–18
  activities 173
  agriculture 5
  corporations 135
  countries 104
  economy 169
capitalists 5, 17–18, 29, 42, 134, 142
capitalization 39, 48, 66n.17, 68, 79, 119, 144, 155, 227
Caplain, M. 124
Carbonnetti, F. 231
Caribbean 55–6, 222
Cariplo 111
Carli, G. 192, 195
Carnegie, A. 26
Carosio, G. 231
Carosso, V. 28n.42
cartels 119–20
Carter, A. 43n.10
Cartesegna, F. 114
Caruso, S. 38n.86
Casardi, A. 86
Cassaro, R. 115
Cassel, G. 66n.20, 69n.26, 73n.41
Cassis, Y. 3n.6, 4, 9–10, 18n.8, 41n.3, 42n.4
Castelbolognesi, G. 72, 113
Catherine the Great 41
CCF 120
central bankers 12, 15, 20n.16, 62–4, 73–4, 81, 87n.87, 180, 182–4, 187–91, 193–4, 197–8, 200, 202, 206–7, 211, 217
central banking 65, 69–70, 76, 78, 80–2, 90–1, 177, 183, 191, 200, 203
Central Bank of Albania 77
central banks 15–16, 64, 69–70, 74, 76–82, 84–6, 130, 182–3, 185–92, 195–7, 199–202, 204–6, 210, 212–15, 218, 226
  elite 182–5, 187–9, 191–7, 199, 202–6, 207, 217, 220
  governors 16n.39, 182–3, 185–6, 190–1, 196, 198, 201, 203, 205, 208–10, 213–14, 219, 221
  leaders 184–5, 196, 203
Cenzato, G. 114
Cerchiai, F. 116
Ceriana, F. 113
certificates 28n.43, 129–30, 150
Cerutti, G. 86, 88

Cesaroni, A. 115
CGP 123n.11
Chambers, D. 147
Chance, C. 161n.6, 172
Chapman, S. D. 5n.15
charity 147, 149n.55
Charleston 55
charters 137, 152, 154
Chase National Bank 28n.42
Chase Securities Corporation 28n.42
Chatillon, D. 124
chemistry 108, 116
Cherest, A. 44n.13
Chiesi, A. M. 96
Chiomenti, P. 115
Church 47, 51
Churchill, W. 8
Ciancarelli, B. 86
Cicé, C. de 45
Cirla, G. 116
City bankers 3–4, 5n.15
City of London 3–4, 6, 26, 75, 141, 160, 165, 177, 180n.95, *see also* London
City of London Club 219
civil
  courts 15, 165, 177
  servants 12–13, 15, 61n.1, 63, 72, 74, 76–7, 84, 87–9, 91, 118–20, 122–4, 130, 131n.19, 132, 155, 187, 189–91, 195, 199, 204–6
  service 71, 124, 131
Claeys, T. 43n.8
Clappier, B. 205
Clarke, R. 235
Clarke, Sir K. 160
Clavarino, G. 115
Clavin, P. 74n.44
CNEP 120
Cobbold, C. 192, 204
Cochrane, S. 146n.48
Cockayne, Sir B. 76
Cofimer 128
Coleby, A. L. 234
Coljé, H. 218, 226
collective biographies 5–6, 15, 212, *see also* prosopographic
Collegi sindacali 98
Colombo, A. 116
colonial
  authorities 55–6
  goods 53
  government securities 134
  governments 135
  millionaires 148
  power 55
Coltorti, F. 92n.1
commercial
  activities 43

241

Index

commercial (*cont.*)
  banking 9, 13, 25, 32n.61, 72, 83
  banks 24, 119, 122, 124, 187, 216, 220
  bills 55
  cities 55
  classes 164
  company 49
  competences 119
  court 165, 177–80
  crisis 169
  decision-making 171
  disputes 180
  distress 168
  elites 173
  exchanges 55
  expertise 174
  interests 172, 175
  law 15, 160, 164, 166
  operations 49
  orders 51
  parties 164
  relationships 55
  sector 164
Commissariat au contrôle des banques 232
Commissariat général du Plan 122–3, 130
Commission de privatization 132
Commission on Currency and Exchange Rates 74, 76n.55
communications 29n.45, 102, 104, 134, 140
Compagnie bancaire 128
Compagnie d'assurance de la Flandre autrichienne (Assurance Company of the Austrian Flanders) 43
Compagnie La Hénin 124
Companies Acts 152n.66, 153, 154n.73
Companies Clauses Consolidation Act (CCCA) 152–3, 154n.74, 155
Comptroller of the Currency 213–17, 220, 235–6
Conciato, A. 115
Concordat 224–5
Conover, T. 236
Conseil économique et social 122, 125
conservatism 35, 75, 117, 123, 197, 222
consolidation 11, 226–7
consumer price index 156n.85
Conti, E. 113–14, 116
Cooke, P. 213, 218–23, 225n.58, 234
Cooley, T. 19n.10
cooperation 63–4, 69, 71, 74, 76, 78, 88–90, 106n.39, 200, 207, 211, 227, *see also* international cooperation, monetary cooperation
coordinated market economy 12, 94
Cope, S. R. 42n.7
Copenhagen 214

corporate
  bankruptcy 149
  boards 137, 192
  bonds 134
  capital 141
  charters 137, 152
  documentation 149
  economy 135
  elites 97, 104–6, 108–9, 111–12
  equity 141
  finance 148, 160n.5, 161n.6
  governance 14, 110, 132, 135, 138, 152–5
  groups 107
  identity 38
  incentive structures 147
  interlocks 96–7
  IPOs 141
  ladder 124
  laws 152–4, 160n.5, 161n.6
  lawyers 85, 87
  networks 13, 88n.90, 92, 95–7, 98n.29, 100, 102–5, 108, 111–12
  organizations 105
  ownership 30
  policies 141
  sector 8, 36, 142
  securities 134–5, 137–8, 152, 154n.74
  systems 13, 93, 96
Corporation of Foreign Bondholders 149n.57
Corporation of London 146n.48
corporations 89n.92, 93, 123, 135, 138, 148, 154, 156, 158, 169–70, 193
corruption 7, 148
Corsi, G. 115
Cortellazzo, G. C. di 86
Cortesi, G. 115
cosmopolitan
  bankers 54
  character 70
  financial elites 30n.50, 64
  financiers 90
  outlook 142
  private bankers 12
cosmopolitanism 62, 87
Costa, G. M. 115
Cottrell, P. I. 29n.45, 42n.4, 76n.55, 139n.20, 140n.29
courts 15, 44, 137, 139, 149n.55, 161–5, 173nn.56, 64, 175, 177–80
Covi, A. 113
Crediop (Consorzio di Credito per le Opere Pubbliche) 72, 83
credit 30, 34, 37, 39, 46, 49–50, 53–6, 57n.41, 66n.20, 80, 82, 95, 120–4, 128, 130, 139, 168, 188, 235
  banks 26
  creation 69

expansion 202
growth 193
institutions 65, 72, 73n.39, 83, 87, 103, 111
market 119
policy 126–7
ratings 152
risk 178n.88
squeeze 127
Crédit Agricole 123
Crédit du Nord 120
Credit industriel et commercial 124
Crédit Lyonnais 120–2, 125, 128, 152
Credito Italiano 67n.22, 68, 72, 76–7, 85, 87, 102–3, 110–11
creditors 46, 57
criminal
  courts 15, 177
  culpability 170
  law 152, 165–6
  liability 165, 170–2, 175–7
  offence 165
  proceedings 175
  prosecutions 147n.51, 149n.55, 170, 177
  sanctions 170
  trials 170, 172–5
criminalization 174–6
Cross, S. 235
Crouch, C. 20n.12
Cullen, Lord 76
cultural
  approach 15
  capital 11, 211
  context 2
  dimension 22, 32
  direction 20
  frameworks 169
  history 6
  representations 224, 229
  ties 161
  values 2
cumulation ratio 99
Cunard 141
Cunliffe Committee Report 73
currency 34n.70, 75, 79, 129
  crisis 79, 83
  inconvertibility 69, 90
  instability 83
  markets 62, 82
  policy 79
  rehabilitation 79

D'Agostino, A. 85
Dalgety & Co 154
Dall'Oglio, G. 86
Dangerfield, G. 20n.12
Daunton, M. J. 4n.13, 5n.15, 35

David, T.
  The Power of Corporate Networks 98, 101, 104n.34
Dawes Plan 79
Da Zara, G. 113
Dealtry, M. 219, 236
Debenture Corporation 145
debentures 145, 151
De Biasi, V. 114
De Bonis, R. 68n.24
debts 40, 42, 44–7, 50, 54, 57, 63, 65, 69–70, 82, 90, 123, 126, 141, 148n.52, 191, 194, 222, *see also* inter-allied debts
De Castro, O. 113
Declaration of the Occupation of New York City 33n.64
defaulters 57, 146n.46, 149n.57, 153
deficits 73–4, 128
deficit spending 123, 127, 129
Deflassieux, J. 127–8
deflation 65, 75, 78, 82
deflationary
  cooperation 77
  effects 79, 82
  measures 69
  options 78
  phenomena 66
  policies 34, 66, 82
  programmes 76
  strategy 63, 76
deindustrialization 3
De Kock, M. H. 62n.7
de La Genière, R. 205
Delaware 153
Delfino, A. 116
Della Porta, D. 33n.64
Della Torre, L. 72, 76–7, 113
della Vida, E. L. 72n.38
Del Vecchio, G. 86
democratization 28, 32n.62
Denmark 182n.2, 225
density index 100, 102
dependent variables 6, 13
depoliticization 15, 204
depredations 14, 137, 148–9
deregulation 7, 36, 125, 131–2, 196–7, 201
De Stefani, A. 79, 81
Destefanis, G. P. 115
de Strycker, C. 187, 194
Deutsche Bank 122
devaluations 186, 193–4
Deventer 57
Dictionnaire historique des inspecteurs des finances 122
Dillon, C. 28n.42
Dillon Read & Co 25, 28n.42
diplomacy 71, 74, 83

243

Index

diplomatic
  relations 55
  service 84–6
Ditchley Foundation 215, 219
Dodd–Frank Wall Street Reform and Consumer
    Protection Act 19
Doidge, C. 155n.78
domestic
  capitalization 155
  centres/markets 121–2, 180
  cooperation 70
  credit 69, 122
  crises 64, 199
  economies 71, 189
  financial system 90
  financing 127, 148
  instability 63–4, 70, 90
  investment 129
  issues 145
  manufacturing 140
  political climate 207
  regulation 61
  rules 14, 118
  scene 62n.8
  securities 134n.2
  share issues 144
  trust 135
Dondelinger, A. 215–16, 218–19, 232
Donegani, G. 114
Dosi, M. 115
dos Reis, A. A. 36n.77
Dow, C. 152n.67
Dow, S. 207n.64
Drach, A. 158
Dublin 145n.45
Duke of Westminster 142n.33
Dunlap, A. 136
Dunlop 148
Dutch
  bankers 41, 43, 56–7
  banks 12, 43–4
  capital 54
  central bank 189, 191, 226
  clients 54, 57
  companies/firms 54, 142
  conference delegates 216, 219
  governors 205
  interests 59
  investors 43
  markets 41, 58
  merchants 54, 56
  see also Netherlands

Eastman, G. 148
Ecole des Hautes Etudes Commerciales de Paris
    (HEC) 119
Ecole Polytechnique 119

economic
  actor 36
  affairs 48
  capital 11, 211
  change 118
  collapse 11
  conditions 15, 78, 203, 205
  conferences 63, 70, 84, 86–7
  consequences 20, 22
  context 29, 183
  crises 3, 20, 27, 33n.63, 187, 199
  cycles 31, 158, 193, 195
  debate 47
  decisions 52
  decline 193
  democracy 131
  depression 27
  development 193, 199, 202, 206
  differences 222
  disasters 155
  disequilibria 75
  distress 34, 207
  effects 199
  elites 11n.31, 13, 122
  environment 183–4, 188, 197, 206
  growth 8, 70, 95, 189, 194, 199, 205
  historians 31, 92–3, 138
  history 3–5, 40n.1
  incentives 153
  institution 47
  interdependence 30
  interests 44, 52
  life 8, 22
  performance 192, 206
  policies 62, 70, 78, 83, 127, 129, 133, 188,
      190, 192–3, 205, 207
  power 4, 18
  project 16
  prosperity 176
  rationale 10n.28
  reality 9, 23n.26, 35
  recessions 183, 202
  reconstruction 120
  recovery 123n.11, 189
  reforms 207
  relations 70–1
  research 202
  sphere 8
  studies 123, 231
  system 13, 20, 69, 104, 188
  theology 38n.86
  theories 37, 131, 193–4, 202
  transformations 10
  uncertainty 168
  world 59
Economic and Financial Organization 70
Economic Mission in England 85

244

Index

economics 23n.26, 31–2, 38, 107–8, 112–16, 192–6, 198–204, 217, 230–6
economists 2, 18, 30–1, 37–8, 93, 122, 130, 135, 139, 189, 193, 195, 197–8, 202–3, 215, 217, 232–5
Edict of Nantes 48
Edinburgh 142–3, 145n.45
Edison 109
education 2, 11, 16, 88, 106, 108, 112–16, 133, 136n.8, 142, 183, 185, 188, 192, 200–1, 203–4, 213, 217–18, 220, 230–6
EEC 126, 129, 215, 218, 222, 225–6, 228, 232
Efficient Market Hypothesis 38n.86
Ehrsam, P. 233
Eichengreen, B. 69n.29
Einzig, P. 34n.70
electrical/electricity
  companies/firms 96, 102–4, 109, 141, 144
  industry 96, 100, 103, 105, 111–12
  sector 102
Ellerman, J. 141, 143
Ellerman Lines 143
Elysée Palace Hotel 144
Emilia-Romagna 107, 113–16
E. M. Warburg Pincus & Co 217, 235
engineering/engineers 31, 87, 107–8, 112–16, 119, 141, 145, 230
England 15, 24, 43, 45, 48, 54, 137, 154n.74, 162, 180
English
  bankers 4, 48
  law/legal system 162, 179
  market 51
  merchant banking 4
  merchants 48, 50–2
  principle of sovereign rule 47
  stock market 52
  system 47
Enron 136
entrepreneurial
  capitalism 143
  class 105
  groups 110
  investments 142
entrepreneurs 3, 33, 35, 39, 77, 87, 88, 123–4, 143, 146n.46
Epargne mobilière 121
Epargne-Valeur 121
equity 27, 29, 134, 156–7, 179
  capital 66, 68, 73n.39
  issues 141
  markets 154
  options 137
Ermotti, S. 39n.89
Escher, H. 53
Escher, J. 54
Espenlaub, S. 155n.77

Esterle, C. 109, 113
Eton 192, 213, 236
eurobond markets 31, 121
eurocredit market 121
Eurocurrency Standing Committee (ECSC) 218–19
eurodollar market 31, 196
Europartners Securities Corporation 122
European Central Bank 200
European Commission 212, 215–16, 230
European Monetary Union (EMU) 199–200
European Options Exchange 126
European Parliament 19
European Union (EU) 19, 129, 131, 199–200
European University Institute (EUI) 23n.25, 92n.1, 182n.1
Eurozone lenders 19
Evans, P. 163–4

Fabriz, P. L. 116
failures 23, 29, 53, 73, 75, 88, 110, 138, 165, 169n.38, 171nn.47–8, 174, 181, 194, 209, 222, 224
Faina, C. 110–11, 114
Falck, A. 116
Falck, B. 115
Falck, G. 114
Falco, G. 74n.45
Falcone, G. 113
Falco, R. 85
Fama, E. F. 10n.28
Fanet, P. 214, 220, 230
Farquhar, Lord 147n.51, 149
Farrant, R. 215, 217–18, 235
fascist
  government 79–80, 94
  hardliners 18
  regime 11, 87, 88
Favre, J. E. 30
Fazio, A. 187
Federal Bank Examination Council 220
Federal Banking Commission (Switzerland) 214, 233
Federal Deposit Insurance Corporation 19n.11, 214
Federal Office of Supervision (Germany) 214, 223
Federal Open Market Committee 207
Federal Reserve Act 205
Federal Reserve Bank 19n.11, 21n.16, 38, 82, 184, 189, 192, 195–7, 205, 220, 222, 230, 235
Federal Reserve Bank of New York 184, 213, 216–17, 233, 235
Federal Reserve System 204
Feldman, G. 32, 36, 38n.85, 61n.1
Feltrinelli, C. 77, 90, 113

245

Index

Ferme Générale 50–1
Ferraris, M. 85, 87
Ferrerio, P. 114
Ferri, G. 96, 108
Fevre, J. P. 216, 220, 230
Fiat 103, 110
Financial Crisis Inquiry Commission (FCIC) 33, 39
Financial Interrelation Ratio 29n.45
Financial Services (Banking Reform) Act 165, 171
financiers 4–5, 7, 9–10, 12, 21, 24, 28–32, 33n.64, 36, 38n.86, 39, 43, 53, 64, 70, 77, 88–90, 108n.43, 109–12, 124, 128, 142, 144, 146n.47, 147n.51, 149, 177
Fink, C. 74n.45
Finland 182n.2, 186–7, 198–9, 225
Fiss, P. C. 22n.22
Flandreau, M. 149n.57
Fore Street Warehouse 142
Foreman-Peck, J. 140nn. 25, 27, 150n.58, 156n.83
Formentini, P. 86
Fortunati, I. R. 85
Foster & Braithwaite 144
Fouchier, J. de 119, 124, 128
France 13, 18, 24, 26–9, 40–2, 44–56, 58–9, 74, 76, 94, 101, 117, 119, 121–4, 129–31, 133, 138, 140, 142, 144n.41, 149, 154n.74, 182n.2, 186, 189, 191–2, 196, 202, 205, 213–20, 222, 226–7, 230–1
  Assembly of Notables 41, 44, 47
  Consulate 53
  Directory 42, 52–3, 57
  Estates General 47
  Fifth Republic 124
  Gaullist party 131n.22
  inspecteurs des finances 13–14, 118–19, 122–3, 125, 127–8, 131n.19, 132
  Jacobin authorities 53
  Minister of Finance 12, 48, 119–21, 123–4, 125, 130, 131n.19, 132, 205
  National Assembly 41–2, 47–8, 50–1, 59–60
  Old Regime 41, 51, 58
  Second Empire 5n.16
  Terror 40, 42n.7, 52–3, 59
  Third Estate 47
Francese, M. 65n.13
Francès, J. 124
François-Poncet, M. 132n.23
Frankfurt 26
Franks, J. 139–40
fraud/fraudsters 14, 28, 36n.77, 136–7, 147, 149, 152, 156, 162, 172, 225
free
  capital mobility 8, 75
  company 81

market 8, 36, 134, 144
trade 8, 34n.70, 50n.29, 58, 75
Freeland, C. 236
Freeman, M. 140n.23
French
  annuities 43–4
  army 55
  authorities 55
  bankers 5, 14, 47, 57n.40, 117
  banks 14, 25, 122, 127
  bonds 57–8
  bourgeoisie 3n.7
  brokers 126–7, 130
  capital 41–2, 44, 47, 52
  capitalism 132, 133
  Caribbean 55
  conference delegates 212–13, 215–16
  credit 46
  Crown 42, 47
  currency 129
  debt 46, 54, 57
  difficulties 42n.5
  economy 40, 59, 123, 127–8, 131, 133
  elites 13–14, 117–18, 192
  Empire 41
  exports 216
  finances 40, 42n.6, 46
  firms 120, 126, 131–2, 154
  franc 79
  governors 192
  Haiti 56n.36
  Keynesian policy 129
  légende noire 18
  market 41, 43, 50–1, 58–9
  merchants 52
  monarchy 40, 43
  people 48
  pirates 56n.36
  political course 52
  political scene 12
  privatization 131
  railways 135
  Republic 55
  republican authorities 56
  state 216
  stocks 44
  system 45, 47, 117, 122–3, 125
  wine 53
French–American trade 53n.32
French East India Company 47–51, 58
French Revolution 10–11, 40–1, 42n.5, 47, 58, 60
Frere, M. 183, 192
Freshfield Bruckhaus Deringer 172, 174
Freshfield, C. 174
Fried, J. 10n.28
Friedman, M. 20n.16, 184, 195–6

Index

Friedman, T. 32n.62
Friesland 57
Friuli-Venezia Giulia 107, 113–15
Furness 144
futures market 126–7, 130

G10 16n.39, 209–10, 214, 218, 222, 224, 227, 229
G20 8
Gaggia, A. 113–14
Galbraith, J. K. 28n.40
Garbagni, M. 113
Garrino, G. L. 115
Garuzzo, G. 115
Gates, B. 136
GDP 65, 66n.16, 138, 155, 160, 191, 194
Gemmill, R. F. 217, 220, 235
Genoa Conference 63, 70, 76–8, 80, 84–7, 89
Genton, J. L. A. 56n.37
Genton, S. V. 56n.37
George, E. 192, 204
Georges-Picot, J. 124
Gérard, M. 52n.31
German
  authorities 223, 227
  Bank Enquête 18
  bankers 5
  banks 26, 151, 184, 195, 197, 200
  bourgeoisie 3n.7
  business 26
  company charters 154
  conference delegates 223
  D-Banken 35
  foreign policy 29
  governors 204
  mixed banks 67, 72
  system 98n.29
  universal banks 25, 100, 105, 112
Germany 16, 19n.10, 24, 26–7, 29, 35n.73, 61n.1, 79, 94, 101–2, 112–13, 129, 138, 140, 144n.41, 154, 182n.2, 186–8, 190–1, 198–9, 202, 209–10, 214, 218–19, 222, 227, 231
Gerschenkron, A. 95
Geyler and Jordan 57n.40
Giannini, F. 85
Giddens, A. 3n.6
Glass–Steagall Act 25
global
  advisory firms 160
  approach to stabilization 70
  crises 19, 24, 137, 166, 182, 202, 206–7, 229
  disasters 155
  economy 73, 179, 189
  elites 32, 165, 178, 180, 182
  indignation 33
  institutions 161

investors 152n.67
law firms 160n.5, 161n.6
manufacturers 144
markets 29, 151, 178
power 138
securities index 152
stock exchange 153
system 70, 178
trade association 178
Global Financial Institutions 217
globalization 9, 20, 26, 29–31, 34n.70, 36–7, 62, 121, 123, 131, 134, 199–200, 211
Glorious Revolution 4
Glyn, Mills & Co 3
Goff, Lord 164
Gold Standard 34, 62, 66, 69–70, 72–3, 75, 78–80, 82–3, 188
Gold-Diskonto Bank 79
golden age 100, 187, 189, 191, 193, 206
Goldman Sachs 38
Goldschmied, L. 85
Goodhart, C. A. E. 69n.25, 211–12, 214, 216–18
Goodwin, A. 44n.13
Goodwin, F. 136
governors 5n.16, 15, 16n.39, 62n.7, 76–7, 80, 90, 167–8, 182–7, 190–2, 194–201, 203–5, 208–10, 213–14, 219, 221, 224–8, 233, 235
Gramsci, A. 9n.27
Grandi, A. 115
Grand Livre de la dette publique 57
Grassi, P. 114
Grazzi, U. 86
Great Depression 9–10, 17–23, 25, 27–9, 36, 94, 96, 102, 188, 202
Great Illusion 30
Great Inflation 194
Great Moderation 202
Great Recession 1–2, 9, 17, 19–23, 27, 29, 34, *see also* recessions
Greek refugees loan 79
Greider, W. 31n.54
Grièges, D. de 124
Grossman, R. 150n.63, 156n.83
Groupe de Contact 214–15, 218, 222, 226, 228
Group of Thirty 215, 219
Guarneri, F. 86, 88
Guinness 141, 148
Gulf countries 222

Haberer, J.-Y. 125, 128
Hague Conference 77, *see also* The Hague
Haiti 55–6
Haldane, A. 166–8
Hall, P. 12
Halmael, A. van 57
Hämäläinen, S. 187

247

Index

Hambros Bank 25, 74n.45, 141, 234
Hammer, J. P. 36n.78
Hancock, Rt. Hon. M. 171n.47
Hannah, L. 140nn. 25, 27, 147n.50, 150n.58, 151n.65, 152n.66, 156n.83
Hardman, J. 44n.13
Harris, J. 4
Harrison, G. 81
Harvard 132n.23, 213, 217, 235
Hauri, K. 219, 233
Hautcoeur, P.-C. 154n.73
HBOS 32n.60
hedge funds 27, 64n.10
hegemony 78, 93
Heimann, J. 213, 215–17, 219–20, 235
Herries & Co 43, 50
Herries, C. 49–50
Herries, W. 43
Heyvaert, F. 230
Higgins, A. 56n.35
Hilferding, R. 3, 30–1, 93
Hirsh, P. M. 22n.22
Hobson, J. A. 3, 30
Hockema, P. 57n.38
Hokkaido Tanko Kisen 153
Holtrop, M. 191–2, 195, 200
Homo Economicus 38n.86
Hong Kong 215, 234–5
Hooley, Sir E. 147n.51, 148–9
Hope & Co 12, 43–4, 49
Hopkins, A. 4
Hottinguer, J.-C. 11–12, 52–4, 56–60
Hounslow & Metropolitan Railway 142
HSBC 32n.60, 135
Huber, B. 47, 48n.21, 50
Hudson's Bay 154
Huertas, T. F. 34n.67
human
  capital 11, 191, 200–1, 203–4, 208
  motivation 14, 137
humanism 6n.20

Icard, A. 216, 230
Iceland 225
ideology 20, 31n.54, 33, 93, 123
Ifo Institute for Economic Research 195
Ikawa, M. 215, 217, 232
immigrants 139n.22, 140, 143
Imperial Court of Vienna 43
Imperial Paper (Canada) 144
incentives 10, 25, 27, 135, 137, 153
income 1–2, 9, 24, 26, 38, 89, 120, 146, 156
incompetence 148, 156–7, 184
Indian
  banks 154
  railways 135, 154
  trade 49

industrial
  Britain 34
  capital 30, 93
  capitalism 169, 173–4
  capitalists 5
  countries 30
  credit 96, 103
  decline 4
  depression 34
  districts 146
  firms 95–7, 108–10, 112, 127, 132
  interests 4
  investments 83, 95
  managers 122
  policy 34
  sector 3, 95, 123n.11, 132, 134
  securities 94, 103, 134
  triangle 106
industrialists 4, 109–12, 146, 148
industrialization 29, 95, 104–6, 138, 140
Industrial Revolution 95, 100, 104, 106–7, 110, 112
inflation 40, 65–6, 69, 73–5, 90, 123, 129, 183–4, 188, 193–5, 197, 202
inflationary
  effects 81
  forces 194
  outcomes 66
  period 123
  phenomena 66
  pressures 68
infrastructural
  investments 83, 142
  networks 72
infrastructure 178n.88
innovations 7, 11, 14, 29n.45, 31, 32nn. 60, 62, 45, 63, 65, 90–1, 118, 120–7, 132–3, 136n.8, 152, 159, 170, 176
Institut d'etudes politiques de Paris 217, 230–1
institutional
  alignment 190
  architecture 88
  arrangements 70
  autonomy 184
  breakups 94–5, 100, 103
  change 2, 6, 13
  choices 79
  constraints 163
  design 7, 19
  devices 78
  embeddedness 20
  entrenchment 165
  evolution 210
  factors 93
  failure 171n.48
  framework 89, 190
  innovation 63

248

Index

investors 32n.58
links 191
patterns 89
reforms 188, 190, 197, 205–6
response 64, 69, 83, 90–1
settings 61n.1, 200
set-ups 92, 207
structure 78
transformations 10, 13
Institut Monétaire Luxembourgeois 232
instrumentalism 6n.20
insurance 39, 72, 87, 95–6, 102–3, 131–2, 142–4, 146, 214
inter-allied debts 12, 63–5, 69–70, 73, 76–7, 80, *see also* debts
intergenerational
  adjustment 62n.8
  transmission 11
intergovernmental organizations 63, 71
interlocking
  directorates (IDs) 13, 30, 88n.90, 95, 105, 108–10, 112
  directorships 132
  partnerships 147
interlocks 95n.18, 96–8, 100n.33, 102–3, 108–9, 111
intermediaries 14, 51, 63, 65, 72, 81, 90, 96, 104, 118, 126, 130, 135, 137, 141–2, 144–5, 147–8, 156
international
  bankers 125
  banking 209–10, 219, 221–2, 224–6
  banks 222, 225, 227
  community 69, 74
  conferences 12, 64, 65, 71n.31, 78, 83, 89, 214, 221, 223, 227
  cooperation 12, 61, 69–71, 73–6, 78, 81, 196, 200, 225
  environment 63–4, 79, 82, 123
  experts 8, 221
  financial system 16, 209, 212, 220–1, 223–4
  monetary system 8, 78
  standard-setter institution 209
International Bankers Association 216
International Banking Regulation 220
International Chamber of Commerce 219
International Financial Conference, *see* Brussels International Financial Conference
internationalism 74n.44
internationalization 62n.8, 121, 125, 127, 209–11, 223, 225, 229
International Mercantile Marine (IMM) 146n.46, 148
International Monetary and Investment Affairs 235
International Monetary Fund (IMF) 161n.6, 202, 215, 217, 230–1, 233–5

International Swaps and Derivatives Association 178
investment
  analysts 152, 158
  bankers 38n.84, 123, 147–8, 155n.77
  banking 6, 9, 13, 25, 32, 72, 83, 144
  banks 25–6, 28n.42, 35, 37–8, 119, 121–2, 130, 216
  certificates 129
  house 32n.58
  interests 145n.45
  projects 110
  prospects 169
  quality 149
  research 152
  strategy 143
  trusts 28n.40, 29n.43, 32n.58, 137, 141, 146
Investment Commission 125
investments 30, 42–3, 52–4, 59–60, 72, 83, 95, 110, 121, 127, 129, 141–3, 151, 157, 194
investors 14, 28, 32n.58, 41–3, 47, 51, 64n.10, 93–4, 121, 130, 132, 135–40, 143–5, 147–8, 150–2, 154–6, 169, 179n.89
IPOs 137n.11, 141, 144, 146–8, 150n.58, 151–3, 154n.72, 155n.77
ISDA Master Agreement 178–9
Israel–British Bank 224
Istituto Mobiliare Italiano (IMI) 83, 86
Istituto per la Ricostruzione Industriale (IRI) 94, 102, 105
Italian
  bankers 66–7, 75, 94
  banks 19n.9, 68, 80, 82, 110, 187
  business 111
  capitalism 96, 104
  central authorities 79
  chambers of commerce 98
  companies/firms 13, 94
  conference delegates/delegation 72–4, 77–8, 81n.74, 83–9
  corporate network 13, 88n.90, 92, 95–6, 100, 103, 105, 107–8, 111–12
  corporate system 13
  economy 12, 64–5, 73n.39, 74, 83
  financial elites 12–13, 61, 64, 71, 76, 84, 89–90, 94, 106n.39, 109–10
  financial system 12
  government 64, 74–5, 80, 83, 87
  governor 187
  industrialization 95
  interests 12
  joint-stock companies 95–8, 104
  lira 79, 82
  Pareto 11
  railways 102
  stabilization 81
  stock exchanges 97

249

Index

Italian Banking Association 76n.57
Italian People's Party 111
Italy 12, 18, 61n.1, 65, 68, 70–2, 74, 76–81,
   83–8, 90, 94–7, 101–5, 110–12, 182n.2,
   188–90, 192, 195–6, 204, 219, 231
   Minister of Finance 77, 79, 86, 88
   Ministry for University and Scientific
      Research 92n.1
   Ministry of Agriculture 71, 86

J & P Coats 144, 146
Jaans, P. 232
Jaffré, P. 132
Japan 24, 94, 182n.2, 184–7, 193, 196,
   198n.50, 199, 203, 205, 207, 212, 214–15,
   222, 226–7, 231–2
Japanese
   conference delegates 214
   economy 189, 199
Jaquinto, R. 116
Jefferson, T. 55
Jenkins, P. 39n.89
Jenkinson, T. 148n.53
Jensen, M. C. 10n.28
Jobs, S. 136
Joel, O. 113
Johnson, P. 147n.51
Johnson, S. 61n.2
joint-stock companies 25n.33, 85, 87,
   95–8, 104
Jones, H. 148n.53
Jopson, B. 19n.11
journalists 3, 21–2, 32n.62
JPMorgan 25, 28nn.42–3, 38, 79–80, 81n.74,
   82, 147, *see also* Morgan, J. P.
judges 15, 156, 159, 162, 164, 175–6, 180
Jung, G. 77, 86, 88

Kahn, A. 28n.42
Kane, E. 7
Kaplan, S. N. 2n.3
Karjalainen, A. 186
Kettl, D. 184
Keynesian
   approach to economics 192
   economic thinking 202
   economics 194
   economists 193, 198
   equilibrium 8
   policies 127, 129, 183, 188, 190
   prescriptions 3
   programmes 206
Keynesianism 15, 31
Keynes, J. M. 71n.31, 75, 88n.89
Keynes-sceptic economists 195
Khurshed, A. 155n.77
Kindleberger, C. 21

King, M. 167n.28, 202
Klassen, K. 195
Klauser, P. 233
Kleinwort 25
Kocka, J. 3n.7
Kodak 148, 154
Köhler, I. 200
Kuhn Loeb & Co 25, 28nn.42–3
Kuznets cycles 73
Kylsant, Lord 136

La Borde 49
Lamont, T. 28n.42, 79n.67
Landes, D. 63n.9
Latin America 141, 222
Latin countries 94
Latium 107, 114–16
lawyers, *see* attorneys/lawyers/solicitors
Layton, W. 72
Lazard Brothers 73n.43, 75
Lazzerini, P. G. 85
League of Nations 63, 66n.20, 69n.26, 70–2, 76
Le Couteulx & C. 53
Le Couteulx de Canteleu, J.-B. 53
Lee Higginson & Co 25
legal
   actors 159–60, 172, 174
   advice 171–2, 231
   advisers 15, 160
   architecture 6
   arguments 179
   assessments 171
   communities 171
   competences 119
   concepts 159, 162
   culture 175, 181
   depredations 137
   discourse 173
   doctrine 163
   documents 159
   elites 160, 163, 165–6, 168, 171–2, 174,
      177–8, 180–1, 211
   frameworks 7, 159, 169, 177, 227
   guidance 153
   historians 152, 168
   histories 153, 159
   innovation 159, 170
   institutions 163
   intervention 175
   legitimacy 159
   liability 172
   norms 162, 181
   profession 160–2
   protection of investors 93–4
   recourse 156
   reforms 7, 166
   requirements 149, 152, 154

services 160, 171
system 162–3, 165, 177, 181
see also attornies/lawyers/solicitors
legislators 7, 45–6, 145n.45
Le Havre 53
Lehman Brothers 1, 8–9, 18–19, 20n.13, 22, 24, 32, 33n.64, 37, 136, 144
Leverhulme, Lord 136, 146n.46
Lévy-Lang, A. 132n.23
liabilities 29, 52, 68, 72, 82–3, 142, 144n.42, 145, 165, 170–2, 175–7
liberal
  environment 224
  faith 143
  market economy 12, 94
  narrative 36
  programme 131
  reforms 127
liberalism 8, 20, 133, *see also* neoliberalism
liberalization 14, 51, 118, 120, 123, 125, 127, 130–1, 196, 198, 221, 229
Liberati, L. B. 85
Liberati, T. 115
Libor 167
Liebig's Extract of Meat 154
Lieuze, M. 231
Liguria 106–7, 113, 115–16
Liikanen Commission 19
Lipton's Tea 144
liquidity 39, 65–6, 75, 82, 130, 150, 153, 225–6
Lisle-Williams, M. 4
listing rules 138, 149–50, 154
Lloyd George, D. 74n.45
lobbying 7, 14, 86, 118, 121–2, 131, 133, 161
Locke, J. 37
Lodolo, A. 113
Lolli, E. 115
Lombard banks 103, 111
Lombard Street 163–4
Lombardy 96, 106–7, 113–16
London 8, 28n.41, 36n.77, 41, 49, 51, 53, 59, 63, 74n.45, 77, 81–2, 88, 121–2, 140–3, 145, 147–8, 150, 152–3, 155, 179, 196, 221
  bankers 173n.56
  Big Bang 125
  brokers 126, 144
  business services 146
  commodity markets 151
  financial markets 180
  financial world 148
  hegemony 78
  IPOs 151–2
  merchant banks 3–4, 25, 34, 73n.43
  see also City of London
London & Brazilian Bank 154
London & Westminster 141
London Court of International Arbitration 177

London Institute of Bankers 30
London Monetary and Economic Conference 12, 78, 84–9, 225, 227
London Stock Exchange (LSE) 126, 134, 143, 145, 148–9, 150n.58, 151–4
Lopez-Morell, M. A. 141
Lorain, M. 125
Louis Philippe 54
Louis XVI 44, 46
Louis XVIII 45n.17
Louisiana 55
Lucas, R. 195
Luxembourg 126, 210, 215–16, 218–19, 232
Luxembourgian Banks and Bankers' Association 216
Luzzati, L. 74
Lyons 52, 153

Maastricht Treaty 200
MacDonald, R. 35
MacGregor, G. 137
Machiavelli, N. 11
MacKenna, R. 71n.31
Mackenzie, D. 23n.26, 32
macroanalysis 3
macroeconomic
  adjustment 91
  environment 78
  functions 69n.25
  imbalances 63
  issues 22
  objectives 69
  perspective 219
  policies 70–1, 84
  stability/stabilization 69, 72, 82–3
Madoff, B. 137
Magic Circle 15, 160–1, 172
Maglione, G. 114
Malthusianism 117
Manchester 134n.1
Manchester Ship Canal 141
Mangili, C. 113
Manichella, D. 192
Maple & Co 150
Marche 107, 114
Marchesano, E. 114
Marcussen, M. 204
Margairaz, D. 44n.11, 90n.93
Margerie, B. de 125
marginal firms 100–1
Mariani, M. 86
Mariotti, M. 85
Marsh, D. 184, 195
Martin, M. 190–2, 205
Marxist
  approach 93
  theorist 9n.27

251

Index

Marx, K. 37
Massai (*née* Lepoivre), F. 214, 230
Masturzo, T. 115
mathematics 31, 108, 113–14, 130–1, 200
Matsushita, Y. 187
Mattioli, F. 115
Mattoni, A. 33n.64
Mauritius 215, 234
Mauroy, P. 127
Mayer, A. 4
Mayer, H. 217, 219, 236
Mayntz, R. 19n.10
Mayoux, J. 123
Mazzoni, C. 113
McKenna, R. 34n.71
Meckling, W. H. 10n.28
Mediobanca 92n.1, 98, 103
Memory of Financial Crises 23n.25
Menichella, D. 83, 90, 190, 195
Mentone, C. F. R. 86
mergers 27, 30, 67n.22, 111, 120n.3, 143
Merrill Lynch 38, 217, 235
Meulen, T. C. E. 71n.31, 75
Micchi, L. 115
Michie, R. C. 3n.6, 12, 146n.48, 147n.51
microanalysis 3
microeconomic
　functions 69n.25
　issues 22
Middle Eastern countries 33n.64
Midland Bank 34n.71
Milan 111
　stock exchange 110
Milanese private banker 72, 76
Miller, W. 186, 191, 204
millionaires 26, 142, 148
Mill, J. S. 139
Minard, P. 44n.12
Minas Geraes 28n.43
mines/mining 99, 140nn.27–8, 145, 149n.55
Mintz, B. A. 98n.30
Mion, G. 116
Mishkin, F. 194
Mitchell, C. 27n.38, 28n.42
Mitterrand, F. 127, 129
Mohamed, A. 155n.77
Moland, T. 186–7
Mollan, S. 146n.48
monetarist policies 8
monetarists 195–6, 198
monetary
　authorities 20n.16, 64–5, 89
　committee 215, 219
　constraint 125
　cooperation 12, 62, 77
　governance 212
　growth 197

instability 68, 90
issues 87
market 130
policies 15, 20n.16, 62n.5, 66–7, 69–70, 78, 82–3, 119, 128–9, 182–4, 186, 190, 193, 197, 200, 202, 205, 207, 233
powers 200
stabilization 74–5, 77–8, 81–2, 90
standards 73–4
systems 8, 63, 78
Money Trust 31
Monnet, J. 71–2, 133
monopoly 8, 72, 80, 126, 130, 149
Monte dei Paschi di Siena 67n.22
Montecatini 111
Montedison 103
Moody, J. 152
Morgan Grenfell 25
Morgan, J. 28n.42
Morgan, J. P. 26, 37–8, 71n.31, 142, 143n.35, 146nn.46–7, 147–8, *see also* JPMorgan
Morgan Stanley 216, 235
Morin, F. 132
Moroni, A. 116
Morpurgo, E. 114
Morrison, A. D. 25n.33
Morrison, C. 142–3
Morris, R. 50–1
mortgages 38, 72, 142
Motta, G. 110, 113–14
Moussa, P. 119, 125, 128
Müller, B. 233
Muller, H. 224–5, 232
Munich 195
Musch, F. 216, 218–19, 232
Mussolini, B. 77, 79–80, 83
mutual funds 32n.58, 121, 125

Nagashima, A. 231
Namierization 62n.3
Nancy 52
Nantes 48, 53
Naouri, J.-C. 130
Nardozzi, G. 195
Nathan, J. 77, 81, 84–6, 88
National Bank of Belgium 188, 194, 214, 219, 230
National City Bank 24, 27n.38, 28n.42
National City Company 28nn.42–3
National Insurance Institute 73n.39
National Investment Bank 35
nationalization 14, 20, 35, 47, 89, 96, 100, 102–3, 111–12, 118–19, 127–8, 188
National Monetary Commission 205
nation states 30, 74n.44, 89
Nazi regime 192
Necker, J. 12, 45–8, 51

Index

Nederlandsche Bank 216, 224, 232
negotiable options market 130
Nendick, D. A. C. 215, 234
neoliberalism 20, 133, *see also* liberalism
Netherlands 144n.41, 182n.2, 185–6, 192, 195, 198, 200, 218–19, 221, 226–7, 232, *see also* Dutch
Netherlands Bank 76
Netherlands Land Enclosure 142
Nettine 49
New Jersey 153
New York 25, 31, 33n.64, 52n.31, 55, 82, 122, 148, 160, 179, 184, 213, 216–17, 230–1, 233, 235
New York Stock Exchange (NYSE) 28n.42, 134, 135n.4, 145, 146n.47, 148–51, 152n.66, 153, 154n.72, 155, 157
New Zealand 222
New Zealand & Australian Land 154
Niemeyer, O. 77
Nitti, F. S. 74n.45
Nixon, R. 194–5
Nizzola, A. 114
Nonet, P. 164
Nordic
 countries 225
 financial crisis 199
 group 222
Norman, M. 75–6, 78–82, 88n.89
North British & Mercantile Insurance 142–3
Northern Ireland 162n.7
Northern Rock 167, 171–2
Norway 154, 186, 188, 198n.50, 199, 225
Notizie statistiche sulle principali società italiane per azioni 97
Nuffield, Lord 136
Nuovo Banco Ambrosiano 111
Nussbaum, F. L. 50n.28

O'Brien, L. 196, 204
Obstfeld, M. 69
Occupy Wall Street 33n.64
O'Hagan, H. O. 141, 146
oil 99, 191, 194
O'Kean, J. M. 141
Olson, M. 33n.65
Optima 121
Orléan 133
O'Rourke, K. H. 29n.45
Ortona, E. 86, 115
Over the Counter (OTC) 178–9
Overend, Gurney and Co 175–6
Overseas Bankers Club 216
owner-managers 10, 24, 26–7

Pace, A. 65n.13
Pagani, F. 86, 88

Pagliano, E. 85
Palmerston, Lord 169, 170n.42
Panzarasa, R. 113
Pareto, V. 11
Paribas 119, 120, 122, 124–5, 128, 132n.23, 217, 235
Paris 28n.41, 42n.7, 44, 48–9, 51, 69, 87, 125, 134–5, 144, 152, 217, 230–1
 market 41–3, 50, 52–4, 56, 59–60
Paris Bourse/Stock Exchange 41, 54, 57, 126
Parisi, E. 114
Paris-Lyons-Méditerranée Railway 153
Parmalat 136
Parr's Bank 149
Parson, E. 56n.36
partnerships 25, 37, 121, 147, 158, 169
Patriarca, M. 217, 236
Pazzaglia, G. 86
Peace Conference 64n.11, 69, 87
Pearson, R. 140n.23
Pecora, F. 28, 33–4
Pennings, J. M. 98
Pennroad Corporation 28n.43
Peruvian government loans 28n.43
Pesenti, C. 111, 114–15
Pessoa, F. 37
 O Banqueiro Anarquista 17, 36
Peyrelevade, J. 128
pharmaceuticals 144, 145n.42
Philadelphia 50
Philipps, J. 141
Phillips & Drew 141
Phillips, K. 31n.54
philosophy 108, 116, 131, 230, 236
physics 108, 116
Piedmont 106–7, 113–15
Pierson, Heldring & Pierson 232
Piketty, T. 1n.2
 Capital in the Twenty-First Century 93
Pillsbury 154
Piluso, G. 73n.39, 106n.39
Pirelli, A. 64n.11, 77, 86–8, 90, 114
Piserchia, G. 86
Plan Comptable 220
Plessis, A. 5n.16
pluralism 16, 31
Poland 79, 113
Poland, H. B. 174
Polanyian social countermovement 8
political
 actors 33, 41, 59, 184
 affinities 128
 battleground 14
 centre 56
 changes 60, 127, 155
 choices 41
 collapse 11

253

Index

political (*cont.*)
  connections 52, 54, 74
  consequences 20, 22, 40
  considerations 5, 52
  content 71
  continuity 131
  decisions 122
  developments 46
  disenfranchisement 33
  dissension 43
  domain 104
  economy 93
  elites 2, 11, 13, 183, 187, 190, 192–6, 205–6
  entrepreneurs 33, 35, 39
  evaluations 47
  events 41
  evolution 42, 47
  field 20
  fortunes 12
  framework 41, 58
  governors 195
  ideas 224
  impulse 130
  independence 197, 205, 207
  influence 4, 5n.15, 12, 190, 197
  influence 200
  institutions 41, 47, 89
  interference 128
  interventions 206
  issues 61
  leaders 30, 122, 186, 188, 207
  mechanisms 135
  motivation 18
  offices 190, 195, 197
  philosophers 38n.86
  polarization 3
  positions 44
  power 84, 124, 210
  pressures 76n.55, 128, 184, 222
  process 8
  profile 15
  reforms 7
  regimes 54
  responsibilities 75n.52
  scenario 41
  science 201
  scientists 2, 20, 31, 92–3
  spectrum 30
  sphere 20
  system 48, 188
  tendencies 2
  theory 37
  transformations 10
  turbulences 20
  weight 5
politicians 8, 15, 21–2, 32n.62, 72, 117, 155, 187

politico-financial scandals 29
Pollone, E. 113
Ponti, G. G. 113
Portugal 36n.77
Portuguese escudo 36n.77
post-war
  co-management of regulation 118
  decade 62, 67, 89
  economic recovery 189
  experiences 88
  financial regime 8
  generation 124
  instability 73
  international monetary system 8
  Japan 205
  period 69n.29
  twentieth century 194
pre-war
  capitalism 89
  cooperation model 90, 106n.39
  dynamics 66
  financial world 63
  Gold Standard 69n.29
  parities 34, 75
  values 75
  world 69, 73
Preziosi, G. 30
Price, J. M. 50n.28
PricewaterhouseCoopers 216, 232, 235
Prinetti, C. 114
private
  act of parliament 152
  action 156
  bankers 12, 26, 37, 42n.4, 64, 72, 76, 88–9, 142
  banks 3, 25–6, 43, 103, 111, 128, 143
  business 137n.11, 170
  citizens 56
  contract 138
  credits 82
  dispute resolution 179
  entrepreneurs 87
  financial elites 122, 132
  financial world 71
  financiers 43, 89
  firms 129
  global trade association 178
  institutions 63, 188, 216
  interests 8
  joint-stock company 85, 87, 102
  law 159, 162
  legal practice 180
  manufacturers 88
  mechanisms 12
  order institutions 153n.70, 155
  prosecution 170, 175
  rules 154

Index

savings 43
sector 62, 64, 70, 74, 76–7, 84–8, 90, 106n.39, 123, 135, 152, 191–2, 194, 197–9, 204, 210, 216–17, 220, 235–6
structure 69, 70, 83, 89
transactions 159
privateers 55–6
privatizations 89, 95, 100, 102–4, 111–12, 125, 128, 131–2, 201
probate inventories 142n.33, 143
profitability 67–8, 137
profits 11, 26, 27n.38, 31n.54, 42, 51, 52, 133, 137, 149, 157, 170
Profumo A. 116
prosopographic
  analysis 97
  approach 84, 93
  study of the big linkers 97
  see also collective biographies
Public Finance Commission 73n.43, 75
Pujo inquiry 31
Punishment of Frauds Act 172

Quartieri, F. 85, 87
Quinn, B. 217, 234

Raggio, A. 113
railways 24, 99, 102, 134–5, 142, 144, 153–4, 169
Rajan, R. G. 155
Rallo, P. 86
Randfontein Estates 149n.55
Randlords 148–9
Ras 103
Rastelli, P. 115
Rational Choice Theory 38n.86
Rauh, J. 2n.3
RBS 32n.60, 167n.23
Reagan, R. 196
real estate 102, 110, 199
Rebaudengo, E. 114
recessions 183, 202, 206, see also Great Recession
Redwood, M. 53
regulation 7–8, 12–14, 16, 18–19, 25, 32n.62, 33, 35–7, 50n.29, 52, 61–5, 78, 81–3, 90–1, 106n.39, 118–22, 128, 132–4, 139, 145, 147, 153n.70, 155–6, 158, 161n.6, 180, 196, 200, 209–12, 214, 218–21, 224, 226, 228–9, see also deregulation
regulators 2, 7, 19n.11, 64n.10, 138, 148, 159, 161n.6, 166–7, 180, 199n.51, 212
regulatory
  action 162
  aftermath 168
  architecture 6, 12, 63
  authorities 16, 122, 181

avoidance 7
bodies 161–2
capture 7, 163
context 2
cycle 79, 83, 89
definition 39
dialectic 7, 118
elites 13, 211
framework 16, 229
institutions 213, 220
legislation 34
model 64, 83
path 166
patterns 89
power 62, 229
principles 90
programmes 206
reforms 19, 167, 207
regime 117, 188, 197, 205
responses 18
scheme 88
standards 159
system 118–19, 121
terms 155
Reichlin, L. 19n.9
Reichsbank 77, 204
Reid, Lord 162n.8
Reinhart, C. M. 21
Reitmayer, M. 5n.16
remuneration 10, 23, 26–7, 38–9
Renouvin, P. 45n.17
rentiers 11n.31, 31n.54
Ricaldone, P. 114
Ricci, V. R. 85, 87
Richardson, M. 19n.10
Riksbank 194, 196, 205
Riley, J. C. 41n.2, 43n.10
Rinaldi, A. 88n.90, 96
Rio de Janeiro City Improvements 154
Rio Tinto 141
Ripa di Meana, V. 116
Roberts, R. 6n.18
Robespierre, M. 42
Robinson, J. A. 61n.2
Robinson, Sir J. 149
Rocca, G. 116
Rockefeller, J. D. 26
Rogoff, K. S. 21
Rolls-Royce 144
Roman law 162n.7
Rome 80, 106, 221, 231
Romiti, C. 115
Rooth, I. 205
Rosa, C. 85
Roselli, A. 29n.45
Rossello, M. 113–14
Rossi, A. 71n.31, 75n.50, 77, 85

255

Index

Rossi, C. E. 115
Rotary Club 219
Rothschilds 25, 26, 135, 141–2, 144, 147, 156
Rougemont & C. 54
Rougemont, D. 53
Rousseau, J.-J. 37
Rowe & Pitman 144
Royal Bank of Scotland 167, 169n.38, 170
Royal British Bank 170n.43, 173n.64, 174n.66, 175–6
Rubinowicz, C. 130
Rubinstein, W. 3–4
Russian Empire 41
Russian railways 135

Saccomani, F. 231
Saint-Geours, J. 125
Sankt Pauli 154
San Martino, E. P. di 85
Sardinia 107, 114–15
Sauvy, A. 28n.41
Savage, M. 6n.20
Scandinavian countries 94
Schaus, J. N. 218, 232
Schlesinger, H. 195
Schmidt, V. A. 20n.14, 132–3
Schneider, M. 218, 231
Schroders 25
Schumpeter, J. A. 31, 33
  Theorie der Wirtschaftlichen Entwicklung 29
Schwarz, A. 184
Schwarz, M. 98n.30
Schweppes 148
Sciences Po 119, 132n.23
Scotland 143, 162n.7
Scott, J. 210–11
Scottish
  banker 42–3, 46–7
  immigrants 143
  island ferries 142
SEANZA countries 222
Secretariat List 88n.88
securities 25, 28, 34n.67, 42, 59, 94, 102–3, 121–2, 129–30, 134–5, 137–8, 141, 143–5, 147, 151–2, 154n.74, 155
securitization 31, 32n.57
Selznick, P. 164
Senior Managers and Certification Regime 165, 170
service industry 99
share
  allocations 145
  capital 97–8, 152, 156n.83
  issues 144
  ownership 28
  participations 103
  portfolios 143

premiums 157
relationships 96
trading 144
shareholder
  protections 153
  responsibility 159
  rights 153
  trust 136
  value 31n.54, 38n.84, 136
shareholders 10n.28, 14, 24, 57n.38, 132, 135–40, 142–5, 148–9, 152–3, 155–7, 169–70
shares 28, 49–50, 95, 132, 135, 137, 143, 145, 149–51, 156
Shell 141, 191
Shimmelpenninck, W. 57n.38
shipping/ships 49, 55, 56n.35, 99, 134, 143–4
Shirakawa, M. 202
Sicily 67, 107, 114
Siemens Brothers 154
Siepmann, H. A. 75n.53, 81, 88n.89
Siklos, P. 184
Silverman, J. L. 34n.67
Silvestrini, A. 68n.24
Simon, C. J. 152n.66, 155n.77
Single European Act 126
Sinigaglia, O. 77
Sir Samuel Scott Bart & Co 141
Slinn, J. 174n.67
Smith Barney & Co 217, 235
Smith, A. 37, 135
Snowden, P. 35
social
  actors 33
  advance 52
  analysis 2
  capital 11, 122, 124, 200, 211
  change 6
  consequences 20, 22
  considerations 5
  contract 168
  countermovement 8
  echelons 173
  embeddedness 15
  esteem 136
  fictions 17
  group 89
  history 3
  Keynesian policies 127
  ladder 41, 54
  market 139
  media 33
  movement 174
  networks 11
  order 23
  prominence 4
  reality 9, 23, 35

Index

sciences 6n.20, 31, 201
scientists 3, 15, 92, 93
stability 120
standards 165
status 5, 122, 185
structure 104
ties 163
Socialists 118, 127–9, 131–2
social-psychological processes 22n.22
Società Bancaria Italiana 102, 110
Società Italiana per le Strade Ferrate Meridionali 102–3
Société Générale 120–2, 125
Sociétés d'investissements à capital variable (SICAV) 121
socio-cultural representation 23
socio-economic
  context 22
  transformations 10
sociologists 2, 31, 92–3
socio-political supremacy 4
socio-professional
  recruitment 119
  status 24
Sogevar 121
Soginter 121
solicitors, see attorneys/lawyers/solicitors
Solimano, A. 64n.10
solvency 225–6
Solza, M. 85, 113
Soskice, D. 12
South African High Court 149n.55
South African Reserve Bank 62n.7
South American stock 28n.43
Spada, M. 108n.43, 114–15
Spain 33n.64, 51, 58
Spanish Crown 58
Spear, D. 56n.35
speculation 8, 27, 43, 53, 79, 82, 169, 199
speculators 11n.31
Speyers 148
stabilization 7, 59, 62–4, 66, 69–70, 72–3, 75–83, 90
stagflation 8
Standard Chartered 32n.60, 234
Stanworth, P. 3n.6
Stapleton, J. 173n.64
state
  actors 8, 36
  apparatus 197
  borrowing 135
  capitalism 133
  control 127n.14
  guarantee 83
  intervention 3, 25, 117, 127, 133, 190, 196, 206
  monopoly 72

officials 117
power 160
primacy 83
ruling 131
supervision 14, 155–6
state-backed bond market 73
state-based system 133
state-controlled attitude 123
state-influenced market economies 94
state-led regulation 90, 106n.39
state-level corporate law 153n.70
state-oriented capitalism 117
state-owned
  banking 119
  banks 118, 120
  companies 120
  conglomerate 94
  enterprises (SOEs) 84, 86, 100, 102–4, 106, 112, 192
  holding 102
  institutions 95, 103, 122, 188–9, 192, 198
  sector 95, 105
Stavisky affair 29
stockbrokers 118, 121, 126, 130, 141, 143–6,
  see also brokers
Stock Exchange Official Intelligence 151
stock exchanges 28, 31, 41, 54, 110, 123, 126–7, 134–5, 137–8, 143–5, 151, 153, 155
stock market 43, 52, 59, 73, 82, 121, 138
  boom 199
  capitalization 119
  crash 168–9, 184
  crisis 27
  downturns 143
  functioning 79
  operations 28
  volatility 81
St Petersburg 134–5
Strahan, Paul and Bates 173nn. 56, 62, 65
Strauss-Kahn, D. 202
Stringher, B. 64n.11, 71–2, 76–7, 79–83, 87n.87
Strong, B. 75, 78–82, 184
Suez 120, 124, 128
suicide 53, 136n.8, 147n.51
Suvich, F. 86
Sweden 73n.41, 182n.2, 186, 196, 198n.50, 199, 205, 219, 225–6, 233
Swedish
  conference delegate 226
  Crown 41
  Riksbank 194, 196
Swedish Central Railway 142
Sweezy, P. 18, 93

257

Index

Swiss
  bankers 5, 41, 52–5, 57, 59
  banks 39n.89, 225, 227
  clients 54
  government 220
Swiss Federal Banking Commission 233
Swiss National Bank 233
Switzerland 54, 114, 128, 210, 214, 217, 219–20, 227, 233
System Steering Committee on International Banking Regulation 220
systemically important financial institutions (SIFI) 167, 171

Talleyrand-Périgord, C.-M. de 53–4, 58n.44, 60
Tancarville, B. de 43n.9
Targetti, R. 85
Tatò, F. 116
tax/taxation 46, 160
  advantages 25
  affair 187
  farmers 43n.9, 50
  income tax 156
  land tax 45–7
taxpayers 19, 20
Taylor, A. M. 69
Taylor, J. 140n.23, 147n.51, 152
technocracies 63–4, 80, 90, 210
technocratic
  elite 89, 177
  model 90, 106n.39
  monetary policy 15
technocrats 12, 63, 74n.44, 77, 88–90
telecommunications, *see* communications
Tett, G. 32n.57
Thane, P. 4
Thatcher, Margaret 125, 196
Thatcher, Mark 20n.14, 133n.27
The Hague 56, 58n.44, 179, *see also* Hague Conference
Théret 133
Tilman, S. 5n.16
Tino, A. 115
tobacco 48, 50–2, 58–9
Toeplitz, G. 71n.31, 90, 113
Tokyo 214, 221, 232
Toniolo, G. 65nn.13–14, 16
Torchiani, T. 114–15
Tornqvist, A. 233
Tosh, J. 167, 168n.29
total assets 13, 65–8, 97–8, 111, *see also* assets
Towers, G. 204
trade unions 17, 123n.11
trading 144, 148, 151
  activities 127
  companies 49, 50, 99
  deflation 34, 50, 126

investment 25
system 123
tramway companies 99
transatlantic, *see* Atlantic/transatlantic commerce/trade
transnational
  committees 218
  dimension 14–15, 33n.64
  elites 215
  networks 15
Treaty of Versailles 63
Trentino-Alto Adige 107, 113
Trento, S. 96, 108
Trump, D. 19, 207
Trust & Loan Company of Canada 142
Tucker, P. 167n.26, 168
Turner, J. D. 140, 150nn.58–9
Tuscany 107, 114–16

UEIF 120
Umbria 107, 114, 116
Undertakings for Collective Investment in Transferable Securities (UCITS) 121
underwriting 141, 143–6, 148, 151
unemployment 188, 194
Unioncamere (Association of the Italian Chambers of Commerce) 92n.1, 98
United Kingdom (UK) 74, 94, 101, 125–6, 137–40, 142, 144, 146–9, 150n.58, 151–5, 160–1, 162n.7, 165, 178–80, 182, 186, 192, 196, 202, 209–10, 218–19, 233–6
  Central Criminal Court 173nn. 56, 64
  Commercial Court 177–9
  Court of Queen's Bench 177
  House of Lords 149n.55, 150n.59
  judiciary 180
  Parliamentary Commission on Banking Standards 167
  Privy Council 149n.55
  Treasury Select Committee 167, 171
  Vickers Commission 19
  see also Britain, England, Northern Ireland, Scotland, Wales
United States and Foreign Securities Corporation 29n.43
United States and International Securities Corporation 29n.43
United States (US) 16, 18n.8, 19–20, 21n.16, 24–8, 29n.43, 32–5, 37n.80, 38, 50n.28, 53–6, 59–60, 94, 101, 125, 129, 134n.1, 138, 139n.22, 142, 145n.45, 146n.46, 147–9, 151–5, 169, 182n.2, 184–6, 189–94, 196, 198, 202, 204–5, 207, 209, 212–14, 216–17, 219–20, 222, 226–7, 235–6
  Democratic leadership 33
  dollar 65, 82
  monetary policy 21n.16

258

Index

Republican leadership 33
Securities and Exchange Commission 155
Senate Committee on Banking and
  Currency 18, 28, 33, 37
Senate investigation 28, 31
see also America, American
urban
  centres 57
  proprietaries 140n.23
urbanization 140
US Steel 153
Useem, M. 3n.6
Utrecht 56

Valerio, G. 114
Valletta, V. 110
Vandenyver Frères & C. 44
Vanderhoeven & Co 57n.40
Vanleeuw, W. 230
Van Staphorst, Willink & Co 57
Vassar-Smith, R. V. 71n.31
Vasta, M. 88, 95–6, 97n.25
Velde, F. R. 42n.5, 57n.38
vendors 137n.11, 145, 147, 149–50, 154n.72
Veneto 107, 111, 113–14, 116
Venini, L. 115
Ventimiglia, G. 85
Verdun, A. 203n.58, 204
Versailles 44, 46–7
  Peace Conference 64n.11, 69, 87
  Treaty 63
Veuve Nettine & C. 43
Vezzalini, G. 115
Vickers 141
Vickers Commission 19
Victorian
  banking failures 165
  banking prosecutions 177
  Britain 14, 152
  criminal courts 15
  England 15, 137
  financial intermediaries 14
  legal liability 172
  politicians 155
  system of collective action 149n.57
  world 143
Vienna 43, 134
Viénot, M. 125
Villa Falletto, F. di 86
Vissering, G. 71n.31, 76
Vocke, W. 191, 204
volatility 11, 38, 59–60, 63, 65, 67–9, 81, 90, 202
Volcker, P. 184, 191, 195n.39, 196–7, 204, 222
Volpi, G. 77, 79–80
Volpin, P. 94

Voombergh, D. J. 57–8
Voombergh, Halmael and Borski 57

Wagg 144
Walckiers, É. de 43
Wales 162, 180
Wall Street 19, 28n.42, 33n.64
  bankers 28, 38n.84, 37
  Crash 22, 27
  probe 18
Walter, I. 19n.10
Warburg 122
Warburg, P. 71n.31
Warburg, Paribas Becker 235
Warburg Pincus & Co 217, 235
Washington 8, 216, 221
Waterlow and Sons 36n.77
waterworks 144
wealth 1, 3, 9, 24, 26, 38, 45, 64n.10, 89,
  141–3, 148, 156
Weber, A. 202
Weir, D. R. 42n.5
Wellink, A. 205
Werner, R. 184, 199
Wernher Beit 147
Wernher, Sir J. 148, 149n.55
Westerhuis, G.
  The Power of Corporate Networks 98, 101,
  104n.34
White, E. N. 42nn.5–6
White Weld 122
Whitney, R. 28n.42
Wiggin, A. 28n.42
Wilhelm, W. J. 25n.33
Willey, D. 213, 216–17, 219, 235
Williams, K. 6n.20
Williamson, J. G. 29n.45
Williamson, P. 3n.6, 35
Wilson, C. 146n.46
Wilson, S. 174nn.71–2, 175n.77
Wimbledonization 6
Workum 57
World Bank 215
Wright, W. 136, 147n.51, 149, 156n.82

Yellen, J. 19n.11

Zambia 215, 234
Zander, C. 113
Zijlstra, J. 195
Zingales, L. 155
Zuberbühler, D. 233
Zurich 52
  bankers 56, 57
  merchant 53